Washington, D.C.
FOR
DUMMIES®
4TH EDITION

by Tom Price

BICENTENNIAL
1807
WILEY
2007
BICENTENNIAL

Wiley Publishing, Inc.

Washington, D.C. For Dummies,® 4th Edition
Published by
Wiley Publishing, Inc.
111 River St.
Hoboken, NJ 07030-5774
www.wiley.com

WILEY

About the Author

Tom Price has lived in and written about Washington, D.C., for more than two decades. As a journalist who focuses on government and politics, he knows the ins and outs of official Washington. As the parent of a college-age Washington native, he's discovered the best Washington places for kids of all ages. As a longtime D.C. resident, he's found fun and interesting Washington experiences for adults of all ages as well, having repeatedly explored the city with his family and visiting friends. From late 1982 through 1995, Tom was a correspondent in the Cox Newspapers Washington Bureau. Since then, he has been a freelance writer whose work has appeared in books, magazines, and newspapers and on Internet sites. With his wife, Susan Crites Price, Tom is coauthor of *The Working Parents Help Book: Practical Advice for Dealing with the Day-to-Day Challenges of Kids and Careers,* which won a Parents' Choice Award, was a Scholastic Book Club selection, and has been featured by "Today," "Oprah," and other broadcast and print media. His most recent book, written with former U.S. representative and ambassador Tony Hall, is *Changing the Face of Hunger: One Man's Story of How Liberals, Conservatives, Democrats, Republicans and People of Faith Are Joining Forces to Help the Poor, the Hungry and the Oppressed.* Tom also is author of Frommer's *Irreverent Guide to Washington.* Previously, Tom, a Pittsburgh native, reported for newspapers in Pennsylvania and Ohio.

Dedication

For Susan and Julie, who make me happy and proud.

Author's Acknowledgments

First, I want to thank Elise Ford, an accomplished travel writer who brought me to Frommer's in the first place and has provided invaluable guidance ever since. I also want to thank my mother, Anna Mae Price; my daughter, Julie, who continually helps me learn new things about Washington; and, of course, Susan, who is always my most important collaborator.

Publisher's Acknowledgments

We're proud of this book; please send us your comments through our Dummies online registration form located at www.dummies.com/register.

Some of the people who helped bring this book to market include the following:

Editorial

Editors: Katie Robinson, Production Editor; Jamie Ehrlich, Development Editor

Copy Editor: Doreen Russo

Cartographer: Roberta Stockwell

Editorial Assistant: Melinda Quintero

Senior Photo Editor: Richard Fox

Cover Photos: Front cover, © Rich LaSalle/Getty Images; back cover, © Joseph Sohm; Visions of America/Corbis

Cartoons: Rich Tennant (www.the5thwave.com)

Composition Services

Project Coordinator: Lynsey Osborn

Layout and Graphics: Claudia Bell, Joyce Haughey, Julie Trippetti

Special Art: Anniversary Logo Design: Richard Pacifico

Proofreaders: Laura Albert, Susan Moritz, Aptara

Indexer: Aptara

Publishing and Editorial for Consumer Dummies

Diane Graves Steele, Vice President and Publisher, Consumer Dummies

Joyce Pepple, Acquisitions Director, Consumer Dummies

Kristin A. Cocks, Product Development Director, Consumer Dummies

Michael Spring, Vice President and Publisher, Travel

Kelly Regan, Editorial Director, Travel

Publishing for Technology Dummies

Andy Cummings, Vice President and Publisher, Dummies Technology/General User

Composition Services

Gerry Fahey, Vice President of Production Services

Debbie Stailey, Director of Composition Services

Contents at a Glance

Maps at a Glance

Table of Contents

Chapter 16: Bars, Stars, and Gee-tars: D.C. at Night 281

Part VI: The Part of Tens *293*

Chapter 17: Top Ten D.C. Views.....................................295

Chapter 18: If You Must Drive: Ten D.C. Roadside Attractions...301

Introduction

• •

*W*hen you visit Washington, D.C., you're visiting the capital of the world — a city with more power than any other on the planet, and one filled with world-class tourist attractions as well.

It wasn't always this way. Almost nothing stood on the sites of the White House, Capitol, and other current U.S. government buildings when George Washington selected the spot to become the new nation's capital city in 1791, primarily because of its central location between the already quarrelling North and South and its nearness to his beloved home, Mount Vernon. As recently as the 1960s, critics described Washington as a cultural backwater, a sleepy Southern town, a place without decent restaurants where the sidewalks were rolled up at dusk.

Washington has long had its shrines to freedom and its halls of government — the Washington Monument, Lincoln Memorial, Library of Congress, and the other government companions to the White House and Capitol. But the city now also has many fine restaurants and hotels, museums, galleries, and performing arts organizations.

Along with New York, Washington was a target of the terrorist attacks of September 11, 2001. American Airlines flight 77 was flown into the Pentagon, across the Potomac River from D.C. in Northern Virginia. United Airlines flight 93, which crashed in rural Pennsylvania, was believed to have been destined for the White House or the Capitol. As I write this book, tours of the White House and Pentagon are given only to select groups, security has been ratcheted up everywhere, and ugly concrete barriers block traffic and mar beautiful views throughout the city. But, like New Yorkers, Washingtonians have been determined to resume normal activities, which include playing host to many visitors. There is little that you could have done here on September 10, 2001, that you can't do today.

I've loved Washington since long before I moved here. For a journalist who focuses on politics and government, there's no better place to live and work. Having lived in D.C. for more than 20 years now, I've come to know it as deeply as I love it. I'm thrilled to be able to share that knowledge with you.

About This Book

You probably picked up this particular book because you're too busy to wade through an overwhelming mass of information or you aren't interested in spending weeks planning a five-day trip. Perhaps you're a first-time visitor to Washington, and you don't know where to begin. Or maybe you're frustrated by all the detail in conventional guidebooks. (You know what I mean: You want to find out when a museum opens, and the author tells you how to *build* one.) Armed with *Washington, D.C. For Dummies*, 4th Edition, you'll feel like a capital insider in no time.

Think of this as a reference book. You can read it from cover to cover if you like (I'll be flattered!), but more likely you'll want to dip into the chapters or sections that are the most interesting or important to you at a particular moment. The Table of Contents and Index allow you to find what you need when you need it — hotels, restaurants, sights, stores, nightspots, and more.

This book doesn't overwhelm you with choices, but it does give you enough information to pick what's best for you. When money is involved, you'll find options at various price levels.

 Please note that travel information is subject to change at any time — and this is especially true of prices. I therefore suggest that you write or call ahead for confirmation when making your travel plans. The authors, editors, and publisher cannot be held responsible for the experiences of readers while traveling. Your safety is important to us, however, so we encourage you to stay alert and be aware of your surroundings. Keep a close eye on cameras, purses, and wallets, all favorite targets of thieves and pickpockets.

I've offered lots of D.C. travel tips to visiting friends and family over the last two decades, and that's exactly what I'm offering you. When you've finished your visit and are heading back home, I expect you'll have acquired some of the affection that I feel for this town and that you'll want to come back.

Conventions Used in This Book

To help you get information quickly, I use some abbreviations and symbols throughout this book. Washington, D.C., is referred to as "Washington," "D.C.," or "the District." (Its formal name is "Washington, District of Columbia.")

Dummies Post-it® Flags

As you're reading this book, you'll find information that you'll want to reference as you plan or enjoy your trip — whether it be a new hotel, a must-see attraction, or a must-try walking tour. Mark these pages with the handy Post-it® Flags included in this book to help make your trip planning easier!

Reviews of hotels and restaurants are organized alphabetically. Handy indexes help you locate them quickly by location, price, and cuisine.

Credit cards accepted are listed this way:

AE: American Express

DC: Diners Club

DISC: Discover

MC: MasterCard

V: Visa

The dollar signs that accompany the hotel and restaurant reviews give you a sense of their prices, as shown in the following table. For a hotel, the dollar signs represent the average of the lowest and highest undiscounted rate for a double-occupancy room for one night during high season. For each restaurant, I've averaged the highest and lowest prices for an appetizer or salad, main course, and dessert at dinner per person, not including taxes and tips.

Cost	*Hotel*	*Restaurant*
$	Less than $125	Less than $20
$$	$125–$225	$20–$29
$$$	$226–$300	$30–$39
$$$$	$301–$400	$40–$50
$$$$$	More than $400	More than $50

In the individual reviews, I give more specific information about costs. I can't, of course, tell you about all the special discounts that hotels and restaurants sometimes offer, but I do mention hotels that often give especially attractive deals. And prices, as you know, are subject to change, so it's a good idea to call ahead to confirm hours and prices and to ask about special offers and discounts when you make your reservations.

You'll find three kinds of listings in the hotel section — first reviews of the best hotels in each price range, then a listing of some runners-up. Don't be shy about picking from the second list if you're unable to get a room at one of the best. The runners-up also are fine places to spend the night. I've also compiled a collection of some of the best bed-and-breakfast accommodations in a wide range of prices. People often think B&Bs are found only in small towns or the countryside, but they also provide some of the most interesting — and sometimes most economical — places to stay in the city, too.

For hotels, restaurants, and attractions that are plotted on a map, a page reference is provided in the listing information. If a hotel, restaurant, or attraction is outside the city limits or in an out-of-the-way area, it may not be mapped.

Foolish Assumptions

I've written this book for both the frequent flier and the inexperienced traveler. The assumptions I've made about both (and, truthfully, I hope they're not foolish!) are:

- ✔ As an inexperienced traveler, you may be trying to determine whether or not to visit Washington, or you may be looking for help in deciding when and how to make the trip.

- ✔ As an experienced traveler, you don't want to spend much time planning your trip, or you don't have much time to spend in the city once you arrive. You want quick, expert advice on how to get the most out of your time and how to enjoy a hassle-free visit.

- ✔ Whatever your degree of travel experience, you're not looking for a book that provides every piece of information available about Washington sights or one that lists every hotel and restaurant in the city. Instead, you want a book that focuses on the best places to eat and sleep in all price ranges and the best ways to enjoy your limited time here.

If you fit any of these criteria, *Washington, D.C. For Dummies,* 4th Edition, is the book you're looking for.

How This Book Is Organized

The Table of Contents at a Glance and complete Table of Contents at the front of this book are useful tools for finding information quickly. At the back of the book is an Appendix, which lists helpful service information and phone numbers, and the index, the most useful tool for navigating the book. The heart of *Washington, D.C. For Dummies,* 4th Edition, is divided into six parts. Within each part are chapters that delve into specifics. Each chapter is written so that you don't have to read what comes before or after it. When necessary, I refer you to other sections of the book for more information.

Part 1: Introducing Washington, D.C.

Here's an overview of Washington and a taste of what you can expect to encounter when you visit. I've compiled a brief list of the best of everything D.C. has to offer, as well as information about the weather, seasons, and special events, to help you decide when you'd like to visit.

Part II: Planning Your Trip to Washington, D.C.

What do things cost in Washington? What's the best way to get here? This part is where I tell you what you need to know to plan your visit successfully. I also include information for travelers with special needs or interests, such as families with kids, people with disabilities, seniors, and gay and lesbian visitors.

Part III: Settling into Washington, D.C.

Okay, here's where I really get into the good stuff. Meet D.C.'s best hotels and restaurants in all price categories. Find out how to get around and how to get along. Come with me through the city's most interesting neighborhoods. Discover the wonders of the underground Metrorail system.

Part IV: Exploring Washington, D.C.

The sights, of course, are why you're coming. In Part IV, I tell you what you want to know about the top sights (and some particularly interesting lesser known attractions) and give you the skinny on tours and shopping. I toss in some itineraries — at no extra charge (you're welcome) — as well as suggestions for excursions nearby.

Part V: Living It Up After Dark: D.C. Nightlife

This part is where you find out what's going on after the museums close and the government goes to sleep for the night. Washingtonians may be known as workaholics who think "party" must be preceded by "Republican" or "Democratic," but D.C. has a vibrant after-dark scene as well, from country, rock, and jazz clubs to world-class symphony, dance, opera, and theater.

Part VI: The Part of Tens

Not as famous as the FBI's Ten Most Wanted list, perhaps, but the *For Dummies* Part of Tens nevertheless is full of cool information. In this part, you find the best places to view the city's breathtaking skyline as well as places that are worth driving to see — the only time driving is worthwhile in D.C., I should add.

Appendix

At the back of the book is your Quick Concierge, a compendium of handy information you may need while visiting Washington. In it, I include phone numbers and addresses for area hospitals and pharmacies, tips for finding ATMs, information about where to take a broken camera or which radio station plays your music, and other useful tips. Check out this Appendix when searching for answers to the little questions that may come up as you travel.

Icons Used in This Book

You find the following icons (little pictures) scattered throughout the margins of this guide. They call your attention to particular kinds of information.

Cut your costs with these money-saving suggestions or alerts to great deals.

 Best of the Best highlights the very best Washington has to offer in all categories.

 The Capitol Dome identifies events and attractions that are unique to D.C.

 This worried fellow warns of tourist traps, rip-offs, hazards, activities that aren't worth your time, and other pitfalls.

 These icons call your attention to hotels, restaurants, and attractions that are especially good for children.

 These are details or plans that you should take care of before you leave home.

 This bull's-eye alerts you to facts, hints, and insider information that can help you make the best use of your time.

Where to Go from Here

Now that you know what to expect from this book, you can start to plan your visit — or, if you're already in D.C., you can decide what to do right now. See and do all you can. And have fun. Your tax dollars help to pay for much of what you'll encounter here, so go get your money's worth.

Part I

Introducing Washington, D.C.

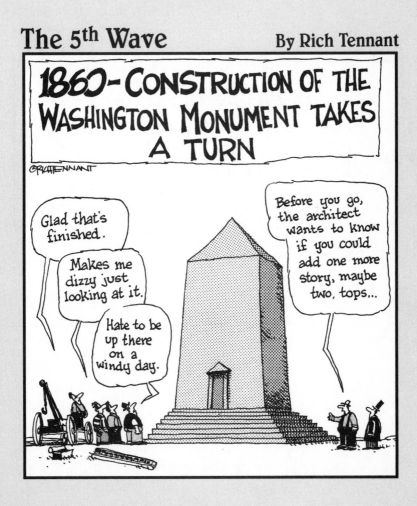

In this part . . .

In this part, I take a look at D.C. in a nutshell. You get a quick tour of the top attractions, places to eat, and places to stay. I also include some historical information, which is a big part of D.C.'s lure, and I tell you about the seasons and provide a calendar of annual events to help you decide when you'd like to visit.

Chapter 1

Discovering the Best of Washington, D.C.

In This Chapter

▶ Discovering the best restaurants and hotels
▶ Enjoying the best attractions
▶ Taking advantage of the best free shows
▶ Finding the best stuff for kids

*W*ashington, D.C., is much more than just the home of the United States government. D.C. offers hotel choices that range from the ultra-ritzy to the ultra-cheap; restaurants that feature many of the world's ethnic cuisines; and rich cultural, historical, scientific, and educational museums and monuments.

One of Washington's best selling points is that many of these top attractions are free. Unlike in London, Paris, Rome, or other major capitals, you don't have to open your wallet before you can open the doors to most of the popular museums, galleries, and other sights. You don't even have to open doors to enjoy another pleasant sight — Washington's impressive landscape.

The car-free National Mall — lawns, gardens, ponds, and walkways — stretches from the Lincoln Memorial to the Capitol and is bordered by many of the Smithsonian's facilities. The cherry trees along the tidal basin are spectacular in the spring.

Whether you're interested in touring the brick and cobblestone streets of Georgetown or enjoying the Latin-influenced nightlife in Adams-Morgan, this chapter shows you the best Washington, D.C., has to offer.

 You can find the details on each location or activity later in this guide. Throughout the book, look for the "Best of the Best" icon to highlight my very top picks.

The Best Hotels

For more information on the hotels listed, see Chapter 9.

- ✔ **Best power palaces:** If you've got money, connections, or both — or just want to act like you do — try staying at one of these spots where lobbyists and government officials hang their hats, or just hang out. You can't beat the location of the opulent **Willard InterContinental,** which has both the White House and D.C.'s city hall in its sights. That's why the powerful and those who seek to influence them have been staying here since the middle of the 19th century. Across Lafayette Square from the White House, the **Hay-Adams** is another favorite among the rich and the politically connected. Less expensive, but close to the Congressional action, the **Capitol Hill Suites** counts U.S. representatives among its long-term residents. Short-term tourist guests get dining privileges at the Republican Party's nearby Capitol Hill Club.

- ✔ **Best charming hotels:** Amidst all of Washington's wealth and pretensions, some accommodations become distinct by daring to be true to themselves. The **Tabard Inn** exudes character and charm in three adjacent town houses on a tree-lined street near Dupont Circle. It also offers especially low prices in some rooms for guests willing to share a bathroom down the hall. Exuding upscale character and charm, **The Jefferson** is quiet and elegant and keeps its guests coming back for its personalized service. The **Morrison-Clark Historic Inn and Restaurant** scatters period antiques throughout two 1864 Victorian Mansions that are listed on the National Register of Historic Places.

- ✔ **Best B&Bs:** The **D.C. Guest House** is a 19th-century mansion, renovated to the eclectic taste of its owners who lavish warm attention on their guests. Equally striking is the 19th-century **Swann House.** This luxurious mansion feels just like it must have when its wealthy occupants lived the lush life in the early 20th century. For the budget-minded, the **Kalorama Guest House at Woodley Park** offers clean, comfortable, and relatively spacious rooms starting at $55 single and $60 double. The afternoon sherry hour offers a touch of elegance.

- ✔ **Best suites:** Suites with cooking facilities — and sometimes separate sleeping quarters — are wonderful for families looking to save money on meals and to enjoy a little privacy. You get lots of choices at **Georgetown Suites,** from a one-room studio to more luxurious town house and penthouse accommodations. **One Washington Circle** also offers a variety of floor plans, from "guest quarters" with sleeping and sitting areas in one large room to "grand staterooms" with separate bedroom, dining area, living area, and one and a half bathrooms. Most have kitchens and balconies. Business travelers and families are attracted to **The River Inn** because of spacious studios, large one-bedroom suites, and occasional super-duper deals that drop the $300-plus rack rates to less than $120.

✔ **Best hotels with international appeal:** Because it stands not far from the State Department, World Bank, Kennedy Center, and George Washington University, the **State Plaza** attracts diplomats and other international travelers bound for those government, artistic, and educational venues. The location of Irish-owned **Jurys Normandy Inn** — near diplomatic facilities in the exclusive Kalorama neighborhood — makes it a popular spot for diplomats and other international visitors as well. The French own the **Sofitel Lafayette Square** and are quite proud of serving up *art de vivre* — "the art of French living" — in the hotel's restaurant food, bar drinks, gift shop gifts, room décor, and even the staff's uniforms.

✔ **Best budget digs:** Youthful idealists in Washington on a shoestring and other budget-minded visitors find **Hostelling International** to be a simple but adequate place to spend the night, with rock-bottom prices for dormitory-style rooms. For families and cost-conscious touring groups, the centrally located **Hotel Harrington** provides large rooms and suites starting at $99. The low-cost **Red Roof Inn** chain operates an urban version of its roadside motels near the Verizon Center, Convention Center, Chinatown, and many attractions of the fast-growing Penn Quarter entertainment and arts neighborhood.

The Best Restaurants

For more information on the restaurants listed here, see Chapter 10.

✔ **Best power palaces:** So you want to watch James Carville and Mary Matalin duke it out over dinner? Grab a table at the **Palm,** where the famous feast on steak and lobster. Senators and Supreme Court justices hang out at **The Monocle** on Capitol Hill. Located near the White House, the **Occidental** attracts presidential aides, journalists, and lobbyists. Check out the photos of the powerful and the famous who have been dining on this site for the last 100 years.

✔ **Best for big spenders:** Pretend you're a member of Congress, for whom (other people's) money is no object, and sample the best Washington food that lots of money can buy. Entrees start at $29 and the tasting menus are $110 to $145 at **Le Paradou,** an exquisite contemporary French restaurant that opened in mid-2004. Also exquisite and French (or "French/Californian," as Chef Michel Richard terms it) is **Michel Richard Citronelle,** where fixed-price meals range from $85 to $150 and a seat at the chef's table starts at $275. Chef Roberto Donna's private dining room at **Galileo,** which he calls **Laboratorio,** charges atmospheric prices for spectacular Italian food. All of which makes **CityZen**'s New American tasting menus seem like bargains at $75 for three courses and $90 for five — plus wine, of course.

Galileo closed for renovations in 2006 and was scheduled to reopen by fall 2007.

✔ **Best for fighting the deficit:** In all-American tradition, **Luna Grill & Diner** offers old-fashioned blue-plate specials and new age green-plate specials for vegetarians. **Booeymonger,** a local deli chain, is open from breakfast to late in the city, till not quite so late in the suburbs. Another local chain, **Firehook Bakery,** offers inventive sandwiches on its own breads and pours D.C.'s best coffee, locally roasted Quartermaine.

✔ **Best for debating foreign policy:** It's dreadfully undiplomatic to pick out a handful of best international restaurants from the zillions that do business in this very international town. But, here goes: **Montmartre** really tastes and feels like France, as does **Cafe La Ruche** for a lot fewer francs. Chef Vikram Sunderam terms **Rasika's** cuisine "modern Indian." It's superb and probably unlike any other Indian dishes you've come across in the past. Authentic Italian cooking comes from the kitchen at **Obelisk,** a small cafe near Dupont Circle that offers a fixed-price menu with a few wonderful selections each evening. **City Lights of China** serves up good Chinese food in attractive surroundings, while the surroundings at **Eat First** are as plain as its name but the food is a joy. For a fun night out with a group, go sit on the floor and eat with your fingers at Moroccan **Marrakesh.**

✔ **Best for inexpensive international fare:** You get real Neapolitan pizza at **Pizzeria Paradiso** and **2 Amys.** To nibble your way through small plates of various nationalities, try **Zaytinya** for Mediterranean *meze* or **Jaleo** for Spanish tapas.

✔ **Best for romancing your number-one constituent:** In cold weather, reserve the table nearest the fire in **Sea Catch's** front dining room, where the walls are made of stone and wood paneling and floor-to-ceiling windows overlook the C&O Canal. Fireside tables also beckon in **1789 Restaurant,** which occupies a 19th-century, Federalist-style home in Georgetown. In warm weather, dine on the balcony over-looking the C&O Canal.

✔ **Best for prevoters:** Kids as well as grownups cast ballots for **2 Amys** and **Pizzeria Paradiso.** Not only is the food kid-friendly, but these places are cheerful and noisy. The Tex-Mex **Austin Grill** restaurants also are gaily noisy, and — downtown and in the suburbs — gaily decorated. The **Old Ebbitt Grill** draws White House staff and pleases adult palates, but the large menu also includes much of interest to children — burgers and finger-food appetizers, for example. And kids' wandering attention can be directed to the hunting trophies and other odd stuff that's scattered throughout this large restaurant/pub.

The Best Attractions

For more information on the attractions listed here, see Chapter 11 unless otherwise indicated.

✔ **Best memorial:** For me, the **Thomas Jefferson Memorial** wins hands-down because of its idyllic setting on the Tidal Basin, its gorgeous views of cherry trees and other Washington landmarks, its suggestion of Tom's home of Monticello, and the inspiring words engraved around the rotunda. It also helps that Jefferson is my favorite founding father. The **Abraham Lincoln Memorial** is a close runner-up, however, for similar reasons. The view from the top of the memorial's steps is a breathtaking sweep of the entire National Mall to the Capitol dome, Lincoln's words are engraved on the walls, and this was the site of many historical events, including Martin Luther King, Jr.'s, "I Have a Dream" speech.

✔ **Best art galleries:** The **National Gallery of Art** is one of the world's great art museums, and it keeps getting better. But the top spot in Washington at this moment has to go to the **American Art Museum** and the **National Portrait Gallery,** which share the Old Patent Office Building in Penn Quarter. Reopened in mid-2006 after a six-year renovation, the galleries' art and venue both will wow you.

✔ **Best places for art that moves:** Hands down, this award has to go to the **John F. Kennedy Center for the Performing Arts,** which is home to the National Symphony, Washington Opera, Washington Ballet, Washington Performing Arts Society, and many traveling shows, both classical and popular. See Chapter 15 for more information.

✔ **Best spot to be emotionally moved:** Somewhere there may be someone who was untouched by a visit to the **U.S. Holocaust Memorial Museum,** but I have yet to meet him. More than a reminder of Nazi atrocities, this museum also conducts memorable programs about genocide. At **Arlington National Cemetery,** the endless rows of plain white grave markers tug at your heart, silently proclaiming the sacrifice of America's military men and women. Many famous Americans have more elaborate memorials here, including presidents Kennedy and Taft. Emotions at the **Vietnam Veterans Memorial** flow from the controversial nature of that war and the constant presence of veterans and friends and relatives of the dead, who search out specific names on the black granite wall. The simplicity of young Chinese-American architect Maya Lin's design became a prototype for many later memorials erected around the country.

✔ **Best government building:** The surroundings are a mess as I write because of construction of an underground visitor center and ugly, stop-gap security barricades, but the **Capitol** remains Washington's preeminent building. The dome is the number-one symbol of American democracy. And the interior is a fascinating mix of the American democratic spirit and ornate old European decoration. With some luck, the construction will be done during the shelf-life of this book, but don't bet your tax refund on it.

The Best Free Shows

For more info on the performing arts events listed, see Chapter 15.

✔ **Best free classical music:** For the best music ever written, performed by a world-class orchestra, for free, under the stars, you just can't top the **National Symphony**'s free summer concerts at the Carter Barron Amphitheater in Rock Creek Park and on the Capitol's west lawn.

✔ **Best free play:** You can equal the National Symphony's excellence (see preceding entry) with the best plays ever written and performed by a world-class troupe, for free, under the stars. That would be the **Shakespeare Theatre**'s no-charge summer performances, also at Carter Barron.

✔ **Best free military music:** The Army, Navy, Marine Corps, and Air Force bands present **military concerts** — where else? — at Carter Barron and outside the Capitol.

✔ **Best free who-knows-what:** In the **Kennedy Center**'s Grand Foyer, the Millennium Stage presents free performances every single day at 6 p.m. Performers range from storytellers to headliners such as Bobby McFerrin or the Pointer Sisters, although most are not well known.

The Best Stuff for Kids

For more information on the attractions listed, see Chapter 11.

✔ **Best animals:** With 2,400 animals on 163 acres of land, the **National Zoological Park** — better known as the National Zoo — can keep kids hopping till they run out of juice. If you get here during 2007, you may be able to see Tai Shan, the first giant panda cub born and surviving in D.C., before he's sent off to his parents' native digs in China.

✔ **Best things to touch that you wouldn't think you'd want to touch:** Children squeal with delight and parents feel a bit squeamish at the **National Museum of Natural History**'s insect zoo. Pet a tarantula. Hold a giant hissing cockroach. Crawl around in a model termite mound.

✔ **Best printed products:** You wouldn't think the **National Postal Museum** would be a big hit with the small set, but the little museum's interactive exhibits have made it a children's favorite. Kids also like to tour the **Bureau of Engraving and Printing,** where stamps, currency, government bonds, and White House invitations are made. Part of the reason is the jovial tour guides, whose red neckties are decorated with images of dollars.

✔ **Best flying objects:** Because kids love things that go zoom, the **National Air and Space Museum** is must-see D.C. for families. Luckily, for parents, big folks find this place fascinating as well.

Chapter 2

Digging Deeper into Washington, D.C.

*W*ashington, D.C., is a city where knowledge is power, so it helps to arrive knowing some background information (even if you don't intend to run for office). You should know who Pierre L'Enfant is and where Lincoln was assassinated. And if you expect to carry on conversations with local politicos, you should know the different between "pork" and "POTUS."

History 101: The Main Events

It all began, of course, with dinosaurs, then saber tooth tigers, and then human beings who eventually came to be called Native Americans. But what is now called Washington didn't really start its journey to becoming the capital of the United States until those Europeans started exploring what they thought of as the New World. Capt. John Smith, of Pocahontas fame, poked around the Potomac River near Washington in 1608, and another group of early European immigrants began to settle along the Anacostia River here in 1622.

Midway through the next century, the river port of George Towne (now Georgetown) was founded, named for King George of England, not the father of the still-unfounded United States. (The Old Stone House, built there in 1765, has survived to become one of modern Washington's very oldest buildings, on bustling M Street.) With George Towne, Maryland, and Alexandria, Virginia, developing as river ports, the colonies didn't look to this area for anything related to government until the end of the

Revolutionary War, when the Continental Congress began casting about for the best place to locate the new nation's capital.

In 1790, the new U.S. Congress, in one of many North-South compromises, authorized President Washington to select a site on the Potomac River, in the northern reaches of the Southern states. Washington, a surveyor by trade, picked the confluence of the Potomac and the Anacostia, a few miles upstream from his home at Mount Vernon, and hired French engineer Pierre L'Enfant to design the city. The District of Columbia, named for Christopher Columbus, was a perfect diamond, 10 miles on each side, straddling the Potomac River, with 69 of its square miles donated by Maryland and the remaining 31 by Virginia. (Virginia reclaimed its land in 1846, making the Potomac Washington's southwestern border.)

The federal government finally moved to D.C. in 1800, with the Capitol and the Executive Mansion still unfinished. Fifteen years later, those seminal structures of American democracy had to be rebuilt after being burned by the British in 1814 during the so-called War of 1812. The refurbishers painted the president's house white, and it's been called the White House ever since.

In the succeeding centuries, Washington has grown with the government it houses and changed with the nation that government leads. During the Civil War, President Lincoln ringed the capital city with forts and insisted on completing the Capitol's dome. As the government expanded to fight the depression, the New Deal's Works Progress Administration hired the unemployed to build the new bureaucracies' headquarters. The Pentagon, the world's largest office building, sprang to life during World War II. Magnificent Union Station was opened during the heyday of railroad travel in 1907, National Airport when commercial aviation was coming into its own in 1941, and Metrorail in 1976 when the Washington region's leaders realized they needed a subway system to move their booming population off the ever-more-congested highways and streets. In this new era of terrorism, on September 11, 2001, hijackers crashed American Airlines flight 77 into a section of the Pentagon, which was rebuilt and reopened in a year. (See the "Years to remember" sidebar in this section.)

Many visitors don't know this fact, but we D.C. residents don't enjoy the full benefits of U.S. citizenship because we don't live in a state. We have no voting representation in Congress, and Congress can override the actions of our elected mayor and council. We are subject to all the obligations of citizenship, however, including federal taxes and the draft. That's why the slogan on our license plates reads, "Taxation without representation."

Years to remember: A D.C. timeline

A lot can happen to a city over the course of 400 years. Here are just a few noteworthy events.

1608: Capt. John Smith explores the Potomac River.

1622: Europeans begin to settle along the Anacostia River.

1751: George Towne is founded.

1765: Old Stone House, now one of Washington's very oldest buildings, is erected in George Towne.

1790: The confluence of the Potomac and Anacostia rivers is selected as the site for the U.S. capital.

1800: The federal government moves to the District of Columbia.

1814: The British burn the Capitol and Executive Mansion during the War of 1812.

1817: The restored Executive Mansion is painted white and dubbed the White House.

1846: The land south of the Potomac is returned to Virginia.

1861–65: Washington is ringed with forts during the Civil War.

1865: The Capitol dome is completed. Lincoln is assassinated in Ford's Theatre.

1907: Union Station opens.

1941: National Airport opens.

1943: The Pentagon is completed.

1976: The first Metrorail stations open.

2001: The Pentagon is hit in September 11, 2001, terrorist attacks.

2002: The damaged Pentagon section reopens.

2007: A new Congress takes office, with Washington residents still on the outside looking in.

Architectural Basics

Washington architecture is a hodge-podge that just gets hodgier and podgier as time runs on. Even though the city's street plan largely follows architect L'Enfant's original diamondlike approach, the buildings that line the streets have been constructed willy-nilly according to the whims of the owners and the tastes of the time.

Much like a medieval cathedral, the **Capitol** — D.C.'s most prominent building — grew over the decades, and each section reflects not only the vision of an architect but the on-site alterations of construction managers as well. The Capitol Dome, perhaps the best-recognized symbol of American self-government, wasn't added until 1865. The West Front terraces were built between 1884 and 1892 and the East Front extension from 1958 to 1962. As I write, the East Lawn is a mess, as an underground visitor center is constructed.

You can find a real cathedral, the **Washington National Cathedral,** in the residential Upper Northwest area. (See Chapter 8 for a description of the neighborhood.) Under construction from 1907 to 1990, it was built the old-fashioned way, "stone-on-stone," with no structural steel for support.

The **White House,** designed by Irish architect James Hoban, was modeled after an Irish country home. Columned porticos on the north and south fronts were added later. The **Old Executive Office Building** next door, sporting 900 Doric columns, is a surreal wedding cake in a style dubbed Second Empire. **Arlington House** in Arlington National Cemetery, once the home of Robert E. Lee, is a classic plantation house, built by slaves in Greek Revival style. It's made of brick and covered by cement, which was scored and painted to look like marble and sandstone. **Union Station** is a marvelous Beaux Arts structure, built for the thriving railroad business at the beginning of the 20th century and restored as a bustling transportation, shopping, eating, and entertainment center at the century's end.

Many government buildings and monuments pay tribute to ancient Rome and Greece, with architects and committees again imposing their own twists on the classical recipes. On a smaller, domestic scale, the residential streets of Georgetown and Capitol Hill are lined with 19th-century town houses and mansions.

The Restaurant Scene

Washington doesn't really have a distinct cuisine, and that's not necessarily a bad thing. Because every community in America is represented in Congress, nearly every cuisine in America makes its way to at least one eating establishment here. The same is true for the cuisines of the world, because nearly every nation sends diplomats, journalists, and business people to monitor and try to influence the U.S. government.

To the extent that any dishes can be called local, they've probably been borrowed from Maryland's nearby shore. If they're in season and the waiter assures you that they're good, order up a crab-cake dinner or sandwich. Or engage in the labor-intensive celebration of digging the meat out of hard-shell crabs, an activity usually conducted on paper-covered tables and accompanied by generous quantities of beer. Soft-shell crabs, the same animal caught when it's between hard shells, are easier to eat.

The exception to the borrowed-cuisine rule is the half-smoke — a mild sausage usually served on a hot dog bun. You'll find half-smokes at nearly every sidewalk food cart and in many short-order eateries. The only thing special about this sausage is that it doesn't seem to be sold under that name anyplace else.

For a more detailed look at D.C. food and restaurants, see Chapter 10.

The Local Lingo

What Washington lacks in unique food, it more than makes up for in unique language — the jargon of politics and government. You'll hear it spoken not only when you tour the halls of Congress but when you eavesdrop on conversations in a restaurant, along the sidewalk, or on a Metrorail train.

If you're fluent in this jargon, then you know that a lawmaker doesn't propose a piece of legislation; he *drops a bill.* The heads of the powerful House subcommittees that control spending bills are not chairmen; they're the *college of cardinals.* A *gaggle* is not a gathering of geese but a gathering of reporters around a news source. You could write a book about this stuff. In fact, several people already have. Check out *Hatchet Jobs & Hardball: American Political Slang,* by Grant Barrett (Oxford University Press).

Here are a few definitions of words or phrases you may hear and wonder about as you wander about D.C.

- ✔ **Advance man:** A political operative who prepares an event before the candidate arrives.
- ✔ **Background:** Interviewer-interviewee agreement by which the information imparted can be reported but the source's identity must be kept confidential.
- ✔ **Carpetbagger:** Politician who moves into a new community to seek power.
- ✔ **Dark horse:** Candidate who probably can't win.
- ✔ **Eleventh Commandment:** GOP tradition — often honored in the breach — that Republicans should not speak ill of other Republicans.
- ✔ **Fat cat:** Someone with lots of money.
- ✔ **Gentle lady:** What the gentlemen of the House call their female colleagues because, for some reason, just plain "lady" doesn't suffice.
- ✔ **Gerrymander:** To draw odd-shaped legislative districts in order to benefit the party in power.
- ✔ **Hack:** A low-ranking party worker who does what he's told.
- ✔ **Junket:** A government official's all-expenses-paid trip that has questionable value to government.

✔ **Lame duck:** Government official who has been defeated or can't run for reelection.

✔ **Off the record:** Information that can't be published.

✔ **The other body:** What the House calls the Senate and the Senate calls the House.

✔ **Pork:** Legislated benefits for a small group rather than for the national interest.

✔ **POTUS:** In acronym-obsessed Washington, the President of the United States.

✔ **Red tape:** Bureaucratic rules that slow down action.

✔ **SCOTUS:** The Supreme Court of the United States.

✔ **Smoke-filled room:** Where politicians cut deals without public scrutiny, and where today smoking probably isn't allowed.

✔ **Think tank:** Organization that conducts research and analysis.

✔ **Veep:** The vice president.

✔ **Waffle:** Not taking a clear stand.

Recommended Movies and Books

My journalistic background may bias my analysis, but I think the best tell-it-like-it-is Washington movie is *All the President's Men,* starring Robert Redford and Dustin Hoffman as then-young *Washington Post* reporters Bob Woodward and Carl Bernstein, who broke the Watergate scandal. This wonderful flick somehow manages to be entertaining while showing how reporters really go about their (often tedious) jobs. A spectacular overhead shot of Woodstein (as the pair was nicknamed) doing research in the **Library of Congress**'s Main Reading Room marvelously evokes two little guys tackling an enormous challenge. My favorite slice of dialogue occurs when a big-shot politician issues the quintessentially Washingtonian threat that if Woodward publishes certain information, "our relationship will be over." The young and politically unconnected Woodward ponders for a moment and then replies, "We don't have a relationship."

You can find many good books about Washington and the game of politics, starting with the real Woodward and Bernstein's *All the President's Men* (Simon & Schuster), upon which the movie was based. Their boss, Washington Post Co. publisher, president, and chair Katharine Graham, collected and annotated more than 100 pieces about Washington that were published posthumously as *Katharine Graham's Washington* (Vintage) in 2002. The annotations record the Washington of her lifetime, from 1917 to preterrorist 2001, and showcase (sometimes surprisingly) the words of John Dos Passos, Russell Baker, David Brinkley, Will Rogers,

James Thurber, Simone de Beauvoir, and many more people. Theodore H. White's ***The Making of the President 1960*** (Buccaneer) chronicles the inside workings of the Kennedy-Nixon campaign race and changed political reporting forever. In ***The Boys on the Bus*** (Random House), Timothy Crouse reveals how the campaign press corps gets its inside stories. Woodward again — this time with co-author Scott Armstrong — exposed the inside workings of the Supreme Court in ***The Brethren*** (Island).

Not all Washington books are nonfiction — or particularly serious. This town has spawned quite a few good mystery writers. Margaret Truman, President Harry's daughter, writes the **"Capital Crime Series,"** with (so far) more than a dozen murder-mysteries set in various Washington locations: ***Murder in the White House*** (Fawcett), ***Murder in Georgetown*** (Fawcett), ***Murder at the Library of Congress*** (Fawcett), ***Murder at Ford's Theatre*** (Ballantine), ***Murder on Capitol Hill*** (Fawcett), ***Murder in the Supreme Court*** (Fawcett) . . . You get the bloody picture. Elliott Roosevelt, son of President Harry's predecessor, wrote such a successful murder-mystery series that, since his 1990 death, his publisher (St. Martin's Minotaur) keeps issuing **"Elliott Roosevelt Mysteries"** written by other (still living) authors. The detective-hero is Elliott's mother, First Lady Eleanor Roosevelt, and the murders often take place in a very violent White House. While alive, Elliott penned such titles as ***The White House Pantry Murder*** (St. Martin's), ***Murder in the Oval Office*** (Avon), and ***Murder in the Rose Garden*** (St. Martin's).

For hard-boiled private-eye action set in Washington's mean streets not often traversed by politicians or tourists, check out George Pelecanos's works, such as ***Right as Rain, Hell to Pay*** (both published by Warner), or, most recently, ***The Night Gardener,*** in which homicide victims' bodies turn up in D.C.'s community gardens.

Chapter 3

Deciding When to Go

*L*ife in Washington is affected by two kinds of seasons — Mother Nature's and Congress's. Deciding when to visit will determine what you can see, how much you pay, how many people you battle at the attractions, and how your body feels about the weather.

Discovering the Secret of the Seasons

You can't choose a bad time to visit D.C. if your primary goal is to see the sights and you're not concerned about the crowds, the temperature, or the humidity. You can tour the museums, monuments, and government buildings any season. Cultural, entertainment, and sports activities are always going on. And shops are happy to provide their wares whenever you walk in with money.

 Overall, the best times to visit D.C. are spring and fall — April through mid-June and September through mid-November. Temperature and humidity tend to be moderate. Flowers are on display in the spring. The weather in the fall can be close to ideal. Congress is likely to be at work, and cultural and entertainment activities are running full force.

Unfortunately, spring also brings crowds. I've always believed that all Americans should visit Washington at least once. But it's easy to grumble as you pick your way through gangs of middle-school students blocking sidewalks as they wait for their tour buses to arrive.

In terms of expense, visiting in the spring means that you find fewer lodging bargains, especially during the work week when business travelers fill the hotels. In addition, events like the Cherry Blossom Festival are so popular that hotels and restaurants can charge top prices.

You can find more bargains in hotter summer months, as hotels try to fill the rooms that empty during Congressional vacations by offering money-saving package deals. You can also enjoy a great deal of free, outdoor entertainment in the summer.

If you're anxious to see government in action, keep in mind that Congress tries to take lengthy recesses in August and near year's end. Another strike against August is that it can feel like an equatorial rainforest — excruciating heat, even more excruciating humidity, and frequent, vicious thunderstorms. The National Weather Service says July is hotter and has more rain, but August always feels worse.

Washington does get a real winter most years, usually with snow and some periods of extreme cold in January and February, even though for many years the city government seemed not to understand the concept of snow and how to plow it. If you don't mind the cold, Washington looks gorgeous after a snowfall, especially when the Congressional Christmas tree is on display at the foot of Capitol Hill. And the city has lately been doing a better job of clearing the streets when the snow falls.

That said, why don't you slip Vivaldi into your CD player and consider the pros and cons of Washington's four seasons?

Spring: Blooming beautiful in D.C.

Spring is a popular time for D.C. visits because:

- ✔ The days are clear and comfortable, and Washington is at its most lush and beautiful.

- ✔ Gardens on and around the Mall (around the entire city, for that matter) bloom with tulips, daffodils, cherry blossoms, dogwoods, and azaleas.

 However, keep in mind the following springtime pitfalls:

- ✔ Washington's weather is always fickle. Scattered among the gorgeous spring days are an occasional preview of summer's heat, humidity, and thunderstorms, along with a sporadic period that feels a bit too cool. Wear layers of clothing and bring rain gear.

- ✔ Tourists, especially busloads of schoolchildren, pour in like a monsoon. Expect crowds, longer lines, and more traffic.

Summer: Having fun in the D.C. sun

Benefits of a summer visit include:

- ✔ The kids are out of school.

- ✔ Many hotels offer money-saving packages.

✔ Many museums offer extended hours.

✔ Free events, such as outdoor concerts, are plentiful.

On the other hand:

✔ Summer means *major* heat, folks. And humidity. Both make frequent appearances until well after Labor Day. (See Table 3-1 for month-by-month averages of D.C.'s temperature and rainfall.)

✔ The influx of summer vacationers can mean longer-than-usual lines at attractions and cold-drink vendors.

✔ Some theaters are dark (or at least darker) in July and August. If you're hoping to see a production by one of Washington's theater companies, check to make sure that it has summer offerings.

Table 3-1 Washington, D.C.'s, Average Temperatures (°F/°C) & Rainfall (in inches)

	Jan	Feb	Mar	Apr	May	June	July	Aug	Sep	Oct	Nov	Dec
Avg. High	43/ 6	47/ 8	56/ 13	66/ 19	75/ 24	84/ 29	88/ 31	86/ 30	79/ 26	68/ 20	57/ 14	47/ 8
Avg. Low	27/ −3	30/ −1	37/ 3	46/ 8	56/ 13	65/ 18	70/ 21	69/ 21	62/ 17	50/ 10	40/ 4	32/ 0
Rainfall	3.21	2.63	3.6	2.77	3.82	3.13	3.66	3.44	3.79	3.22	3.03	3.05

(Source: U.S. National Weather Service.)

Fall: Harvest good times in Washington

If you don't have to worry about school schedules, fall probably is the best time to travel to D.C.:

✔ The weather is as good as it gets. Heat and humidity drop as the calendar wears on.

✔ Lines are shorter; crowds are smaller.

✔ Entertainment and cultural opportunities abound.

But watch out for:

✔ Congress reconvenes, and the convention scene heats up, filling up hotels and restaurants, particularly during the work week.

✔ Traffic can be worse than in summer. (But you're too smart to drive around Washington anyway, aren't you?)

Winter: A great place to celebrate the holidays

Winter brings visions of softly falling snowflakes and holiday cheer, although the snow often holds off until the holidays are over. Advantages of a winter visit mean:

- ✔ You don't need to worry about heat and humidity.

- ✔ Lines at museums and other attractions are short or nonexistent.

- ✔ Colorful, often free, holiday events are plentiful from December into January.

- ✔ Airlines and tour operators offer good deals.

- ✔ When snow piles up on the ground, you get picture-postcard views of the Capitol, the White House, and other photogenic buildings and monuments.

- ✔ Congress and the White House set up their competing Christmas trees. (The Congressional tree is better!)

Winter does have its downsides, however:

- ✔ While its average temperatures look good on paper, Washington always is visited by some extremes. A damp, windy, 40-degree day on the Mall can feel colder than zero in Alaska. And D.C. does get real cold and windy winter weather — subzero temperatures and even the occasional blizzard — if only for short spells.

- ✔ You have fewer opportunities for outdoor activities.

Washington's Calendar of Capital Events

D.C.'s date book is jam-packed with special events. Some holidays celebrated throughout the country are extra-special here (Independence Day, for example). I list available dates and times (note that D.C. is in the Eastern Time Zone), but please double-check specifics before planning your vacation around an event; they're subject to change. See the Friday "Weekend" section of the *Washington Post* for comprehensive, up-to-date listings.

Because the easiest way to get around D.C. is by Metrorail — the local subway — the event listings include the Metrorail stops closest to them. The site listings in Part IV give detailed directions. Unless otherwise noted, the events are free.

January

Martin Luther King, Jr.'s, Birthday (☎ 202-426-6841; www.nps.gov/linc; Metro: Foggy Bottom–George Washington University) is celebrated in word and music on the third Monday in January at the Lincoln Memorial, site of the great civil rights leader's "I Have a Dream" speech.

Inauguration Day, U.S. Capitol (Metro: McPherson Square, Federal Triangle, Archives-Navy Memorial, Federal Center Southwest, Capitol South, Union Station), occurs at noon on January 20 every fourth year, the day the president is sworn in at the Capitol. A **parade** along Pennsylvania Avenue from the Capitol to the White House follows the swearing in. You need political contacts to get a seat on the Capitol lawn or on the parade route bleachers. (A friend with an office window or balcony that overlooks the route is good, too.) Otherwise, head for that long stretch between Congress's and the president's workplaces that morning — the earlier, the better. The next presidential inauguration is January 20, 2009.

January is Washington's coldest month, so the inauguration can be a bone-chilling event. Be prepared!

February

During **Black History Month,** African Americans' struggles and achievements are commemorated in numerous ways throughout the city. Museums, libraries, and other sites feature readings, speeches, musical performances, and other events. Check these Web sites: National Park Service (www.nps.gov/ncro/PublicAffairs/Calendar.htm), Smithsonian Institution (www.si.edu/events), and the Washington Convention and Tourism Corp. (www.washington.org).

On February 12, at noon, at the Lincoln Memorial, wreath-laying, band music, and a dramatic reading of the Gettysburg Address mark **Abraham Lincoln's Birthday,** Lincoln Memorial (☎ 202-426-6841; www.nps.gov/linc; Metro: Foggy Bottom–George Washington University).

March

As with Black History Month, many Washington institutions commemorate the achievements of women during **Women's History Month,** various locations. You can find information on the Internet from the National Park Service at www.nps.gov/ncro/PublicAffairs/Calendar.htm, the Smithsonian Institution at www.si.edu/events, and the Washington Convention and Tourism Corp. at www.washington.org.

March to April

At the **Smithsonian Kite Festival,** Washington Monument grounds (☎ 202-633-1000; Metro: Smithsonian), you can compete, watch the experts, or just find a place to fly your own kite. The Smithsonian Associates and the National Air and Space Museum sponsor this carefree Washington tradition, usually in late March or early April, in conjunction with the Cherry Blossom Festival.

Daily events bloom all over town during the **National Cherry Blossom Festival,** at various locations (www.nationalcherryblossomfestival.org), which runs for about two weeks in March and April. The official highlight is the **parade** near the end of the festivities. But the real stars are the cherry blossoms, especially those around the Tidal Basin, and they make their appearances whenever they darn well please. Click "Bloom Watch" at the festival's Web site for info on projected peak blooming dates. The blooms provide a great backdrop and canopy for a picnic at the Tidal Basin or on the Washington Monument Grounds.

Since 1878, presidents have invited children to roll eggs on the White House lawn the Monday after Easter at the **White House Easter Egg Roll** (☎ **202-456-7041;** www.whitehouse.gov/easter; Metro: McPherson Square). Modern presidents have added entertainment — inside and outside the White House grounds — to occupy the youngsters during the inevitable waits in line. Free tickets timed for entrance are distributed first-come, first-served at the Ellipse Visitor Pavilion on the southwest corner of 15th and E streets NW. Most tickets are distributed beginning at 7:30 a.m. Saturday, with some additional tickets made available beginning at 7:30 a.m. Monday. Lines can be gargantuan. Children of all ages can attend, as long as at least one child is 7 or younger and no more than two adults are in the group.

Note: Rules for Egg Roll admission are subject to change from year to year, so be sure to check before your visit. Outdoor events are also affected by bad weather.

April

For four days in mid-April, more than 100 artisans from around the country, selected from more than 1,000 entrants, display their expertise at basketry, ceramics, decorative fiber, furniture, glass, jewelry, leather, metal, mixed media, paper, wearable art, and wood during the **Smithsonian Craft Show,** National Building Museum, 401 F St. NW (☎ **888-832-9554;** www.smithsoniancraftshow.org; Metro: Judiciary Square). The Smithsonian calls this "the nation's most prestigious juried exhibition and sale of contemporary American crafts." Admission is $15 for adults; $12 for seniors, students, military, and Smithsonian Associates; free for children 12 and younger (but strollers are not permitted). If you come with 11 friends, you can purchase 12 tickets in advance for $120.

May

What better place to mark **Memorial Day** than Washington, D.C., the site of so many memorials? Ceremonies abound at monuments to American heroes of the past. One of the most moving begins with a **wreath-laying** at 11 a.m. at the Tomb of the Unknowns in Arlington National Cemetery, where members of the Army's 3rd Infantry, the Old Guard, place flags at more than 260,000 graves just prior to the weekend (☎ **703-607-8000;** www.arlingtoncemetery.org). Usually, the president or another high-ranking government official participates.

One of the most pleasant places to be on Memorial Day weekend is on a blanket or a folding chair on the Capitol's West Lawn as the National Symphony Orchestra presents its **Memorial Day Concert** at 8 p.m. on

Sunday (☎ **800-444-1324** or 202-467-4600; www.kennedy-center.org/ nso; Metro: Capitol South, Union Station, Federal Center Southwest). The rain date is Memorial Day itself, but the concert is rarely postponed unless the weather is truly terrible. With the performers enclosed in a band shell and a national audience looking on via PBS, the concert isn't rescheduled lightly. This event is eclectic, with classical, popular, and patriotic music performed by the orchestra and glamorous guest stars, and it draws a big crowd.

You can catch the **dress rehearsal** at 7:30 p.m. the day before the National Symphony's Memorial Day concert at the Capitol.

June

Traditional music, crafts, and ethnic foods from the United States and around the world fill the Mall with enticing sounds, sights, and scents from late June through early July during the **Smithsonian Festival of American Folklife** (☎ **202-275-1150;** www.folklife.si.edu/center/ festival.html; Metro: Smithsonian). One of Washington's premier outdoor events, the festival typically highlights one or two states and foreign countries.

July

The nation's capital does it up big for the nation's **Independence Day Celebration.** Highlights include the **parade** along Constitution Avenue starting a little before noon, the National Symphony Orchestra **concert** (again with big-name guests) on the Capitol's West Lawn at 8 p.m., and the **fireworks** launched from around the Lincoln Memorial Reflecting Pool shortly after 9 p.m. Oh, and the **Smithsonian Festival of American Folklife** (see preceding entry) is in full swing! Expect big crowds, especially at the Capitol for the concert. Popular spots for viewing the fireworks include the Mall, the Jefferson Memorial, the Ellipse behind the White House, the Marine Corps (Iwo Jima) Memorial, and areas along the Virginia side of the Potomac River that can be reached from George Washington Memorial Parkway parking lots.

Since the 2001 terrorist attacks, July 4 visitors to the Mall have had to pass through security checkpoints. You can't have alcoholic beverages, glass bottles, fireworks, or grills on the Mall or other surrounding federal land, including the banks of the Potomac and Anacostia rivers.

Here's another place the locals go to watch the fireworks: the Key Bridge, which crosses the Potomac River between Georgetown and Arlington. Get there early to grab a railing-side spot. There's no seating, and you can stand on the sidewalks only (not in the traffic lanes).

To avoid the July 4 crowds, you can catch the same show (sans fireworks) at the Capitol concert **dress rehearsal** at 7:30 p.m. July 3.

August

On an August evening each year, the U.S. Army Band performs Tchaikovsky's rousing **"1812 Overture"** (Sylvan Theater at the Washington Monument; ☎ **703-696-3399;** www.mdw.army.mil; Metro: Smithsonian), accompanied by cannon fire from the Presidential Salute Gun Battery of The Old Guard (the 3rd Infantry Regiment). Call or check the Web site for the exact date (☎ **800-444-1324** or 202-467-4600; www.kennedy-center.org/nso).

September

Washingtonians mark the end of summer by toting blankets and folding chairs to the Capitol Lawn and listening to the National Symphony Orchestra perform its **Labor Day Concert** (☎ **800-444-1324** or 202-467-4600; www.kennedy-center.org/nso; Metro: Capitol South, Union Station, Federal Center Southwest) with some guest celebrities. The concert starts at 8 p.m. on the Sunday of Labor Day weekend.

During the **Kennedy Center Open House,** Kennedy Center (☎ **800-444-1324** or 202-467-4600; www.kennedy-center.org; Metro: Foggy Bottom–George Washington University), the hall and grounds of the performing arts center showcase performances in music, theater, and dance, along with special activities for kids. This event is popular, so be prepared to encounter lines for the inside events.

Hundreds of thousands of parents, grandparents, and children flock to the National Mall for the two-day **Black Family Reunion** (☎ **202-737-0120;** www.ncnw.org/events/reunion.htm; Metro: Smithsonian), a celebration of African-American heritage. The festival features music, food, arts, crafts, and pavilions dedicated to such subjects as health, sports, and education.

If reading's your thing, you can get your fill of books, book-signings, author speeches, and other things literary at the **National Book Festival** (☎ **888-714-4696;** www.loc.gov/bookfest; Metro: Smithsonian). It's free, on the Mall, and sponsored by the folks at the Library of Congress, who know a thing or three about the subject at hand.

October

The famous **Marine Corps Marathon** (☎ **800-786-8762;** www.marine marathon.com) is so popular that registration for the 34,000 (!) runners' slots fills up in less than three days. Go to the Web site to find out when registration opens (probably in May). The race, on the last Sunday of October, is nicknamed the "Marathon of the Monuments" for good reason. It starts near the Iwo Jima statue at the edge of Arlington Cemetery and winds through Georgetown and the core of D.C., passing the major memorials, Smithsonian museums, White House, Capitol, and Pentagon before returning to the starting point. You don't have to be a world-class runner to participate. Many highly fit amateurs rise to this challenge. If you're not a runner, stake out a spot along the route and watch.

November

During the **Veterans' Day Ceremony** at Arlington National Cemetery
(☎ **703-607-8000;** www.arlingtoncemetery.org; Metro: Arlington
Cemetery), the president or another high-ranking government official
lays a wreath at the Tomb of the Unknowns at 11 a.m. November 11.

December

In early December, a member of the First Family throws a switch to light
the large Christmas tree in the Ellipse. The **White House Christmas Tree
Lighting** (www.pageantofpeace.org/opening.htm; Metro: Federal
Triangle) kicks off the Pageant of Peace, which continues most of the
month. Features include a Yule Log, a circle of smaller trees — each decorated on the theme of a state, territory, or the District of Columbia —
and musical performances from 6 to 8:30 p.m. most nights. Free tickets
for the lighting are distributed first-come, first-served at the Ellipse
Visitor Pavilion on the southwest corner of 15th and E streets NW. One
person can get four tickets, and they can disappear in less than an hour.
People have been known to get in line nine hours early! Tickets usually
are distributed on the first Saturday in November. Check this Web site
for details: www.nps.gov/whho/pageant.htm. Tickets aren't needed for
the rest of the pageant.

Keep in mind that it gets bitterly cold in Washington in the winter from
time to time. If it's cold when you visit, bundle up good, or you may
spend all your time at the pageant huddled beside the burning Yule Log.

During the **Kennedy Center Holiday Celebrations** (☎ **800-444-1324** or
202-467-4600; www.kennedy-center.org; Metro: Foggy Bottom–George
Washington University), the performing arts center hosts holiday-
themed events throughout the month, including dancing in the Grand
Foyer on New Year's Eve and a Christmas Eve performance of Handel's
Messiah by the National Symphony and the National Cathedral's Choral
Society.

Part II
Planning Your Trip to Washington, D.C.

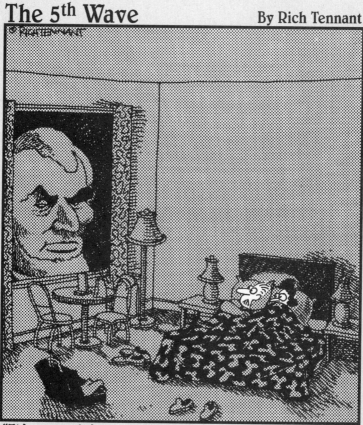

"It's creepin' me out too, but you're the one who wanted a hotel room close to the Lincoln Memorial."

In this part . . .

This part helps you get serious about planning your visit. Here you find the nitty-gritty about options — and costs — for your trip. I compile some tips for keeping your possessions safe and what to do if you lose something. Then I give advice for folks with special needs or interests: families, seniors, travelers with limited mobility, and gay and lesbian visitors to D.C.

Chapter 4

Managing Your Money

- -

In This Chapter

▶ Planning your budget
▶ Cutting costs — but not the fun
▶ Handling money
▶ Dealing with a lost or stolen wallet

- -

*W*hen I was a newspaper reporter, a joke around the Washington bureau was that the only guy on staff who thought D.C. living costs were reasonable was the guy who transferred from Tokyo! Washington is not a cheap place to live, especially when it comes to housing. But, believe it or not, the District can be a reasonably priced place to visit. Many attractions and events are free, and you can take cheap public transportation to most places. You also can use this book to find good deals at places where prices often are sky high.

Planning Your Budget

No matter how clever a traveler you are — unless you're staying with friends who feed you and schlep you around town — you can't avoid opening your wallet to eat here, sleep here, get here, get around here, and enjoy some of Washington's entertainment options.

Transportation

D.C. offers many forms of local transportation. Some are easier on your pocketbook — and stress level — than others.

The most expensive — and nerve-shattering — is **driving yourself.** If you drive to D.C., park your car when you get here and don't touch it until you leave. Even then, you may be charged $20 or more each night for parking at your hotel. (For a list of other typical D.C. costs, see Table 4-1.) No one in his or her right mind drives while sightseeing here. The streets are too crowded. There's not enough street parking. Garage parking fees reach the stratosphere. All the circles, squares, and meandering avenues make for mind-numbing traffic patterns. Washington is full of important people — or people who think they're important — and they drive as though the function of all other vehicles is to get out of their way.

Table 4-1   What Things Cost in Washington, D.C.

Item	Cost
Taxi from Reagan National Airport to downtown	$12
Metrorail from National to Metro Center: Rush hour (5:30–9:30 a.m. and 3–7 p.m. weekdays)	$1.65; normal hours $1.35
Taxi from Dulles Airport to downtown	$55
SuperShuttle van service from Dulles to downtown	$22 first passenger, $10 each additional
Express Metrobus from Dulles to L'Enfant Plaza	$3
SuperShuttle from Baltimore/Washington International Airport (BWI) to downtown	$31 for first passenger, $11 each additional
Taxi from BWI	$60–$65
Pay telephone call (local)	50¢
Metro	$1.35–$1.85 (most trips within D.C.)
Taxi	$6.50 (within one zone)
Admission to all Smithsonian museums	Free

The good news is that **cabs** are relatively cheap, the **Metrorail** subway system is one of the best in the world, and the **Metrobuses** can take you just about any place you want to go.

Metrorail (☎ **202-637-7000;** www.wmata.com) is the first choice for moving around town, because it's fast, clean, comfortable, and reasonably priced. You can find stations near most major attractions. It starts running at 5 a.m. Monday through Friday, 7 a.m. on weekends, and closes at midnight Sunday through Thursday, 3 a.m. Friday and Saturday. Fares, based on distance traveled, range from $1.35 to $2.35 per trip, except during weekday rush hours and after 2 a.m. Friday and Saturday; then, the range is $1.35 to $3.90. When you travel among the main attractions from Capitol Hill to Dupont Circle and Foggy Bottom, you pay just $1.35 at any time. Up to two children ages four and younger ride free with a paying adult. If you travel during peak morning and evening commute time, expect standing-room-only, packed-like-sardines crowds on the trains. Get comprehensive information about routes, schedules, and fares at the service windows in the Metro Center Station. Informational signs and manned kiosks are located at every station entrance.

Most **Metrobuses** (☎ 202-637-7000; www.wmata.com) run all the time, but less frequently in the wee hours and on weekends. The fare is just $1.25, unless you stumble onto one of the few express buses that cost $3.

Bus-to-bus **Metro Transfers** are free. Transferring from Metrorail to Metrobus costs 35¢. Get the transfer from a machine in the station where you enter the Metrorail system. There is no bus-to-rail transfer discount.

Taxis cost less than in most big cities, but the bizarre fare structure can baffle longtime residents as well as first-time tourists. D.C. taxis don't have meters. Instead, the city is divided into zones, and you're charged according to the zones you travel through. You see a map — with north NOT at the top! — posted in the back seat of the taxi. A cab ride to a destination within the same zone costs $6.50. Crossing into another zone makes the fare $8.80, and it continues to increase as more zones are entered. Then add $1.50 for each passenger older than five who accompanies you, $1 for trips during the 7 to 9:30 a.m. or 4 to 6:30 p.m. weekday rush hours, 50¢ to $2 for luggage handled by the driver depending on its size, and $2 if you telephone for a cab instead of hail it on the street. There's a $1.75 surcharge for single passengers at National Airport and a $2.50 surcharge when the DC Taxicab Commission declares a snow emergency. If you take a D.C. cab into the suburbs (to an airport, for example), you're charged by the mile as the cabby reads it on his odometer. The good news for tourists is that Zone 1 contains many major attractions, including the Capitol, White House, and Smithsonian museums on the Mall. The bad news is that humidity, air pressure, and phases of the moon can alter the fare calculations — or, at least, it seems that way. The fare downtown from National Airport is about $12. It's about $55 from Dulles and $60 to $65 from Baltimore/ Washington International. D.C. cabbies are allowed to pick up additional passengers without the consent of the original passenger, as long as the original passenger doesn't have to go more than 5 blocks out of the way. (The driver needs the original passenger's consent if the subsequent passenger has a pet or other animal, unless it's a service dog.) In that circumstance, each passenger pays full fare for his or her trip, so it's to the cabby's advantage to double up. But it seldom happens. Washington cabbies cruise major government/business/tourist areas and usually are easy to find during the day and early evening. Off-hours and off-the-beaten-track, cabs can be nearly impossible to hail. Try outside a major hotel. Or pay the surcharge to summon a taxi by phone. Two of the bigger D.C. taxi organizations are **Diamond Cab** (☎ 202-387-6200) and **Yellow Cab** (☎ 202-544-1212).

To find out a fare before you ride, call the D.C. Taxicab Commission at ☎ 202-645-6018, or check out the D.C. government's cool fare calculator at www.citizenatlas.dc.gov/atlasapps/taxifare.aspx.

Another option is to sit back and relax on **Tourmobile** (☎ 202-554-5100, 888-868-7707; www.tourmobile.com), an open-sided tram that makes about 15 stops near top tourist sites daily except December 25. The

Tourmobile is a great way to get an overview of the top attractions and is especially attractive to families, the elderly, travelers with disabilities, and the weary of all ages. For $20 ($10 for children 3 through 11, free for younger kids), you can get off and reboard as many times as you want between 9:30 a.m. and 3:30 p.m. and ride until 4:30 p.m. You can buy tickets from the driver (no credit cards) or at Tourmobile ticket booths.

The final good news for travelers watching their wallets is that D.C. is pedestrian friendly. Because many of the top sights are close to each other, **walking** often is the best way to travel between them. Just watch for those self-obsessed Washington drivers.

Lodging

You can spend as little as $32 a night for a bed in dormitory-like rooms at **Hostelling International** (☎ 202-737-2333; hiwashingtondc.org) or pay $4,200 for a night in the best suite at the **Willard InterContinental** (☎ 888-424-6835 or 202-628-9100; www.washington.intercontinental.com). In between those extremes, you'll find it just about impossible to obtain undiscounted, high-season rates below $125. Without landing a special deal, you'll have to view anything less than $200 as a modest price. But deals abound. If you make like Sherlock Holmes, you may be able to sleuth your way to a room for less than $100 at a no-frills hotel or a B&B. (See Chapter 9 for hotel listings.)

If you have a flexible schedule, you can save by visiting D.C. when things are slow and hotels slash prices to fill rooms. That would be Thanksgiving through New Year's, July, August, and weekends year-round.

 You also can save by putting a little extra effort into your hotel search. Check a couple of online travel agencies, such as **Expedia.com** and **Travelocity.com**. If a hotel has a toll-free phone number, call it and the local number as well. Check the hotel's Internet site, too. After a reservation clerk quotes you a price, ask whether he's got anything better. Then ask again. It's amazing how often you'll find different prices with each query. Also be sure to mention your membership in AAA, AARP, frequent-flier programs, hotel frequent-sleeper programs, and any other corporate rewards programs. Government employees often qualify for discounts.

Dining

As with lodging, you can spend whatever you want to dine in D.C. One Italian chef, the highly regarded Roberto Donna, illustrates this fact by himself. Prices at **Galileo** (☎ 202-331-0880; www.robertodonna.com), Donna's downtown restaurant, are high. But Donna also runs restaurants within that restaurant, where prices are both substantially higher and downright bargains. In **Laboratorio,** Donna's private dining room with open kitchen, you'll pay $125 for a weekend dinner, or $200 with perfectly matched wines. Galileo's bar serves inexpensive lunches, and at dinner offers appetizers, pastas, main courses, side dishes, and desserts for $12 or less. Also at lunch, Donna periodically fires up a barbecue and sells sandwiches for less than $10.

Galileo was scheduled to be closed for remodeling until late summer or early fall of 2007.

Food bargains are scattered throughout the city. Not surprisingly, many Asian and Mexican/Southwestern restaurants offer tasty meals at modest prices. D.C. is experiencing a boom in restaurants that serve little dishes in the $5 to $10 range — Spanish *tapas* and Mediterranean *meze,* for instance. And the District has some home-grown diners, delis, and bakeries that serve inexpensive salads, sandwiches, and soups — even blueplate specials — for less than $10.

You also can save while sampling expensive restaurants by opting for early-bird specials, post-theater menus, and fixed-price deals, as well as eating your main meal at lunch when prices are lower. (See Chapter 10 for restaurant listings.)

Sightseeing

Seeing the sights is Washington's best bargain. You can walk into almost all of D.C.'s top attractions for free. (See Chapter 11 for attractions listings.)

Shopping

Washington's no New York, London, or Paris when it comes to shopping. And, in this case, the comparison's not in D.C.'s favor. Once again, you can spend at any level. Major department stores and other national chain shops are scattered around town. But the most interesting shopping is that which is unique to Washington or at least special to Washingtonians.

Most museums and galleries have shops built upon their exhibits — jewelry, textiles, and other crafts at the **American Indian Museum** (☎ **202-633-1000;** www.nmai.si.edu), astronaut ice cream at the **Air and Space Museum** (☎ **202-633-1000;** www.nasm.si.edu), prints of the **National Gallery**'s paintings (☎ **202-737-4215;** www.nga.gov), and the annual White House Christmas ornament at the **White House Visitor Center** (☎ **202-208-1631;** www.nps.gov/whho/planyourvisit/ indooractivities.htm). Washingtonians tend to be avid readers, so you can choose from many bookstores, from those at many museums to niche stores devoted to gay/lesbian, feminist, African-American, and New Age literature.

Quaint and rowdy **Georgetown** is stuffed with quaint and rowdy shops that sell antiques, art, vintage comic books, movie posters, biker boots, and exotic clothing. **Union Station** (☎ **202-289-1908;** www.unionstation dc.com) contains a multilevel shopping mall with chain stores and small shops specializing in American and international crafts. Washingtonians frequent **Adams-Morgan,** the city's most ethnically diverse neighborhood, for imports, unusual clothing, and secondhand goods.

For flea market action, head for Capitol Hill's Victorian-era **Eastern Market** (☎ 202-544-0083; www.easternmarket.net) on Sundays. For a miniature version of Beverly Hills' Rodeo Drive, explore Wisconsin Avenue where it crosses the D.C.-Maryland border in the **Friendship Heights** neighborhood. If your vacations must include a discount mall visit, drive 26 miles south on I-95 (yuck!) to enormous **Potomac Mills** (☎ 800-826-4557, 703-496-9301; www.potomacmills.com).

Nightlife

If you want to catch a big show, concert, or major dance performance, you'll pay $20 to $80 for most seats. If your budget won't stretch that far, Washington — the land of the freebie — will come to your rescue.

The Kennedy Center's **Millennium Stage** (☎ 202-467-4600, 800-444-1324; www.kennedy-center.org/programs/millennium) serves up free entertainment nightly throughout the year. The **National Symphony Orchestra** (☎ 202-467-4600 and 800-444-1324; www.kennedy-center.org/nso) and **military bands** play free outdoor concerts at several sites throughout the summer. The **Shakespeare Theatre** (☎ 202-547-1122; www.shakespearetheatre.org) performs outdoors for free for about a week each summer.

Most Washington bars and nightclubs don't impose cover charges, although you may be unpleasantly surprised at what they charge for beverages.

TicketPlace (☎ 202-842-5387; www.ticketplace.org) sells tickets at a discount for same-day performances Tuesday through Saturday. Sunday and Monday tickets are sold on Saturday, and there are some other advance sales. You can call for recorded information around the clock. The TicketPlace box office, at 407 7th St. NW between D and E streets, is open Tuesday through Friday from 11 a.m. to 6 p.m. and Saturday from 10 a.m. to 5 p.m. You also can purchase some tickets online Tuesday through Friday from noon to 4 p.m. Some tickets are available only online and not at the box office. After service charges are added, the box office sells tickets for 62 percent of face value. Online sales are 67 percent of face value.

Cutting Costs — But Not the Fun

To conserve your cash, follow these tips:

✔ **Visit in the off season.** In Washington, that means Thanksgiving through New Year's, July, August, and weekends year-round. That's because Congress tries to be away at those times, so fewer business travelers are in town.

✔ **Travel midweek.** You sometimes can find cheaper flights on Tuesday, Wednesday, and Thursday. When you ask about airfares, see whether you can get a cheaper rate by flying on a different day. For more tips on getting a good fare, see Chapter 5.

✔ **Package it.** You sometimes can save money by booking a package that includes airfare, hotel, sightseeing, restaurant perks, and maybe even ground transportation. For particulars, call a travel agent or visit an online travel agency (see Chapter 5).

✔ **Rent a kitchen.** Dining out three times a day adds up, even if you take all your meals at hamburger joints and pizza parlors. Book a hotel room or suite with a kitchen, and you can make breakfasts and late-night snacks for a lot less than you'd pay at restaurants. A refrigerator and microwave are particularly handy when you're traveling with kids.

✔ **Opt for kids-stay-free hotels.** You can save money at hotels that let kids stay free in their parents' room. Ask whether two double beds or a sofa bed or rollaway is available.

✔ **BYOM (bring your own munchies).** Toss pre-purchased snacks into your backpack each day. They're cheaper than buying them in vending machines or from tourist-area stands. Easy access to appropriate munchies helps keep the younger tourists contented.

✔ **Bring a water bottle for each member of your party.** Refill the bottles from water fountains as you trek around town. This way, you avoid paying for pricey sodas or bottled H_2O. And having water on hand makes it easy for you to stay hydrated — an important health concern in hot weather.

✔ **Take Metrorail or hoof it.** You can get around D.C. on the cheap by utilizing the subway and your feet. If you're planning to take at least five Metrorail (☎ 202-637-7000; www.wmata.com) trips in a day, purchase an all-day fare card for $6.50, and you can get on and off the subway as many times as you like after 9:30 a.m. on weekdays and all day on weekends and holidays. For $22, a seven-day short-trip pass covers any fare up to $2.20, which will take you between most tourist attractions. You can pay the extra cost of more-expensive trips at the Exitfare machine when leaving the station. An unlimited seven-day pass costs $33. You can buy the passes at station vending machines marked "Passes/Farecards," and from sales personnel at the Metro Center Metrorail station and some retail stores. When you're not taking the subway, walk. Or hop the 30-series buses for trips along all of Wisconsin Avenue, most of Pennsylvania Avenue, and M Street in eastern Georgetown. Passes for unlimited bus riding (except on special express buses) cost $3 for a day and $11 for a week.

✔ **Always ask for discount rates.** Membership in AAA, frequent-flier plans, trade unions, AARP, or other groups may qualify you for savings on car rentals, plane tickets, hotel rooms, and even meals. Ask about everything; you may be pleasantly surprised.

✔ **Try expensive restaurants at lunch instead of dinner.** Lunch tabs are usually a fraction of what dinner would cost at a top restaurant, and the menu often boasts many of the same specialties.

✔ **Skip the souvenirs.** Your photographs and your memories may be the best mementos of your trip. If you're concerned about money, you can do without the FBI T-shirts, Washington Monument key chains, and other trinkets.

Handling Money

You're the best judge of how much cash you feel comfortable carrying or what alternative form of currency is your favorite. That's not going to change much on your vacation. True, you'll probably be moving around more and incurring more expenses than usual (unless you happen to eat out every meal when you're at home), and you may let your mind slip into vacation gear and not be as vigilant about watching your wallet. But, those factors aside, the only type of payment that won't be quite as available to you away from home is your personal checkbook.

Using ATMs and carrying cash

The easiest and best way to get cash away from home is from an ATM (automated teller machine). The **Cirrus** (☎ **800-424-7787**; www.master card.com) and **PLUS** (☎ **800-843-7587**; www.visa.com) networks span the globe; look at the back of your bank card to see which network you're on and then call or check online for ATM locations at your destination. Make sure that you know your personal identification number (PIN) before you leave home, and don't forget to find out your daily withdrawal limit before you depart. Also keep in mind that many banks impose a fee every time your card is used at a different bank's ATM. On top of this charge, the bank from which you withdraw cash may add its own fee. To compare banks' ATM fees within the United States, go to www.bankrate.com and click on the "checking and savings" tab. For international withdrawal fees, ask your bank. You can find 24-hour ATMs on nearly every street corner in D.C., it seems, as well as in hotel lobbies, many public buildings, and some grocery stores and restaurants.

Charging ahead with credit cards

Credit cards are a safe way to carry money: They also provide a convenient record of all your expenses, and they generally offer relatively good exchange rates. You also can withdraw cash advances from your credit cards at banks or ATMs, provided you know your PIN. If you've forgotten yours, or didn't even know you had one, call the phone number on the back of your credit card and ask the bank to send it to you. It usually takes five to seven business days, though some banks will provide the number over the phone if you tell them your mother's maiden name or some other personal information.

Some credit-card companies recommend that you notify them of any impending trip abroad so that they don't become suspicious when the card is used numerous times in a foreign destination and block your charges. Even if you don't call your credit-card company in advance, you can always call the card's toll-free emergency number if a charge is refused — a good reason to carry the phone number with you. But perhaps the most important lesson here is to carry more than one card with you on your trip; a card may not work for any number of reasons, so having a backup is the smart way to go.

Toting traveler's checks

These days, traveler's checks are less necessary because most cities have 24-hour ATMs that allow you to withdraw small amounts of cash as needed. Keep in mind, however, that you'll likely be charged an ATM withdrawal fee if the bank is not your own. So, if you're withdrawing money every day, it may be cheaper to pay the traveler's checks fee — provided that you don't mind showing identification every time you want to cash one.

You can get traveler's checks at almost any bank. **American Express** offers denominations of $20, $50, $100, $500, and (for cardholders only) $1,000. You pay a service charge ranging from 1 percent to 4 percent. You also can get American Express traveler's checks over the phone by calling ☎ 800-221-7282; AmEx gold and platinum cardholders who use this number are exempt from the 1-percent fee.

Visa offers traveler's checks at Citibank locations nationwide, as well as at several other banks. The service charge ranges between 1.5 percent and 2 percent; checks come in denominations of $20, $50, $100, $500, and $1,000. Call ☎ 800-732-1322 for information. AAA members can obtain Visa checks without a fee at most AAA offices and for a fee by calling ☎ 866-339-3378. **MasterCard** also offers traveler's checks. Call ☎ 800-223-9920 for a location near you.

 If you choose to carry traveler's checks, be sure to keep a record of their serial numbers separate from your checks in the event that they're stolen or lost. You can get a refund faster if you know the numbers.

Dealing with a Lost or Stolen Wallet

Be sure to contact all your credit-card companies the minute you discover that your wallet has been lost or stolen, and file a report at the nearest police precinct. Your credit-card company or insurer may require a police report number or record of the loss. Most credit-card companies have an emergency toll-free number to call if your card is lost or stolen; they may be able to wire you a cash advance immediately or deliver an emergency credit card in a day or two. Call the following emergency numbers in the United States:

- ✔ **American Express** ☎ **800-221-7282** (for cardholders and traveler's check holders)

- ✔ **MasterCard** ☎ **800-307-7309** or 636-722-7111

- ✔ **Visa** ☎ **800-847-2911** or 410-581-9994

For other credit cards, call the toll-free number directory at ☎ **800-555-1212.**

If you need emergency cash over the weekend when all banks and American Express offices are closed, you can have money wired to you via **Western Union** (☎ **800-325-6000;** www.westernunion.com).

Identity theft and fraud are potential complications of losing your wallet, especially if you've lost your driver's license along with your cash and credit cards. Notify the major credit-reporting bureaus immediately; placing a fraud alert on your records may protect you against liability for criminal activity. The three major U.S. credit-reporting agencies are **Equifax** (☎ **800-766-0008;** www.equifax.com), **Experian** (☎ **888-397-3742;** www.experian.com), and **TransUnion** (☎ **800-680-7289;** www.transunion.com).

Taxing Matters

The D.C. general sales tax is 5.75 percent, restaurant tax is 10 percent, and hotel tax is 14.5 percent. Maryland's sales and restaurant taxes are 5 percent. An additional 1-percent to 10-percent lodging and amusement tax may be imposed by Maryland localities. Virginia's general sales tax is 4.5 percent, with local options for taxes on lodging, restaurants, and admissions to events.

Chapter 5

Getting to Washington, D.C.

. . . .

In This Chapter

▶ Figuring out how to get here

▶ Comparing Washington's airports and train station

▶ Finding the best fares

▶ Considering a package tour

. . . .

*O*ne of Washington's assets is an abundance of ways to get here. D.C. has terrific train service between here and New York. If train travel is your thing, you can find service up and down the East Coast, with less appealing routes to and from the west. Metropolitan Washington also has three major airports, all served by major airlines. And, of course, the city is connected to the Interstate Highway System — though driving into town is no fun, and driving in town is even worse.

Flying to Washington, D.C.

The city's three major airports compete with each other and encourage price competition among the airlines. Each has distinct advantages and disadvantages for the traveler.

Check if your hotel offers free or inexpensive transportation to and from the airport or offers a discount on the SuperShuttle van.

Ronald Reagan Washington National Airport (☎ 703-417-8000; www. metwashairports.com/national), known to locals simply as "National," is the most convenient. **Washington Dulles International Airport** (☎ 703-572-2700; www.metwashairports.com/dulles), known, naturally, as "Dulles," is 26 miles west of downtown in what used to be the Virginia countryside. **Baltimore/Washington International Thurgood Marshall Airport** (☎ 800-435-9294; www.bwiairport.com) is 33 miles northeast of D.C. and is known by its acronym, "BWI."

Ronald Reagan Washington National Airport

Republican members of Congress, who didn't think enough things had been named for the 40th president, bestowed this rather lengthy moniker on the airport. (It's located in Arlington, Virginia, and is managed by a regional authority.) The locals, for the most part, still call it National.

Nomenclature aside, National is a marvelous airport. The original terminal, opened in 1941 on the eve of America's entry into World War II, is a historic structure that is being restored and will stay in use. The new terminal, opened in 1997, is a striking, modern architectural triumph, with picture-window views across the Potomac River to Washington's landmarks. The views from planes arriving from the north and west are spectacular as well, especially after dark, as you can clearly see Washington's most familiar buildings and monuments from the approaching aircraft. The new terminal was designed by renowned architect Cesar Pelli and has original art incorporated throughout it.

The food options at National are decent for an airport, including a few sit-down chain restaurants such as Legal Sea Foods and T.G.I. Friday's. If you find yourself in need of last-minute gifts or souvenirs, you can choose from a couple dozen shops, including a Smithsonian Institution store.

The airport is compact and easy to get around. With all the security added in the wake of September 11, 2001, National is probably the safest airport in the world to fly into or out of. And you can't beat the convenience.

Metrorail Yellow Line and Blue Line trains connect National with downtown D.C. stations in less than 20 minutes for about $1.35 to $1.65. A taxi to downtown costs about $11 to $12 (before tip) and takes 15 to 20 minutes (depending, of course, on Washington's notorious traffic). **Super-Shuttle** (☎ **800-258-3826;** www.supershuttle.com) provides door-to-door shared van service to downtown for about $13 for one passenger, $8 for each additional passenger.

National's downside includes the fact that it *is* "national." If you want to fly here nonstop from outside the United States, Montreal, Toronto, or Bermuda, you have to touch down at Dulles or BWI. The airport also has fewer long-distance flights within the United States. Noise restrictions limit traffic late at night and early in the morning. And, because it's so close to the city, the airport has a high demand for its flights, so you find fewer bargains at National than at Dulles or BWI. "Fewer" doesn't mean "none," however. If you book early and follow the tips listed in the section "Getting the best deal on airfares," later in this chapter, you can find good prices at National as well.

The following airlines serve National Airport: Air Canada, Air Tran, Alaska, American, ATA, Continental, Delta, Frontier, Midwest, Northwest, Spirit, United, and US Airways. The airport also is served by the regional carriers Allegheny and American. (See the Quick Concierge at the back of this book for complete listings of phone numbers and Web sites.)

Washington Dulles International Airport

Like Reagan Airport, Dulles also sports impressive architecture: the soaring main terminal. Designed by highly regarded architect Eero Saarinen, it opened to many *oohs* and *ahs* in 1962. The airport's main

D.C. Metropolitan Area

attractions today are its international and long-haul domestic service and its sometimes-better fares than those found at National. At Dulles, you can even catch a flight on Aeroflot . . . should you happen to *want* to catch a flight on Aeroflot.

Dulles's main disadvantage is location — of the airport itself, within metropolitan Washington, and of the facilities within the airport. The cab ride to D.C. takes about 45 minutes in favorable traffic and costs about $55.

The **SuperShuttle** (☎ **800-258-3826;** www.supershuttle.com) van charges $22 for the first passenger and $10 for each companion.

Travel within the airport is a bit of a challenge as well. Dulles has grown and grown. As new terminals were added, airport architects didn't bother to connect them. Not many of Dulles's gates are at the main terminal. As a result, for most travelers, entering the terminal is just the beginning of their airport journey. If you land at Dulles, you'll probably deplane at one of the so-called "midfield" terminals. You then make your way to a loading zone where you board a monstrous bus (euphemistically called a "mobile lounge"). You then debus at the main terminal. Some of these contraptions take passengers directly to and from the planes.

One time when I flew out of Dulles, I hopped onto the wrong mobile lounge, which took me to the wrong midfield terminal, which left me puzzling for a bit over why I didn't see any signs to my gate. When I figured out what I had done, I had to take another mobile lounge back to the main terminal and then another back to the right midfield terminal. Fortunately, because I had arrived at the airport early, I still caught my flight. This escapade is one of many reasons I always leave myself a lot of extra time when I set out for an airport — and even more when the airport is Dulles.

 The cheapest trip from Dulles to D.C. is by the **5A express Metrobus,** which drops you at L'Enfant Plaza, a couple blocks south of the National Mall, which has a Metrorail station, or at the Rosslyn Metrorail station in Virginia, across the river from Georgetown. The ride costs $3. It departs Dulles every 40 to 50 minutes from 5:50 a.m. to 11:40 p.m. on weekdays. Hourly weekend service is offered from 6:32 a.m. to 11:40 p.m.

Airlines serving Dulles Airport are: Aeroflot, Air Canada, Air France, Air Tran, ANA, American, Austrian, British Airways, Continental, Delta, Ethiopian, JetBlue, KLM Royal Dutch, Korean Air, Lufthansa, Max Jet, Northwest, SAS, Saudi Arabian, South African, Southwest, Sun Country, TACA, TED, United, US Airways, and Virgin Atlantic. (See the Quick Concierge at the back of this book for complete listings of phone numbers and Web sites.)

Baltimore/Washington International Thurgood Marshall Airport

 BWI's mouthful of a moniker exceeds even National's, but at least it was the locals who decided to add the name of the native son who grew up to become a prime leader of the Civil Rights movement and the first black justice of the Supreme Court. BWI's prime attraction is price. Its distance from Washington means airlines have to try a little harder to attract D.C. clientele. That means that often — though not always — you can find cheaper airfares at BWI than at National.

BWI's disadvantage is, like Dulles's, location. By cab, you're 45 to 60 minutes and $60 to $65 away from downtown D.C., if the traffic flows smoothly. The **SuperShuttle** (☎ **800-258-3826;** www.supershuttle. com) van service sets you back $31 for the first passenger and $11 for each companion. At least when you walk into BWI's terminal, though, you don't have to take a bus to your plane.

As at Dulles, **Metrobus** runs a $3 express from BWI — this one to the Greenbelt Metrorail station. The B30 bus leaves the airport every 40 minutes between 6:58 a.m. and 10:50 p.m. weekdays, 9:38 a.m. to 10:48 p.m. weekends. From the Greenbelt station, the Metrorail ride to Penn Quarter costs between $2.35 and $3.05 and takes about 25 minutes.

On weekdays, you also can ride the **MARC train** (☎ **800-325-7245;** www.mtamaryland.com) from BWI to Union Station for $6. Trains run between 5 a.m. and 9:46 p.m. The interval between trains varies from 13 minutes to two hours, but usually is less than an hour. The trip takes 25 to 35 minutes. **Amtrak** (☎ **800-872-7245;** www.amtrak.com) runs trains frequently on the same route from before 7 a.m. until after midnight. Tickets range from $11 to $37, and the trip takes 25 to 35 minutes.

BWI is served by these airlines: Air Canada, Air Jamaica, Air Tran, American, British Airways, Continental, Delta, Frontier, Icelandair, Mexicana, Midwest, North American, Northwest, Pan Am Clipper Connection, Southwest, United, US Airways, and USA3000. (See the Quick Concierge at the back of this book for complete listings of phone numbers and Web sites.)

Getting the best deal on airfares

Deregulation of the U.S. airline industry has brought a flood of discounted fares to the market. The problem is . . . a flood of different fares is on the market. How do you find the best one for you?

If money's no object, you may choose to fly first class or the less pricey but still premium business class. If money is an object, but you must buy a ticket on short notice, you can be stuck with a full-fare coach ticket. The high cost of full-fare coach — theoretically, the low-cost way to travel — can be shocking. Susan and I had to travel between D.C. and Chicago several times on business a few years ago. We were able to plan several weeks ahead on all but one occasion, and we were able to buy round-trip tickets for between $200 and $300 each. Once, however, our client summoned us on short notice, and each ticket cost more than $1,200 — on the client's tab, thank goodness.

If you want bargains, then you don't want plain vanilla coach fares. You want . . . bargain fares. And you, or your travel agent, have to work a bit to find the best ones.

Checking many sources to save

Taking full advantage of the magic of computers, airlines now practice what is called *yield management*. Ticket prices are adjusted day-by-day — hour-by-hour, minute-by-minute — based on what the computer knows about the history of ticket-purchasing on a particular flight and how sales are going right now. The goal is to fill the plane and sell every ticket at the highest possible price. That means you're not going to get a bargain on a flight that's heading toward a sellout. But, because the airline wants to fill every seat — the seat's always there, and if no one's in it, it's not producing any income — you can find cut-rate fares on flights in danger of taking off without a full load.

The way for you to take advantage of this system is to check every possible source of information about ticket prices and to keep your travel plans as flexible as possible. That's because studies have shown that the cheapest ticket doesn't always show up in the same information source. To maximize your chances of finding it, you need to telephone the airlines, visit their Internet sites, check for newspaper ads, call a travel agent, and visit online travel agencies as well.

Finding bargains on the Internet

If contacting multiple sources is more hassle than you're willing to endure and you're comfortable on the Internet, checking several Web sites probably is your best bet. Visit a couple online travel agencies, such as **Travelocity** (travelocity.com), **Expedia** (expedia.com), and **Orbitz** (orbitz.com). (Canadian travelers should try www.expedia.ca and www.travelocity.ca; U.K. residents should try expedia.co.uk and opodo.co.uk.) For last-minute trips, **Site59** (www.site59.com) in the United States and **LastMinute** (www.lastminute.com) often have better deals than the major-label sites.

Finally, visit the Web sites of the airlines that the online agencies say have the lowest fares to see whether you can get them even lower. Check the sites of airlines that you know fly the route you want to travel. And, if you try to collect miles in a particular frequent-flier program, check that airline's Web site, too.

Start your search as early as possible, but check back at the last minute as well; prices can drop on flights that aren't selling well. At the airlines' and travel agencies' Web sites, you can register for e-mail notices that alert you to last-minute deals on routes you specify or on any routes in case you may find one tempting.

If you can be flexible about travel dates or time of day, you increase your chances of finding the best bargain. Be alert for packages that save money by combining airline, hotel, and other reservations in a single purchase.

Be aware that the cheapest tickets are likely to carry the stiffest restrictions — no refunds and high penalties for making changes in your itinerary.

If you're willing to give up some control over your flight details, **Priceline** (www.priceline.com) offers low prices in exchange for travel on a "mystery airline" at a mysterious time of day, often with a mysterious change of planes en route. The mystery airlines are all major, well-known carriers — and the possibility of being sent from Philadelphia to Chicago via Tampa is remote. But your chances of getting a 6 a.m. or 11 p.m. flight are pretty high. *Note:* In 2004, Priceline added nonopaque service to its roster. You now have the option to pick exact flights, times, and airlines from a list of offers — or opt to bid on opaque fares as before.

 Another online travel service is **SideStep** (`www.sidestep.com`). It purports to "search 140 sites at once" and allows you to open a browser and purchase flights from the sites that they search. The advantage is that it searches low-cost airlines — such as Southwest — while other online travel agencies do not.

 Some airlines offer discounts to older passengers. If you think you may qualify, be sure to ask. The discounts may not apply to the lowest fares, however, so it still pays to search. Southwest Airlines is notable for offering senior discounts on its already low fares.

Many airlines offer free tickets to children younger than two who don't occupy a seat. I urge you to think carefully about the implications of this arrangement before you take advantage of it. There's a reason that airplanes have seat belts and that the pilot urges you to keep your seat belt fastened when you're not standing in line at the potty. Things — including passengers — can get thrown around the cabin if the plane runs into turbulence, and sometimes the turbulence is unexpected. Picture your child flying out of your lap in that situation. The Federal Aviation Administration recommends that children who weigh less than 40 pounds ride in an approved child safety seat (car seat) that is properly belted into the airplane seat. Make sure that your safety seat is labeled "certified for use in motor vehicles and aircraft." To encourage this practice, some airlines offer discounted tickets for children younger than two.

To give your kids — and you! — a little more room on your flight, request seats behind the bulkhead. You'll have to store all your bags in the overhead bins, however, because you won't have a seat in front of you to place them under.

Adults can get more leg room by asking for a seat in the emergency exit row. Usually you can't do this till you arrive at the airport, and some airlines now are charging extra for the extra space.

Getting to D.C. without Leaving the Ground

You don't have to fly into Washington. D.C.'s railway station is a tourist attraction in its own right. The bus probably is the cheapest way to get here. And you can always drive, although dealing with your car once you arrive can be a major headache.

Riding the rails

Whenever I travel up the East Coast, as far as New York, I take the train. Rail tickets aren't necessarily cheaper than airfare, but the train is *soooo* much more pleasant. The seats are bigger and much more comfortable. You can walk about with ease. You can sit at a table in the club car and eat, or play cards, or have a cup of coffee or beer while spreading the newspaper out before you. You can work, if you're so inclined. You arrive at and depart D.C. right on Capitol Hill. Union Station — built at the beginning of the 20th century in the heyday of rail travel — is a marvelous place, with Metrorail and tour-bus stations inside and a taxi stand outside. The food court has a huge selection of places where you can buy great eats for the trip. Whenever the Price family goes to New York for an outing, the vacation starts as the train pulls out, and we picnic on food we bought at the station.

The trip between New York and Washington takes from about 2 hours and 45 minutes to 3 hours and 30 minutes, depending on which train you choose. The **Acela Express** is faster and more comfortable than the garden variety trains that make more stops along the way. In my experience, the premium service isn't worth the premium price. Like the airlines, Amtrak (☎ **800-872-7245**; www.amtrak.com) offers special deals. Except for weekday Acela service, up to two children ages 2 to 15 can ride for half price with a paying adult, and one younger child can ride free on an adult's lap. Students and veterans can buy discount cards. Discounts also are offered to riders 62 or older, military personnel, and members of some organizations, such as AAA or AARP.

In the Washington–New York corridor, train travel can be faster than flying. You can arrive minutes before the train departs the station. You travel from and to the heart of each city. It's a rare day when rain, fog, or snow disrupts the schedule. You can catch a train in the Boston-Washington corridor just about any time you want. Service from elsewhere is less frequent and not competitive with air travel in terms of time.

Taking a car

I live in D.C. Therefore, I drive in D.C. But you don't have to, and I advise you not to.

Driving *to* D.C. is another issue. For a family, it can be less expensive than air or rail travel, and some people just prefer to drive. The traffic on the region's highways is horrendous, especially at rush hour (which starts earlier and ends later with each passing day). But once you're in town, you can park your car and leave it alone until you're ready to go home. However, be aware that parking fees tend to be as horrendous as the traffic, often $20 or more per day. When you make your reservation, ask your hotel whether it offers parking and what it charges. Make sure that you're sitting down when you ask this question.

If you're driving to Washington, you may save money by booking a suburban hotel that offers free parking and is near a Metrorail station. It may take you longer to get to your first sightseeing stop of the day, but Metro remains fast and cheap, even from the farthest suburb. From Shady Grove, at one end of the Red Line in suburban Maryland, for example, the 34-minute trip to Metro Center costs $3.90 in rush hour and $2.35 at other times. When you're researching hotels, ask how long it takes to walk to the Metro station, whether there's free shuttle service, or what it costs to take a cab and how easy it is to get one. You can park at some Metrorail stations, but competition for the spaces is heavy and starts before the rooster crows.

If you do drive to Washington, you encounter the **Capital Beltway** (I-495), which surrounds the city like a medieval moat — filled with raging drivers instead of raging sea monsters. Beware all who enter: There are speeders, chronic lane-changers, and vicious road-ragers . . . or one enormous parking lot. Surviving the Beltway is challenge number one. Challenge number two is to actually get into the city.

Assuming that you're traveling to Washington on the Interstate Highway System:

- ✔ If you arrive from the northwest, you'll be on I-270; follow the I-495 signs to Virginia. Immediately after crossing the American Legion Memorial Bridge into Virginia, take the George Washington Parkway east to I-66 east. That will take you across the Theodore Roosevelt Memorial Bridge into Washington on Constitution Avenue near the Lincoln Memorial.

- ✔ From the west, I-66 is a straight shot onto Constitution Avenue.

- ✔ From the south, take I-95 to I-395 and then follow signs into Washington.

- ✔ From the northeast on I-95, there is no direct route into town. The easiest way (using that term loosely) probably is to stay on I-95 south after it merges with I-495, and then take the Baltimore-Washington Parkway (Maryland Route 295) south to U.S. 50 west, which runs through the heart of D.C.

- ✔ From the east, you'll probably be on U.S. 50, which you can take into the middle of town.

Easily accessible on foot and by the Metrorail, Washington is your worst driving nightmare: confusing traffic circles, often poor signage, and streets that dead-end and then resume their course farther along. That's not to mention scarce and expensive parking. Traffic is heavy from predawn to post-sunset. One wrong turn in D.C., and you may end up in Virginia. I had lived in Washington for years — I do mean years! — before I could consistently negotiate the drive from National Airport to my home in Upper Northwest without missing a turn and finding myself on a freeway to Virginia after I had entered the District.

AAA (☎ **800-763-9900;** www.aaa.com) and some other automobile clubs offer free maps and driving directions to their members. If you're a member, give your club a call.

Riding the bus

For travelers on a tight budget, the bus probably is the cheapest way to reach D.C. from most cities in the Northeast. Bus fares typically cost less than half the price of regular train tickets. As I write this book, **Peter Pan** (☎ **800-237-8747;** www.peterpanbus.com) and **Greyhound** (☎ **800-231-2222;** www.greyhound.com) both were charging $37 for one-way tickets between Washington and New York.

Both bus lines run express service between Washington and New York City. Travel time on the express routes is listed at 4 hours and 20 minutes, but with good road conditions, the drivers can cut some time off the run. The D.C. bus terminal, 1005 1st St. NE, is a 4-block walk to the Union Station Metrorail stop that you would not want to make at night, so plan on cabbing to your destination if you arrive then.

If you decide to ride the bus to D.C., make sure that you book express service, or you may end up spending a lot more time on the road than you expected.

Choosing a Package Tour

Sometimes you can save money by purchasing a *package tour.* This type of tour doesn't mean that you have to follow a guide around town. It's simply a way of buying your airfare and accommodations at the same time. Because the packager buys in bulk, it sometimes can sell to you for less than you'd pay by shopping on your own. Some packages also include local transportation, meals, admission to events or attractions, and local tours.

Prices can vary greatly. Some packages offer a better class of hotel than others. Some offer the same hotels for lower prices. Some offer flights on scheduled airlines. Others book charters. In some packages, your choice of accommodations and travel days may be limited. Some let you choose an escorted tour. Others allow you to add on just a few excursions or escorted day trips without booking an entirely escorted tour.

The best place to start looking for packages is the travel section of your local Sunday newspaper or in the nearest major newspaper if your paper is too small to attract this kind of advertising. You also can find packages in the back of national travel magazines, at the Internet travel agency sites, and at the Internet sites of many airlines and hotel chains. The Internet sites often let you build a package by choosing among hotels, flight times, and other options. Car rentals are offered, too, but you really don't want a car in D.C. unless you plan to use it to leave town.

Driving to D.C.

DRIVING INTO D.C.

If you drive to Washington, ask your hotel for directions.

IN GENERAL:

• **From the Northwest:** *Take I-270, follow I-495 signs to Virginia, go east on George Washington Parkway, then go east on I-66, which will take you onto Constitution Ave.*

• **From the West:** *Take I-66 onto Constitution Ave.*

• **From the South:** *Take I-95, go north on I-395, then follow signs into Washington.*

• **From the Northeast:** *Take I-95, then go west on U.S. 50, which becomes New York Ave.*

• **From the East:** *Follow U.S. 50 into town.*

Liberty Travel (☎ 888-271-1584; www.libertytravel.com) is one of the biggest packagers in the Northeast. **American Express Vacations** (☎ 800-297-2977; www.americanexpress.com/travel) is another good option. Their Web sites can direct you to the office nearest your home if you want to meet a travel agent face-to-face.

Airlines also offer packages to varying destinations. If you've already picked your hotel, ask whether it offers land/air packages.

If you're unsure about the pedigree of a smaller packager, check with the Better Business Bureau in the city where the company is based, or go online at www.bbb.org. If a packager won't tell you where it's based, find another packager.

Chapter 6

Catering to Special Travel Needs and Interests

. . . .

In This Chapter

▶ Making vacation fun for your kids
▶ Reaping the benefits of age (finally!)
▶ Dealing with disabilities
▶ Exploring gay-friendly D.C.

. . . .

*W*hen you travel, do you need to find places that interest and accommodate children? Do you have special interests or needs related to your age? Do you need to find places with easy access for the disabled? Do you want to seek out gay-friendly activities and venues? This chapter is the right spot to find what you're looking for. And don't worry: Washington is friendly to everyone.

Finding Family-Friendly Fun in D.C.

Washington is one of the most family-friendly destinations around. Those yellow school buses migrate here all year round for good reason: Class trips to Washington are rites of passage, like braces and pimples.

Many attractions have special sections and programs for children. Washington's abundant parkland offers countless places for kids to let off steam. Restaurants entice the young and restless with kids' menus or half-portions, booster seats and high chairs, crayons, coloring books, and other pacifiers. The best ones offer menus for children that range far beyond the traditional hot dogs, french fries, and peanut-butter-and-jelly sandwiches.

When you check hotels, ask about special rates for families and perks such as free or lower-priced food for kids in hotel restaurants. When you want some time *without* the kids, many hotels can link you up with baby sitters. Ask the concierge.

When you're traveling with kids, a suite with kitchen facilities can be a great place to stay. With a refrigerator and microwave, you can eat breakfast before setting out on your adventures, and you can return for a midday snack and nap, which is a great way for the little ones to recharge. Separate sleeping areas — perhaps a bedroom and a living room with foldout sofas — let your kids enjoy their own space (and TV), while you relish some peace and privacy. Bring some snacks.

Many Washington attractions offer colorful, age-appropriate workbooks that enhance youngsters' visits. Some host family film sessions, workshops, and educational programs for children. In museums, ask at the information desk. Kid-friendly food is available at most museum restaurants as well. At National Park Service sites, ask about the Junior Ranger program.

Some national parks' Web sites have a button labeled "for kids" that takes you to information about kid-friendly places and activities. Washington's parks are listed at this Web site: `data2.itc.nps.gov/parksearch/state.cfm?st=dc`.

Hands-on exploring in D.C.

Children want to do more than look when they're on vacation. Here's a small sampling of the things kids can *do* in D.C.

- ✔ Pet a tarantula (well, kids think it's cool!) at the **National Museum of Natural History**'s insect zoo.

- ✔ Touch a moon rock and peer into John Glenn's Friendship 7 space capsule at the **National Air and Space Museum.**

- ✔ Attend a **family concert** at the Kennedy Center and touch the musical instruments during the "petting zoo" period.

- ✔ Ride the **carousel** on the National Mall.

- ✔ Say "hi" to the pandas at the **National Zoo.**

And that list is just a teeny-tiny sampling.

Frolicking in wide, open spaces

Washington's parks offer an open invitation for your kids to behave like, well, kids. They can run around, ride the carousel, or fly a kite on the mammoth lawn known as the National Mall. If they'd prefer to frolic on water, your family can rent pedal boats under Mr. Jefferson's gaze on the Tidal Basin. Or you can take a hike in the middle of the Potomac River on Theodore Roosevelt Island. For more detailed information on the best activities for families, check out *Frommer's Washington, D.C. with Kids.*

Drafting a plan for your clan

To start your family vacation off right, let your kids get involved in the planning. They can start by writing to the **Washington, D.C., Convention and Tourism Corp.,** 901 7th St. NW, 4th Floor, Washington, DC 20001, or going to the Web site www.washington.org for general information.

The computer-literate can find useful and interesting information at the Web sites listed throughout this book. In addition to the preceding park service site, check out:

✔ Smithsonian Institution for children: smithsonianeducation.org/students

✔ White House Web site for kids: www.whitehouse.gov/kids

✔ National Zoo: natzoo.si.edu

Throughout this book, this Kid Friendly icon marks the best places and activities for children.

Making Age Work for You: Tips for Seniors

If you're a senior citizen, you're (finally!) eligible for some special benefits when you travel. *Senior citizen* can be defined as being a lot younger than many may expect — 50 years old for AARP membership, for example, and 55 for many discount programs.

Elderhostel (☎ 800-454-5768; www.elderhostel.org) includes Washington in its educational tours for travelers 55 and older (and a spouse or companion of any age). Nine D.C. programs, ranging from one to five nights, are being offered as I write this book. A one-day program, organized with the American Foreign Service Association (the professional association of U.S. diplomats), looks at the United States' foreign policy challenges. A six-day program explores the Smithsonian in depth. Another visits major memorials, monuments, museums, and historic sites.

Savings for the senior set

As you plan your trip, and after you arrive, always ask whether any restaurant, lodging, attraction, or form of transport has a senior rate. Carry identification that shows your age, and you may end up with significant savings over your younger counterparts.

You may want to check out the benefits of joining **AARP** (known as the American Association of Retired Persons prior to setting its focus on recruiting baby boomers *before* they reach retirement age). Various discounts are available to AARP members, and local chapters run programs — including tours — for members. Information is available at ☎ 888-687-2277 or at the AARP Web site at www.aarp.org.

American citizens and permanent residents who are at least 62 can buy a **Golden Age Passport,** which gives you lifetime free entrance to all properties managed by the **National Park Service** (☎ **888-467-2757;** www. nps.gov/fees_passes.htm) and some other federal facilities. At places that charge a per-vehicle fee, the passport admits all passengers. If the fee is per person, the passport admits you, your spouse, and your children. The passports are sold for $10 at park service facilities that charge an entrance fee. Besides free entry, the passport gets you a 50 percent discount on federal-use fees charged for such facilities as camping, swimming, parking, boat launching, and tours, although the discount sometimes applies only to the pass holder.

Most park service sites in Washington are free anyway. The pass does save you a few bucks at the Great Falls parks in Maryland and Virginia, which I recommend for a nearby excursion, and at the Frederick Douglass National Historic Site.

Here are some additional ways for you to save money just by revealing your birth date:

✔ Many hotel chains offer senior discounts. Always ask when making a reservation. You may have to register and pay a fee to join a seniors club.

✔ Although most U.S. airlines no longer routinely offer lower fares to older travelers, you still can find special deals for seniors. **American** (☎ **800-433-7300;** www.aa.com) offers lower fares to 65-and-older travelers on some flights, for example. **United** (☎ **800-720-1765;** www.silverwingsplus.com) has created a "Silver Wings Plus" program for those who are at least 55, but it costs $240 a year. **Southwest** (☎ **800-435-9792;** www.southwest.com) offers discounts on its already usually low fares to travelers 65 and older. So, when you book your flight, it pays to ask.

✔ **Amtrak** (☎ **800-872-7245;** www.amtrak.com) travelers ages 62 and older receive a 15 percent discount on most train tickets and 10 percent off the North America Rail Pass for 30 days worth of travel in the United States and Canada. The discount doesn't apply to weekday Acela Express service, to sleeper accommodations, or on the Auto Train between Washington's Northern Virginia suburbs and Florida.

✔ Seniors 65 and older can buy half-price Metrorail fare cards in the Metro Center Station ticket office (12th and F streets NW) and at many stores, including Safeway and Giant grocery stores. You also can ride buses for 50¢. In both cases, you must provide some proof of your age (driver's license, birth certificate, or passport).

Asking about senior discounts pays off, even if you don't consider yourself to be a senior citizen. You don't necessarily have to be 65. Many establishments — restaurants, theaters, and museums — offer discounts at age 62, while some even begin as early as age 55.

More senior resources

For more information on senior traveling, check out these publications: the magazine *Travel 50 & Beyond* (www.travel50andbeyond.com), and the book *Unbelievably Good Deals and Great Adventures That You Absolutely Can't Get Unless You're Over 50* (McGraw-Hill), by Joann Rattner Heilman.

Traveling without Barriers: D.C. for the Disabled

Washington is a highly accessible city for disabled visitors, and all major transportation providers offer services to help the disabled traveler get here in the first place.

To scope things out, check out **Access-Able Travel Source** (☎ 303-232-2979; www.access-able.com). The Web site lists travel agents who have experience serving individuals with disabilities and provides some information about accessibility to lodging, transportation, and attractions for major cities around the world, including D.C. It also provides leads for renting wheelchairs and other health-care equipment.

Getting to, and around, town

Tell your air, rail, or bus carrier ahead of time if you need any assistance — both when you make your reservation and again when you check in at the airport or station. If you travel with a Seeing Eye dog or other service animal, ask about rules for taking it with you.

If you need special accommodations or assistance, **Amtrak** asks you to make your reservation by telephone (☎ 800-872-7245) or at a ticket counter, rather than online. The railroad also operates text telephone service (TDD/TTY) from 5 a.m. to 1 a.m. Eastern time at ☎ 800-523-6590. If you need accessible sleeping accommodations on an overnight train, Amtrak suggests you reserve at least 14 days before your trip. The railroad makes all bedrooms available to all passengers after that time.

Amtrak offers discounted fares to disabled passengers. You must purchase tickets by phone or at a ticket counter, and you must show documentation of your disability at the ticket counter and when boarding the train. Acceptable documentation includes a transit system disability ID card, a membership card from a disabilities organization, or a letter from a physician.

If you require the assistance of a personal care attendant and provide notice 24 hours in advance, Greyhound (☎ 800-752-4841; www.greyhound.com) lets the attendant travel for half fare. If you're traveling alone and alert Greyhound 48 hours prior to your travel, the company can arrange assistance along your route.

The National Park Service offers a **Golden Access Passport** that is essentially the same as the **Golden Age Passport** described earlier in this chapter in the section "Savings for the senior set." The access passport is free to citizens or permanent residents who are visually impaired or permanently disabled, regardless of age. You can get one at a park service facility that charges a fee by showing proof of medically determined disability and eligibility for receiving benefits under federal law. In addition to the benefits conferred by the Golden Age Passport, the Golden Access Passport covers admission for a care assistant if you travel with one. You can get more information at ☎ **888-467-2757** or www.nps.gov/fees_passes.htm.

Visitors with disabilities find **Metrorail** an excellent way to get around D.C. Every station has elevators, as well as fare-card vending machines, entrance gates, and telephones, all built to accommodate wheelchairs. For the hearing-impaired, blinking lights along the edge of the track announce the arrival of trains, and (for everyone's convenience) newly installed announcement signs give information about the approaching train. A bumpy surface has been placed along platform edges to help the vision-impaired locate the edge. Elevator control panels and signs in the stations contain Braille. On the train, bells chime and announcements occur when the doors are about to open or close, and the driver announces each station. All **Metrobuses** kneel for easier access, and almost all have low floor ramp or a lift. The TTY number for Metro information is ☎ **202-638-3780.**

Metro gives passengers with disabilities the same discounts available to seniors, but they must possess valid proof of disability. If the individual doesn't already have a Medicare card, however, the discount probably isn't worth the paperwork for someone who's visiting for a few days or even a few weeks.

 Unfortunately, Metrorail's elevators are notorious for breaking down, a minor inconvenience for most passengers but a major problem for anyone with a mobility problem. (Metro management was severely embarrassed a few years ago when a frustrated man in a wheelchair — who had encountered several out-of-service elevators — screamed an obscenity and was ticketed. Management quickly apologized, tore up the ticket, and gave the man complimentary passes.) When entering the Metrorail system, ask the attendant whether elevators are working at your destination. You can also call ☎ **202-962-1212** for information on elevator outages. When elevators are out, Metro provides shuttle buses to serve those stations. Ask the attendant where to catch them.

All **Tourmobile** trams are accessible to passengers who can climb two or three steps. The company also has vehicles with wheelchair lifts which must be ordered in advance. For information, call ☎ **703-979-0690. City Scooter Tours** (☎ **888-441-7575;** www.cityscootertours.com) rents and offers guided tours of the Mall and Tidal Basin areas on sit-upon powered "mobility scooters."

Building accessibility

The **Smithsonian Institution**'s museums, as well as most other public museums and attractions, are accessible to individuals with disabilities. Many films aired in museum theaters offer narrated audiotapes for the vision-impaired. Most live theaters have infrared headsets for the vision- and hearing-impaired. Live productions often feature at least one signed performance during the run. Call the theater for specifics. Some older facilities are less accessible than the newer ones, but that's far from universal. The best bet is to call ahead to make sure that the facility can accommodate your needs.

The Smithsonian, including the Zoo, offers many accommodations to visitors with disabilities. Get information at www.si.edu/visit/visitors_with_disabilities.htm. The Smithsonian's central information number is ☎ **202-633-1000** (TTY 202-633-5285). Service animals and power scooters are permitted in all Smithsonian facilities. Most exhibition videos are captioned or have scripts available. You can get scripts for audio tours. Manual wheelchairs can be borrowed for free on a first-come, first-served basis at information desks. Companion-care restrooms are available at the National Air and Space Museum, National Museum of Natural History, and Hirshhorn Museum, and more are planned.

You may find that some old properties, historic inns, and bed-and-breakfasts are inaccessible, but most major D.C. hotels and restaurants are. Ask specifically when you make a reservation. If you book through a travel agency or tour group, be sure to make your needs known.

For more information

Organizations that offer assistance to disabled travelers include **Moss-Rehab** (www.mossresourcenet.org), which provides a library of accessible-travel resources online; **SATH (Society for Accessible Travel and Hospitality)** (☎ 212-447-7284; www.sath.org; annual membership fees: $49 adults, $29 students and seniors 63 and older), which offers a wealth of travel resources for all types of disabilities and informed recommendations on destinations, access guides, travel agents, tour operators, vehicle rentals, and companion services; and the **American Foundation for the Blind (AFB)** (☎ 800-232-5463; www.afb.org), a referral resource for the blind or visually impaired that includes information on traveling with Seeing Eye dogs.

Also check out the quarterly magazine *Emerging Horizons* ($16.95 per year, $21.95 outside the U.S.; www.emerginghorizons.com).

Resources for Gay and Lesbian Travelers

Washington has a large and vibrant gay and lesbian community, so the city is a welcoming place for GLBT (gay, lesbian, bisexual, and transgender) visitors. Just ask our two gay City Council members, one of whom was a Republican until he turned independent to protest the GOP's "indifference, intolerance, and injustice." The traditional center of gay life is Dupont Circle, but gay and lesbian Washingtonians are thoroughly integrated into neighborhoods throughout the city. Gay and lesbian tourists are likely to be made welcome wherever they decide to visit.

Gathering gay and lesbian information about Washington

The prime source of news for and about D.C.'s gay community is the *Washington Blade* (www.washingtonblade.com), a weekly newspaper that's been hitting the streets here since 1969. It's filled with local, national, and international news, plus information about entertainment and community resources. It's widely available for free throughout the city.

Washington's premier gay and lesbian bookstore is **Lambda Rising,** at 1625 Connecticut Ave. NW (☎ 202-462-6969; www.lambdarising.com). The **Human Rights Campaign,** the nation's largest gay-rights political action organization, operates an Action Center and Store at 1629 Connecticut Ave. NW (☎ 202-232-8621).

The following travel guides are available at most travel bookstores and gay and lesbian bookstores, or you can order them from **Giovanni's Room** bookstore, 1145 Pine St., Philadelphia, PA 19107 (☎ 215-923-2960; www.giovannisroom.com): *Spartacus International Gay Guide* (Bruno Gmünder Verlag; www.spartacusworld.com/gayguide), a good guidebook focused on gay men, and the *Damron* guides (www.damron.com), with separate annual books for gay men and lesbians.

Getting to and staying in D.C. the gay-friendly way

Many travel agencies offer tours and itineraries specifically for gay and lesbian travelers. **The International Gay and Lesbian Travel Association (IGLTA)** (☎ 800-448-8550 or 954-776-2626; www.iglta.org) is the trade association for the industry and offers an online directory of gay-friendly travel businesses. **Above and Beyond Tours** (☎ 800-397-2681; www.abovebeyondtours.com) offers tours and independent travel arrangements for gay travelers. **Now, Voyager** (☎ 800-255-6951; www.nowvoyager.com) is a well-known San Francisco–based gay-owned and -operated travel service.

Among the gay-friendly hotels listed by IGLTA are:

✔ **Hotel Helix.** 1430 Rhode Island Ave. NW. Metro: Farragut North or McPherson Square (☎ **202-462-9001** or 800-706-1202; www.hotel helix.com).

✔ **Hotel Madera.** 1310 New Hampshire Ave. Metro: Dupont Circle (☎ **202-296-7600** or 800-430-1202; www.hotelmadera.com). See Chapter 9.

✔ **Hotel Rouge.** 1315 16th St. NW. Metro: Dupont Circle (☎ **202-232-8000** or 800-738-1202; www.rougehotel.com). See Chapter 9.

✔ **Topaz Hotel.** 1733 N St. NW. Metro: Dupont Circle (☎ **202-393-3000** or 800-775-1202; www.topazhotel.com).

For really special accommodations, make a reservation at the **D.C. Guest House** (1337 10th St. NW 20001; Metro: Mt. Vernon Square; ☎ **202-332-2502;** www.dcguesthouse.com), a recently renovated 1876 mansion. Gourmet breakfast is served in an elegant dining room. You'll feel like guests in a home because this place is lovingly restored and operated by four friends who spread their personal, eclectic tastes throughout the truly stunning mansion.

Chapter 7

Taking Care of the Remaining Details

In This Chapter

▶ Getting the lowdown on rental cars and travel insurance

▶ Staying healthy on your trip

▶ Accessing the Internet and using your cellphone

▶ Planning ahead for the latest airline security measures

"*A*re we there yet?" Well, not quite. But after I share with you a few more details, you'll be ready to stick your plans in your pocket and begin enjoying D.C.

Renting a Car — Not!

I live in D.C. Therefore, I drive in D.C. But you don't have to, and I advise you not to. (See Chapter 5 for reasons why you don't want to get behind the wheel.) Ask all who live here. They'll tell you that, even with the grid system, getting from place to place can be confusing, and the cost of parking can take a large chunk out of your budget. You can rely on shuttle, taxi, bus, or rail service from the airport or train station. Use Metrorail and your own two feet for sightseeing — or buses and taxis when necessary.

If you decide you really want or need to drive despite my warnings, see the next section.

Getting the best rental rate

If you insist on renting a car, keep in mind that car-rental rates vary widely. The price depends on many factors: the size of the car, the length of time you keep it, where and when you pick it up and drop it off, where you go in it, and a host of other factors. Asking the following key questions can save you big bucks:

✔ **Is the weekend rate lower than the weekday rate?** Ask whether the rate is the same for a Friday morning pickup as it is for one on Thursday night. If you keep the car five or more days, a weekly rate may be cheaper than the daily rate.

✔ **Are you charged a drop-off fee if you return the car to a location that's different from where you picked it up?** If, for example, you're leaving town from a different airport from the one you arrived at or you're driving to another city in a rental car, the company may tack on a hefty charge to leave it in a location other than the original pickup point.

✔ **Is the rate cheaper if you pick up the car at the airport instead of a location in town?** One location may be more practical than the other, so don't forget to factor convenience into your decision.

✔ **Do you get a special rate for being a member of AAA, AARP, frequent-flier programs, or other organizations?** Such memberships can get you discounts ranging from 5 percent to 30 percent.

✔ **Can you have the discounted rate you saw advertised in the local newspaper?** Be sure to ask for that specific rate; otherwise, you may be charged the standard (higher) rate.

✔ **Is age an issue?** Many car-rental companies add on a fee for drivers younger than 25, while some don't rent to younger drivers at all.

Adding up the costs of renting a car

On top of the standard rental prices, you need to watch out for other charges that may be applied. The *Collision Damage Waiver (CDW)* absolves you of responsibility to pay for damage to the vehicle in exchange for a hefty daily fee. Check with your auto insurance agent and the credit-card company you use to rent the car. You're probably already covered.

Car-rental companies also may try to sell you *liability insurance* (to cover you if you harm others in an accident), *additional liability insurance* (to increase the coverage you already have), *personal accident insurance* (to cover injury to yourself or your passengers), and *personal effects insurance* (to cover possessions that you carry in the rental car). If you don't know whether you're already covered, check with your auto and homeowner's insurance agent(s). You may not need to purchase this extra coverage. If your own insurance doesn't cover you for rentals, however, or if you don't have auto insurance, definitely consider the additional coverage. Ask the car-rental agent to explain it to you thoroughly and make sure that you understand the explanation. Unless you're toting around the Hope diamond — and you don't want to leave that in your car trunk anyway — you probably can skip the personal effects insurance. But driving around without liability or personal accident coverage is never a good idea. Even if you're a good driver, other people may not be, and liability claims can be complicated.

Some rental-car companies also offer *refueling packages,* which means that you pay for an entire tank of gas up front and don't face extra charges if you fail to return the car with a full tank. This service may be convenient, but the best way to save money is to fill the tank yourself at a gas station just before you return to the rental lot. The refueling package makes sense only if you routinely run late and face penalty charges for returning the car without a full tank.

Frequent fliers can cheer themselves up with the knowledge that most car rentals are worth at least 500 miles in their frequent-flier accounts. Be sure to show your card.

Booking a rental car on the Internet

As with other aspects of planning your trip, using the Internet can make comparison-shopping and renting a car much easier. The major online travel agencies — such as **Travelocity** (www.travelocity.com), **Expedia** (www.expedia.com), **Orbitz** (www.orbitz.com), and **Smarter Living** (www.smarterliving.com) — have search engines that dig up discounted car-rental rates. Enter the size of the car you want, the pickup and return dates, and the city where you want to rent, and you'll be quoted prices. Pick the deal you want and make your reservation at the site. As with buying airline tickets, checking the car-rental companies' sites can pay off, too.

Travel and Medical Insurance: To Buy or Not to Buy?

Three primary kinds of travel insurance are available: *trip cancellation, lost luggage,* and *medical.* Trip cancellation insurance is a good idea for some people, but lost luggage and additional medical insurance don't make sense for most travelers. Be sure to explore your options and consider the following insurance advice before you leave home:

✔ **Trip cancellation insurance.** If you pay a large portion of expensive vacation costs up front, consider purchasing this type of insurance. When you buy a package tour, insurance comes in handy if the packager or tour company defaults, a member of your party becomes ill, or (heaven forbid!) you experience a death in the family and aren't able to go on vacation. You probably won't be reimbursed if you cancel your trip just because you change your mind. Reasons that qualify for reimbursement can range from sickness to natural disasters to the State Department declaring your destination unsafe for travel. Insurers usually don't cover general fear — as many travelers discovered when they tried to cancel trips in October 2001 because they were wary of flying.

Note: Many tour operators include insurance in the cost of the trip or can arrange insurance policies through a partnering provider, a convenient and often cost-effective way for the traveler to obtain insurance. Make sure that the tour company is a reputable one, however. Some experts suggest you avoid buying insurance from your tour or cruise company, saying it's better to buy from a "third-party" insurer than to put all your money in one place.

✔ **Lost luggage insurance.** Your homeowner's insurance should cover stolen luggage if your policy encompasses off-premises theft. Check your existing policies or ask your insurance agent before you buy any additional coverage. Airlines are responsible for up to $2,500 for checked luggage they lose on domestic flights. If you plan to check items more valuable than the standard liability — and if your valuables aren't covered by your homeowner's policy — get baggage insurance as part of your comprehensive travel-insurance package or buy "BagTrak" from **Travel Guard** (see listing later in this section). Don't buy insurance at the airport, because it's usually overpriced. Be sure to take any valuables or irreplaceable items with you in your carry-on luggage, as many valuables (including books, money, and electronics) aren't covered by airline policies.

If your luggage is lost, immediately file a lost-luggage claim at the airport, detailing the luggage contents. For most airlines, you must report delayed, damaged, or lost baggage within four hours of arrival. The airlines are required to deliver luggage, once found, directly to your house or destination free of charge.

✔ **Medical insurance.** If you get sick while on vacation, your existing health insurance should cover your expenses. But keep in mind that some HMOs may differ on the benefits they offer while you travel. You may want to review your policy or ask your agent before leaving home, especially if you're coming to Washington from overseas.

If you think you need additional insurance, make sure that you don't pay for more coverage than you need. You also should call around to find a good deal on insurance. Here are some reputable issuers of travel insurance:

- **Access America** (☎ 866-807-3982; www.accessamerica.com)

- **Travel Guard International** (☎ 800-826-4919; www.travelguard.com)

- **Travel Insured International** (☎ 800-243-3174; www.travelinsured.com)

- **Travelex Insurance Services** (☎ 888-457-4602; www.travelex-insurance.com)

Protect yourself further by paying for the insurance with a credit card. By law, consumers can get their money back on goods and services not received if they report the loss within 60 days after the charge is listed on their credit card statement.

Staying Healthy When You Travel

If you suffer from a chronic illness, consult your doctor before your departure. For conditions like epilepsy, diabetes, or heart problems, wear a **MedicAlert Identification Tag** (☎ **888-633-4298** or 209-668-3333; www.medicalert.org), which immediately alerts doctors to your condition and gives them access to your records through MedicAlert's 24-hour hotline.

Most health insurance policies cover you if you get sick away from home — but check, particularly if you're insured by an HMO or traveling from overseas. Always carry your insurance ID card with you.

Pack **prescription medications** in your carry-on luggage and carry prescription medications in their original containers with labeling showing they were prescribed for you. Also bring along copies of your prescriptions in case you lose your pills or run out. And don't forget sunglasses and an extra pair of contact lenses or prescription glasses.

CVS (www.cvs.com), Washington's major drugstore chain (with more than 40 D.C. area locations), has three stores with 24-hour pharmacies near tourist-frequented neighborhoods:

✔ Dupont Circle: 6 Dupont Circle NW (Metro: Dupont Circle; ☎ **202-785-1466**)

✔ West End: 2240 M St. NW (Metro: Dupont Circle; ☎ **202-296-9876** pharmacy, 202-296-9877 main)

✔ Upper Northwest: 4555 Wisconsin Ave. NW (Metro: Tenleytown; ☎ **202-537-1587**)

If you need immediate medical attention, head for the **emergency room** at one of the following District hospitals. In a true emergency, call ☎ **911** for an ambulance. If it's not an emergency and you drive, call for directions.

✔ **Children's National Medical Center,** 111 Michigan Ave. NW, Upper Northwest (☎ **202-884-5000**)

✔ **George Washington University Hospital,** 900 23rd St. NW, downtown (☎ **202-715-4911**)

✔ **Georgetown University Hospital,** 3800 Reservoir Rd. NW, Georgetown (☎ **202-444-2119**)

✔ **Sibley Hospital,** 5255 Longboro Rd. NW, Upper Northwest (☎ **202-537-4000**)

✔ **Washington Hospital Center,** 110 Irving St. NW, Upper Northwest (☎ **202-877-7000**)

Washington's hospitals also can **refer you to a physician** if you don't really need emergency room care. Try calling one of the following hospitals for a referral:

- ✔ George Washington University Hospital (☎ 888-449-3627)
- ✔ Georgetown University Hospital (☎ 202-342-2400)
- ✔ Sibley Hospital (☎ 202-537-4638)
- ✔ Washington Hospital Center (☎ 202-877-3627)

If you need a dentist, call the District of Columbia Dental Society Referral Service (☎ 202-547-7615).

Avoiding "economy-class syndrome"

Deep vein thrombosis — or, as it's known in the world of flying, economy-class syndrome — is a blood clot that develops in a deep vein. It's a potentially deadly condition that can be caused by sitting in cramped conditions, such as an airplane cabin, for too long. During a flight (especially a long-haul flight), get up, walk around, and stretch your legs every 60 to 90 minutes to keep your blood flowing. Other preventative measures include frequent flexing of the legs while sitting, drinking lots of water, and avoiding alcohol and sleeping pills. If you have a history of deep vein thrombosis, heart disease, or other condition that puts you at high risk, some experts recommend wearing compression stockings or taking anticoagulants when you fly; always ask your physician about the best course for you. Symptoms of deep vein thrombosis include leg pain or swelling, or even shortness of breath.

Staying Connected by Cellphone or E-mail

It used to be that travelers wondered if their hotel room would have a phone and if they should use a pay phone anyway to save money. Now it seems everyone travels with a cellphone and an e-mail account, and the question becomes whether your cellphone works in a strange city and where you can find Internet access.

Using a cellphone across the United States

Just because your cellphone works at home doesn't mean it'll work elsewhere in the country (thanks to our nation's fragmented cellphone system). It's a good bet that your phone will work in Washington. But take a look at your wireless company's coverage map on its Web site before heading out. If you need to stay in touch at a destination where you know your phone won't work, you can **rent** a phone that does from **InTouch USA** (☎ 800-872-7626; www.intouchglobal.com) or at a rental-car location. Beware that rates can be steep.

If you're not from the United States, you'll be happy to know that **GSM (Global System for Mobiles)** service is available in Washington. But, to be safe, you should ask your wireless provider whether your phone will work here.

Accessing the Internet away from home

Travelers have many ways to check the Internet and e-mail on the road. Using your own laptop or hand-held device gives you the most flexibility. A growing number of hotels offer Internet access in rooms or at a business center — or by wireless anywhere in the facility. Ask about charges first, or you may be unpleasantly surprised at check-out time. Call your hotel in advance to see what your options are.

You also can take advantage of a growing number of cybercafes, where you can go online while you sip a beverage or nibble at lunch, often for a fee. At **Kramerbooks & Afterwards** (1517 Connecticut Ave. NW, just above Dupont Circle; ☎ 202-387-1400; www.kramers.com), you can check e-mail for free at the bar. Many **Starbucks** offer wireless Internet access. You can search for other Washington cybercafes at www.cybercaptive.com and www.cybercafe.com.

All D.C. public libraries (☎ 202-727-0321; www.dclibrary.org) offer free Internet access. The main library is the downtown **Martin Luther King Library** (901 G St. NW at 9th Street; ☎ 202-727-0321). The **West End Branch** (☎ 202-724-8707) is at 1101 24th St. NW at L Street. The **Georgetown Branch** (☎ 202-282-0220) is at 3260 R St. NW at Wisconsin Avenue. On Capitol Hill, the **Southeast Branch** (☎ 202-698-3377) is at 403 7th St. SE at D Street. Call for hours, which vary.

To retrieve your e-mail, ask your **Internet Service Provider (ISP)** if it has a Web-based interface tied to your existing e-mail account. If your ISP doesn't have such an interface, you can use the free **mail2web** service (www.mail2web.com) to view and reply to your home e-mail. For more flexibility, you may want to open a free, Web-based e-mail account with **Yahoo! Mail** (http://mail.yahoo.com). Your home ISP may be able to forward your e-mail to the Web-based account automatically.

Some Internet Service Providers (ISP) have **local access numbers** around the world, allowing you to go online by simply placing a local call. Check your ISP's Web site or call its toll-free number and ask how you can use your current account in Washington, and how much it will cost. If you're traveling outside the reach of your ISP, you can get Internet access through **i2roam** (☎ 866-811-6209 or 920-235-0475; www.i2roam.com).

Bring your own **connection kit** — extension electric cord, phone cord, and Ethernet cable — or find out if your hotel supplies them to guests.

If you need to access files on your office computer, look into a service called **GoToMyPC** (www.gotomypc.com). The service provides a Web-based interface for you to access and manipulate a distant PC from anywhere — even a cybercafe — provided that your "target" PC is on and has an always-on connection to the Internet. The service offers top-quality security, but if you're worried about hackers, use your own laptop rather than a public computer to access the GoToMyPC system.

Keeping Up with Airline Security

Post-9/11 security procedures have made flying a lot less fun than it used to be. Generally, you're fine if you arrive at the airport **one hour** before a domestic flight and **two hours** before an international flight. Add at least another half hour to work your way through Dulles, maybe an extra hour if you're checking bags. If you're in line and worrying that you might miss your flight, tell an airline employee and you'll probably be moved up in line if necessary.

Bring a **current, government-issued photo ID,** such as a driver's license or passport. Keep your ID ready to show at check-in, the security checkpoint, and sometimes even the gate. (Children younger than 18 don't need government-issued photo IDs for domestic flights.)

In 2003, the Transportation Security Administration (TSA) phased out **gate check-in** at all U.S. airports. In addition, **E-tickets** have made paper tickets nearly obsolete. Passengers with E-tickets can beat the ticket-counter lines by using airport **electronic kiosks** or even **online check-in** from your home computer. Online check-in involves logging on to your airline's Web site, accessing your reservation, and printing your boarding pass — airlines even offer you bonus miles when you do so! If you're using a kiosk at the airport, bring the credit card you used to book the ticket or your frequent-flier card. Print your boarding pass from the kiosk and simply proceed to the security checkpoint with your pass and a photo ID. If you're checking bags or looking to snag an exit-row seat, you'll be able to do so using most airline kiosks. Even the smaller airlines are employing the kiosk system, but always call your airline to make sure that these alternatives are available. **Curbside check-in** is also a good way to avoid lines, although not all airlines offer it; call before you go.

Repeated changes in airport security rules can confuse passengers and lead to long checkpoint lines. If you have trouble standing for long periods of time, tell an airline employee; the airline can provide a wheelchair. Speed up your trip through security by removing all metal items (keys, watches, jewelry, coins, buttons, hair decorations, large belt buckles, cellphones, and so on) from your pockets and your body and placing them in you carry-on bag. Don't wear a bra with metal wiring. If you've got metallic body parts, a note from your doctor can prevent a long chat with the security screeners.

At the metal detector, you'll have to remove your shoes and coats and put them in a bin for examination by the X-ray machine. If you haven't put your metal items in your luggage, you'll have to put them in a bin as well. If you carry liquids, gels or aerosols on board (mouthwash, toothpaste, deodorant, shaving cream, and so forth) they must be in 3-ounce or smaller containers. And all of them must be placed in a single, quart-size, zip-top, clear plastic bag. The bag must be placed on the X-ray conveyor belt or in a bin.

You can bring larger amounts of prescription and over-the-counter medications as well as other liquids, gels, and aerosols that are medically necessary, including prosthetics. You can bring baby formula or breast milk if you are traveling with the baby or small child who consumes it. These need to be separated from other items and declared to a security screener.

If you're carrying a laptop computer, you must take it out of its carrying case and place it on the X-ray conveyer belt.

You cannot take other liquids, gels, or aerosols — such as coffee or soft drinks — past the screening area. You can by them in the secure area, then carry them onto the plane with you.

The list of prohibited items is long but based on common sense: things you could use to hurt other people, especially sharp objects and items you could wield like a weapon. In other words, no knives, scissors with blades longer than 4 inches, baseball bats, ski poles, guns, ammunition, hatchets, hammers, screw drivers more than 7 inches long, brass knuckles, martial arts weapons, explosives, fuels . . . you get the picture.

Travelers in the United States are allowed one carry-on bag, plus a "personal item," such as a purse, briefcase, or laptop bag. Carry-on hoarders can stuff all sorts of things into a laptop bag; as long as it has a laptop in it, it's still considered a personal item.

Airport screeners may decide to search your checked luggage by hand. You can purchase luggage locks that allow screeners to open and relock a checked bag if hand-searching is necessary. Look for Travel Sentry certified locks at luggage or travel shops and Brookstone stores (you can buy them online at www.brookstone.com). Luggage inspectors can use a special code or key to open these locks, which are approved by the TSA. For more information on the locks, visit www.travelsentry.org. If you use something other than TSA-approved locks, your lock will be cut off your suitcase if a TSA agent needs to hand-search your luggage.

Keep in mind that only **ticketed passengers** are allowed past security, except for folks escorting disabled passengers or children. If you're an escort, you have to get a pass at the check-in counter.

For the latest word on all airport security rules, visit the Transportation Security Administration's Web site at www.tsa.gov.

Part III
Settling into Washington, D.C.

The 5th Wave   By Rich Tennant

"Six of Jennifer's goldfish died today, and, well, I just don't think it's worth the three of us keeping our reservations at Takara's Sushi Restaurant tonight."

In this part . . .

In this part, you get into the real details: Washington's best hotels (and a few runners-up), the best restaurants, and the best places to catch a quick snack or have a drink with a capital view. Because you need to know how to get to all these great places, I also give you the lowdown on D.C.'s spectacular subway system, comprehensive network of bus routes, confusing taxi fares, and state-themed avenues (on which you should never, ever drive).

Chapter 8

Arriving and Getting Oriented

In This Chapter

▶ Arriving in Washington by plane, train, or auto
▶ Discovering Washington's neighborhoods
▶ Acquiring visitor information
▶ Making your way around town

*Y*ou can get to Washington easily by train or plane and, in a sense, by automobile. Once you're here, a car is not the best bet for local transportation — D.C.'s world-class Metrorail system is. After you settle in, you'll discover that Washington's most interesting neighborhoods are fairly close to each other and easy to navigate.

Finding the Way to Your Hotel

The train takes you right to Capitol Hill, where Union Station is an easy cab or subway ride away from the hotels that are most attractive to tourists. National Airport is nearly as convenient, but you'll face a bit of a trek from Dulles or Baltimore/Washington International.

Signs for taxis and other ground transportation are posted in the airports' baggage claim areas, as well as outside the terminals. Taxis stop at Union Station's main front doors. At National Airport and Union Station, you also see signs to on-site Metrorail stations.

From Ronald Reagan Washington National Airport

National is Washington's most convenient airport. It's close to town, is easy to get around, and has terrific transportation connections. It's also an attraction in its own right, thanks to the eye-popping terminal that opened in 1997. The new terminal has been divided in half and given the names Terminal A and Terminal B. The old terminal is called C.

Two **information desks** are located on the main concourse in the new terminal, and one is near the baggage claim area of the old terminal.

ATMs are on the main concourses in the old and new terminals and in the baggage claim area of the new terminal. **Currency exchange** services are offered at two customer service centers in the new terminal's main concourse.

Before you leave home, find out whether your hotel offers complimentary shuttle service. If not, the cheapest and quickest way into town is **Metrorail.** You pay $1.35 ($1.55 in rush hour) for a 12-minute ride on Metrorail's Yellow Line from National to the Archives-Navy Memorial Station, which is about halfway between the White House and the Capitol. The trip to Metro Center takes about 18 minutes and costs an extra dime in rush hour because you have to change trains or take a long loop on the Blue Line. Rush-hour fares are charged on weekdays before 9:30 a.m. and from 3 to 7 p.m. You also pay the surcharge when the trains run after 2 a.m. Usually trains run from 5 a.m. till midnight Monday through Thursday, 5 a.m. to 3 a.m. Friday, 7 a.m. to 3 a.m. Saturday, and 7 a.m. until midnight Sunday. Hours may vary on holidays and during special events.

A **taxi** to downtown costs about $11 to $12 (before tip) and takes about 15 minutes (depending, of course, on Washington's notorious traffic).

To avoid price gouging, ask for the fare before you get in a cab. D.C. cabs don't have meters. (The suburban cabs do.) Fares are calculated according to an arcane zone system, which is displayed on a nearly indecipherable map in the cab's back seat. To be safe, ask your hotel ahead of time to estimate the fare from the airport. Allow plenty of time to get to the airport for your return flight if you travel weekdays from 6 to 10 a.m. and 3 to 8 p.m. For more information on taxi fares, see Chapter 4.

From Dulles International Airport

Dulles is in suburban Virginia, about 26 miles from downtown D.C. To get into town, pick from the following options.

✔ The **cab** ride to downtown Washington takes about 45 minutes in favorable traffic and costs about $55.

✔ The **SuperShuttle van** (☎ **202-296-6662** or 800-258-3826; www.supershuttle.com) charges $22 for the first passenger, $10 for each companion.

✔ The best bargain is the **5A express Metrobus,** which runs from Dulles to L'Enfant Plaza near the National Mall in D.C. or to Rosslyn, Virginia, just across the river from Georgetown. At both stops, you can enter the Metrorail system or hail a taxi. The bus costs $3. It departs Dulles every 40 to 50 minutes from 5:50 a.m. to 11:40 p.m. on weekdays, and hourly from 6:32 a.m. to 11:40 p.m. weekends.

Dulles's **ATMs** are on both levels of the main terminal and on midfield concourses A, B, C, and D. **Currency exchange** services are located on the upper level of the main terminal and on midfield concourses B, C, and D. An **information counter** is on the lower level of the main terminal.

Washington, D.C., Airports

Getting into town from the Airports

• From Dulles International Airport:

Take the Dulles Airport access road (the only road out) to I-66 east through the Virginia suburbs and over the Theodore Roosevelt Bridge (still I-66), which lands you on Constitution Avenue and the western edge of the national Mall near the Lincoln Memorial.

• From Baltimore Washington International Airport:

Take the airport access road to Highway 295 (Gladys Spellman Parkway; also known as the Baltimore-Washington Parkway) south to Route 50 west (New York Avenue).

• From Reagan National Airport:

Take the George Washington Memorial Parkway north to the 14th Street Bridge, which dumps you onto...14th Street! Just follow the signs to Washington.

From Baltimore/Washington International Airport

BWI often has the least expensive airfares. But it's also the farthest away from the heart of D.C., so getting from the airport to your hotel takes longer and costs more money.

By **cab,** you're 45 to 60 minutes and $60 to $65 away from downtown Washington if the traffic flows smoothly. The **SuperShuttle** (☎ 800-258-3826; www.supershuttle.com) van service charges $31 for the first passenger and $11 for each companion.

As at Dulles, **Metrobus** runs a $3 express from BWI — this one to the Greenbelt Metrorail station. The B30 bus leaves the airport every 40 minutes between 6:58 a.m. and 10:50 p.m. weekdays and 9:38 a.m. to 10:48 p.m. weekends. From the Greenbelt station, the Metrorail ride to Penn Quarter costs between $2.35 and $3.05 and takes about 25 minutes.

On weekdays, you also can ride the **MARC train** (☎ 800-325-7245; www.mtamaryland.com) from BWI to Union Station for $6. The interval between trains varies from 13 minutes to two hours, but usually is less than an hour. The trip takes 25 to 35 minutes. **Amtrak** (☎ 800-872-7245; www.amtrak.com) runs trains frequently on the same route from before 7 a.m. until after midnight. Tickets range from $11 to $37, and the trip takes 25 to 35 minutes. A courtesy shuttle operates between BWI Airport and the nearby BWI Rail Station.

ATMs and **information** desks are scattered throughout the airport. **Currency exchange** services are available on the upper level by Pier C and on both levels of the International Pier.

From Union Station

Amtrak has great service in the Northeast Corridor. In my experience, it's the most efficient way to travel from New York to Washington and from points between. Trains arrive a few blocks from the U.S. Capitol at historic **Union Station,** a tourist attraction unto itself (see Chapter 11). You can make taxi and Metrorail connections here.

From the Union Station **Metrorail** station, you pay $1.35 to ride a few minutes to most hotels you'd be likely to stay at in central D.C. **Taxi** fares are more complicated. (See Chapter 4 for an explanation.) To get from Union Station to most of Washington's prime tourist areas, you'll pay the cabbie $6.50 to $8.80, plus $1.50 for each additional passenger, plus possibly more add-ons — plus a tip.

An Amtrak **information** station is in the middle of the gates area, and there's a tourist information stand in the Main Hall.

Arriving by car

They say you shouldn't subject yourself to seeing the making of either law or sausage. To that, I will add driving in Washington. Driving *to*

Washington isn't much fun, either — at least not when you get close to D.C.'s infamous Beltway. If you do drive here on a weekday, try to schedule your arrival at the Beltway between 10 a.m. and 3 p.m. — or after 8 p.m. — to avoid the worst of the rush-hour insanity, which seems never to go away entirely.

When you make your hotel reservations, ask for directions. To help visualize the territory, see the "Driving to D.C." map on p. 53.

Once you get to your Washington destination, park your buggy and leave it parked until you leave. You'll be much happier if you get around town via Metrorail, Metrobus, taxi, or your own two feet.

If you drive to a hotel in town, be prepared to pay $20 or more to keep your car in a garage each day.

Figuring Out the Neighborhoods

Many first-time visitors are surprised to find that Washington is not all marble and memorials. Even in the most populated areas, you can find grass, trees, flowers, and places to chill. You can discover much more in Washington than the White House, the Capitol, and the other familiar places featured on the nightly news. In fact, the District has several distinct and distinctive neighborhoods. You can explore their different facets during your visit and leave with a kaleidoscope of impressions. To get you started, here are thumbnail sketches (and a handy map) of D.C.'s major 'hoods.

Adams-Morgan

Vibrant and diverse — that's **Adams-Morgan,** whose main crossroads are 18th Street and Columbia Road NW, north of Dupont Circle. This neighborhood's ethnic restaurants, boutiques, and jumping nightlife draw fun-seekers, especially in the evening and on weekends. Then, Adams-Morgan is packed, and parking is nearly impossible. The Dupont Circle and Woodley Park-Zoo Metrorail stations are a hike, but doable for the physically fit. There are no hotels in Adams-Morgan, and after partying at night most people head to other parts of town to sleep. After dark, take a taxi or the no. 98 Metrobus, which runs from the Woodley Park-Zoo Metrorail Station from about 6 p.m. to 3:15 a.m. weeknights, from 9:50 a.m. to 3:15 a.m. Saturdays, and from 6:05 p.m. to 12:15 a.m. Sundays. Be sure to exercise your street smarts.

Capitol Hill

The Hill, as it is known around Washington, extends from the U.S. Capitol in three directions: north, south, and east. Two of the three branches of the federal government live here, as do a lot of people. In addition to housing the Congress and the Supreme Court, **Capitol Hill** is a charming residential neighborhood, with 19th-century houses, brick sidewalks,

Washington, D.C., Neighborhoods

• *ADAMS-MORGAN*
This neighborhood is vibrant and diverse. Come here to enjoy ethnic restaurants, boutiques, and nightspots.

• *CAPITOL HILL*
Congress dominates Capitol Hill, and the Supreme Court has its digs here, too. But the Hill also is a charming residential neighborhood, with a bustling old-fashioned market and gorgeous old Union Station.

• *CHINATOWN*
D.C.'s Chinatown is quite small, but it's got some very good restaurants and a large ornamental gateway.

• *DUPONT CIRCLE*
Day or night, there's always something doing in Dupont Circle. Pop into the galleries, restaurants, boutiques, and nightspots that abound there.

• *FOGGY BOTTOM/WEST END*
As laid back as Dupont is lively, Foggy Bottom boasts quiet residential streets, George Washington University, the State Department, and the Kennedy Center.

• *GEORGETOWN*
The oldest part of D.C., Georgetown encompasses exclusive residential streets, Georgetown University hangouts, lots of wildly diverse shops, restaurants, and nightspots.

• *NATIONAL MALL*
The Mall is lined with museums, dotted with memorials, and bordered by government headquarters buildings.

• *PENN QUARTER*
A constantly expanding collction of galleries, restaurants, nightspots, and theaters makes Penn Quarter a lively center of arts and entertainment.

and tree-lined streets. You also find Union Station, the National Postal Museum, the Folger Shakespeare Library, the historic — and lively — Eastern Market, and quite a few restaurants, watering holes, and mom-and-pop stores popular with the lawmakers, congressional staffers, lobbyists, and journalists who work — and sometimes live — here. The neighborhood brims with vitality and a persona uniquely its own.

Unfortunately, the area closest to the Capitol has become an eyesore and a travel nightmare because of construction projects and stop-gap security devices thrown up around government buildings. The Hill is another place to watch your step after dark, particularly beyond the Capitol grounds and the first few blocks of Pennsylvania Avenue SE.

The perks of staying on Capitol Hill are

- ✔ In addition to having easy access to the Hill's attractions, you can walk to the Mall or hop Metrorail to anywhere. The Hill is served by Red, Blue, and Orange Line stations.

- ✔ If you arrive and depart by train, your lodging is conveniently close to Union Station, which also is a great place to eat and shop.

- ✔ This area is easier on your pocketbook than many other D.C. neighborhoods.

On the downside

- ✔ Although the area has its *pocket parks* (small, welcome green spots in the midst of urban surroundings), it has less elbow room than other sections of the city.

- ✔ You won't encounter many problems in the immediate vicinity of the major hotels and attractions, but the farther you go from the Capitol, the less safe you'll be at night.

Downtown

Office buildings, shops, hotels, restaurants, and some government headquarters (including the White House) vie for space in this central area, which runs roughly from 10th to 22nd streets NW, north of Pennsylvania Avenue and south of the Dupont Circle neighborhood. Once as scintillating as white bread, the area now attracts nighttime and weekend visitors thanks to redevelopment along Pennsylvania Avenue, the addition of high-quality restaurants, and the endurance of long-standing theaters. Downtown's K Street is used as shorthand for lawyers and lobbyists, even though most of them have their offices elsewhere. Connecticut Avenue sports high-class shopping.

The advantages of staying downtown are

- ✔ You're within walking distance of major attractions and Metrorail stations for the Red, Blue, and Orange lines.

> ✔ Many of the city's best restaurants are located here, as are a large
> number of inexpensive eateries frequented by downtown workers
> at lunch time.

On the other hand

> ✔ You can pay a high price for the convenient location.
>
> ✔ Much — though not all — of the area loses its vitality when the
> office workers go home for the night.

Dupont Circle

One of Washington's liveliest neighborhoods around the clock, the
Dupont Circle area is an ideal spot for people-watching. (Check out the
street musicians and chess players in the heart of the circle itself.) Early
in the morning, workers arrive at the embassies, businesses, think tanks,
and other nonprofit organizations that set up their headquarters here.
The area's many restaurants feed people from breakfast through dinner.
The neighborhood is filled with art galleries and specialty shops. The
nightspots keep hopping until well after midnight. Kramerbooks ("open
early to late, seven days a week," and never closing on weekends)
offered food, drink, and live music long before that became de rigueur
for all bookstores. Dupont Circle is the traditional hub of Washington's
gay community, which parties in the neighborhood's gay-oriented night
spots and shops — among many other places — at Lambda Rising bookstore and the Human Rights Campaign store.

On the upside

> ✔ This area is hip, trendy, lively, colorful, more interesting, and less
> homogenized than most of the other neighborhoods in town.
>
> ✔ You're close to some of the city's best nightlife and dining.
>
> ✔ You can find reasonable prices here, too.

The drawbacks are

> ✔ You're further from major tourist attractions than you would be in
> several other areas, although you can easily hop onto Metro.
>
> ✔ All that after-dark partying means the area can get very noisy at
> night.
>
> ✔ In a city full of traffic and parking horrors, this neighborhood can
> be particularly nightmarish.

Foggy Bottom/West End

Insiders call the State Department **"Foggy Bottom"** because that's the
neighborhood in which its headquarters stand, and the name seems perfect for the obfuscating parlance that marks much diplomatic dialogue.
George Washington University also occupies an ever-expanding portion

of the neighborhood. That leaves an ever-shrinking piece of the pie to Foggy Bottom's charming residential streets of brick row houses, Lilliputian gardens, and mature trees. Here, you also find the Kennedy Center, the Watergate complex, and quite a few hotels. The neighborhood got its name, by the way, because much of it was low, swampy land that produced much fog and mist, and later was an industrial area (called "Funkstown") that was engulfed in smoke and smog.

Foggy Bottom encompasses the area west of the White House, east of Georgetown, and south of Pennsylvania Avenue. **West End** refers to the small neighborhood surrounded by Foggy Bottom, downtown, Dupont Circle, and Georgetown. There you find office buildings and a few hotels and restaurants.

The pros:

✔ You're close to the White House, Kennedy Center, State Department, George Washington University, the infamous Watergate, and Georgetown.

✔ You can hop Metrorail or the 30-series Metrobuses for longer trips.

✔ A very pleasing European ambience pervades the neighborhood.

✔ Foggy Bottom is quieter than other sections of town.

The only con is that the quiet also means that the area usually has less excitement than elsewhere.

Georgetown

One of Washington's best-known neighborhoods was established before the District of Columbia was a gleam in George Washington's eye. Fragments of a former era, when **Georgetown** was a bustling tobacco port, endure in the residential architecture and the cobblestone and brick streets off the main drags.

On Wisconsin Avenue and M Street, however, the mood is far from genteel, especially on weekends. A mix of shops, restaurants, and nightspots draws the young — and the young at heart — from D.C., the suburbs, local universities, and all over the world. Georgetown University, Dumbarton Oaks, the C&O Canal, the "*Exorcist* Steps" (featured in the movie), and some of the city's most exclusive residences contribute to Georgetown's enduring cachet.

Georgetown has no Metrorail station, but 30-series Metrobuses run on Wisconsin and on M to Pennsylvania Avenue. You can hike in from the Foggy Bottom–GWU Metrorail Station. Georgetown Metro Connection shuttle buses run from the Foggy Bottom, Dupont Circle, and Rosslyn stations from 7 a.m. to midnight Monday through Thursday, 7 a.m. to 2 a.m. Friday, 8 a.m. to 2 a.m. on Saturday, and 8 a.m. to midnight Sunday. Fare's $1.50 — or 35¢ with a Metrorail transfer. Another bus, the DC Circulator, runs from Union Station, through downtown, to Wisconsin

Avenue and M Street, Georgetown's main intersection. Tickets cost a buck, 35¢ with transfer. The bus runs from 7 a.m. to 9 p.m. every day.

Staying in Georgetown is great because

- ✔ Like Dupont Circle, Georgetown jumps a lot more than most of Washington.

- ✔ An abundance of shopping, dining, and nightlife is within walking distance.

- ✔ Walk just northwest of Wisconsin and M, and you're in another college community — Georgetown University.

- ✔ Walk just northeast and you enter Washington's most exclusive residential neighborhood, home to some of the richest, most powerful, and most famous people in the world.

On the other hand

- ✔ If you seek tranquillity, especially at night, stay elsewhere. The noise on weekends (when the student population comes out to party) can grow very loud.

- ✔ Georgetown has no Metrorail station, so you have to hail a cab, hop a bus, or hike to Foggy Bottom or (believe it or not) the Rosslyn Station in Virginia.

- ✔ Georgetown can get very crowded. Traffic is bad at all times and is particularly horrendous during rush hour, on weeknights, and throughout the weekends.

The National Mall

Washington's long, long lawn stretches from the Capitol to the Lincoln Memorial and is where you find many museums, monuments, and memorials. The **Mall** is lined by major Smithsonian Institutions and is across the street from major federal government offices. You encounter somber contemplation at places such as the Vietnam War Memorial and joyful play on the grass and walkways (kite-flying, cycling, jogging, strolling, and squirrel-watching).

There's no point reviewing the pluses and minuses of staying on the Mall, because there's no place to sleep there (unless you pitch a tent, which tends to be frowned upon).

Penn Quarter

Not so long ago, Penn Quarter was just an obscure, run-down corner of Downtown. Now it's one of *the* places to go, for several reasons. Bordered by 10th Street, 6th Street, Pennsylvania Avenue, and Massachusetts Avenue, Penn Quarter booms with a constantly increasing number of restaurants, shops, galleries, and the Verizon Center sports and concert arena. The area also encompasses much of what's left of D.C.'s minuscule **Chinatown.**

You'll like Penn Quarter because

✔ It's equaled — maybe surpassed — Georgetown, Dupont Circle, and Adams-Morgan as a place to cut loose at night.

✔ It's got several superb, and moderately priced, restaurants.

✔ If art galleries are your thing, you'll find plenty here.

You may have second thoughts when

✔ You realize how noisy and crowded the place can be at night and on weekends.

Upper Northwest

The **Upper Northwest** area is essentially everything north and west of what I describe in the preceding sections. It's mostly nice residential neighborhoods, D.C.'s best public schools, some office buildings, and the restaurants, theaters, and retail establishments that serve them. Some hotels and tourist attractions, notably the Washington National Cathedral and the National Zoo, are here. I live in this neighborhood, but I take visitors elsewhere to sightsee. Where Wisconsin Avenue crosses into Maryland is an area that I refer to as Washington's Rodeo Drive — a number of exclusive stores (plus some discounters) for those who are inclined to expend substantial vacation bucks on shopping.

Some good points for staying here:

✔ Families appreciate the area's proximity to the National Zoo, a major child-pleaser, on Connecticut Avenue.

✔ You find Washington's answer to Beverly Hills' Rodeo Drive near the Friendship Heights Metrorail Station.

✔ Washington National Cathedral is on upper Wisconsin Avenue.

The only bad thing is that you'll be taking Metrorail, Metrobus, or a taxi to see most of the sights.

Gathering Information after You Arrive

If you need information after you arrive in Washington, head for one or more of these spots:

✔ **Washington, D.C., Visitor Information Center,** on the ground floor of the Ronald Reagan International Trade Center Building, 1300 Pennsylvania Ave. NW, at the Federal Triangle Metrorail Station (☎ 866-324-7386; www.dcvisit.com). From March 15 through

Labor Day, the center is open 8:30 a.m. to 5:30 p.m. weekdays and 9 a.m. to 4 p.m. Saturdays. The rest of the year, it's open 9 a.m. to 4:30 p.m. weekdays, closed weekends.

This center is a full-service spot. Staff members can answer your questions, and you can pick up free brochures. You can buy Metro fare cards, theater tickets, and sightseeing tickets. You can use its computers to find out information about hotels, restaurants, and events and can even book a hotel reservation.

✔ **The White House Visitor Center,** in the Commerce Department Building, 15th and E streets NW, near the Federal Triangle Metrorail Station (☎ 202-208-1631; www.nps.gov/whho/planyourvisit/index.htm). At press time, White House tours are limited to groups of at least ten who get tickets from a member of Congress. But the National Park Service continues to operate this visitor center, which isn't in the White House.

It's open 7:30 a.m. to 4 p.m. every day except Thanksgiving, December 25, and January 1. You can find information here about other parts of Washington in addition to the White House. You can use restrooms, telephones, and water fountains and obtain first aid if you need it.

✔ **The Smithsonian Information Center,** in the "Castle," 1000 Jefferson Dr. SW, on the National Mall, near the Smithsonian Metrorail Station (☎ 202-633-1000; TTY 202-357-1729; www.si.edu/visit/infocenter/start.htm; e-mail info@si.edu). Stop here for information about the Smithsonian and other attractions. Watch an 18-minute video for an overview of the institution. Peruse a model of the Mall to help you locate your first stop. Find attractions and Metro and Tourmobile stops using an electronic map. Pick up a free guide in any of seven languages. Grab a bite to eat in the cafe.

This center also has information about events elsewhere in the city. Your kids can access information from the video-display monitors while you challenge the staff with your questions. If you're on overload, ask one of the volunteers for help in planning your itinerary. On your way out, you may want to pay your respects to British subject James Smithson, whose bequest gave birth to the institution. His crypt is just inside the Jefferson Drive entrance. The center is open 8:30 a.m. to 5:30 p.m. daily except December 25.

Getting Around Washington

Washington can be a challenge to navigate, particularly for a newcomer. But once you know the basics, you can negotiate the tourist areas with ease.

D.C. has streets, avenues, roads, drives, places, squares, circles — and probably some other arteries that have slipped my mind. The avenues, roads, drives, and places go every which way. Roadways run into physical barriers and disappear, only to reappear again several blocks away. Circles and squares pop up in your way and leave you searching for your route on the other side. But the street-naming system is based on a grid that extends throughout the city. If you understand how the street-naming system works, you can find almost any address and figure out where you are most of the time.

The key to the city: Getting from here to there

When D.C. was created from land ceded by Maryland and Virginia, it was a perfect square, 10 miles on a side, with one corner pointing due north. In due course, Virginia was given back most of Southwest D.C. and a portion of Northwest, which is why the district now has an irregular shape defined by the Potomac River along its border with Virginia.

The street-naming system, based on the original square, has endured. The city is divided into quadrants, and all the streets are known by the quadrant they're in: Northwest (NW), Northeast (NE), Southeast (SE), and Southwest (SW).

Understanding the District's directions

The Capitol dome is the center of D.C. geography. Three streets — North Capitol, East Capitol, and South Capitol — run in those directions from the Capitol grounds. You won't find a West Capitol Street, but you can imagine it running due west from the Capitol down the center of the National Mall. These streets define the boundaries of the four quadrants.

All of Washington's numbered streets run north-south, counting from the Capitol. First Street NE is the first street east of North Capitol Street. First Street NW is the first street west of North Capitol Street. First Street SE is the first street east of South Capitol Street. Just to confuse things, here and there you encounter a Half Street, which is closer to Capitol Street than a portion of First Street.

Washington's east–west-running streets all have names that — in most cases — work through the alphabet as they get further north and south of East Capitol Street and the middle of the National Mall. The streets closest to East Capitol and the middle of the Mall are named for letters — A Street, B Street, and so on. As you continue north and south and the alphabet is exhausted, you run into streets with two-syllable names — Adams, Bryant, Channing, and so on. Then you hit three-syllable names (Allison, Buchanan).

Unfortunately, you find numerous exceptions to these rules. For some reason — or perhaps for no reason at all — no J, X, Y, or Z streets exist. Some streets break the alphabet and syllable rules. And the roadways that aren't streets — avenues, roads, drives, places — do whatever they feel like doing.

If you understand the basic street grid, you can find almost any address and figure out where you are most of the time. If you're looking for 450 H St. NW, you know it's in the Northwest quadrant of the city, eight streets north of the middle of National Mall, between 4th and 5th streets. If you're looking for 850 4th St. NE, you know it's in the Northeast quadrant, between H and I streets.

You'll notice I said "almost." The numbered streets don't mess around. But some named streets defy the alphabet and syllable standards. And, because there is no J Street, the block between K and L is the 1000 block. I'm sorry. At least you'll be able to estimate locations within a few blocks. (And then you can ask directions!)

Movin' around on Metro

Washington's extensive public transportation system makes getting around the city a cinch. **Metrorail,** called Metro by locals, is the city's subway system. Rail stations open at 5 a.m. on weekdays and at 7 a.m. on weekends. Final trains leave stations around midnight Sunday through Thursday and around 3 a.m. Friday and Saturday. If you're traveling late at night, check the exact time of the last train leaving the station you'll be using. The schedule is posted at the kiosks in each station. You can reach Metro information at ☎ **202-637-7000** (TTY 202-638-3780) or online at www.wmata.com. Request a **Metro Visitor's Kit** by calling ☎ **888-638-7646** or 202-962-2733. You can find visitors information online at www.wmata.com/riding/visitors/visitors.cfm.

Finding Metrorail stations

To find a Metrorail station on Washington's streets, look for the brown pole topped by the letter M and the station name. You should see a *colored stripe* beneath the M to indicate the line or lines that stop there. The different Metrorail lines are named for colors — Red, Blue, Orange, Yellow, and Green. Trains are well marked, but sometimes trains from different lines (such as Blue and Orange) use the same tracks. If you're unsure, ask the station manager or another waiting passenger. If you find yourself on the wrong train, hop off and take a train back to the station where you made the mistake.

Metrorail's cars are air-conditioned, and the seats are upholstered. Stations are clean and well lighted. Though Metrorail is showing its age (not unlike most people), a major effort is underway to replace tired escalators, refurbish old trains, and put new trains on the rails.

Trains run every few minutes during rush hour, less often at other times, least often late at night. I always carry reading material for use when I'm sitting on the train and waiting at the station. Or you can use your transportation time to people-watch.

Washington, D.C., Metro Stops

Paying your way on Metro

Getting around via Metrorail is relatively inexpensive. Fares are based on distance traveled and time of day. Off peak, the minimum fare is $1.35. You pay less than $2.25 for most trips within D.C., even during rush hour (weekdays before 9:30 a.m. and from 3 to 7 p.m.). There's also a surcharge after 2 a.m. You can buy fare cards from vending machines inside the stations. The machines accept coins (from nickels to quarters) and bills (from $1 to $20). Some machines take credit cards. Bear in mind that the machines return up to only $5 in change — *in coins only* — so make sure that you use small bills when you buy a low-value fare card. Experiencing difficulty? Ask the station manager — or a nearby local — for help.

Estimate the amount of fare you need throughout your D.C. stay and buy one fare card per person with that amount on it. That way, you don't have to stop at a fare card vending machine each time you want to take a ride.

Each passenger needs a fare card. One or two children younger than 5 can ride free with a paying passenger. Disabled persons and seniors 65 and older can ride for half price with a special fare card, but they must possess valid proof of disability or age. For the senior discount, identification can be a driver's license or birth certificate. If the disabled person doesn't have a Medicare card, however, the discount probably isn't worth the paperwork for someone who's visiting for a few days or even a few weeks. A convenient place to purchase the half-price fare cards is the sales office inside the Metro Center Metrorail Station. You can get to it through the station's 12th and F streets entrance or by taking a train to the station. The sales office is open weekdays from 7:30 a.m. to 6:30 p.m. The cards also are sold at some stores, including some Safeway and Giant groceries.

One-day rail passes cost $6.50 and allow unlimited rides for a single weekday after 9:30 a.m. or all day Saturday and Sunday. You can buy them at all Metrorail stations.

After you insert your fare card in the entrance gate, it's stamped and returned. Don't walk off without it (as many visitors do). You need to reinsert it in the exit gate at your destination, where the card is returned if value is left on it. If you underestimate the fare, you can add what's necessary at the *Addfare* machines found near the exit and entrance gates.

Hints for smooth riding on Metrorail

First-time passengers sometimes find the system intimidating. Follow these tips, and you should enjoy a smooth ride. (Should you start to hyperventilate, just ask a station attendant for help.)

> ✔ **Use the maps.** Wall-mounted maps and the lists of station-to-station fares are posted in Metrorail stations. Take your time in locating the station closest to your destination. When in doubt, ask the station manager. You can get maps at Metrorail stations. You can download a map from the Metro Web site at `www.wmata.com/metrorail/colormap.pdf`.

✔ **Hold onto your fare card** when it's returned to you. Keep it handy for reinsertion at your destination.

✔ **Don't board the wrong train.** It sounds obvious, but the minute (or two) that you take to note the station stops, listed on columns inside the stations, is worth it.

✔ **Do not eat, drink, or smoke on Metro or in the stations.** *This rule is serious!* Washington's Metro is one of the cleanest subway systems in the world, and this rule is the reason for it. The police will fine — *and even arrest* — you for sipping a soft drink or nibbling on potato chips in a station or on a train. Keep your snacks in your backpacks.

✔ **Get a transfer ticket** if you're switching from Metrorail to Metrobus. You can get one from a machine where you enter the Metrorail system to start your trip, and it lets you transfer to a regular bus for 35¢ and to an express bus for $2.10. You can't get a bus-to-subway transfer.

✔ On the escalator, **stand to the right and walk on the left.** Blocking walkers by standing on the left is considered exceedingly rude. A columnist for the *Washington Post* staged a contest a few years ago to come up with a name for people who stand to the left. The winning entry: "Tourists."

Traveling by Metrobus

Metrobuses run throughout Washington and its Maryland and Virginia suburbs. Metrorail is faster and more comfortable. But the subway doesn't go to as many places as the buses do. For tourists, the 30-series buses are quite useful.

All 30, 32, 34, 35, and 36 buses travel down Wisconsin Avenue from the D.C.-Maryland border to M Street in the heart of Georgetown. They then go through the heart of downtown and along part of the National Mall on their way to Capitol Hill and beyond.

To find Metrobus stops, look for the red, white, and blue signs with route numbers. You can request a free **map** of all Metrobus Routes in D.C. and Virginia, which is probably all you need to hit the major sights, by phoning ☎ **202-637-7000.** A map of the D.C. and Maryland routes is available, as well. You can download bus and rail maps at this Web site: www. wmata.com/maps/maps.cfm. You also can get the maps at Metrorail stations and Metro sales offices.

Bus fare is $1.25, except for some suburban express routes that cost $3. Bus-to-bus transfers are free; ask the driver of your first bus. Drivers don't make change, so you need to carry exact fare. Most buses run daily around the clock — frequently during rush hour, infrequently in the wee hours.

Up to two children younger than 5 ride free with a paying passenger. Seniors 65 and older and persons with disabilities can ride for 60¢. Valid proof of age or disability must be presented when boarding. For seniors, a driver's license or birth certificate works. A disabled person needs a Medicare card or a special Metro ID that, for a visitor, probably is more trouble to get than it's worth.

Other buses

The D.C. Circulator (http://dccirculator.com) and the Georgetown Metro Connection (www.georgetowndc.com/shuttle.php) offer other ways to get around central D.C.

The Georgetown shuttle buses connect this popular but Metrorail-starved neighborhood with the Foggy Bottom, Dupont Circle, and Rosslyn Metrorail stations. Buses run from 7 a.m. to midnight Monday through Thursday, 7 a.m. to 2 a.m. Friday, 8 a.m. to 2 a.m. on Saturday, and 8 a.m. to midnight Sunday. Fare's $1.50, or 35¢ with a Metrorail transfer. The Connection's two routes intersect at Wisconsin and M. One travels mostly on M between Rosslyn and Dupont Circle. The other runs mostly on Wisconsin and K, from Foggy Bottom to Wisconsin's intersection with R.

The Circulator has three routes. One runs mostly along K Street and Massachusetts Avenue between Union Station and Wisconsin and M. Another circles the National Mall on Independence Avenue, Constitution Avenue, 17th Street, and 4th Street. The third travels north–south, mostly on 7th and 9th streets, between the Convention Center and the Southwest Waterfront. A ride costs $1 – 35¢ with Metro transfer. The Circulator bus operates 7 a.m. to 9 p.m. every day.

Taxi! Cabbing it in D.C.

Hailing a cab in Washington usually is a snap, except for late at night. Stand on a main street, by a busy intersection, or in front of a hotel or large office building to better snag a taxi. When I need to order a cab, I call **Diamond** (☎ **202-387-6200,** 202-797-5916, 202-797-5915, or, for airport service, 202-387-2600). Diamond's not perfect, but I seem to get a higher percentage of well-maintained cabs with knowledgeable drivers with Diamond than with some other companies.

Strangers to D.C. may find the zone fare system baffling — as do the locals. But if you ride a Washington cab, you have to deal with it. For details, see Chapter 4.

Items left in a cab are supposed to be turned in to the D.C. Taxicab Commission (☎ **202-645-6018,** fax 202-889-3604; http://dctaxi.dc.gov/dctaxi). If you leave something in a cab, phone, fax, or e-mail the commission with this information: your name, daytime telephone number, a brief description of the item (include model and phone number for cellphone), and the date it was lost. Also have the name, ID number, and vehicle license plate number of the cab, if you know it. If you have a

Taxicab Zones

ZONE FARES	Single Passenger and Shared Riding Rate Per Passenger
1 Zone	$6.50
2 Zones	$8.80
3 Zones	$11.00
4 Zones	$12.60
5 Zones	$14.00
6 Zones	$15.50
7 Zones	$17.80
8 Zones	$18.90

Group Rates:
$1.50 extra for each additional passenger after first passenger in group

Rush Hour:
(7–9:30 a.m., 4–6:30 p.m.)
Surcharge—$1.00 per trip

Radio Dispatch:
Surcharge—$2.00

NOTE:
Fares are doubled during periods of snow emergency as declared by the District of Columbia Taxicab Commission.

receipt, enlarge it to double its original size and fax it. The commission's office hours are 8:15 a.m. to 4:45 p.m. Monday to Friday, except holidays.

Taking a ride on Tourmobile

An excellent alternative mode of transportation for tourists is **Tourmobile** (☎ **202-554-5100,** 888-868-7707; www.tourmobile.com), the tram that stops by major tourist attractions and at points in Arlington Cemetery. The $20 fare ($10 for children 3 through 11 and free for younger kids) lets you ride all day with unlimited reboarding privileges. That means you can ride the full route, listening to the tour guide's narrative, and get a good overview of most of the big attractions. Then you can use the Tourmobile as a bus to go from place to place for the rest of the day. A two-day pass is $30 or $15.

Trams stop about every 20 minutes at the red, white, and blue Tourmobile signs from 9:30 a.m. until 4:30 p.m. daily except December 25 and January 1. Final reboarding is at 3:30 p.m. You can buy tickets from the driver or at Tourmobile ticket booths.

All Tourmobile trams are equipped with priority seating for individuals with disabilities and wheelchair storage space. Individuals with disabilities who can transfer from their wheelchairs and climb three steps can board any Tourmobile. Vehicles with lifts are dispatched when a request is made to a Tourmobile driver or at a ticket booth. You can schedule service by a lift-equipped vehicle in advance by calling ☎ **703-979-0690** between 8 a.m. and 5 p.m. daily except December 25 and January 1. Disabled riders can leave the tram at any stop and arrange a reboarding time with the driver.

Walking through Washington

Like Nancy Sinatra's boots, Washington is made for walking. In these health- and budget-conscious times, putting mileage on your feet instead of your wallet, fare card, or car makes sense. On foot, you discover things that you may otherwise miss, things that make a trip special. (When you get home, please write and tell me what they are.)

 Try a Mall crawl, walking from museum to museum between the Capitol and the Washington Monument. The museums are air-conditioned; you can rest and rejuvenate in a restaurant or snack bar. Or stroll through the residential side streets of Foggy Bottom and/or Georgetown.

 Keep your wits about you when you walk. That's not to say that D.C. isn't safe to walk around. It is, especially in the major tourist zones. It just pays to be prepared.

Stride with a sense of purpose; dawdlers appear vulnerable, which is just what professional pickpockets and muggers look for. Be alert in crowds, where a bump from a pickpocket can easily be missed. Be aware of your surroundings. Stow wallets, cash, credit cards, and travelers checks in front pockets or a money pouch worn under your clothing. Wear your purse across one shoulder and over the chest — bandolier style. Lock your hotel room door, car doors, and trunk. Don't leave luggage or other items visible in your car when you park it. Lock valuables in a safe deposit box (if not in your room, then at the front desk). Keep a close eye on your pocketbook and camera. Hold onto your purse in a restaurant. Don't leave a purse or other bag unattended in public. Not only might you lose it to a purse snatcher, you might lose it to law enforcement officials who worry that there's a bomb inside. Leave the family jewels at home; what you do bring, don't flash.

The safe zones include the major tourist areas and Metro. At night, use the buddy system and stick to the well-lighted, highly populated, main commercial blocks — especially in Adams-Morgan, the U Street Corridor, and Capitol Hill. The Mall used to feel safe round the clock, but a couple of well-publicized muggings after dark in 2006 challenged that complacency — as did a mugging that became a murder on a residential street in Georgetown. If Metro's service has stopped for the night, and you're still out on the town, take a taxi. Know your destination before you set out. Hold your kids' hands on city streets and sidewalks, on all Metro escalators, and on Metro platforms.

On Capitol Hill, you won't encounter many problems in the immediate vicinity of the major hotels, restaurants, and attractions. But the farther you go from the Capitol, the less safe you'll be at night.

Driving your car

I have yet to meet a person who enjoys driving in Washington. The traffic is oppressive and constantly getting worse. Washington also seems to be cursed by an ever-growing number of drivers who drive as if no one else is on the road. Street parking is at a premium. Garage parking will consume your family's lunch money.

If you plan on arriving by car, ask about parking rates at your hotel when you make a reservation. It may prevent your requiring treatment for shock when the final hotel tab is totaled up.

Chapter 9

Checking In at D.C.'s Best Hotels

*B*ecause so many different kinds of people come to Washington with regularity, the city has a wide variety of accommodations. The idealistic young and penniless come here, perhaps to protest, to volunteer for the many do-gooder groups in town, or just to see the sights. At the other extreme, high-rolling lawyers and lobbyists arrive with no worries about expense accounts because their clients will be picking up whatever tab is presented. The rest of the world, in the vast middle between those extremes, is looking for budget, moderate, or moderately luxurious accommodations. Fortunately, visitors can find them all.

Finding the Best Room at the Best Rate

Some folks call a hotel, ask for a rate, and pay it with no more questions asked. These are the same folks who go to an automobile dealer and pay sticker price. You, however, aren't going to mimic these people by paying the first price you're quoted, because you're going to use the tips that follow to find the best hotel room for your money.

Finding the best rates

If you walk in off the street and ask for a room for the night, you'll be told the hotel's maximum charge for that room — its *rack rate*. (During your next hotel stay, take a peek at the fire and/or emergency directions posted on the back of your door; the rack rates usually are posted on or near these notices.) If a hotel can get away with collecting its rack rate for a room, the management is very happy. But here's the scoop: Hardly anyone forks over the rack rate. Avoiding the rack rate is surprisingly simple: Ask whether the hotel offers a cheaper or discounted rate. You almost always get a better price! Better yet, don't walk in off the street. Make reservations ahead of time.

Room rates change with the season, as occupancy rates rise and fall. If a hotel is close to full, it's less likely to extend discount rates; if a hotel is close to empty, it may be willing to negotiate. D.C. hotels are more likely to negotiate with you on weekends and during low season.

Low season — low prices

The three best times of year to find deals on hotel rooms in D.C. are:

- ✓ **Thanksgiving through New Year's.** Fewer travelers leave home and hearth.

- ✓ **July and August.** Congress is in recess, and the city is in siesta mode.

- ✓ **Weekends** throughout the year. Politicians (and the folks who follow them) get outta town, leaving space for everyone else.

Between Thanksgiving and early January, the pace here slows down. Many members of Congress take very long breaks from Washington. (The House calls them "district work periods." The Senate calls them "recesses." They're usually actually a bit of both.) And folks in the rest of the country are less likely to pack up for a Washington vacation during the year-end holidays. With fewer people in town, hotels cut their rates. During July and August, when the Senate and House office buildings are morguelike because the elected officials are away for their summer recess/ work period, hotels woo visitors with lower charges. (For more on Washington's high and low seasons, see Chapter 3.) And on the weekends, the gang on the Hill heads home again, as do the visiting lobbyists, and hotel rates again take a dip.

High season — high prices

High season in Washington is:

- ✓ **Mid-March through June.** Everyone wants to visit D.C. in the spring, and who can blame them? The city blossoms in the warm weather, but, alas, so do hotel prices.

- ✓ **September through mid-November.** Congress is back in session, and Capitol Hill is hopping in fall. The weather outside may be delightful, but it's a safe bet that hotel prices will be frightful.

In spring, the Cherry Blossom Festival, good weather, and school districts' spring breaks historically draw visitors to the city in huge numbers. The weather is usually mild into June, and that keeps the crowds coming. High season also occurs when the Capitol is a beehive of activity, and those who want to influence Congress converge.

Hotels in Washington, D.C.

WASHINGTON'S BEST HOTELS
Capitol Hill Suites **32**
Four Points by Sheraton **39**
Four Seasons **8**
Georgetown Suites
    30th Street **7**
Georgetown Suites
    29th Street **9**
George Washington
    University Inn **12**
Hay-Adams **25**
Henley Park Hotel **37**
Holiday Inn on the Hill **33**
Hostelling International **38**
Hotel Harrington **30**
Hotel Lombardy **14**
Hotel Madera **17**
Hotel Monaco **35**
Hotel Washington **27**
The Jefferson **22**
Jurys Normandy Inn **4**
Jurys Washington **18**
Mandarin Oriental **31**
Morrison-Clark Historic Inn
    and Restaurant **40**
One Washington Circle **15**
Red Roof Inn **36**
Renaissance Mayflower **24**
Ritz-Carlton Washington **16**
The River Inn **11**
Sofitel Lafayette Square **26**
State Plaza **13**
Tabard Inn **20**
Willard InterContinental **28**

WASHINGTON'S BEST B&Bs
D.C. Guest House **41**
Kalorama Guest House at
    Woodley Park **1**
Swann House **19**
Woodley Park Guest House **2**

RUNNER-UP HOTELS
Georgetown Inn **5**
Hotel George **34**
Hotel Rouge **21**
J.W. Marriott **29**
Latham Hotel **6**
Omni Shoreham **3**
Washington Plaza **23**
Washington Suites
    Georgetown **10**

Surfing the Web for hotel deals

You can use the Internet to gather information and make hotel reservations. In fact, because so many different deals are available, your best bet is to use both the telephone and the Internet when you search for the best prices. Check several online sources as well.

Major hotel chains — and many individual hotels — book rooms online the same way that airlines and Amtrak book transportation. (See the Quick Concierge for chains' Web addresses and phone numbers.)

Expedia offers a long list of special deals and "virtual tours" or photos of rooms so that you can see what you're paying for (a feature that helps to counter claims that the best rooms are often held back from bargain booking Web sites). **Travelocity** posts unvarnished customer reviews and ranks its properties according to the AAA rating system. Also reliable are **Hotels.com** and **Quikbook.com**. Be sure to **get a confirmation number** and **make a printout** of any online booking transaction, in case questions about your reservation arise.

In the opaque Web site category, **Priceline** is even better for hotels than for airfares; you're allowed to pick the neighborhood and quality level of your hotel before offering up your money. On the down side, many hotels stick Priceline guests in their least desirable rooms. You must pay up front, and the fee is nonrefundable. Be sure to go to the **BiddingForTravel** Web site (www.biddingfortravel.com) before bidding on a hotel room on Priceline; it provides information about recent winning bids to help you decide how much to offer. *Note:* Some hotels don't provide loyalty program credits or points or other frequent-stay amenities when you book a room through opaque online services.

 Room rates change with the season, as occupancy rates rise and fall. But even within a given season, room prices are subject to change without notice, so the rates quoted in this book may be different from the actual rate you receive when you make your reservation.

Reserving the best room

The amount you spend to bed down eats a big chunk of your travel dollars. In all but the smallest accommodations, the rate you pay for a room depends on many factors — chief among them being how you make your reservation. Prices change, sometimes faster than room service can deliver coffee and a bagel.

Calling your friendly travel agent

A travel agent may be able to negotiate a better price with certain hotels than you can get by yourself. Often, the hotel gives the agent a discount in exchange for steering his or her business toward that hotel.

Your travel agent may suggest a package deal (with airfare) and/or traveling with a group. (See Chapter 5 for more on package tours.) Booking with a group can be the best way to get the best deal. Not only do you hand over the responsibility of planning the trip to someone else — the tour operator — you often get a better rate. Hotels, joyful at the prospect of booking 20 rooms instead of one or two, give tour operators a discount that's passed on to you.

Making your own hotel reservations

Hotel chains take telephone reservations through a central toll-free number and at the individual hotels. (See the Quick Concierge at the back of the book for toll-free numbers for the major chains.) Sometimes the toll-free number and local numbers produce different rates. Your best bet is to call both and see which provides a better deal.

 Be sure to mention membership in AAA, AARP, frequent-flier programs, and any other corporate rewards programs, or whether you're a government employee, when you make your reservation. You never know when doing so can save you a few dollars off your room rate.

After you make your reservation, ask a few more questions. These inquiries can go a long way toward making sure that you secure the best room for the best price.

 ✔ **Always ask whether a corner room is available at the same price.** Sometimes a corner room has more space and more windows (with views). And the corner location may mean a quieter environment. If you're located at the end of the hall, you don't hear neighbors passing your room or using the elevator all night.

✔ **Steer clear of construction zones.** Be sure to ask whether the hotel is renovating. If it is, request a room away from the renovation site. The noise may be more than you want to deal with on your vacation.

✔ **Request smoking or nonsmoking rooms.** Be sure to indicate your preference. Otherwise, you may get stuck with a room that doesn't meet your needs.

✔ **Inquire about the location of the restaurants, bars, and nightspots.** These areas of the hotel can be sources of irritating noise. On the other hand, if you want to be near the action, or if you have a disability that makes it difficult for you to get around, you may choose to be close to these amenities.

 Even if you secure a relatively quiet room, strange noises, loud TVs, and snoring partners can wreak havoc with your sleep. Carry earplugs when you travel.

Arriving without a Reservation

Arriving in D.C. and *then* looking for a place to stay is not the preferred way to find a bargain — or a room of any kind, for that matter. If you do find yourself in this bind, call the major hotel chains and ask what they have available. (See the Quick Concierge at the back of this book for their phone numbers.) Or try some local reservation services, such as **Capitol Reservations** (☎ **202-452-1270,** 800-847-4832; www.washington dchotels.com), and **Washington, D.C. Accommodations** (☎ **202-289-2220,** 800-503-3330; www.dcaccommodations.com).

When it's open, the **Washington, D.C., Visitor Information Center** (Ronald Reagan International Trade Center Building, 1300 Pennsylvania Ave. NW; Metro: Federal Triangle; ☎ **866-324-7386;** www.dcvisit.com), helps walk-ins book hotel rooms. From March 15 through Labor Day, it's open 8:30 a.m. to 5:30 p.m. weekdays and 9 a.m. to 4 p.m. Saturdays. The rest of the year, it's open 9 a.m. to 4:30 p.m. weekdays, closed weekends.

Washington's Best Hotels at All Prices

In this section, I get down to the really important stuff: D.C.'s best hotels at various price levels.

I provide reviews of these hotels and list them alphabetically. I also include two indexes to help you quickly find the hotels you want to consider. One index lists the hotels by price range, the other by neighborhood. And I show the hotels' locations on a map. In case these inns are booked, I offer a list of runners-up.

Table 9-1 explains what the dollar-sign ratings in each listing mean. The price range reflects the average of the highest and lowest prices quoted for a standard double room for one night in high season.

Table 9-1	Key to Hotel Dollar Signs	
Dollar Sign(s)	*Price Range*	*What to Expect*
$	Less than $125	In this category, you may share a dorm-like room at a hostel; stay in an older, no-frills hotel; stay at a B&B (perhaps with a shared bathroom); or check into a plain, budget motel. Your room will be clean, but sometimes won't include a TV or phone. Don't expect room service or extra frills.
$$	$125–$225	The rooms in this category may be smallish or in older buildings, but you usually can count on a TV and other amenities (coffeemaker, soaps, shampoos). You can find some good bargains in housekeeping suites in this price range.

Dollar Sign(s)	Price Range	What to Expect
$$$	$226–$300	These rooms are in full-service hotels or nice B&Bs minus the most luxurious of amenities, or they're nice all-suite properties. Expect hair dryers, irons, coffeemakers, and TVs. You may get room service, on-site restaurants, and access to exercise facilities (on- or off-site).
$$$$	$301–$400	Now you're talking luxury. Besides a large, well-decorated room, you'll likely enjoy a spacious bathroom with ample towels and a terry robe — as a loaner, so don't pack it as a souvenir. Expect a full range of amenities, multiple phones, a dataport, minibars, on-site restaurant(s), room service, and access to exercise facilities. The staff pays great attention to the hotel's appearance and to high-quality service.
$$$$$	More than $400	You pay for the prestigious name, location, service, and opulence. Expect round-the-clock concierge and room service, sumptuous lobbies and room furnishings (entertainment centers, in-room safes), one or more restaurants for fine dining, a bar and/or lobby cocktail lounge, on-site exercise facilities, and staff who trip over themselves to serve you.

Capitol Hill Suites
$$$ Capitol Hill

You become an instant Capitol Hill insider when you bed down here. You're 2 blocks from the Capitol Grounds and across the street from the Library of Congress's Madison Building. You get dining privileges at the nearby Capitol Hill Club, the Republican Party social club that's next door to GOP National Committee headquarters. And you may bump into one of the lawmakers who take advantage of the hotel's long-term rates to make this their Washington home. All suites have kitchenettes. The junior suites are one-room efficiencies, with one queen bed and an armchair with ottoman or sofa bed. Superior suites have two queen beds, an alcove for the kitchenette, and a sitting area with an armchair and ottoman or a sofa bed. The one-bedroom suites have a king or queen bed and a separate living room with a sofa bed. In decorating the hotel, the operators tried to capture what they call the "traditional Capitol Hill" look. That means lots of navy blue and burgundy, leather, marble, and cherry wood. Room rate includes continental breakfast and use of a nearby health club. Valet parking is available. The Capitol South Metrorail Station is about a block away.

See map p. 100. 200 C St. SE (at 2nd Street). ☎ *866-716-8114 or 202-543-6000. Fax: 202-547-2608.* www.capitolhillsuites.com. *Metro: Capitol South. From escalator exit, walk 1 block east on C Street to 2nd Street. From elevator exit, walk 1 block east on D Street and then 1 block north on C Street. Parking: $28 per night. Double room: $209–$319. Children under 18 stay free in parents' room. Rates include continental breakfast. AE, DC, DISC, MC, V.*

Four Points by Sheraton
$$$ **Downtown**

This hotel has a room with a view, but it's not the room you'll be sleeping in. Rather, it's the heated indoor pool on the roof, one of many amenities that make this place a good buy, especially if you snag an off-peak deal that can run $125-a-night or less. From the pool, you get a panoramic look at D.C., including the Capitol dome. Four Points offers concierge services, room service, valet parking, fitness center, business center, and an on-site restaurant. Each room has high-speed Internet access, two-line phones with dataports and voice mail, a coffeemaker, and security safe designed to accommodate a laptop computer. You can ask for a microwave and minifridge. Rooms come with one queen bed, one king bed, or two double beds. Studio and one-bedroom suites with kitchenettes also are available. This hotel is a place where corner rooms are a bit bigger.

See map p. 100. 1201 K St. NW (at 12th Street). ☎ *888-481-7191 or 202-289-7600. Fax 202-349-2215.* www.fourpointswashingtondc.com. *Metro: Metro Center. From G and 12th streets exit, walk 3 blocks north on 12th to K Street. Limited parking: $28 per night. Double room: $245. Children younger than 18 stay free in parents' room. AE, DC, DISC, MC, V.*

Four Seasons
$$$$$ **Georgetown**

Where Foggy Bottom meets Georgetown, you find one of Washington's most celebrity-friendly (and kid-friendly) hotels. The rich and famous love this place because of its luxury and the staff's discretion and impeccable service. The concierge can rent you a tux, find you a toothbrush, or get you theater tickets. You can take high tea or sip a cocktail in the Garden Terrace. An indoor pool and a health club offer all imaginable amenities. If you want to work — *what?* — the hotel has every imaginable business service as well. George Washington never slept here, but Tom Hanks, Sheryl Crow, and Nicolas Cage have. The hotel also brags about its service to "VICs" (Very Important Children). Kids receive gifts and snacks at check-in. They can use the hotel's board games, videotapes, coloring books, kid-sized terry bathrobes, toddler slippers, and teddy bears. Parents can request baby necessities, such as a crib, high chair, and bottle-warmer. Children's menus are offered for meals and at tea. The hotel can get you an experienced, bonded, and insured baby sitter.

See map p. 100. 2800 Pennsylvania Ave. NW (at 28th Street). ☎ ***800-819-5053*** *or 202-342-0444. Fax: 202-944-2076.* www.fourseasons.com/washington. *Metro: Foggy Bottom–George Washington University. Walk 1 block north on 23rd Street to traffic circle, go left around circle to Pennsylvania Avenue, and then go left onto Pennsylvania for 4 blocks. Parking: $35 per night. Double room: $565 and up. One child younger than 18 stays free in parents' room. AE, DC, DISC, MC, V.*

Georgetown Suites
$$ Georgetown

This Georgetown accommodation can be good for families because the suites with bedrooms allow for some privacy and the kitchens enable you to cook. I know cooking isn't what most vacationers put on their itineraries. But vacationing with kids can be much more pleasant when you can return to your lodgings for meals, snacks, and naps. Here, your meal options include a free continental breakfast. Your lodging choices include a one-room studio "suite" (queen-size bed and sitting area with loveseat), a "double double suite" (two double beds and a sitting area), or a one-bedroom suite (king bed and separate living room with pull-out queen-size sofa). A two-bedroom suite has two bathrooms, master bedroom with king bed, a second bedroom with full bed, and a living room with queen sofabed. All have a kitchen with refrigerator, coffeemaker, microwave, and dishwasher. More-luxurious town house and penthouse accommodations are available. The hotel has an exercise room and business center. The suites are in two buildings. The main building, at 1111 30th St. NW, is quieter. Additional perks: Local phone calls and high-speed Internet access are free.

See map p. 100. Main building: 1111 30th St. NW (just below M Street); second building: 1000 29th St. NW (at K Street). ☎ ***800-348-7203*** *or 202-298-7800. Fax: 202-348-7203.* www.georgetownsuites.com. *Metro: Foggy Bottom–George Washington University. Walk 1 block north on 23rd Street to traffic circle, go left around circle to Pennsylvania Avenue, go left onto Pennsylvania for 5 or 6 blocks, and then turn left on 29th or 30th street. Or take Georgetown Connection Route 1 shuttle bus from Foggy Bottom–GWU Metrorail Station or a 30-series Metrobus. Parking: $18 per night. Rates for studios to one-bedroom suites: $195–$225; others higher. AE, DC, DISC, MC, V.*

George Washington University Inn
$$$ Foggy Bottom/West End

Located in a quiet, tree-lined residential section of Foggy Bottom, the George Washington University Inn is an ideal place to park your suitcase if you're visiting the university or sampling the performing arts at the Kennedy Center. The inn is essentially on the GWU campus; it's about 3 long blocks from the Kennedy Center. The short walk to the Foggy Bottom–GWU Metrorail Station and to the 30-series Metrobus routes on Pennsylvania Avenue makes visiting the rest of the city easy, too. The 95 rooms (31 of which are one-bedroom suites) are relatively large, decorated in colonial Williamsburg style, and come with mini refrigerators, microwaves, and coffeemakers. Some suites have full kitchens. You get free access to a fitness facility 2 blocks away, and valet parking is available if you want it. You often can find deep discounts.

See map p. 100. 824 New Hampshire Ave. NW (between H and I streets). ☎ **800-426-4455** *or 202-337-6620. Fax: 202-298-7499.* www.gwuinn.com. *Metro: Foggy Bottom–George Washington University. Walk west on I Street, across 24th Street, and then left on New Hampshire. Parking: $22. Double room: $269–$309. Children younger than 12 stay free in parents' room. AE, DC, MC, V.*

Hay-Adams
$$$$$ Downtown

The Hay-Adams is such a Washington institution that its reopening after an $18-million renovation was front-page news in the *Washington Post*'s business section. It's hard to imagine a better location for an upscale hotel — directly across picturesque Lafayette Square from the White House. Built in 1928, the Hay-Adams long has been a top choice of the rich, the powerful, and the simply famous. Sure, Warren Beatty, Annette Bening, and Meg Ryan have stayed here. But so have Charles Lindbergh, Amelia Earhart, and Sinclair Lewis. The prime attraction of the Hay-Adams always will be what it always has been — that location. Windows in the higher-level rooms on the south side look across Lafayette Square to the White House, with the Washington Monument in the distance. Now, all the amenities are 21st-century state-of-the-art. Impressed by hotel rooms with two telephones? Every Hay-Adams room has *three* two-line phones, including a cordless phone. You also get voice mail, a high-speed Internet connection, a component audio system, 24-hour room service, business services, valet parking, and — of course — the concierge. Will you pay mightily for this luxury? Well . . . if you have to ask . . .

See map p. 100. One Lafayette Square (at 16th and H streets NW). ☎ **800-853-6807** *or 202-638-6600. Fax: 202-638-2716.* www.hayadams.com. *Metro: McPherson Square. From the Vermont Avenue–White House exit, walk south 1 block on Vermont, turn right on H, walk 1 more block, and cross 16th. Valet parking: $30. Double room: $600. Children younger than 17 stay free in parents' room. AE, DC, DISC, MC, V.*

Henley Park Hotel
$$$ Penn Quarter

I have a friend who always tries to stay here because he appreciates the attentive service and the effort the staff makes to get to know regular guests. The rooms are small but comfortable and feature two-line speaker phones with voice mail and dataports, irons and ironing boards, terry cloth robes, coffeemakers, 24-hour room service, and safes. Guests also get free access to an off-site fitness center and outdoor pool. The comfort and attentiveness spill over to the on-site Blue Bar, where a pianist performs Thursday, Friday, and Saturday evenings, and to the Coeur de Lion restaurant. Rates less than $110 are sometimes available.

See map p. 100. 926 Massachusetts Ave. NW (between 9th and 10th streets). ☎ **202-638-5200** *or 800-222-8474. Fax 202-638-6740.* www.henleypark.com. *Metro: Mount*

Vernon Square. Walk 2 blocks south on 7th Street, then right across Mount Vernon Square, and right on Massachusetts. Valet parking: $22. Double room: $259–$329. Children younger than 12 stay free with parents in some rooms. AE, DC, DISC, MC, V.

Holiday Inn on the Hill
$$$$ Capitol Hill

This Holiday Inn enjoys a choice location, about 2 blocks from Union Station and the Capitol grounds, and within walking distance of other attractions. This hotel is more stylish than your typical Holiday Inn — and charges higher prices to match. Staff wear designer uniforms, and the facilities are strikingly decorated. Standard rooms now come with one king bed and easy chair or sofa, or two queen beds with an easy chair. Every guest room has free high-speed Internet access. The lobby, restaurant, and meeting rooms enjoy Wi-Fi access. A large rooftop pool, which provides a great view of the area, is open in summer. The fitness center has treadmills, steppers, circuit trainer, free weights, and recumbent bicycles. Many of the hotel's employees have been here a long time, and that translates into staff and visitor satisfaction. Discounts to below $200 are sometimes available.

See map p. 100. 415 New Jersey Ave. NW (between D and E streets). ☎ **800-638-1116** *or 202-638-1616. Fax: 202-638-0707.* www.hionthehilldc.com. *Metro: Union Station. From the Union Station Shops/Massachusetts Avenue exit, cross Massachusetts, walk around the circle to Louisiana, turn right on Louisiana, right on D, and right on New Jersey. Parking: $30. Double room: $399. Children 18 and younger stay free with their parents. AE, DC, DISC, MC, V.*

Hostelling International
$ Downtown

I promised you accommodations in all price ranges, and this one is the lowest price you're gonna get — at least anywhere you'll *want* to stay, unless you're visiting a friend with a spare bed or space on the floor. If you want candy, you better bring it with you because you don't get Godiva on your pillow here. And you can't watch TV in bed. Whaddaya expect at these prices? This 270-bed facility is basic. It is, however, clean and comfortable, with dorm-style rooms (all air-conditioned), and it's just 3 blocks from Metro Center. The rooms, some coed, sleep 4 to 12 guests. Bathrooms are down the hall. But you get free continental breakfast, high-speed Internet access, and use of a theater-style TV room with a 60-inch screen, kitchen, dining room, luggage storage, lockers, and coin laundry. The hostel organizes activities for guests, such as walking tours. The savvy staff can help you with your itinerary. Families and couples can reserve private rooms for themselves, but you must do so *at least* a month in advance.

See map p. 100. 1009 11th St. NW (at K Street). ☎ **202-737-2333.** *Fax: 202-737-1508.* hiwashingtondc.org. *Metro: Metro Center. From 11th Street exit, walk north on 11th Street 3 blocks. Parking: Use commercial garages in the area. Rates: $32 per person ($29 for Hostelling members) in dorm rooms, $89–$93 per room for private room. MC, V.*

Hotel Harrington
$ Downtown

When you think bargain and no frills, think Hotel Harrington. Family-owned since it opened in 1914, the Harrington caters to groups, families, and others looking for good value. It's an easy walk to the White House, the National Mall, and many other attractions, such as the FBI headquarters, Ford's Theatre, the National Theater, and MCI Center. In addition, the Metro Center Metrorail Station is 2 blocks away for access to anyplace else you'd like to go. If you're traveling with your kids, a family suite is a good idea. The suite includes two rooms (queen bed in one, two twin beds in the other), two bathrooms, compact refrigerator, and coffee/tea maker. Some extra-large rooms sleep up to six. You can have a fridge put into many rooms. Toss in a load at the self-service laundry on the premises. The hotel has three on-site restaurants, all reasonably priced, and plenty of other nearby food options. Trivia note: In 1938, the Harrington became the first hotel in Washington to air-condition all of its rooms.

See map p. 100. 436 11th St. NW (at E Street). ☎ *800-424-8532 or 202-628-8140. Hotel fax: 202-347-3924. Fax for guests: 202-393-2311.* www.hotel-harrington.com. *Metro: Metro Center. From 11th Street exit, walk 2 blocks south to E. Parking: 4 blocks away $10. Rates: $99–$125 double, $125–$169 for larger rooms. AE, DC, DISC, MC, V.*

Hotel Lombardy
$$$ Foggy Bottom/West End

The Lombardy was built as an apartment building in 1929, and it keeps that old-fashioned elegant and homey feel today with the panel of brass mailboxes off the lobby, the elevator with white-gloved operator, and the touches of a comfortable past in the guest rooms. The rooms are large and furnished with antiques, wrought-iron beds, and brocade fabrics. Most have kitchenettes with dining areas, as well as bathrooms with the original tile and period pedestal sinks. In a nod to the modern, the innkeepers also provide two-line phones with dataports and voice mail, coffeemakers, and terry robes. The multilingual staff is friendly. Discounts to below $120 available off peak.

See map p. 100. 2019 Pennsylvania Ave. NW (actually on I Street between 20th and 21st). ☎ *800-424-5486 or 202-828-2600. Fax: 202-872-0503.* www.hotellombardy. com. *Metro: Farragut West. From 18th Street exit, walk 2½ blocks west on I Street. Parking: $28. Double room: $229. Children stay free with parents in some rooms. AE, DC, DISC, MC, V.*

Hotel Madera
$$$$ Dupont Circle

The Madera is one of several boutique hotels that have brought creative, avant-garde, sometimes way-over-the-top style to this traditionally buttoned-up city. The Madera is a strikingly attractive place with fairly large rooms, a complimentary evening "wine hour," and personalized service that focuses right down to the amenities you might find in your room.

"Cardio rooms" have exercise equipment; "flash rooms" hold a computer with high-speed Internet access; "entertainment rooms" provide DVDs to go with the DVD player and extra TV; and "snack rooms" have a kitchenette. Some rooms have balconies. Others, on the upper floors, offer nice views. Rooms are sometimes available for as low as $129.

See map p. 100. 1310 New Hampshire Ave. NW (north of N and west of 20th streets). ☎ *800-430-1202 or 202-296-7600. Fax: 202-293-2476.* www.hotelmadera.com. *Metro: Dupont Circle. From the Dupont Circle exit, walk south on 19th Street briefly, then right on Sunderland Place and across 20th to New Hampshire, and then turn left. Valet parking: $28. Double room: $349–$389. Children stay free with parents in some rooms. AE, DC, DISC, MC, V.*

Hotel Monaco
$$$$ Penn Quarter

You get history with your sleep at the Monaco, a luxury hotel that resulted from a three-year rehabilitation of a 19th-century government palace. It was designed by two noted architects and served first as Washington's general post office and then as the Tariff Commission headquarters. Robert Mills, architect of the Washington Monument, modeled his post office design on the Temple of Jupiter in Rome; it opened in 1842. Thomas Walter, an architect of the Capitol, designed the 1869 addition. As a guest, you get marble columns outside and a mixture of the 19th and 21st centuries inside. The spacious guest rooms have plush furnishings, workspaces, cordless phones, complimentary high-speed Internet access, and a bust of Thomas Jefferson. The hotel even pampers your pet or lends you a goldfish if you long for company during your stay. The Monaco also is well located in D.C.'s new and growing arts and entertainment district. Discounts to below $200 are sometimes offered.

See map p. 100. 700 F St. NW (at 7th Street). ☎ *800-649-1202 or 202-628-7177. Fax: 202-628-7277.* www.monaco-dc.com. *Metro: Gallery Place-Chinatown. From the 7th and F streets exit, look for the gigantic building with marble columns diagonally across the intersection. Parking: $34. Rack rates: $309–$339 double. Children stay free with parent in some rooms. AE, DC, DISC, MC, V.*

Hotel Washington
$$$$ Downtown

Overlooking the White House and an easy stroll from the National Mall, the Hotel Washington boasts convenience and one of the city's best views. (I find myself saying that about a lot of D.C. hotels!) From the Sky Terrace open-air restaurant on the hotel's top floor (open May–Oct), you can look down on the president's mansion while eating a light meal or relaxing with a drink. The adjacent, indoor Sky Room is open year-round. Many guest rooms also feature views of the White House and/or the Washington Monument. (Ask about availability and price.) Once every four years, the inaugural parade marches by, as the president makes the quadrennial pilgrimage from the Capitol to 1600 Pennsylvania Ave. Antique reproductions throughout the hotel help to create an atmosphere of historical charm. Discounts to below $200 sometimes available off peak.

See map p. 100. 515 15th St. NW (at Pennsylvania Avenue). ☎ *800-424-9540 or 202-638-5900. Fax: 202-638-1594.* www.hotelwashington.com. *Metro: Metro Center. From the 12th and F streets exit, walk 3 blocks west on F to 15th. Parking: $28. Rack rates: $299–$399 double. Children younger than 12 stay free with parents in some rooms. AE, DC, MC, V.*

The Jefferson
$$$$$ Downtown

Debuted in 1923, the Jefferson is still considered one of the city's very best hotels because of its intimate atmosphere and personalized service. It's small, quiet, elegant, and expensive, with a top-notch staff that remembers return guests by name. Antiques, original art, and reproductions grace the 67 rooms and 33 suites, many with balconies, some with wood-burning fireplaces. Some rooms include canopied beds, and each room features two-line telephones, speaker-phone, voice mail, fax machine, and Internet access, along with video and CD player. Double-glazed windows mute the traffic noise from 16th and M streets. The hotel has 24-hour room service along with concierge and business services, a good restaurant, a comfortable lounge, and a fitness center. Guests have access to the indoor pool, exercise machines, steam room, and Jacuzzi at the University Club across the street. Discounts to below $200 sometimes available off peak.

As this book was being written, the Jefferson was making plans for renovations in 2007. Check with the hotel to find out if that might affect your plans for staying here.

See map p. 100. 1200 16th St. NW (at M Street). ☎ *866-270-8118 or 202-347-2200. Fax: 202-331-7982.* www.thejeffersonwashingtondc.com. *Metro: Farragut North. From L Street exit, walk 2 blocks east on L, turn left on 16th, and then walk 1 block to M. Parking: $28. Rack rate: $449 double. Children under 12 stay free in parents' room. AE, DC, DISC, MC, V.*

Jurys Normandy Inn
$$$ Dupont Circle

This relatively small, homey hotel is a bit out of the way, but not too far for the accommodations when you can get a discount. It's about 5 blocks north of the Dupont Circle Metrorail Station, in the neighborhood known as Kalorama, and about the same distance from the heart of Adams-Morgan, which are two of D.C.'s most popular entertainment districts, with plenty of restaurants and nightspots. The hotel is located in a neighborhood of imposing residences and diplomatic facilities. (Check out the French ambassador's digs at 2221 Kalorama Rd., for a truly jaw-dropping example.) If you stay here, you can call this intriguing neighborhood your own for a brief spell. Jurys Normandy also truly is a bargain. For relatively little money (for Washington), you get a comfortable room with free high-speed Internet access, two-line phone with dataport, minifridge, coffeemaker, and complimentary newspaper on weekdays. Tea and coffee are served for free in the lounge in the afternoons, and a complimentary wine-and-cheese reception occurs on Tuesday nights. Maybe you can strike up a conversation with a traveling diplomat. Specials drop as low as $89 during slow times.

See map p. 100. 2118 Wyoming Ave. NW (west of Connecticut Avenue). ☎ *800-424-3729 or 202-483-1350. Fax: 202-387-8241.* www.jurys-washingtondc-hotels.com. *Metro: Dupont Circle. From the Q Street exit, walk north 5 blocks on Connecticut Avenue and then turn left on Wyoming. Limited parking: $20. Rack rate: $235 double. Children younger than 12 stay free in parents' room. AE, DC, DISC, MC, V.*

Jurys Washington Hotel
$$$$ Dupont Circle

Unlike its sibling, Jurys Normandy, this hotel is not out of the way at all. It's right on the northeastern edge of the Dupont Circle action. With its more convenient location, Jurys Washington naturally is pricier than the Normandy. But it still often offers really good deals. The Jurys hotels are run by an Irish organization, Jurys Doyle Hotels of Dublin, and that's reflected in the Washington's bar — Biddy Mulligan's — which is styled as an Irish pub, with the bar itself imported from the Old Country. The rooms at Jurys Washington are large, pretty, and comfortable. They come with the usual amenities, including high-speed Internet access. The hotel offers room service, a business center, and an exercise room. Discounted rates sometimes drop below $100.

See map p. 100. 1500 New Hampshire Ave. NW (on northeast edge of Dupont Circle). ☎ *800-424-3729 or 202-483-6000. Fax: 202-328-3265.* www.jurys-washingtondc-hotels.com. *Metro: Dupont Circle. From the Dupont Circle exit, walk around the circle counter-clockwise to New Hampshire. Parking: $20. Rack rate: $325 double. Children younger than 16 stay free in parents' room. AE, DC, DISC, MC, V.*

Mandarin Oriental
$$$$$ Tidal Basin

If you've got the bucks to buy your way in, you'll love the luxury of this gorgeous, comfortable, and pampering hotel. Overlooking the Tidal Basin, just 2½ blocks south of the National Mall, the Mandarin is well located for daytime sightseeing, but not for walking alone at night. The views from the rooms and the public spaces are terrific, especially when the Tidal Basin's cherry blossoms bloom in spring. Depending on where you're located, you can look out to the Potomac River, Jefferson Memorial, Washington Monument, and other highlights of the D.C. skyline. Rooms come with more than the usual amenities, including large bathrooms, three phones, high-speed Internet access, 24-hour room service, and twice-daily house-keeping. Suites on the upper floors have high-definition televisions. Replicas of Asian art from the Smithsonian's Freer and Sackler galleries hang throughout the Mandarin, and the hotel has its own gallery with rotating exhibits. CityZen, one of Washington's very best restaurants, is on-site, as are Cafe MoZU, which serves good breakfast, lunch, tea, and dinner, and the Empress Lounge, where you can get drinks and light fare midmorning into the evening. Guests have access to a fitness center and lap pool, and the Mandarin houses a top-of-the-line spa. Washington-area residents can get a room for less than $200 at some off-peak times. The best deal I could find for the rest of you was a $295 Internet-only rate; click "Tempting Offers" on the hotel's home page.

See map p. 100. 1330 Maryland Ave. SW (west of 12th Street and south of D). ☎ *888-888-1778 or 202-554-8588. Fax: 202-554-8999.* www.mandarinoriental.com/washington. *Metro: Smithsonian. From the Independence Avenue Exit, walk south on 12th Street SW; just past D Street, turn right toward a cul-de-sac where the hotel is located. Take a cab if you're alone at night. Parking: $39. Rack rate: $495–$695 double. AE, DC, DISC, MC, V.*

Morrison-Clark Historic Inn and Restaurant
$$ Penn Quarter

History and attentive service are hallmarks of this charming hotel that waits for gentrification at the northeast edge of the Penn Quarter arts and entertainment district. The name comes from the families who lived in the two Victorian mansions that were combined to create the hotel. Built in 1864, the mansions now are listed in the National Register of Historic Places. The rooms are individually decorated, some with period antiques. Antiques also are on display throughout the public areas. Some rooms that face L Street have porches and are particularly attractive. If you value peace and quiet, ask for a room on the inner courtyard. If you're here between 5:30 and 7:30 p.m. on a Thursday from spring into fall, step outside for the "Big Easy on the Veranda" — free hors d'oeuvres and a cash bar. Try the house specialty, the vodka-and-Cointreau-based Steel Magnolia. Discounts to $109 are sometimes available.

See map p. 100. 1015 L St. NW (at 11th Street). ☎ *800-222-8474 or 202-898-1200. Fax: 202-289-8576.* www.morrisonclark.com. *Metro: Mount Vernon Square. Walk south on 8th Street 1 block, then right on L Street 3 blocks to 11th. Exercise care at night. Valet parking: $25. Rack rates: $199–$239 double. AE, DC, DISC, MC, V.*

One Washington Circle
$$$$$ Foggy Bottom/West End

All but 10 of this hotel's 151 units have kitchens, and most have balconies. Among the deluxe touches: coffee beans and a grinder to use with the coffeemaker. All the units also have a free high-speed Internet connection, two-line cordless telephones, a stereo with a CD player, and a video-game console. The most luxurious units — the "grande staterooms" — feature a separate bedroom with king-size bed, a dining area with table and six chairs, living area with sofa bed, and a bathroom and a half. Even the simplest "guest quarters" feel spacious, with sleeping and sitting areas in one large room that includes a double bed and fold-out sofa or two double beds. The strikingly modern décor is warmed with dark wood and fabrics in beige, gold, and blue. You can take advantage of an on-site fitness center, outdoor pool, concierge services, and a good restaurant, the **Circle Bistro.** Georgetown is an easy stroll away, and the Foggy Bottom–George

Washington University Metrorail station is just around the circle. Deep discounts below $100 per suite are sometimes available.

See map p. 100. 1 Washington Circle NW (Pennsylvania Avenue at New Hampshire Avenue). ☎ *800-424-9671 or 202-872-1680. Fax: 202-887-4989.* www.thecircle hotel.com. *Metro: Foggy Bottom–George Washington University. Walk north on 23rd Street 1 block to Washington Circle and then counterclockwise around the circle to New Hampshire Avenue at the northeast edge of the circle. Valet parking: $22. Rack rates: $449 double, $499–$529 suites. Children younger than 13 stay free in parents' room. AE, DC, DISC, MC, V.*

Red Roof Inn
$$ Chinatown

This hotel is not like the Red Roof Inns you breeze by on the Interstate. Hardly. Close to the Convention Center, Verizon Center (sports and big-name entertainers), galleries, theaters, restaurants, nightspots, and Chinatown, this inn contains 197 rooms on 10 floors. It's a value find for business travelers and families. A king room includes a large desk in work area with dataport and speaker phone. Families can get rooms with two double beds. All rooms feature coffeemakers and large bathrooms. The hotel also has an exercise room and an on-site restaurant. Local phone calls are free. Rates below $120 are sometimes available.

See map p. 100. 500 H St. NW (at 5th Street). ☎ *800-733-7663 or 202-289-5959. Fax: 202-289-0754.* www.redroof.com. *Metro: Gallery Place-Chinatown. From 7th and H streets exit, walk 2 blocks east to 5th. Parking: $20. Rack rates: $200–$225 double. Children 17 and younger stay free in parents' room. AE, DC, DISC, MC, V.*

Renaissance Mayflower
$$$$$ Downtown

This hotel has been hosting big events since it opened in 1925; Cal Coolidge's inauguration was celebrated here. The Mayflower is big, luxurious, and the setting for many meetings, conventions, and other public events. You can bump into any big shot here. The guest rooms, as well as the public areas, feature marble and mahogany. They also have your basic modern traveler's necessities — two-line phones, speaker phones, voice mail, and dataports. Parents can obtain cribs and child care. The hotel has a restaurant, coffee shop, lounge, 24-hour room service, concierge services, and exercise equipment. The location is ideal — midway between Dupont Circle and the White House, on top of the Farragut North Metrorail station. Discounted rates sometimes drop as low as $139.

See map p. 100. 1127 Connecticut Ave. NW (between L and M streets). ☎ *800-228-7697 or 202-347-3000. Fax: 202-776-9182.* www.marriott.com. *Metro: Farragut North. From the L Street exit, look for the hotel. Valet parking: $30. Rack rates: $449–$509 double. AE, DC, DISC, MC, V.*

Ritz-Carlton Washington
$$$$$ Foggy Bottom/West End

This may be Washington's most luxurious hotel — in terms of both facilities and services. You can choose, for example, a 2,250-square-foot suite: living room with fireplace, bedroom, dining room with seating for ten, Jacuzzi, and private terrace. Or you can stay on the private Club Level, where you get a key for the elevator, the lounge offers food and beverage service all day, and a concierge is at your beck and call. If you like package deals, the Ritz offered a special for the 2005 presidential inauguration that included private jet transportation, a personal butler, inaugural ball tickets — and other stuff — for $150,000. The standard rooms feature marble in the bathrooms, goose down or nonallergenic pillows to suit your need, dataports, portable phones, and high-speed Internet access. And then you have the "fitness center," the adjacent Sports Club/LA — 100,000 square feet of just about any exercise and sports facility you can dream of for $12 a day. But it's the service that really marks the Ritz. Beyond daily attentiveness, managers here think creatively about what additional services you might want. For example, noting increased air-travel hassles, the hotel introduced "luggage-less" travel for frequent guests. Leave your clothes in your room, and the hotel will launder, dry clean, press, store them, and then place them in your room when you return. And, on your way out of D.C., grab some of the hotel's "flight bites" to eat on the airplane.

See map p. 100. 1150 22nd St. NW (at M Street). ☎ **800-241-3333** *or 202-835-0500. Fax 202-835-1588.* www.ritzcarlton.com/hotels/washington_dc. *Metro: Foggy Bottom–George Washington University. Walk 1 block east on I Street, turn left on 22nd, and then walk 4 blocks to M Street. Parking: Self $17; valet $35. Rack rates: $599–$649 double. AE, DC, DISC, MC, V.*

The River Inn
$$$ Foggy Bottom/West End

The facilities and services at this all-suites hotel focus on the needs of business travelers. But the kitchens in all units and separate bedrooms in some — coupled with discounts that can drop below $100 — make the River Inn a good option for families as well. Business travelers especially appreciate the large desk and good lighting, the lack of which drives me crazy in many hotels. Every unit also comes with free high-speed Internet access, sofa bed, dressing alcove with vanity, and grinder with beans to use with the coffeemaker. The studios feel spacious. The one-bedroom suites are truly large, with two or three couches and king-size beds. The hotel also has an exercise facility.

See map p. 100. 924 25th St. NW (between I and K streets). ☎ **800-424-2741** *or 202-337-7600. Fax: 202-337-6520.* www.theriverinn.com. *Metro: Foggy Bottom–George Washington University. Walk 2 blocks west on I and then turn right on 25th. Parking: $22. Rack rates: $245 double. AE, DC, MC, V.*

Sofitel Lafayette Square
$$$$$ Downtown

The French-owned Sofitel promises *art de vivre* — the art of French living — and delivers with the excellent **Cafe 15** French restaurant, a bar called **Le Bar,** plus interior décor and staff uniforms created by French designers. Rooms in this 1928 office building — renovated and opened as a hotel in 2002 — are bright, airy, and cheerful. Velvet curtains, thick carpeting, rich-colored upholstery, and black lacquered desks with chrome legs provide the feel of luxury. The overall effect is a melding of early-20th-century Art Deco with 21st-century style and amenities. The bathrooms have separate tubs and showers. You can order room service around the clock and work out in the on-site fitness center. Discounts to below $130 are sometimes available.

See map p. 100. 806 15th St. NW (at H Street). ☎ *800-763-4835 or 202-730-8800. Fax: 202-730-8500.* www.sofitel.com. *Metro: McPherson Square. From Vermont Avenue/White House exit, walk 1 block east on I Street and then turn right on 15th. Valet parking: $34. Rack rates: $559–$609 double. One child younger than 12 can stay free in parent's room. AE, MC, V.*

State Plaza
$$ Foggy Bottom/West End

The spacious accommodations at the all-suites State Plaza provide a home away from home for diplomats, business travelers, performing artists, and educators headed to the nearby World Bank, State Department, Kennedy Center, and George Washington University. The State Plaza is a find for families, too. Kids 18 and younger stay free in their parents' room, and you can save money by cooking meals in the suites' kitchens. On a quiet Foggy Bottom block, the State Plaza feels like a private residence in a condo or apartment building. Spacious is the operative word. The largest suites (the Grand Plaza) have a master bedroom, living room with queen sofa bed and easy chair, a stylish and well-equipped kitchen, and a separate dining area. The **Garden Café** serves breakfast, lunch, and dinner, with outdoor dining in season. Discounts as low as $109 are sometimes available.

See map p. 100. 2117 E St. NW (between 21st and 22nd streets). ☎ *800-424-2859 or 202-861-8200.* www.stateplaza.com. *Metro: Foggy Bottom–George Washington University. Walk 2 blocks east on I Street, turn right on 21st Street, walk 4 blocks south, and then turn right on E Street. Parking: $30. Rack rate: $189–$239 suite. AE, DC, DISC, MC, V.*

Tabard Inn
$$ Dupont Circle

The Tabard is an eclectic and eccentric — and, yes, charming — place. If you've traveled in Europe under Frommer's tutelage, the Tabard will remind you of all those inexpensive but marvelous hostelries that have been cobbled together from adjacent buildings that measure their age in centuries. The Tabard isn't that old, but it was created from three adjacent

Victorian town houses on a tree-lined street in the Dupont Circle neighborhood. Each of the 40 rooms is different, and they're furnished with a combination of antiques and — uh, well — pre-owned items. They're priced according to their size, view, location within the hotel, and whether they have private bathrooms (five don't). All rooms come with free continental breakfast and free admission to the Tabard's fabulously equipped health club — the Capital YMCA around the corner. The Tabard's restaurant is wonderful, both for the setting and the New American cuisine. You can dine in the garden in warm weather or sip a drink beside a fireplace when it's cold. The lounge is the proverbial comfortable old shoe, a well-worn place for luxuriating by the fire, not for luxury. Be warned that the Tabard has no elevator.

See map p. 100. 1739 N St. NW (between 17th and 18th streets). ☎ *202-785-1277. Fax: 202-785-6173.* www.tabardinn.com. *Metro: Dupont Circle. From the Dupont Circle exit, walk south on Connecticut Avenue 1 block, and then turn left on N and cross 18th. Parking in nearby public garages. Rack rates: $103–$208. Additional person: $15. AE, DC, DISC, MC, V.*

Willard InterContinental
$$$$$ Downtown

The Willard is another Washington hotel steeped in history. A stone's throw from the White House and the D.C. government's headquarters, it's been a prime spot for the powerful and the power-seekers to hang their hats since even before Henry Willard bought the old hotel that occupied the site in 1850. Abraham Lincoln stayed for a while in Henry's hostelry. And Calvin Coolidge lived in the current building until Mrs. Harding vacated the White House following her husband's death in 1923. Heads of foreign states stay here now. The current Willard — built in 1901, closed in 1968, opened after a thorough restoration in 1986, and given a major face-lift in 2000 — is a large, ornate, and luxurious domicile. Take a walk through Peacock Alley, the first-floor hallway, even if you don't stay here, and take a peek into the opulent **Willard Room** restaurant. If you do stay here, you'll have a room furnished in antique reproductions and equipped with the latest electronics. The Jenny Lind Suite has a canopy bed and a Jacuzzi that sits beneath a large, circular window that centers on the Washington Monument. The 3,000-square-foot Thomas Jefferson Suite sports an oval dining room that seats ten and looks down Pennsylvania Avenue to the Capitol, a master bedroom with sitting area, a living room, and two bathrooms, one with a Jacuzzi. You can have it for $4,200 a night. Occasionally special deals for standard rooms are available for less than $300.

See map p. 100. 1401 Pennsylvania Ave. NW (at 14th Street). ☎ *888-424-6835 or 202-628-9100. Fax: 202-637-7326.* www.washington.interconti.com. *Metro: Metro Center. From the F Street exit, walk 2 blocks west on F to the hotel's rear entrance between 14th and 15th streets. Parking: $28. Rack rates: $610–$660 double. AE, DC, DISC, MC, V.*

The B&B Alternative

Many people associate bed-and-breakfast facilities with the New England countryside or some quaint small town. In fact, Washington houses quite a few B&Bs in a broad range of prices and styles of living. You can spend what you would at a luxury hotel and be treated like royalty. You can find terrific bargains at small guesthouses. What you're sure to encounter at the B&Bs introduced to you here are clean rooms, comfortable surroundings, and a personal hospitality you would be hard-pressed to find at any hotel.

D.C. Guest House
$$$ **Downtown**

This 19th-century mansion is a wonderful find a bit off the beaten tourist track but just 1 block from the D.C. convention center. It's just what you're looking for in a B&B — a building with character, decorated according to the personalities of the owners who provide attentive service because they really want their guests to enjoy their stay. The four owners have appointed the house with modern furnishings, original art, and African artifacts. The eclectic ambience ranges from country manor to urban chic. Guest rooms are large, warm, and comfortable. Two rooms have working fireplaces, and most have private bathrooms. All rooms have wireless Internet access, satellite TV, DVD player, and access to DVDs. You're served a gourmet breakfast in an elegant dining room. Almost unheard of in Washington, you can park your car for free about a block away. As one of the owners pointed out to me, that puts your car closer to your room here than it would be in the parking garage of many large hotels. The owners, by the way, really know how to shop in Washington. So, if shopping's your thing, ask them for suggestions.

See map p. 100. 1337 10th St. NW (between N and O streets). ☎ ***202-332-2502.*** *Fax: 202-332-6013.* www.dcguesthouse.com. *Metro: Mt. Vernon Square. Walk 2 blocks west on M Street to 10th, then right on 10th across N Street. Take a cab at night. Free parking. Rack rates: $175–$300 double. Rates include breakfast. AE, MC, V.*

Kalorama Guest House at Woodley Park
$ **Upper Northwest**

Excellent location and excellent price mark this homey B&B on a relatively quiet residential street just off busy Connecticut Avenue. Rooms in these two early-20th-century houses are clean, comfortable, and, well, roomy. You're 3 blocks from the elevator and 4 blocks from the escalator at the Woodley Park-Zoo Metrorail station, where you can catch the Blue Line to Washington's top sights. When you get back, you can unwind with cookies and lemonade in the afternoon or sip some sherry in the evening. A single room costs as little as $55, and a double is $60. The highest price is $135 for a two-room suite, with private bathroom, that sleeps up to six. No TV or phone in rooms. Some rooms share bathrooms.

See map p. 100. 2700 Cathedral Ave. NW (at 27th Street). ☎ ***202-328-0860.** Fax 202-328-8730.* www.kaloramaguesthouse.com. *Metro: Woodley Park-Zoo. From escalator exit, walk 3 blocks north on Connecticut Avenue, then left 1 block on Cathedral; elevator exit is 1 block closer on Connecticut. Parking: Space-available $14; must reserve when booking room. Rack rates: $60–$135 double. Rates include breakfast. AE, DC, DISC, MC, V.*

Swann House
$$$ Dupont Circle

Stay here and you can pretend you're visiting rich relatives at the turn of the last century. The mansion was built in 1883 and has been restored and furnished to the opulence it probably displayed in the early 20th century. You have the run not only of your room, but of the entire first floor and the second-floor balcony. Both are splendid for sitting and reading, chatting, or just soaking up the ambience. This preservation of the past is not done at the expense of modern amenities. In addition to fireplaces in some rooms and suites, a couple also sport Jacuzzis. One mind-bending bathroom has a high domed ceiling over an enormous bathtub and a giant rain shower. All rooms have private bathrooms, robes, satin sheets, down pillows, feather beds, TVs, phones, and free Internet access. (If you're allergic to feathers, the innkeepers will give you synthetic bedding.) If you want a VCR or DVD player, ask. There's also an in-ground pool — something you don't find very often in this densely developed neighborhood.

See map p. 100. 1808 New Hampshire Ave. NW (between S and Swann streets). ☎ ***202-265-4414.** Fax 202-265-6755.* www.swannhouse.com. *Metro: Dupont Circle. From Q Street Exit, walk 2 blocks east on Q to New Hampshire, then 5 blocks northwest across S Street. Rack rates: $150–$365 double. Rates include breakfast. AE, DISC, MC, V.*

Woodley Park Guest House
$$ Upper Northwest

The small rooms here sleep just one or two, but they're attractive, comfortable, and modern, having been renovated in 2001. The huge Wardman Park Marriott Hotel sits atop the hill across the street and enjoys a bit of two-way traffic with this guesthouse. Some folks who attend conventions at the big hotel bed down at the Woodley Park to escape the crowds. Guests of the Woodley Park climb to the Wardman to hop on tour buses. Unique touch: This B&B's walls are hung with art available for purchase. If you're an artist, you just might find a market for your work. Each room has a phone, but there is no TV in the building. Some rooms share bathrooms.

See map p. 100. 2647 Woodley Rd. NW (just west of Connecticut Avenue). ☎ ***866-667-0218** or 202-667-0218. Fax: 202-667-1080.* www.woodleyparkguesthouse.com. *Metro: Woodley Park-Zoo. From escalator exit, walk 1 block north on Connecticut Avenue, then left on Woodley; from elevator exit, just walk 500 feet up Woodley. Rack rates: $115–$160 double. Rates include breakfast. AE, MC, V.*

Washington's runner-up hotels

Space limitations prevent me from publishing an encyclopedia of Washington's hotels. If you're stuck and can't find a room, check the Quick Concierge at the back of this book for hotel chains' toll-free reservation numbers or contact the following hotels, all tried and true (until readers of this book tell me otherwise). All offer lower weekend and off-peak rates. How low? Sometimes you can find a room for less than $100 a night, depending on availability.

Georgetown Inn

$$$$ **Georgetown** This well-soundproofed hotel in the heart of Georgetown offers one-bedroom suites and adjoining rooms that can be converted to suites. *See map p. 100. 1310 Wisconsin Ave. NW (between N and O streets).* ☎ *800-368-5922 or 202-333-8900. Fax: 202-333-8308.* www.georgetown collection.com.

Hotel George

$$$$$ **Capitol Hill** Modernistic posters of the first president adorn the hotel, which attracts lobbyists, celebrities, and others who dig hip surroundings and proximity to power. *See map p. 100. 15 E St. NW (at North Capitol Street).* ☎ *800-576-8331 or 202-347-4200. Fax: 202-347-0359.* www.hotel george.com.

Hotel Rouge

$$$$ **Dupont Circle** This super-hip boutique hotel decorated in — take a wild guess — red, serves free Bloody Marys on weekend mornings, and offers a complimentary red wine and beer hour on weekdays. *See map p. 100. 1315 16th St. NW (north of N Street).* ☎ *800-738-1202 or 202-232-8000. Fax: 202-667-9827.* www.rougehotel.com.

J.W. Marriott

$$$$$ **Downtown** This convention hotel is huge, which means many rooms are available and good deals abound when conventions aren't in session. *See map p. 100. 1331 Pennsylvania Ave. NW (at 14th and E streets).* ☎ *888-236-2427 or 202-393-2000. Fax: 202-626-6991.* www.marriott.com.

Latham Hotel

$$$ **Georgetown** Between M Street and the C&O Canal, the Latham offers a variety of units, including two-story carriage suites. *See map p. 100. 3000 M St. NW (at 30th Street).* ☎ *888-876-0001 or 202-726-5000. Fax: 202-337-4250.* www.thelatham.com.

Omni Shoreham

$$$$$ **Upper Northwest** Another enormous — and opulent and historic — hotel that hosts conventions and large meetings. Therefore, you'll find comprehensive services and facilities, along with good deals when the conventioneers and meeters aren't around. *See map p. 100. 2500 Calvert St. NW (west of Connecticut Avenue).* ☎ *888-444-6664 or 202-234-0700. Fax: 202-265-7972.* www.omnihotels.com.

Washington Plaza
$$$ **Downtown** This 1960s hotel boasts redecorated and refurnished rooms, plus a large outdoor pool. *See map p. 100. 10 Thomas Circle NW (at M and 14th streets).* ☎ *800-424-1140 or 202-842-1300. Fax: 202-371-9602.* www. washingtonplazahotel.com.

Washington Suites Georgetown
$$$ **Foggy Bottom/West End** This all-suites hotel offers bargains to families when special discounts bring rates as low as $149 a night. *See map p. 100. 2500 Pennsylvania Ave. NW (at 25th Street).* ☎ *877-736-2500 or 202-333-8060. Fax: 202-338-3818.* www.washingtonsuitesgeorgetown.com.

Index of accommodations by price

$

Hostelling International (Downtown)
Hotel Harrington (Downtown)
Kalorama Guest House at Woodley Park (Upper Northwest)

$$

Georgetown Suites (Georgetown)
Morrison-Clark Historic Inn and Restaurant (Penn Quarter)
Red Roof Inn (Chinatown)
State Plaza (Foggy Bottom/West End)
Tabard Inn (Dupont Circle)
Woodley Park Guest House (Upper Northwest)

$$$

Capitol Hill Suites (Capitol Hill)
D.C. Guest House (Downtown)
Four Points by Sheraton (Downtown)
George Washington University Inn (Foggy Bottom/West End)
Henley Park Hotel (Penn Quarter)
Hotel Lombardy (Foggy Bottom/West End)
Jurys Normandy Inn (Dupont Circle)
Latham Hotel (Georgetown)
The River Inn (Foggy Bottom/West End)
Swann House (Dupont Circle)

Washington Plaza (Downtown)
Washington Suites Georgetown (Foggy Bottom/West End)

$$$$

Georgetown Inn (Georgetown)
Holiday Inn on the Hill (Capitol Hill)
Hotel Madera (Dupont Circle)
Hotel Monaco (Penn Quarter)
Hotel Rouge (Dupont Circle)
Hotel Washington (Downtown)
Jurys Washington Hotel (Dupont Circle)

$$$$$

Four Seasons (Georgetown)
Hay-Adams (Downtown)
Hotel George (Capitol Hill)
The Jefferson (Downtown)
J.W. Marriott (Downtown)
Mandarin Oriental (Tidal Basin)
Omni Shoreham (Upper Northwest)
One Washington Circle (Foggy Bottom/West End)
Renaissance Mayflower (Downtown)
Ritz-Carlton Washington (Foggy Bottom/West End)
Sofitel Lafayette Square (Downtown)
Willard InterContinental (Downtown)

Index of accommodations by location

Capitol Hill

Capitol Hill Suites ($$$)
Holiday Inn on the Hill ($$$$)
Hotel George ($$$$$)

Chinatown

Red Roof Inn ($$)

Downtown

D.C. Guest House ($$$)
Four Points by Sheraton ($$$)
Hay-Adams ($$$$$)
Hostelling International ($)
Hotel Harrington ($)
Hotel Washington ($$$$)
The Jefferson ($$$$$)
J.W. Marriott ($$$$$)
Renaissance Mayflower ($$$$$)
Sofitel Lafayette Square ($$$$$)
Washington Plaza ($$$)
Willard InterContinental ($$$$$)

Dupont Circle

Hotel Madera ($$$$)
Hotel Rouge ($$$$)
Jurys Normandy Inn ($$$)
Jurys Washington Hotel ($$$$)
Swann House ($$$)
Tabard Inn ($$)

Foggy Bottom/West End

George Washington University
Inn ($$$)
Hotel Lombardy ($$$)
One Washington Circle ($$$$$)
Ritz-Carlton Washington ($$$$$)
The River Inn ($$$)
State Plaza ($$)
Washington Suites Georgetown ($$$)

Georgetown

Four Seasons ($$$$$)
Georgetown Inn ($$$$)
Georgetown Suites ($$)
Latham Hotel ($$$)

Penn Quarter

Henley Park Hotel ($$$)
Hotel Monaco ($$$$)
Morrison-Clark Historic Inn and
Restaurant ($$)

Tidal Basin

Mandarin Oriental ($$$$$)

Upper Northwest

Kalorama Guest House at Woodley
Park ($)
Omni Shoreham ($$$$$)
Woodley Park Guest House ($$)

Chapter 10

Dining and Snacking in Washington, D.C.

In This Chapter

▶ Understanding Washington's eating habits

▶ Reviewing the best restaurants in all price ranges

▶ Finding snacks and meals to go

There's a joke around Washington that you can identify the world's trouble spots by checking out the new restaurants in town. People flee trouble overseas, whether it's famine, war, or oppression. Washington — the capital of the free world — is a beacon. Many refugees have started on the road to the American Dream by opening a restaurant. As a result, Vietnamese, Ethiopian, Afghan, and other exotic cuisines took root in the nation's capital when times were particularly bad in the lands that spawned them. Washington's international influences and community provide a hungry and knowledgeable audience for the Chinese, French, German, Indian, Italian, Japanese, Spanish, Thai, Latin American, and Middle Eastern restaurants you can find here. And, with Congress representing every corner of America, a variety of regional cuisines from throughout the United States are represented as well.

Getting the Dish on the Local Scene

This section brings you up to speed on a few trends and technicalities before you get down to the business of eating. You can find more news about D.C. dining in the *Washington Post* (www.washingtonpost.com), and *Washingtonian* magazine (www.washingtonian.com). Click "City Guide" on the *Post*'s home page, and "Restaurants" on *Washingtonian*'s.

The current trends

A key sign that Washington's dining scene really is on a long-term up-tick is the creativity and diversity of its food and chefs.

✔ The number one trend right now is **sheer quality.** This is a big deal, because it wasn't so long ago that the nation's capital was considered the nation's backwater when it came to food. Now, however, a few really, really good restaurants open each year, adding to D.C.'s expanding roster of top-notch dining spots. Among the most recent additions: the New American **CityZen,** whose chef, Eric Ziebold, previously cooked at California's famed French Laundry, and the Modern Indian **Rasika,** where chef Vikram Sunderam works the magic he nurtured first in India and England. They join such established world-class venues as the Italian **Galileo, Kinkead's** seafood restaurant, the French/Belgian **Marcel's,** the French/Californian **Michel Richard Citronelle,** and the French **Le Paradou.**

✔ The biggest things in Washington dining right now continue to be **little things,** and that's a trend that's accelerating. We've discovered the pleasure of strolling into a good restaurant with a group of friends, ordering nice wine, and spending several hours sharing nibbles of small dishes. Mediterranean *meze* is on the menu at **Zaytinya,** a strikingly stylish new restaurant in the Penn Quarter arts-theater-entertainment district. **Jaleo,** in the same neighborhood and in two suburbs, offers an enormous choice of Spanish *tapas.* At **Mini Bar,** a special section within **Café Atlántico** (also in the neighborhood), Chef José Andrés whips up tiny creations that spring from his mind rather than one particular cuisine — potato mousse with caviar and vanilla oil, for example, or foie gras surrounded by cotton candy! Head up to Dupont Circle and dip little pieces of meats, fruits, vegetables, and breads into hot pots of cheeses, broths, and melted chocolate at the **Melting Pot,** a fondue emporium. In Upper Northwest, **2 Amys** offers Italian tidbits along with its superb Neapolitan pizzas. The best way to sample the superb cuisine at the aforementioned **Rasika** is to pick among Sunderam's many small-plate offerings.

✔ The other great trend, which also continues to accelerate, is the proliferation of not-your-father's **hotel restaurants.** A growing number of Washington hostelries are turning their dining space over to great chefs. **CityZen** is in the Mandarin Oriental Hotel, for instance, and **Michel Richard Citronelle** in the **Latham.** Other very good hotel restaurants include **Poste** in the **Hotel Monaco, Circle Bistro** in **One Washington Circle Hotel, Bistro Bis** in the **Hotel George,** and the **Tabard Inn** in, well, the **Tabard Inn.**

The lunch scene

Washingtonians do lunch in just about every way imaginable. The infamous three-martini lunch has pretty much faded into the past. But business lunches remain a big deal — a way for lobbyists, lawmakers, administrators, political operatives, and journalists to share info in a relaxed setting without cutting into their crowded business days. Most Washingtonians on most days, however, gobble quick soups and sandwiches in lunch rooms, grab sandwiches and soft drinks and head for a

Dining in Washington, D.C.

Austin Grill
  Penn Quarter **24**
Austin Grill Upper
  Northwest **3**
B. Smith's **30**
Bistro Bis **29**
Bullfeathers **33**
Busboys and Poets **4**
Café Atlántico **26**
Capital Q **19**
Circle Bistro **6**
CityZen **34**
Clyde's Upper Northwest **1**
Clyde's Penn Quarter **22**
Eat First **17**
Galileo **7**
Georgia Brown's **12**
Jaleo **25**
Kinkead's **8**
Le Paradou **27**
Marcel's **5**
Marrakesh **16**
Matchbox **20**
The Monocle **31**
Montmartre **32**
Nooshi **10**
The Occidental **14**
The Oceanaire Seafood
  Room **15**
Old Ebbitt Grill **13**
Poste **23**
The Prime Rib **9**
Rasika **28**
Tony Cheng's **18**
2 Amys **2**
Vidalia **11**
Zaytinya **21**

park bench, or take their eats back to the office and get back to work with their food at their elbows.

What this routine means to you is that you can find lots of spots for grabbing decent quick lunches. And, because many of the top restaurants are open for lunch, you can sample some of the city's best dining in smaller portions for smaller prices at midday.

Eating like a local

Both high-class and inexpensive eateries are scattered throughout the city. Here's what makes some neighborhoods distinctive, food-wise.

- ✔ **Capitol Hill:** Despite their low standing with the general public, members of Congress and their aides are in general a hard-working bunch, so you can find lots of spots for quick lunches on Capitol Hill. Restaurants, cafeterias, and carry-outs are scattered throughout the Capitol and the congressional office buildings. The food court on the bottom floor of Union Station is one of the largest and most diverse you'll find anywhere.

- ✔ **Downtown:** This area is Washington's business center, so you can find many fine-dining establishments, plus delis and sandwich shops, on most corners. Buy a sandwich, chips, and soft drink and find a nearby park for people-watching.

- ✔ **Georgetown, Dupont Circle, Adams-Morgan, Penn Quarter:** These areas are D.C.'s party spots, so lots of vibrant restaurants and saloons line the streets. You can eat, drink, dance, and check out the street scenes. What's left of Chinatown — a fair number of Chinese restaurants and the Chinatown Gate — occupies a northern section of Penn Quarter.

- ✔ **The National Mall:** The Mall is lined with museums and galleries, and the bigger ones will feed your stomach as well as your eyes. You also can find a lot of street vendors nearby, hawking hot dogs, sausages, chips, candy, and soft drinks.

Making reservations

While you can find lots of spots for lunch without much of a fuss or wait, accomplishing this feat is a bit trickier later in the day. Regarding restaurant dinner reservations: If you can make them, do!

If you know your plans, make your reservations several days in advance — even before you leave home. Reserve for lunch, too, if you can. Otherwise, you can decrease the size of the lunch lines you wait in by arriving before 11:45 a.m. or after 1:30 p.m.

If you're a Web head, you can make reservations at many D.C. restaurants by surfing over to OpenTable at `www.opentable.com` and clicking on the "Washington" link. OpenTable also provides descriptions of the restaurants, reviews, maps, and links to the restaurants' Web sites.

Dining in Adams-Morgan and Dupont Circle

Bistrot du Coin **3**
The Brickskeller **6**
City Lights of China **2**
The Grill From Ipanema **1**
Hank's Oyster Bar **15**

Luna Grill & Diner **13**
Malaysia Kopitiam **11**
The Melting Pot **10**
Mimi's American Bistro **7**
Obelisk **8**

The Palm **12**
Pizzeria Paradiso **9**
Restaurant Nora **4**
Sette Osteria **5**
Tabard Inn **14**

Dressing to dine

Washington is a working town, so it's filled with suits, wingtips, and sensible pumps. You'll encounter them in restaurants at breakfast, lunch, and dinner, as well as in government, media, and business offices. But Washington has a pretty forgiving dress code. Few restaurants block your entrance if you're dressed more casually. (I note those that do in the reviews that follow.) I doubt you'll get thrown out of many places for wearing jeans, although you may feel out of place at the nicer restaurants. If you love to dress up, go for it. Washingtonians don't look down on you for that, either. Though I wouldn't recommend it, you can wear a tux most places without raising eyebrows. Enough black-tie affairs occur in this town that people are used to seeing the penguin look on Metrorail or hustling down the street.

Smoking in restaurants

By law, Washington's restaurants and bars now are smoke-free, except for cigar and hookah bars and outdoor areas such as sidewalk cafes. The ban also covers offices and apartment building lobbies. The law lets you smoke in your hotel room. Establishments, of course, are free to impose stricter limitations of their own, and smoke-free hotel rooms have become pretty ubiquitous.

Trimming the Fat from Your Budget

 Spending oodles on noodles (and steak and swordfish) is easy in D.C., but it's not required. Here are some suggestions for keeping your food bill under control:

- ✔ **When you want to sample an expensive restaurant, do so at lunchtime.** You can still get the acclaimed food, but you don't pay so much.

- ✔ **Buy carryout and picnic on a park bench or on the National Mall.** You can find many lovely, shaded spots among the memorials.

- ✔ **Take advantage of fixed-price, early bird, pre-theater, and post-theater menus.** Check your watch as well as the hours restaurants offer specials. If you arrive five minutes late, you'll pay full price. You snooze, you lose.

- ✔ **Split appetizers and desserts — and even main courses — with your dining companions.** Many restaurants serve sinfully large portions. If you have access to a refrigerator and microwave, ask for doggie bags. You can heat up the leftovers for an in-room meal — like room service without the service (or the service fee).

- ✔ **Ask the prices of the dishes that are described by the waiter rather than listed on the menu.** They can shock you.

Dining in Georgetown

Amma Indian
 Vegetarian Kitchen **3**
Bistrot Lepic & Wine Bar **1**
Café La Ruche **9**
Clyde's **6**
Garrett's **11**
Harmony Cafe **4**
Martin's Tavern **7**
Michel Richard's
 Citronelle **10**
Pizzeria Paradiso **5**
Sea Catch **8**
1789 Restaurant **2**
The Tombs **2**

Washington's Best Restaurants

Now it's finally time to feed your faces, folks! While you loosen your belt buckle, I'll help you figure out where you'd like to eat.

I've compiled reviews of the best restaurants in all price ranges, arranged alphabetically for easy reference. The price range, location, and the type of cuisine follow each restaurant's name. After the reviews, you can find all the restaurants indexed by **location,** so you can find a place near the attractions you visit, by **price,** so that you can budget accordingly, and by **cuisine,** so that you can satisfy your individual tastes. The restaurants also are marked on handy maps.

Restaurants designated as kid-friendly in this chapter have a kids' menu and/or cuisine that appeals to a younger palate.

Each review contains two price indicators. There's a dollar symbol, for a quick look at the average price of a dinner without beverages. I also list the range of prices for main courses on the restaurant's menu. I added up the costs of the least expensive and most expensive appetizer or salad, main course, and dessert at dinner, not including taxes and tips, and then averaged the highest- and lowest-priced meals to come up with the dollar-sign ranking.

Prices change over time, and the cost of your meal obviously depends on what you order. One reason I don't include beverage costs in my price categories is that ordering top-shelf cocktails and expensive wines can produce a $$$$$ bill at a $$$ restaurant. Sticking to a lower-priced entree and drinking coffee (or water) can squeeze a $$$$ restaurant into a $$$ bill (not that I recommend water over wine at gourmet restaurants).

Here's what you can expect meals to cost. Prices in Table 10-1 are per person, not including drinks.

Table 10-1	Key to Restaurant Dollar Signs
Dollar Sign(s)	*Price Range*
$	Less than $20
$$	$20–$29
$$$	$30–$39
$$$$	$40–$50
$$$$$	More than $50

Amma Indian Vegetarian Kitchen
$ **Georgetown INDIAN/VEGETARIAN**

Amma is a wonderful example of the amusing diversity of Georgetown. This quiet, unassuming restaurant — with quiet, unassuming staff — sits right next to the Jinx Proof Tattoos & Piercing Parlor on bustling M Street. Amma offers you numerous ways to sample Indian vegetarian cooking at bargain prices. If you're new to Indian cuisine, try one of the house specials, which let you sample several dishes.

See map p. 131. 3291 M St. NW (near 33rd Street). ☎ *202-625-6652. Reservations accepted. Take Georgetown Connection shuttle bus Route 2 from Dupont Circle or Rosslyn Metrorail Station. Full meals for $11 or less. AE, MC, V. Open: Mon–Thurs 11:30 a.m.–2:30 p.m., 5:30–10 p.m.; Fri 11:30 a.m.–2:30 p.m., 5:30–10:30 p.m.; Sat 11:30 a.m.–10:30 p.m.; and Sun 11:30 a.m.–4 p.m.*

Austin Grill
$$ **Penn Quarter and Upper Northwest SOUTHWESTERN**

Our family hits the Austin Grill often. You get good Tex-Mex food in a festive atmosphere served by friendly staff. The grill gives you lots of choices. You can make a meal from several appetizers. Vegetarians may like the portobello mushroom and spinach quesadilla, although I think it would benefit from some extra spices. I like the Austin Special — one chicken and one cheese enchilada covered with three sauces. The kids' menu has Tex-Mex dishes, along with burgers, a PB&J sandwich, carrot and celery sticks, and free ice cream for dessert. The original, which is a bit funky, is on Wisconsin Avenue above Georgetown. Tourists are more likely to encounter the new and spacious grill in the Penn Quarter arts-and-entertainment area near MCI Center.

See map p. 126. 750 E St. NW (between 7th and 8th streets). ☎ *202-393-3776.* www. austingrill.com. *Reservations not accepted. Metro: Gallery Place. From the 7th and F streets exit, walk 1 block south on 7th and then turn right on E. Main courses: $8–$18. AE, DC, DISC, MC, V. Open: Sun 11 a.m.–9:30 p.m., Mon–Thurs 11 a.m.–10 p.m., Fri–Sat 11 a.m.–11 p.m.*

See map p. 126. 2404 Wisconsin Ave. NW (near 37th and Calvert streets). ☎ *202-337-8080. On the 30-series Metrobus lines. Sun 11 a.m.–10:30 p.m., Mon 11:30 a.m.–10:30 p.m., Tues–Thurs 11:30 a.m.–11 p.m., Fri 11:30 a.m.–midnight, and Sat 11 a.m.–midnight.*

Bistro Bis
$$$$ **Capitol Hill FRENCH**

The food at Bistro Bis is an excellent modern American interpretation of classic French bistro and brasserie cooking. The setting represents a modern American nod toward classic bistro style. From the zinc bar with two-story mirror to the spacious leather booths, Bis is eye-catching, comfortable, bustling, and noisy. The menu changes frequently, so I can't tell you for sure what you'll find. When Susan and I last dined here, we especially liked our main courses — roasted chicken with a sauce that included bits of bacon and spinach, and pan roasted rockfish. For dessert, the passion fruit mousse in a chocolate cup with raspberries is tart and refreshing. The caramel and chocolate tart is rich. The simplest dishes — grilled tuna, seared salmon, or braised short ribs, for example — often are the best. Also very good are seared sea scallops with garlic, tomato, olives, parsley, and eggplant.

See map p. 126. 15 E St. NW (west of North Capitol Street). ☎ *202-661-2700.* www. bistrobis.com/bistro. *Reservations recommended. Metro: Union Station. From the Union Station Shops/Massachusetts Avenue exit, turn right on Massachusetts, then left on North Capitol, and then right on E. Main courses: $23–$32. AE, DC, DISC, MC, V. Open: Mon–Fri 7–10 a.m., 11:30 a.m.–2:30 p.m., and 5:30–10:30 p.m.; Sat–Sun 7–10 a.m. and 5:30–10:30 p.m.*

Bistrot Du Coin
$$$ Dupont Circle   FRENCH

This noisy, bustling, crowded place is jam-packed with people who are enjoying their food and each other's company. The long, narrow, high-ceilinged, brightly lighted room with wooden tables covered by butcher paper feels just like a Paris hangout, where everybody knows the waiters, the waitresses, the bartenders, and the clientele. Sit on the caned chairs, try to translate the French signs on the walls, and admire the French prints. Du Coin serves very good French comfort food — beef burgundy, roast chicken, rabbit stew, snails with garlic butter, and the like. The menu is huge and includes soups, salads, pâtés, sandwiches, and, of course, dessert. If you're partial to Roquefort cheese — which I am — start your feast by ordering the green salad with Roquefort, walnuts, croutons, and a tangy dressing. The mushroom soup's yummy, too.

See map p. 129. 1738 Connecticut Ave. NW (between R and S streets). ☎ *202-234-6969.* www.bistrotducoin.com. *Reservations recommended. Metro: Dupont Circle. From the Q Street Exit, walk 2½ blocks north on Connecticut. Main courses: $8–$24. AE, DC, DISC, MC, V. Open: Mon–Wed 11:30 a.m.–11 p.m., Thurs–Fri 11:30 a.m.–1 a.m., Sat 11 a.m.–1 a.m.*

Bistrot Lepic & Wine Bar
$$$ Georgetown   FRENCH

This neighborhood gathering place in upper Georgetown is filled with diplomats, world travelers, and others who revel in real French food. Chef Bruno Fortin began to learn the art of French cooking in his parents' restaurant in Brittany, then hopped around Europe and North America before settling into Washington and opening Lepic (named for a street he lived on in Paris) in 1995. Like other good French chefs in America, Fortin offers traditional French dishes and his own improvisations on them. Start with the mussel soup with leeks and potatoes. Then try the grilled trout with carrot sauce, potato-crusted salmon, or sautéed sea scallops with ginger broccoli mousse. The dining room is small, bustling, and pleasant, with sunny yellow walls. Fortin added a second-floor wine bar to create space for drinking and nibbling appetizers.

See map p. 131. 1736 Wisconsin Ave. NW (between R and S streets). ☎ **202-333-0111.** www.bistrotlepic.com. *Reservations recommended. Take Georgetown Connection Route 1 shuttle bus from Foggy Bottom–George Washington University Metrorail station or take a 30-series Metrobus. Main courses $17–$27. AE, DC, DISC, MC, V. Open: Sun–Thurs 11:30 a.m.–2:30 p.m. and 5:30–9:30 p.m., Fri–Sat 11:30 a.m.–2:30 p.m. and 5:30–10:30 p.m. Wine bar open daily 5:30 p.m.–midnight.*

The Brickskeller
$$ Dupont Circle AMERICAN

If you've left your college days long behind you, visiting the Brickskeller may make you think you've gone back. Your college town has to have a (smaller) tavern like this one. It's got red brick walls. It's got red-and-white checkered tablecloths. It's got beer cans and bottles as a primary decorating motif. It's got Janis Joplin on the jukebox. It's got surprisingly good food. And, my, does it have beer — more than 1,000 brands are advertised. The fish and chips here are really good. The juicy burgers, spicy chicken wings, and French fries also are good choices. You get an enormous pile of fried onion rings for $3.95. If you crave alternatives to standard pub fare, you can order pasta, salmon, beef steak, and several renditions of buffalo (not the kind with wings).

See map p. 129. 1523 22nd St. NW (between P and Q streets). ☎ **202-293-1885.** www.thebrickskeller.com. *Reservations accepted. Metro: Dupont Circle. From the Q Street exit, walk west on Q to 22nd and then turn left. Main courses: $5.45–$18 (veggie burger–buffalo steak, respectively). AE, DC, DISC, MC, V. Open: Mon–Thurs 11:30 a.m.–2 a.m., Fri 11:30 a.m.–3 a.m., Sat 6 p.m.–3 a.m., Sun 6 p.m.–2 a.m.*

B. Smith's
$$$$ Capitol Hill SOUTHERN

Under the ornate, soaring Beaux Arts ceiling of what once was the President's Room in Union Station, Washingtonians now dine on innovative versions of Southern, Cajun, and Creole cooking. Share the red beans and rice appetizer before diving into your main courses. B. Smith's house special is called Swamp Thing, with mixed seafood over greens in a mustard-based seafood sauce. Executive Chef Rahman Harper also has come up with a dish he calls Southern Surf & Turf — fried lobster tail and molasses braised short ribs with shitake quinoa. Traditional jazz groups entertain on Friday and Saturday nights. Because of the 30-foot ceilings and hard surfaces, this place can get noisy.

See map p. 126. 50 Massachusetts Ave. NE (in Union Station). ☎ **202-289-6188.** www.bsmith.com/restaurant_dc.php. *Reservations recommended. Metro: Union Station. Main courses: $17–$35. AE, DC, DISC, MC, V. Open: Mon–Thurs 11:30 a.m.–3 p.m. and 5–9 p.m., Fri–Sat 11:30 a.m.–3 p.m. and 5–10 p.m., Sun 11:30 a.m.– 9 p.m.*

Bullfeathers
$$ Capitol Hill   AMERICAN

Because of its location near the Capitol and the price and quality of its food and drink, Bullfeathers is a prime lunch, dinner, and elbow-bending spot for House staffers and the journalists who cover them when Congress is in session. When Congress shuts down — around the year-end holidays, for instance — you could hold a paint-ball tournament in here and not hit anybody. Most people come for the burgers and other sandwiches, but the restaurant offers a full dinner menu. There are lots of munchie specials from 3:30 to 6:30 p.m. Monday to Saturday and drink specials from 4 to 8 p.m. The restaurant says its name comes from Teddy Roosevelt's favorite euphemism, which is slung around quite a bit during those aforementioned congressional sessions.

See map p. 126. 410 1st St. SE (between D and E streets). ☎ *202-543-5005.* www. bullfeatherscapitolhill.com. *Reservations accepted. Metro: Capitol South. From the escalator exit, walk 1½ blocks south on 1st. From the elevator exit, look across 1st to the south. Main courses: $7.40–$25 (veggie sandwich–steak, respectively). AE, DC, DISC, MC, V. Open: Mon–Sat 11:15 a.m.–midnight.*

Busboys and Poets
$$ U Street Corridor   AMERICAN

This hip gathering place is a restaurant, bookstore, theater, bar, coffee house, and Internet cafe rolled into one. The food is good and the entertainment eclectic at this new addition to the rapidly gentrifying section of U Street. Busboys and Poets draws writers, activists, singles, and families. The restaurant serves salads, sandwiches, pizzas, and burgers. You also can build full meals around such entrees as crab cakes, meatloaf, and vegetable lasagna. If you like entertainment with your food, check the Web site to see when the next poetry slam, documentary film, or folk guitar player is scheduled in the performance space next to the main dining room.

See map p. 126. 2021 14th St. NW (between U and V streets). ☎ *202-387-7638.* www. busboysandpoets.com. *Metro: U Street. From the 13th and U streets exit, walk 1 block west on U, then right on 14th. Main courses: $6–$19 (veggie sandwiches–crab cakes, respectively). AE, DC, DISC, MC, V. Open: Mon–Thurs 10 a.m.–midnight, Fri–Sun 10 a.m.–2 a.m.*

Café Atlántico
$$$$ Penn Quarter   LATIN AMERICAN

Brightly decorated and filled with greenery and tables scattered over three open floors, Café Atlántico is a lively spot within an easy walk of many tourist attractions and cultural and entertainment venues. The Nuevo Latino cooking draws on the cuisines of South America, Central America, Mexico, and the Caribbean. The food is tasty and can be as rainbow-bright as the interior decorations. The cafe is noted for its exotic mixed drinks and extensive Latin American wine list. Come Saturday or Sunday from

11:30 a.m. to 2:30 p.m. for "Latino dim sum," chefs José Andrés and Katsuya Fukushima's innovative take on *tapas,* small dishes of Spain. At six-seat Mini Bar, on the second floor, Andrés and Fukushima spin out small servings of whatever their imaginations can conjure up (foie gras in cotton candy, for example). The $95 tasting menu is offered Tuesday through Saturday with seatings at 6 and 8:30 p.m. A $56 tasting menu is available in the main dining area, and a $28 pre-theater menu runs from 5 to 6:30 p.m. daily.

See map p. 126. 405 8th St. NW (between D and E streets). ☎ *202-393-0812.* www. cafeatlantico.com. *Reservations recommended (required for Mini Bar). Metro: Gallery Place-Chinatown. From F and 7th streets exit, walk east on F to 8th and then turn left. Main courses: $15–$28. AE, DC, DISC, MC, V. Open: Sun–Thurs 11:30 a.m.– 2:30 p.m. and 5–10 p.m., Fri–Sat 11:30 a.m.–2:30 p.m. and 5–11 p.m.*

Café La Ruche
$ Georgetown   FRENCH

My wife and daughter like to eat in this little restaurant off Georgetown's beaten path because it reminds them of France. From the outside, you can imagine it as a house in the French countryside (if you ignore the surrounding buildings). Inside, it's like a well-worn neighborhood hangout in Paris (though the TV at one end of the dining room intrudes upon the fantasy). Unfortunately, at times, indifferent service can remind you of Paris as well. To start, try the traditional French onion soup. You can make a meal of the *salade Niçoise.* The quiches are delicious. And the desserts are wonderful. (Get the fruit tart, and you can pretend it's health food. I do.) Weekend brunch, from 10 a.m. to 3 p.m., is a treat and, at $11, is one of the best bargains in town. When the weather's nice, you can eat outside.

See map p. 131. 1039 31st St. NW (between M and K streets). ☎ *202-965-2684.* www.cafelaruche.com. *Reservations accepted. Take Georgetown Connection shuttle bus Route 2 from Foggy Bottom–GWU or Rosslyn Metrorail station to 31st and M and then walk south on 31st. Or take a 30-series Metrobus. Main courses: $6–$10. AE, DC, DISC, MC, V. Open: Mon–Fri 11:30 a.m.–midnight, Sat–Sun 10 a.m.–midnight.*

Capital Q
$ Penn Quarter   TEXAS BARBECUE

How's this for incongruity? In Washington's Chinatown stands a tiny restaurant with autographed pictures of U.S. politicians on the walls and Texas barbecue on the menu. Most of the politicians are Texans, which is appropriate since this restaurant is run by transplanted Texan Nick Fontana. Capital Q is authentic enough to attract Texas expatriate diners and was picked to cater the party that House Majority Leader Dick Armey (of Texas) threw for 4,000 of his closest friends at the 2000 Republican National Convention in Philadelphia. Order the beef brisket or pulled pork from the sandwich menu. Or try the beef brisket plate, which comes with two side dishes. Service is cafeteria style. Wanna see what's happening here right now? Capital Q has a live cam on its Web site.

See map p. 126. 707 H St. NW (between 7th and 8th streets). ☎ *202-347-8396.* www. capitalqbbq.com. *Reservations not accepted. Metro: Gallery Place-Chinatown. From the 7th and 8th streets exit, cross 7th on H and look for the restaurant. Sandwiches: $6–$7. Plates: $5.25–$26 (for an enormous serving of ribs). AE, DC, DISC, MC, V. Open: Mon–Wed 11 a.m.–9 p.m., Thurs–Sat 11 a.m.–midnight.*

Circle Bistro
$$$ Foggy Bottom/West End   MODERN AMERICAN

The food at this restaurant off Pennsylvania Avenue is excellent, and you can sample it in several different ways. The most obvious is from the regular dinner menu in the comfortable dining room, which is sleek and modern but warmed by earth-toned décor and windows that look into greenery planted outside. But there's also a bar menu of small plates and salads; a weekday happy hour from 5 to 8 p.m.; an 11:30 a.m. to 2:30 p.m. Sunday brunch; a $35-dollar pre-theater dinner from 5 to 7 p.m. daily; and breakfast every day as well. Try the lemon-dusted brook trout, Alaskan halibut, duckling, or hanger steak.

See map p. 126. 1 Washington Circle NW (at 23rd Street and New Hampshire Avenue). ☎ *202-293-5390.* www.circlebistro.com. *Reservations recommended. Metro: Foggy Bottom–George Washington University. Walk 1 block north on 23rd and then go counterclockwise around Washington Circle to New Hampshire and 23rd. Main courses: $19–$27. AE, DC, DISC, MC, V. Open: Sun 8–10:30a.m., 11:30 a.m.–2:30 p.m., and 5–10 p.m.; Mon–Thurs 7–10 a.m., 11:30 a.m.–2:30 p.m., and 5–10 p.m.; Fri 7–10 a.m., 11:30 a.m.–2:30 p.m., and 5–11 p.m.; Sat 8–10:30 a.m., 11:30 a.m.–2:30 p.m., and 5–11 p.m. Bar open Sun–Thurs 10 a.m.–11 p.m., Fri–Sat until midnight.*

City Lights of China
$$ Dupont Circle   CHINESE

Good food served by a friendly staff in pleasant surroundings — what more do you want in a Chinese restaurant? City Lights has a large and varied menu, and the owners invite you to ask the chef to accommodate your personal tastes. My family has become especially fond of the hot-and-sour soup, spring rolls, and Seafood Delight (shrimp, scallops, crab, and vegetables stir-fried in a light sauce). The restaurant is also noted for its Peking duck, eggplant with garlic, and tangy Szechwan lamb. Many vegetable dishes are on the menu. In addition to serving you inside, City Lights has a substantial takeout menu and delivers to nearby hotels. Keep that thought in mind if you want to picnic on a park bench or collapse in your room after a particularly grueling day of seeing the sights.

See map p. 129. 1731 Connecticut Ave. NW (between R and S streets). ☎ *202-265-6688.* www.citylightsofchina.com. *Reservations recommended. Metro: Dupont Circle. From the Q Street exit, walk north on Connecticut Avenue past R Street. Main courses: $9–$26 (Peking Duck). AE, MC, V. Open: Mon–Fri 11:30 a.m.–10:30 p.m., Sat noon–11 p.m., and Sun noon–10:30 p.m.*

CityZen
$$$$$ Tidal Basin MODERN AMERICAN

There's still a buzz about CityZen, even though it really can no longer be considered a new restaurant, having opened in 2004. The warm colors and soft lighting make this a welcoming, soothing room, with a touch of whimsy. Windows along one wall reach from the floor to the high ceiling. Enormous lamps — shaped like normal table lamps — fit with the soaring height of the room. You can glimpse Chef Eric Ziebold and his assistants preparing your dinner in the open kitchen. You know a great deal of care has gone into preparing an exquisite dining experience when the chef sends out several *amuse-bouche* offerings to begin the meal — on our visit a tasty mushroom fritter, a thin pumpkin soup to be sipped from a small cup, and a quail egg and ham salad which the waiter offers to top with shaved black salt from the Himalayas. Three styles of bread arrive with two kinds of butter, one identified as sweet butter from Pennsylvania, the other as lightly salted butter from Vermont. You order from a tasting menu — $75 for three courses, $90 for five, $80 for a five-course vegetarian tasting. The five-course menu is set by the chef. You're given a half-dozen choices for each course of the three-course tasting. Vegetarians can piece together a three-course veggie dinner as well. The selections change frequently, so making recommendations is problematic. The best of our tastings were two appetizers, artichoke ravioli, and a *tartiflette* with duck confit; a main course of poached fluke topped with lemon sauce and salty, buttery sea urchin; and two complex desserts, a poached pineapple guava with rosemary cake and guava sorbet, and a poached pear with pastry and candied walnut ice cream. CityZen offers a large selection of wines by the glass priced from $10 to $20.

See map p. 126. 1330 Maryland Ave. SW (west of 12th Street and south of D, in the Mandarin Oriental Hotel). ☎ *202-787-6606.* www.mandarinoriental.com/hotel/535000039.asp. *Reservations recommended. Metro: Smithsonian. From the Independence Avenue exit, walk south on 12th Street SW; just past D Street, turn right toward a cul-de-sac where the hotel is located. Take a cab if you're alone at night. Fixed price tasting menus: $75–$90. AE, DC, DISC, MC, V. Thurs 6–9:30 p.m., Fri–Sat 5:30–11:30 p.m.*

Clyde's
$$ Georgetown, Penn Quarter, Upper Northwest AMERICAN

Like its sibling Old Ebbitt Grill, Clyde's of Georgetown was one of my favorite places to eat when I managed to find an excuse to visit Washington long before we moved here. Then, it was a comfortable old saloon with some unusually good food, especially (to my taste) the omelets. A 1996 renovation modernized the place, while aiming to maintain a saloonlike atmosphere — oak bar, plank flooring, checkered tablecloths. But the Garden Room now looks like all those other family-friendly pubs that hang artifacts all over the place. In this case, models of antique airplanes dangle below the skylight. Clyde's is still a place for hamburgers and other bar fare, but the ever-changing menu is quite ambitious, with special attention to incorporating fresh produce from mid-Atlantic farms. Always order the light and fluffy omelet if it's offered. We've also had good luck ordering pear salad with blue cheese and walnuts, linguine with mussels, rockfish, and crab cakes. Clyde's is a local chain now, with Clyde's of Chevy Chase feeding shoppers in the Friendship Heights upscale shopping area that I call Washington's Little Rodeo Drive, and Clyde's of Gallery Place hosting hordes of revelers in the Penn Quarter arts and entertainment district.

See map p. 126. 3236 M St. NW (between Wisconsin Avenue and Potomac Street). ☎ *202-333-9180.* www.clydes.com. *Reservations recommended. Take the Georgetown Connection Route 2 shuttle bus from the Dupont Circle or Rosslyn Metrorail station to M and Potomac or 33rd Street. Or hop a 30-series Metrobus to M and Wisconsin. Main courses: $8–$24. AE, DC, DISC, MC, V. Open: Mon–Thurs 11:30 a.m.–midnight, Fri 11:30 a.m.–1 a.m., Sat 10 a.m.–1 a.m., Sun 9 a.m.–midnight.*

Also in Penn Quarter (see map p. 126): 707 7th St. NW (between G and H streets). ☎ *202-349-3700. Metro: Gallery Place/Chinatown. Restaurant is just south of the 7th and H streets exit. Open: Mon–Fri 11 a.m.–1 a.m., Sat–Sun 10 a.m.–1 a.m.*

Also in Chevy Chase, MD (see map p. 131): 5441 Wisconsin Ave. (north of the intersection of Wisconsin and Western avenues). ☎ *301-951-9600. Metro: Friendship Heights. From the Western Avenue and Military Road exit, walk north on Wisconsin, cross Wisconsin Circle, and then turn right into the Chevy Chase shopping center parking lot. Open: Mon–Sat 11 a.m.–12:30 a.m., Sun 10 a.m.–12:30 a.m.*

Eat First
$$ Chinatown   CHINESE

The name and the exterior appearance of Eat First don't scream "gourmet cooking," but the restaurant serves good food popular with the locals. You need to peruse the various sections of the lengthy menu to locate the best dishes. Try the steamed shrimp from among the house specialties, General Tso's chicken in the poultry section, sliced chicken with ginger and scallion from the clay pot preparations, and the barbecued pork and roasted duck entrees from the barbecue and soy sauce dishes. If you know your Chinese cooking, the chefs are happy to prepare items not on the menu. In an early-to-bed town, this place is one where you can satisfy late-late-late hunger.

See map p. 126. 609 H St. NW (between 6th and 7th streets). ☎ *202-289-1703. Reservations accepted. Metro: Gallery Place-Chinatown. From the 6th and H streets exit, walk less than 1 block east on H. Main courses: $11–$20. AE, MC, V. Open: Sun–Thurs 10 a.m.–2 a.m., Fri–Sat 10 a.m.–3 a.m.*

Galileo
$–$$$$$ Downtown   NORTHERN ITALIAN

Talk about multipurpose! Galileo long has set the bar by which other D.C. Italian restaurants are measured — and charged for the quality. For several years, award-winning chef Roberto Donna also has been offering an even more expensive opportunity to taste additional outstanding dishes in *Laboratorio*, a private dining room where a 10- to 12-course tasting menu

Dining with Dubya: Politico hangouts

So you wonder where the president likes to grab a bite outside the White House? Or where members of Congress and lobbyists feed their faces and bend their elbows between roll calls?

Well, President George W. Bush isn't known to frequent D.C. eateries, and when he does he seems to choose modest digs. Like his father, he's shown up at the **Peking Gourmet Inn** in suburban Falls Church, Virginia (6029 Leesburg Pike; ☎ 703-671-8088). My daughter ran into him one night at the **Cactus Cantina** (3300 Wisconsin Ave. NW, 1 block north of the National Cathedral; ☎ 202-686-7222), a good Tex-Mex spot. (Ironically, she had stopped there before going off on a school field trip to see a play that was highly critical of an execution Bush approved when he was Texas governor.) Nevertheless, one of her bolder classmates approached the president and asked whether he would pose for a picture with the group, and he graciously agreed. Then, every kid with a cellphone — whether red state or blue state in their political leanings — immediately called relatives and friends to tell who was eating at the next table.

You'll find senators, lobbyists, and Supreme Court justices at **The Monocle;** senators, lobbyists, and Senate staffers at **the Dubliner;** Senate staffers and lobbyists at **Bistro Bis.** House staffers and the occasional representative frequent **Bullfeathers.** White House folks hit the nearby **Occidental** and **Old Ebbitt Grill.**

The number-one see-and-be-seen place in town is **The Palm.** You might bump into lobbyists at any of the preceding restaurants because their jobs revolve around government folks, and they have the expense accounts to afford it.

---

is served for $110 on weekdays and $125 on weekends, with an additional $75 option for matched wines. Now he's gone the opposite direction, and he's added bargain-priced meals at lunch and dinner in the bar area and outdoors in nice weather. Donna calls the bar area Osteria del Galileo, and offers lunch and dinner guests appetizers, pastas, main courses, side dishes, and desserts for $12 or less. On some days at lunch in nice weather, he sets up a grill outside and conjures up chicken, pork, sausage, and meatball sandwiches for $5 to $6. You have to call or get on his e-mail list to find out when Galileo's grilling. Epicures are advised to reserve well ahead for one of the 30 coveted seats in *Laboratorio,* but you can't make reservations for Osteria.

Galileo closed for renovations in 2006 and was scheduled to reopen in late summer 2007.

See map p. 126. 1110 21st St. NW (between L and M streets). ☎ *202-293-7191. Laboratorio* ☎ *202-331-0880.* www.robertodonna.com. *Reservations recommended for Galileo, required for Laboratorio, not accepted for bar area meals. Metro: Farragut North. Walk west on L Street 4 blocks and then right on 21st. Main courses: $24–$35 at Galileo, $5–$12 at Osteria, $110–$125 tasting menu at Laboratorio. AE, DC, DISC, MC, V. Open: Mon–Thurs 11:30 a.m.–2:15 p.m. and 5:30–10 p.m., Fri 11:30 a.m.–2:15 p.m. and 5:30–10:30 p.m., Sat 5:30–10:30 p.m., Sun 5–10 p.m. Bar area bargains not available weekends at lunch or Sun and Mon at dinner.*

Garrett's
$$ **Georgetown**   **AMERICAN**

Garrett's is an old-fashioned saloon with a surprisingly pretty little bright and airy dining room, with large windows and a glass roof tucked into a corner of the second floor. Take the stairs just east of the first-floor bar, and you may find the friendly, accommodating staff singing to a child celebrating a birthday. Garrett's menu features soups, salads, pasta, burgers, sandwiches, appetizers, fish and chips, and a couple of main courses. I like the "Huntington Hash" — pulled chicken and roasted potatoes topped with gravy and served with fresh fruit and coleslaw. Desserts include such down-home favorites as bread pudding, brownie a la mode, apple crisp, and ice cream sundaes. The wine list is small, but the wines are good and reasonably priced. They also have some interesting beer selections.

See map p. 131. 3003 M St. NW (west of 30th Street). ☎ ***202-333-1033.*** *www. garrettsdc.com. Reservations accepted. Take Georgetown Connection shuttle bus from Dupont Circle or Rosslyn Metrorail station to M and 30th or Thomas Jefferson Street. Or ride 30-series Metrobus. Main courses: $6–$14 (sandwich–ribs, respectively). AE, DC, DISC, MC, V. Open: Mon–Thurs 11:30 a.m.–1:30 a.m., Fri–Sat noon–2:30 a.m., Sun noon–1:30 a.m.*

Georgia Brown's
$$$$ **Downtown**   **SOUTHERN**

Ready for some "nouveau soul food"? That's how the chef once described the cuisine at Georgia Brown's, a Southern restaurant that bases its cooking on the traditions of South Carolina's Low Country — with a twist. And just what does that produce? How about fried green tomatoes stuffed with herbed cream cheese, served on green tomato relish with lemon-cayenne mayonnaise and watercress? It's a superb, rich dish that four can share as an appetizer or side dish. Or what about sweet potato cheesecake? Or a vegetarian croquette? You can find plenty of traditional home cooking, too, like fried chicken, pork chops, catfish, gumbo, shrimp, and grits. This New South is vegetarian-friendly, with several veggie selections on the menu, including a sampler. Portions are large. The dining room is warm and comfy. A popular jazz brunch occurs from 10 a.m. to 2:15 p.m. Sunday. The place is a hangout for local movers and shakers, and it's one of the most integrated dining rooms in town.

See map p. 126. 950 15th St. NW (between I and K streets). ☎ ***202-393-4499.*** *www. gbrowns.com. Reservations recommended. Metro: McPherson Square. From the Vermont Avenue/White House exit, walk north on Vermont to I and then bear left on 15th. Main courses: $15–$36 (veggie croquettes–filet mignon, respectively); brunch $33 adults, $22 children. AE, DC, DISC, MC, V. Open: Mon–Fri 11:30 a.m.–10:30 p.m., Sat 5:30–10:30 p.m., Sun 10 a.m.–2:15 p.m. (brunch) and 5:30–9 p.m.*

The Grill From Ipanema
$$$ **Adams-Morgan**   **BRAZILIAN**

If you've never enjoyed the complex flavors of Brazilian cuisine, don't miss this favorite, known for its good food and lively neighborhod bar scene.

Beneath the palm trees and tropical colors, get into a Latin American mood with Brazil's national dish, *feijoada* — a rich black bean stew with sausages, smoked meats, dried beef, and pork spooned over rice. Wash it down with Brazil's national cocktail, a *caipirinha,* made with lime, sugar, and sugar cane brandy. Other menu standouts include a variety of seafood stews called *moqueca.* If you want to avoid noise drifting in from the bar, ask for an outdoor table when the weather is nice.

See map p. 129. 1858 Columbia Rd. NW (at Mintwood Place). ☎ *202-986-0757.* www. thegrillfromipanema.com. *Reservations accepted. Metro: Woodley Park Zoo-Adams Morgan. From the Metrorail station, catch the no. 98 Metrobus to Calvert Street and Columbia Road, and then walk south on Columbia 2 blocks. Bus runs 6 p.m.–3:15 a.m. weeknights, from 9:50 a.m.–3:15 a.m. Sat, and 6 p.m.–12:15 a.m. Sun. Or take a taxi. Main courses: $15–$25. AE, DC, DISC, MC, V. Open: Mon–Thurs 5–10:30 p.m., Fri 5–11:30 p.m., Sat noon–11:30 p.m., Sun noon–10 p.m.*

Hank's Oyster Bar
$$$ **Dupont Circle SEAFOOD**

Anxious to hang out her own shingle after succeeding famously at the hotel restaurant 15ria, Chef Jamie Leeds decided to open a local dining spot in her own neighborhood near Dupont Circle. The result is this small seafood house, inspired by the Pearl Oyster Bar in New York and named for her late father, an avid fisherman. Oysters — raw and fried — are, of course, the first order of business here, along with other seafood dishes, notably crab cakes, lobster rolls, oyster po' boys, calamari, popcorn shrimp, and clams. But Leeds was known for comfort cooking at 15ria, and she's brought her "meats and two" specials to Hank's. That would be two sides with a meat dish such as molasses-braised short ribs, smothered pork chops, or roasted chicken. For weekend brunch (11 a.m.–3 p.m.), she adds sourdough French toast and crab-cake eggs Benedict to the menu. Following the neighborly theme, Leeds offers fish sticks, french fries, hamburgers, and macaroni-and-cheese for the kids. Leeds shops for fresh produce at the Dupont Circle farmers' market in season, and buys oysters from oyster farmers whose standards she has checked. This is a small restaurant with tightly packed tables, and it doesn't take reservations. If you don't like crowds or waiting for a table, come before or after normal meal times.

See map p. 129. 1624 Q St. NW (between 16th and 17th streets). ☎ *202-462-4265.* www.hanksdc.com. *No reservations. Metro: Dupont Circle. From the Q Street exit, walk east on Q 3½ blocks. Main courses: $11–$19. AE, MC, V. Open: Sun–Tues 5:30–10 p.m., Wed–Fri 5:30–11 p.m., Sat 11 a.m.–3 p.m. and 5:30–11 p.m., Sun 11 a.m.–3 p.m.*

Harmony Cafe
$ **Georgetown ASIAN**

Tucked in the basement of an unassuming Georgetown storefront, the Harmony Cafe's attractive dining room can please vegetarians and omnivores alike. Most of the Asian dishes, from *kung pao* chicken to pork in garlic sauce, come in vegetarian versions, a testament to the ability of soy products to mimic other foods. The garden salad with a light Asian dressing is a refreshing accompaniment to the large list of entrees. For an appetizer, try the grilled shitake mushrooms. Don't see exactly what you want on the menu? Under the list of Chef's Specialties, one option is "Your Favorite Dish (ask for it)."

See map p. 131. 3287½ M St. NW (east of 33rd Street). ☎ 202-338-3881. Reservations accepted. Take Georgetown Connection shuttle bus Route 2 from Dupont Circle or Rosslyn Metrorail station to M and 33rd or Potomac Street. Main courses: $5–$10. DISC, MC, V. Open: Mon–Sat 11:30 a.m.–11 p.m., Sun 5–11 p.m.

Jaleo
$$ Penn Quarter   SPANISH

Loosely translated, *jaleo* means revelry or racket. Neither is in short supply at this lively, colorful tapas bar and restaurant with walls of windows that look out onto bustling sidewalks. Enjoy flamenco music while perusing a menu of 50 tapas and main courses. Because sharing is an unspoken rule, Jaleo is fun with a group. The Sunday brunch (11:30 a.m.–3 p.m.) attracts locals en route to a nearby attraction or an afternoon siesta. You can graze here nightly for a week and not sample everything. Because I like so many things here, it's hard to focus on a few recommendations. Let me do my duty and steer you toward the spinach sautéed with pine nuts, apples, and raisons; chorizo sausage with garlic mashed potatoes; roasted eggplant with onions; fried calamari; grilled asparagus; and garlic shrimp. Don't eat too many of these choices, though, because you must sample dessert — and share it, too. The warm Basque cake with cream, cinnamon-vanilla sauce, and ice cream is wonderful, as is the flan and the chocolate-nut mousse. A world-traveler friend declared Jaleo's *cafe con leche* "compares favorably with what I've had in Mexico and Spain."

See map p. 126. 480 7th St. NW (at E Street). ☎ 202-628-7949. www.jaleo.com. Reservations accepted for lunch and between 5 and 6:30 p.m. Metro: Gallery Place/Chinatown. From the 7th and F streets exit, walk 1 block south on 7th to E. Main courses: $15–$17; tapas $4.25–$10. AE, DC, DISC, MC, V. Open: Sun–Mon 11:30 a.m.–10 p.m., Tues–Thurs 11:30 a.m.–11:30 p.m., and Fri–Sat 11:30 a.m.–midnight.

Kinkead's
$$$$ Foggy Bottom/West End   SEAFOOD

This restaurant is one of the very best in Washington. Everything is terrific, but chef-owner Bob Kinkead's signature dishes include pumpkin-seed-crusted salmon with crab, corn, and chili ragout; as well as roasted cod accompanied by crab imperial, sweet potato purée, mustard cream sauce, and spoon bread (with ham, corn, and cheddar cheese). At the other extreme, Kinkead offers what he calls "simply grilled fish," such as salmon or tuna with steamed fresh vegetables. And he serves up excellent clams — fried and in chowder. The main dining rooms upstairs are attractive and formal. An informal bar and cafe on the lower level offers live jazz from 6:30 to 10 p.m. Tuesday through Saturday. An added attraction at Kinkead's: Sommelier Michael Flynn can advise you on selecting wine.

See map p. 126. 2000 Pennsylvania Ave. NW (actually on I Street between 20th and 21st streets). ☎ *202-296-7700.* www.kinkead.com. *Reservations recommended. Metro: Foggy Bottom. Walk 2½ blocks east on I. Restaurant entrance is on the right in the middle of the block. Main courses: $26–$30. AE, DC, DISC, MC, V. Open: Sun–Thurs 11:30 a.m.–10 p.m., Fri 11:30 a.m.–10:30 p.m., Sat 5:30–10:30 p.m.*

Le Paradou
$$$$$ Penn Quarter   FRENCH

If you've got 150 bucks to spend on a *nine-course* tasting menu, Le Paradou is the place for you. Superstar chef Yannick Cam and business partner Michael Klein have spared no effort or expense in offering the finest dining experience at this contemporary French restaurant, which opened in mid-2004. The earth-toned décor with commissioned contemporary art is elegant but comfortable. From the pre-appetizer amuse of paper-thin smoked salmon with crème fraîche to the dessert of thin crispy pastry, caramel ice cream, nuts, and warm cherries and quince, the food is exquisite. Ask the waiter's advice when ordering à la carte. If you spring for a fixed-price meal and something doesn't strike your fancy (put off by foie gras?), ask the waiter to suggest a substitute. Be really nice, and maybe he'll bring you the post-dessert dessert, a plate of thumbnail-sized mini treats. I've heard some complaints about the service recently, but no one questions the high quality of the food. You can't eat cheap here, but you can taste Chef Cam's cooking for a lot less in the attractive bar and lounge, at the sidewalk tables in nice weather, or at lunch. Men are expected to wear jackets in the main dining room.

See map p. 126. 678 Indiana Ave. NW (between 6th and 7th streets). ☎ *202-347-6780.* www.leparadou.net. *Reservations recommended. Metro: Archive/Navy Memorial. Walk east across the square to Indiana. Restaurant is ahead on right. Main courses: $29–$40. Tasting menus: Three-course pre-theater $45, six-course $115, nine-courses $150. AE, DC, DISC, MC, V. Open: Mon–Thurs 11:45 a.m.–2:15 p.m. and 5:30–10 p.m., Fri 11:45 a.m.–2:15 p.m. and 5:15–10 p.m., Sat 5:15–11 p.m.*

Luna Grill & Diner
$$ Dupont Circle   AMERICAN

At Luna, you can get bacon and eggs all day and much of the night. This diner offers you plenty of comfort food: meatloaf, mashed potatoes, grilled cheese . . . and burgers. You have alternatives to the traditional meat and potatoes, such as grilled vegetables and vegetarian pasta. Try the fried sweet potatoes or gravied mashed potatoes. There's a Blue Plate Special every day (lasagna, fried chicken, pork ribs) and a Green Plate Special for vegetarians (veggie pasta, portobello parmigiana). How 'bout apple pie and ice cream for dessert? Luna entertains kids with whimsical murals on the walls and booths — and with a menu that contains plenty of kid-friendly items. In nice weather there's an easy-to-overlook outdoor dining area out the back door. Luna doesn't take reservations, but you can call ahead to be placed on a waiting list that moves you to the front of the line when you arrive.

See map p. 162. 1301 Connecticut Ave. NW (at N Street). ☎ **202-835-2280.** www. lunagrillanddiner.com. *Reservations not accepted; call to get on waiting list. Metro: Dupont Circle. From the Dupont Circle exit, walk 1 block south on Connecticut. Main courses: $7–$16, sandwiches $6–$9. AE, DISC, MC, V. Open: Mon–Thurs 8 a.m.–10:30 p.m., Fri 8 a.m.–midnight, Sat 10 a.m.–midnight, Sun 10 a.m.–10 p.m.*

Malaysia Kopitiam
$$ Dupont Circle MALAYSIAN

There's a good chance you've never tasted Malaysian cooking. But, when you do, it'll remind you of other Asian cuisines, notably Chinese, Thai, and Indian. Washington is blessed with a good Malaysian eatery ready to help you understand the unfamiliar. First, the lengthy menu describes the dishes and contains photos to show you what they look like. Next, owner/host Leslie Phoon and his staff stand ready to answer questions and offer advice. (His wife, Penny, is the chef.) On your way in, check the chalkboard for specials. Try not to be distracted by the tiki bar décor. If you want suggestions from me, try the *wok wok* shrimp. The shrimp are served on a bed of lettuce with a sweetish cream sauce. A dining companion likened beef *hor fun* — stir-fried flat rice noodles with beef, bean sprouts, and Chinese spinach — to the ubiquitous Thai dish, *pad thai. Assam sambal* shrimp is stir-fried with red onions and red peppers in a spicy/sour sauce. *Nyonya* chicken is another spicy entree, this one with cucumbers. If you're not into hot stuff, don't worry: An entire menu section lists nonspicy entrees. Vegetarians will appreciate the section devoted to vegetable dishes.

See map p. 129. 1827 M St. NW (between 18th and 19th streets). ☎ **202-833-6232.** www.malaysiakopitiam.com. *Reservations accepted. Metro: Farragut North. From the L Street exit, walk north on Connecticut Avenue and then left on M. Main courses: $7–$23, many under $10. AE, DISC, MC, V. Open: Mon–Thurs 11:30 a.m.–10 p.m., Fri–Sat 11:30 a.m.–11 p.m., Sun noon–10 p.m.*

Marcel's
$$$$$ Foggy Bottom/West End FRENCH/BELGIAN

Chef/owner Robert Wiedmaier describes the fare here as "French cuisine with a Belgian flair." That combination produces such dishes as chicken with caramelized shallots, Gruyère cheese, and potato cake; veal with mushrooms, potato purée, and zinfandel sauce; and rack of lamb with chive potato purée and lamb sausage flavored with cumin and Madeira. Wiedmaier prepares tasting menus costing from $58 (three courses) to $98 (six). Diners can hear live jazz drifting from the bar. And Marcel's offers a unique pre/post-theater deal. For $48, you can eat the first two courses of a three-course dinner, take a complimentary limo to Kennedy Center, and then return in the limo for dessert after the performance. (In case you're curious, Wiedmaier named Marcel's for his son.)

See map p. 126. 2401 Pennsylvania Ave. NW (west of 24th Street). ☎ **202-296-1166.** www.marcelsdc.com. *Reservations recommended. Metro: Foggy Bottom–George*

Washington University. Walk west on I Street and then right on 24th 1½ blocks to Pennsylvania. Main courses: $29–$42. AE, MC, V. Open: Mon–Thurs 5:30–10 p.m., Fri–Sat 5:30–11 p.m., Sun 5:30–9:30 p.m.

Marrakesh
$$ Downtown MOROCCAN

This Moroccan restaurant is just plain fun. Suspend your disbelief, and you can imagine you're out for a night with Humphrey Bogart and Sydney Greenstreet in old Casablanca. The adventure starts when you knock on the closed front door, it opens, and you're escorted through a curtain into an enormous dimly lighted dining room decorated from floor to ceiling in intricate colored patterns. After you settle into cushions around a low brass table, you wash your hands, which are your primary eating utensils for the evening. The seven-course meal is served family style, and you scoop up the food with bread or your fingers. Think eggplant, cucumber, phyllo pastry, almonds, cinnamon, olives, dates, raisons, honey, couscous, two meat courses (one perhaps a kebab), fruit, pastries, and mint tea. This place is most fun with a group — I'd say about ten people — but the restaurant will serve any number. Oh, and there's a belly dancer.

See map p. 126. 617 New York Ave. NW (between 6th and 7th streets). ☎ *202-393-9393.* www.marrakeshwashington.com. *Reservations required. Metro: Mt. Vernon Square. Walk 2 blocks south on 7th and then go left on New York. Restaurant is on left, just before 6th. Fixed price meal: $30. No credit cards accepted. Open: Daily 6–11 p.m.*

Martin's Tavern
$$$ Georgetown AMERICAN

Martin's is a real Washington institution. Every president since Harry Truman has eaten here, and Truman, John F. Kennedy, Lyndon Johnson, and Richard Nixon were Martin's regulars when they served in Congress. A huge proportion of Georgetown University students eat here, too, as do Georgetown residents and other Washingtonians looking for an old-style, neighborhood tavern in which to sip a beer, grab a bite, or enjoy nice weather in the narrow sidewalk cafe. William S. Martin, a 19th-century Irish immigrant, opened this place in 1933 with his son William G. The founder's great-grandson Billy and Billy's wife Gina are the proprietors today. Tiffany lamps and a mahogany bar mark the atmosphere inside. The menu runs to crab cakes, corned beef and cabbage, fish and chips, Welsh rarebit, calves liver, strip steak, burgers, and sandwiches.

See map p. 131. 1264 Wisconsin Ave. NW (south of N Street). ☎ *202-333-7370.* www.martins-tavern.com. *Reservations recommended. Take Georgetown Connection shuttle bus from Dupont Circle, Foggy Bottom–GWU, or Rosslyn Metrorail Station, or ride 30-series Metrobus. Main courses: $8–$27 (Welsh rarebit–strip steak, respectively). AE, DC, DISC, MC, V. Open: Mon–Thurs 10 a.m.–11 p.m., Fri 10 a.m.–12:30 a.m., Sat 8 a.m.–12:30 a.m.; Sun 8 a.m.–11 p.m.*

Matchbox
$$$ Penn Quarter   PIZZA/AMERICAN

The name no longer is quite appropriate for this formerly tiny pizza-and-more spot. Superb thin-crust, New York style pizza from a wood-fired oven is what draws the hordes here. But Matchbox — which expanded in fall 2006 — offers a full menu that ranges from burgers to such entrees as pepper-crusted yellowfin tuna on sesame sticky rice with stir-fried vegetables. I think the veggie pizza is especially good. Non-veggies should check out the delicious and unusual crab cake in crispy phyllo pastry. Matchbox has a half-dozen beers on tap, and the bar's a decent place to eat if you can't get a table due to the restaurant's no-reservations policy.

See map p. 126. 713 H St. NW (at 7th Street). ☎ *202-289-4441.* www.matchbox dc.com. *Reservations not accepted, except sometimes for groups of at least six. Metro: Gallery Place–Chinatown. From the 7th and H streets exit, look across the street. Main courses: $12–$25. Sandwiches: $10–$12. Plain pizza: $9–$15. AE, MC, V. Open: Mon–Fri 11 a.m.–10 p.m. or later, Sat noon–11 p.m. or later.*

The Melting Pot
$$$$ Dupont Circle   FONDUE

As with Marrakesh, the Melting Pot is a great place to bring a group for a festive evening of drinking and dipping and dining (although you also have the choice of a "Lovers Lane" of dimly lighted booths for two). Here, however, you're not dipping your fingers into the pot in front of you. (It's not recommended with boiling oil!) Instead, you're strongly encouraged to use fondue forks. The ambience here is a combination of sophisticated and whimsical. The restaurant is modern and attractive. Lights come in the shapes of forks and pots and tiny spots suspended over the tables. Don't worry if steam from your fondue pot obscures your dining companions across the table. It's from the boiling water beneath the cooking chamber. (A member of my large party here once described the experience "like getting a facial.") The suggested way of proceeding is to begin with melted cheese (my favorite is cheddar with beer, garlic, and other seasonings) into which you dip breads, vegetables, and apples. The main course (shrimp, steak, chicken, scallops, vegetables — even lobster) is dipped in a hot broth. The burgundy-based broth seems best for beef, but many like the simple oil because it doesn't import its own taste to the foods being cooked. You make dessert by dipping strawberries and other items — even marshmallows — into melted chocolate. The more dippers in your party, the more variations you can concoct with the different ingredients to heat and to dip. "Fondue Feasts" — the Melting Pot's version of tasting menus from salad to dessert — serve two dippers for $82 to $92.

See map p. 129. 1220 19th St. NW (between M and N streets). ☎ *202-857-0777.* www. meltingpot.com. *Reservations recommended. Metro: Dupont Circle. From the Dupont Circle exit, walk south on 19th about 1½ blocks. The restaurant is hiding underground on the right. Main courses: $19–$30. AE, MC, V. Open: Sun 4–10 p.m., Mon–Thurs 5–10 p.m., Fri 5 p.m.–midnight, Sat 4 p.m.–midnight.*

Michel Richard Citronelle

$$$$$ **Georgetown FRENCH/CALIFORNIA**

Chef Michel Richard has earned a reputation as one of the best French chefs in America. His restaurant actually bills its offerings as "French/California cuisine" — French recipes with American influences. Citronelle offers fixed-price dinners from $85 to $150 and a chef's table from $275 (all before beverages). The appetizers may include a lobster tart, eggplant gazpacho, or crab tempura. For the main course, how about roasted monkfish with spinach, oyster ravioli and watercress sauce, or wild rockfish with crab risotto and saffron potato purée? For dessert, try a rich and creamy raspberry vacherin cheese or petits fours. At these prices, gentlemen are expected to wear a jacket — and to be gentlemen! You can eat for less — but not for cheap — in the lounge or on the terrace. You also can test Citronelle's wares at breakfast. In addition to serving these haute cuisine dinners, Citronelle is the in-house restaurant for the Latham Hotel.

See map p. 131. 3000 M St. NW (at 30th Street, in the Latham Hotel). ☎ **202-625-2150.** www.citronelledc.com. *Reservations required. Jacket required. Take Georgetown Connection shuttle bus from Dupont Circle or Rosslyn Metrorail station to M and 30th or Thomas Jefferson Street. Or ride 30-series Metrobus. Fixed-price dinner: $85–$275 and up. AE, DC, MC, V. Open: Mon–Thurs 6:30–10:30 a.m. and 6–10 p.m., Fri–Sat 6:30–10:30 a.m. and 6:30–10:30 p.m., Sun 6:30–10:30 a.m. and 6–9:30 p.m.*

Mimi's American Bistro

$$$ **Dupont Circle AMERICAN**

Remember when you were a kid and the gang would get together and say "let's put on a show" or "let's play restaurant"? Well, Mimi's is kind of like that. The dark walls and tables suggest being backstage at a theater, and the waiters sing. Fortunately, they deliver pretty good food. For starters, I recommend the poached pear salad with apple, honey roasted walnuts, cheese, greens, and cranberry vinaigrette. At the end, the Key lime pie is refreshing, the chocolate soufflé tasty. In between, your choices range from sandwiches to steak. Nightly specials and vegetarian options always grace the menu.

See map p. 129. 2120 P St. NW (between 21st and 22nd streets). ☎ **202-464-6464.** www.mimisdc.com. *Reservations suggested. Metro: Dupont Circle. From the Dupont Circle exit, walk clockwise around the circle to P, then 2½ blocks west. Main courses: $15–$24. Sandwiches: $8–$10. AE, DC, DISC, MC, V. Open: Mon–Thurs 11:30 a.m.–11 p.m., Fri–Sat 11:30 a.m.–midnight, Sun 11 a.m.–midnight.*

The Monocle

$$$$ **Capitol Hill AMERICAN**

A stone's throw from the Senate office buildings, the Monocle is an old-style Washington institution. If you're a regular viewer of C-SPAN or CNN, you'll recognize some of the faces you see here (or at least the photos on the walls). John Kerry was a regular before he began his ultimately unsuccessful run in the 2004 presidential campaign and spent most of his life on the road. Now that he's back as a rank-and-file senator, you may bump into him here again. The Monocle staff is solicitous. Steak, lobster, and crab cakes are popular items. The pork rib chop with pommery mustard sauce is especially good. At lunch, go for the hamburger. Not surprisingly, the menu also has a good selection of martinis.

See map p. 126. 107 D St. NE (between 1st and 2nd streets). ☎ *202-546-4488.* www. themonocle.com. *Reservations recommended. Metro: Union Station. From the Union Station Shops/Massachusetts Avenue exit, walk counter-clockwise around the circle to 1st Street NE, then right 1 block to D, then turn left. Main courses: $16–$30. AE, DC, MC, V. Open: Mon–Fri 11:30 a.m.–midnight. Closed two weeks before Labor Day.*

Montmartre
$$$ Capitol Hill   FRENCH

Just a few blocks from the House office buildings and the U.S. Capitol, this little restaurant reminds you of what you love about Paris. Appearances outside and in — including the sidewalk cafe — suggest a modest eatery on some French side street. The food tastes that way, too. The waitress doesn't speak clear English, but she does deliver a mean basket of crispy-crusted French bread. From then on, you have to choose, and I suggest a wonderful salad of endive, walnuts, and blue cheese to start. The sautéed cod with garlic mashed potatoes makes for a homey main course, and the roasted salmon with leeks and risotto tastes pretty darn good, too. For dessert, there's no contest. If it's offered, grab the berry tart.

See map p. 126. 327 7th St. SE (between Pennsylvania Avenue and C Street). ☎ *202-544-1244.* www.montmartre.us. *Reservations recommended. Metro: Eastern Market. Walk across Pennsylvania on 7th. Main courses: $11–$20. AE, DC, DISC, MC, V. Open: Tues–Thurs 11:30 a.m.–2:30 p.m. and 5:30–10 p.m., Fri–Sat 11:30 a.m.–2:30 p.m. and 5:30–10:30 p.m., Sun 11:30 a.m.–2:30 p.m. and 5:30–9 p.m.*

Nooshi
$ Downtown   ASIAN

When the popular Oodles Noodles added sushi, it morphed into Nooshi. It still has an inventive array of Pan Asian noodle dishes such as *mee goreng* — a spicy marriage of Malaysian and Indian-style noodles with vegetables — as well as dishes sans noodles, such as chicken with basil, which you can have prepared mild or spicy. The sushi menu is large and reasonably priced. Other popular dishes include drunken noodles (with stir-fried minced chicken in basil, pepper, and onion sauce), spring rolls, and chicken *satay* (with slightly spicy peanut sauce). The décor is sophisticated, and so is the presentation. Be sure to arrive early. At midday, office workers grab all the tables.

See map p. 126. 1120 19th St. NW (between L and M streets). ☎ *202-293-3138. Reservations accepted for seven or more. Metro: Farragut North, exit west side. From L Street, walk 2 blocks to 19th and turn right. Main courses: $8–$13. Sushi servings: $3–$13. AE, DC, DISC, MC, V. Open: Mon–Sat 11:30 a.m.–11 p.m., Sun 4:30–10 p.m.*

Obelisk
$$$$$ Dupont Circle   ITALIAN

Handmade pasta, fresh ingredients, and a fine wine list are hallmarks of this tiny Dupont Circle trattoria that's up a flight of steps along P Street. So is a knowledgeable and attentive staff. The décor is simple. The fixed-price menu features several choices for each of the five courses. The best table in the house sits at a window overlooking the street.

See map p. 129. 2029 P St. NW (between 20th and 21st streets). ☎ *202-872-1180. Reservations recommended. Metro: Dupont Circle. From the Q Street exit, walk south on 20th to P and turn right. Fixed-price dinner: $60. D, MC, V. Open: Tues–Sat 6–10 p.m.*

The Occidental
$$$$$ Downtown   AMERICAN

The Occidental quite likely fits your image of a Washington power hangout. Two blocks from the White House, it projects an old-fashioned atmosphere with its dark wood paneling, classic bar, and spacious booths. The walls are covered with more than 2,000 autographed photos of Occidental diners, from Buffalo Bill Cody through Huey Long and various Kennedys up to Oprah Winfrey and contemporary politicians. The dining rooms (above the grill is a more formal room with the same menu) were opened in 1986, but the restaurant traces its roots on essentially the same site to 1906. The Occidental had been known for steak and lobster, which remain on the menu. But when Chef Rodney Scruggs took over in 2005, he started tempting diners with such offerings as she-crab soup, wild mushroom ravioli, and a lamb salad. You can spend a lot less for a hamburger or other sandwich at lunch and still soak up the atmosphere.

See map p. 126. 1475 Pennsylvania Ave. NW (in the Willard Hotel complex between 14th and 15th streets). ☎ *202-783-1475.* www.occidentaldc.com. *Reservations recommended. Metro: Metro Center. From the F and 12th streets exit, walk 2 blocks east on F to 14th, then turn left 1 block to Pennsylvania, and then turn right. Main courses: $22–$39. AE, DC, MC, V. Open: Mon–Thurs 11:30 a.m.–10 p.m., Fri 11:30 a.m.–10:30 p.m., Sat 5–10:30 p.m.*

The Oceanaire Seafood Room
$$$$ Downtown   SEAFOOD

This is a festive place that's an especially good restaurant for larger parties. It also just happens to serve good seafood. Many people walk into Oceanaire and feel as if they've stepped onto the set of a 1930s movie. The menu evokes that earlier age, and the restaurant was designed to suggest a 1930s ocean liner. The teens, however, debated whether they were supposed to be inside a ship — or under water, because of the fish mounted on the walls and the blue cast to the lighting. However you interpret the décor, oyster lovers can choose among a dozen varieties. The crab cakes are nearly all meat. The fried foods are tops. It's hard to go wrong ordering the fresh fish broiled. Portions are large — for sharing or taking home for another meal.

See map p. 126. 1201 F St. NW (west of 12th Street). ☎ *202-347-2277.* www.the
oceanaire.com/DC. *Reservations recommended. Metro: Metro Center. From the
F and 12th streets exit, look across the street. Main courses: $19–$40. AE, DISC, MC,
V. Hours: Mon–Thurs 11:30 a.m.–10 p.m., Fri 11:30 a.m.–11 p.m., Sat 5–11 p.m., and
Sun 5–9 p.m.*

Old Ebbitt Grill
$$$ Downtown   AMERICAN

Before we moved to Washington, one of my favorite places to visit here
was the Old Ebbitt Grill, ensconced in a narrow, 19th-century building that
made you feel like Teddy Roosevelt might walk through the door. That
building was demolished in 1983, and the restaurant moved into new digs
just around the corner from the White House. The new Old Ebbitt is a large,
handsome establishment that evokes older times with mahogany, velvet,
marble, and brass, as well as collections of antique steins, hunting tro-
phies, and decoys. This place is a lunchtime and after-work gathering place
for folks employed in the area — including White House staffers — so
many customers order burgers and other bar fare. But the diverse menu
changes daily, featuring what's fresh from local farmers, and there's a sub-
stantial oyster bar. For me, the highlight of one visit — other than spotting
Newt Gingrich with his most recent wife — was superb strawberry short-
cake with whipped cream. The Virginia farm that produced the berries was
credited on the menu. The staff tends to be friendly and nice to kids, and
many kid-friendly items are on the menu — from the very good burgers to
finger-food appetizers.

See map p. 126. 675 15th St. NW (between F and G streets). ☎ *202-347-4800.*
www.ebbitt.com. *Reservations recommended. Metro: Metro Center. Take the 13th
Street exit. Walk 2 blocks west on G and then turn left at 15th. Main courses: $8–$24
(hamburger–steak, respectively). AE, DC, DISC, MC, V. Open: Mon–Fri 7:30 a.m.–1
a.m., Sat–Sun 8:30 a.m.–1 a.m.*

The Palm
$$$$ Dupont Circle   STEAKHOUSE

This is the ultimate old-school Washington power place, even though it's
part of a chain that originated in New York. The walls are covered with
autographed caricatures of Palm patrons past and present, many of whom
will be familiar to you. And you can spot regulars seated at their favorite
tables as easily as you can find them painted upon the walls. (Think Larry
King, James Carville, Tim Russert, and George Bush the First.) One time
Susan was here with an out-of-town companion, and no sooner finished
describing the place as a celebrity magnet when Carville walked in. The
Palm has billed itself as "the place to see and be seen," and that certainly
is true. It's also the place to eat large steaks (how about a 36-ounce New
York strip for two?) and large lobsters (3 pounds or more at market price).
The strip steaks and lobsters are top-notch, by the way, and the fried
onions and creamed spinach come highly recommended as well.

See map p. 129. 1225 19th St. NW (between M and N streets). ☎ *202-293-9091.*
www.thepalm.com. *Reservations recommended. Metro: Dupont Circle. From the*

Dupont Circle exit, walk 1½ blocks south on 19th. Main courses: $18–$41 (pasta–prime rib, respectively). AE, DC, MC, V. Hours: Mon–Fri 11:45 a.m.–10:30 p.m., Sat 5:30–10:30 p.m., and Sun 5:30–9:30 p.m.

Pizzeria Paradiso
$$ Dupont Circle/Georgetown PIZZA

Pizzeria Paradiso is so popular — because it's so good — that the original Dupont Circle spot spawned an offspring restaurant in Georgetown. Then the Georgetown location expanded into its downstairs, creating a beer and pizza parlor dubbed Birreria Paradiso. This is excellent pizza prepared in the traditional Neapolitan manner. The light, thin crust is baked in a wood-burning oven and topped with whatever you request. To taste real Neapolitan pizza, order the Margherita, which comes with tomato, basil, and mozzarella cheese. The Atomica is spicy, thanks to the hot pepper flakes combined with the tomato, salami, black olives, and mozzarella. Paradiso also serves sandwiches, salads, and desserts. And the Birreria offers 80 bottled beers and 17 on tap. But it's the pizza that sets Paradiso apart from Washington's other restaurants, with the exception of the similar 2 Amys in Upper Northwest. It's bustling and it serves pizza, so it's obviously a good place to take kids. It's also a good spot when you're looking for takeout. The restaurants are small — especially the tiny Dupont Circle original — and they don't take reservations. So it's wise to phone ahead to check the likely waiting time for a table.

See map p. 129. Dupont Circle: 2029 P St. NW (between 20th and 21st streets). ☎ 202-223-1245. www.eatyourpizza.com. Reservations not accepted. Metro: Dupont Circle. From the Q Street exit, walk 2 blocks south on 20th and then right on P. Georgetown (see map p. 131): 3282 M St. NW (west of Potomac Street). ☎ 202-337-1245. Take the Georgetown Connection Route 2 shuttle bus from the Dupont Circle or Rosslyn Metrorail station to M and Potomac or 33rd Street. Or hop a 30-series Metrobus to M Street and Wisconsin. Pizzas: $10–$17, more if you pile on the extra ingredients. DC, MC, V. Open: Mon–Thurs 11:30 a.m.–11 p.m., Fri–Sat 11:30 a.m.–midnight, Sun noon–10 p.m.

Poste
$$$$ Penn Quarter MODERN AMERICAN

I'm happy to report that Poste found a chef (Robert Weland) who could keep his job. That's a big deal for this extremely good-looking restaurant that seemed capable of enticing chefs into its kitchen but incapable of developing a long-term relationship. When Weland arrived here in May 2004 (from Guastavino's in New York), he became Poste's third chef since the restaurant's opening in July 2002. Poste occupies one of the most striking and historical spaces in the D.C. dining world — the mail-sorting room of the 1842 General Post Office which, after an 1859 expansion, housed the Tariff Commission. Sixteen feet above the floor is the original cast iron ceiling with skylights. Floor-to-ceiling cupboards, filled with cooking utensils, cover one wall. Another is hung with large mirrors. The plush booths provide comfortable seating, and you have the choice of outdoor tables in nice weather. The place can get noisy, and the trip to the bathroom becomes an adventure; you have to walk through the lobby of the adjacent Hotel Monaco, then climb the stairs or take the elevator to the second floor. As for the food, Weland prepares a seasonal menu, and he's so into freshness that he's put a greenhouse on the terrace so he can take herbs straight from the plant to the kitchen as he cooks. If it's on the menu, try the salmon poached in olive oil with horseradish and chives. If you like rabbit, this is the place to get it — braised in red wine with poppy seed egg noodles, caramelized fennel, and wild mushrooms. The Key lime tart makes for a refreshing dessert. If you're a crème brûlée aficionado, Poste's version is fabulous.

See map p. 126. 555 8th St. NW (between E and F streets). ☎ **202-783-6060.** www. postebrasserie.com. *Reservations recommended. Metro: Gallery Place/ Chinatown. From the 7th and F streets exit, walk 1 block south on 7th, then 1 block right on E, then turn right on 8th. Or take a shortcut through the hotel entrance at 700 F St. (between 7th and 8th). Main courses: $24–$28. AE, DC, DISC, MC, V. Open: Mon–Thurs 7–10 a.m., 11:30 a.m.–2:30 p.m., and 5–10 p.m.; Fri 7–10 a.m., 11:30 a.m.–2:30 p.m., and 5–10:30 p.m.; Sat 9 a.m.–4 p.m. and 5–10:30 p.m.; Sun 9 a.m.–4 p.m. and 5–9 p.m.*

The Prime Rib
$$$$$ Downtown STEAKHOUSE

If you want to visit the first half of the last century during your D.C. vacation, eat at Oceanaire one night and Prime Rib the next. At Prime Rib, the 1940s atmosphere comes from subdued lighting, black lacquered walls, brass trim, leather chairs and booths, tuxedoed waiters, a piano and bass playing supper club music after 7:30 p.m., and the requirement that gentlemen wear jacket and tie. The food is impeccable — prime beef, of course, but also a wide selection of seafood, plus a little lamb, pork, veal, and chicken. This place is called the Prime Rib for a reason, so you ought to have a good excuse for ordering something else. If you crave seafood, order the crab cake for your appetizer.

See map p. 126. 2020 K St. NW (between 20th and 21st streets). ☎ **202-466-8811.** www.theprimerib.com. *Reservations recommended. Metro: Farragut West. From the K Street exit, walk 3½ blocks west on K. Main courses: $20 (grilled chicken)–$44 (rib eye steak). AE, DC, MC, V. Open: Mon–Thurs 11:30 a.m.–3 p.m. and 5–11 p.m., Fri 11:30 a.m.–3 p.m. and 5–11:30 p.m., Sat 5–11:30 p.m.*

Rasika
$$$ Penn Quarter MODERN INDIAN

The food here is just plain wonderful. Executive Chef Vikram Sunderam — who came to Washington from his native India via London's Bombay Brasserie — insists he does traditional Indian cooking, deviating only by substituting fresh locally grown meats and produce for some traditional Indian ingredients. But there's clearly a creative touch in this chef's hands. The result — which the restaurant labels "modern Indian cuisine" — is quite pleasing. You can order a multicourse meal, with appetizer, salad, main course, and dessert. Or you and your dining companions can graze among Rasika's small-plate offerings. The *palak chaat* is a spectacular salad of crispy, deep-fried baby spinach, served with sweet yogurt and tamarind date chutney. The *tandoori* black cod is moist, tender, rich, and truly melts in your mouth. For dessert, pick the apple *jalebi,* which a fellow diner described as an Indian beignet. It's a crispy battered and deep-fried apple ring, topped with a sweet glaze and served warm with cardamom ice cream. Rasika also offers a three-course pre-theater menu for $28, a chef's tasting menu for $50 ($70 with paired wines), and a vegetarian tasting menu for $36 ($56 with the wines). Rasika's décor is modern, light, and airy, suggesting India with hanging silk panels and strings of glass beads. Lots of hard surfaces means the dining room can become noisy. The large windows along the front wall unfortunately look out on the loading docks of buildings across D Street.

See map p. 126. 633 D St. NW (between 6th and 7th streets). **202-637-1222.** www. RasikaRestaurant.com. *Reservations accepted. Metro: Archives/Navy Memorial/Penn Quarter. Walk north on 7th Street, then right on D. Main courses: $15–$28. Small plates: $3–$12. AE, DC, DISC, MC, V. Restaurant open: Mon–Thurs 11:30 a.m.–2:30 p.m. and 5:30–10:30 p.m., Fri 11:30 a.m.–2:30 p.m. and 5:30–11 p.m., Sat 5:30–11 p.m. Lounge serves light meals: Mon–Thurs 11:30 a.m.–11 p.m., Fri 11:30 a.m.–midnight, Sat 5:30 p.m.–midnight.*

Restaurant Nora
$$$$$ Dupont Circle   AMERICAN/ORGANIC

This is PC food for people with lots of organically grown greenbacks. Everything possible on Nora's menu is produced without chemicals, hormones, or other additives. Anything that's not certified organic is marked with an asterisk. Most likely, it's wild fish or foraged mushrooms, for which no certification exists. The water is triple-filtered to remove chlorine, bacteria, and metals. The coffee is purchased from small, farmer-owned cooperatives that grow their crops beneath the forest canopy to protect native trees and wildlife. Even the staff's shirts are made from organic yarn, and Nora strives to patronize winemakers who don't use chemicals in their vineyards. Oh, and did I say the food is sophisticated and delicious and that the dining room — decorated with antique quilts — is attractive and comfortable?

See map p. 129. 2132 Florida Ave. NW (north of R Street). ☎ **202-462-5143.** www. noras.com. *Reservations recommended. Metro: Dupont Circle. From the Q Street exit, walk 1 block north on Connecticut Avenue, then go left on R for 2 blocks, and then turn right on Florida. Main courses: $28–$35. Tasting menu: $75. Vegetarian tasting menu: $65. AE, MC, V. Open: Mon–Thurs 5:30–10 p.m., Fri–Sat 5:30–10:30 p.m.*

Sea Catch
$$$$ Georgetown   SEAFOOD

Hidden in the back end of a courtyard off 31st Street, between M Street and the C&O Canal, Sea Catch is a surprisingly large restaurant that offers an attractive place to eat good food year-round. In warm weather, tables on an outdoor terrace overlook the canal. When it's cold, you still can view the canal through floor-to-ceiling windows. Fireplaces in two of the dining rooms make this restaurant a pleasant and romantic place to dine when it's really cold. I especially like the front dining room, which has stone walls, windows facing onto the canal, wood paneling, ceiling beams, and one of those fireplaces. To start your meal here, try the mixed green salad topped with grapefruit, avocado, and crushed hazelnuts. You can't beat the crab cakes for your main course or appetizer. The lobster is quite good, too. If you like your tuna rare, Sea Catch holds that out as a signature dish. Susan's word for the crème brûlée here is "wonderful."

See map p. 131. 1054 31st St. NW (south of M Street at the C&O Canal). ☎ *202-337-8855.* www.seacatchrestaurant.com. *Reservations recommended. Take Georgetown Connection Route 2 shuttle bus from Dupont Circle or Rosslyn Metrorail station to M and 31st or Thomas Jefferson Street and then walk south on 31st and look for the courtyard on the right. Or take a 30-series Metrobus. Main courses: $22–$49 (grilled trout–crab-stuffed lobster, respectively). AE, DC, DISC, MC, V. Open: Mon–Sat noon–3 p.m. and 5:30–10 p.m., Sun 11 a.m.–3 p.m. and 5:30–9 p.m.*

Sette Osteria
$$$ Dupont Circle   ITALIAN

Sette Osteria is a popular haunt in bustling Dupont Circle. By fairly early in the evening, you're likely to find young professionals three-deep at the bar, standing, drinking, chatting, glancing at the large-screen TVs, and juggling slices of superb pizza from the wood-fired oven. This is a modern, airy, attractive restaurant that's full of hard surfaces: bare tables, bare walls, tile floors, and floor-to-ceiling windows onto R Street and Connecticut Avenue. Combined with the lively bar scene, this makes for a lot of noise — and, by the way, kid-friendliness — as a result. (On a recent visit we saw children in high chairs and an infant being passed from lap to lap around a table as the adults took turns eating.) Sette's pizzas boast a thin, chewy crust under excellent toppings. Sharing one is a great way to start your meal. I really like the *pizza ai funghi,* which is topped with mushrooms, mozzarella, and tomato. Other good choices include the four-cheese pizza and the *salsiccia e cime di rapa,* which is topped with mozzarella, pork sausage, chili peppers, and broccoli rabe. For the main course, I highly recommend the *cavatelli* pasta with mild Italian sausage, broccoli rabe, and pecorino cheese. If you like gnocchi — many people find this pasta too dense and pasty — Sette's *gnocchi alla Sorrentina* is served in a fine sauce of tomato, mozzarella, and basil.

Sette doesn't take reservations. To avoid a wait, arrive by 6 or 6:30.

See map p. 129. 1666 Connecticut Ave. NW (at R Street). ☎ *202-483-3070.* www.sette osteria.com. *Reservations not accepted. Metro: Dupont Circle. From the Q Street exit, walk 2 blocks north to R. Pizza: $10–$13, more if you pile on extra toppings. Main courses: $11–$19. AE, DC, DISC, MC, V. Open: Mon–Thurs 11:30 a.m.–1 a.m., Fri–Sat 11:30 a.m.–2 a.m., Sun 11:30 a.m.–midnight.*

1789 Restaurant

$$$$$ Georgetown   AMERICAN

Washington gastronomes held their collective breath when Executive Chef Ris Lacoste turned in her toque at this Georgetown institution. Could a successor maintain 1789's status as one of D.C.'s very best restaurants for romance and special occasions? The answer, we now know, is "yes." Since commandeering the kitchen at the beginning of 2006, Nathan Beauchamp has preserved the best of 1789 while steadily putting his own stamp on the place. You're still served by attentive, knowledgeable, tuxedoed waiters in long white aprons and busboys in white jackets. Male guests are still required to wear jackets, and everyone seems happy to dress up for the formal dining rooms anyway. The first-floor room with a fireplace is still the best spot to dine, especially if you're sharing a special meal with a significant other. When I first sampled Beauchamp's fare — with my significant other, by the way — Susan and I were blown away from the start by the escargot in a crispy pastry shell with garlic-onion-mushroom purée. The crab soup was a light broth with generous helpings of lump crabmeat, corn, scallions, and other vegetables. The moist pork chop was accompanied by tasty/sweet greens. The dessert pastries — mine lemon, Susan's peach — were equally appealing. Beauchamp offers a three-course, pre- and post-theater menu for $35 and a five-course tasting menu for $65. The restaurant, which takes its name from the birth year of the United States government and Georgetown University, occupies a 19th-century Federal-style house. It's decorated with antiques and historical prints. It's the opposite of hip and attracts a lot of older diners. But younger folks come, too, for the romantic setting — and superb food.

See map p. 131. 1226 36th St. NW (north of Prospect Street). ☎ *202-965-1789.* www.1789restaurant.com. *Reservations recommended. From the Dupont Circle or Rosslyn Metrorail station, take the Georgetown Connection Route 2 shuttle bus to M and 33rd or 34th streets, walk up the hill 1 block on 33rd or 34th, then walk left on Prospect, and then turn right on 36th. Or take a taxi. Main courses: $23–$38. AE, DC, DISC, MC, V. Open: Mon–Thurs 6–10 p.m., Fri 6–11 p.m., Sat 5:30–11 p.m., Sun 5:30–10 p.m.*

Tabard Inn

$$$ Dupont Circle   MODERN AMERICAN

This is one of my wife's favorite Washington restaurants — for the setting as much as for the food. It truly is an inn, with sleeping, eating, and drinking facilities scattered among three adjoining town houses near Dupont Circle. The dining rooms are comfortable and lively at meal times. You can have a drink by the fireplace in the winter and dine in the garden when it's warm. Chef Pedro Matamoros worked at the Tabard under two previous, well-regarded, chefs — David Craig and Andrew Saba. Though Matamoros is a native of Nicaragua with a special interest in French and Italian cuisine, he is keeping alive the Tabard's tradition of Modern American cooking, with changing seasonal menus and an emphasis on fresh local ingredients. The seafood dishes always have tended to be the best here.

See map p. 129. 1739 N St. NW (between 17th and 18th streets). ☎ *202-833-2668.*
www.tabardinn.com/rest.htm. *Reservations recommended. Metro: Dupont
Circle. From the Dupont Circle exit, walk south on Connecticut Avenue 1 block and
then turn left on N and cross 18th. Main courses: $19–$26. AE, DISC, MC, V. Hours:
Mon–Thurs 7–10 a.m., 11:30 a.m.–2:30 p.m., and 6–9:30 p.m.; Fri 7–10 a.m., 11:30
a.m.–2:30 p.m., and 6–10 p.m.; Sat 8–9:30 a.m., 11:30 a.m.–2:30 p.m., and 6–10 p.m.;
Sun 8–9:30 a.m., 10:30 a.m.–2:30 p.m., and 6–9 p.m.*

The Tombs
$$ Georgetown   AMERICAN

Bill Clinton ate and drank in this basement pub, as has nearly every other
student who has wandered the halls of Georgetown University since 1962.
Faculty and townsfolk frequent the place, too. It is, on the one hand, a col-
lege tavern. But it's an unusually good-looking and well-maintained one.
And the food is quite good, too, thanks to the Tombs' relationship with the
fabulous 1789 Restaurant upstairs. The crab cakes are superb — sweet,
moist, and perfectly seasoned. The veggie burger is fat and juicy. The
french fries are sublime — tasty, salty, crisp on the outside, moist in the
middle. The waiters automatically refill your iced tea and soft drinks as
well as your coffee.

See map p. 131. 1226 36th St. NW (north of Prospect Street). ☎ *202-337-6668.*
www.tombs.com. *Reservations not accepted. From the Dupont Circle or Rosslyn
Metrorail station, take the Georgetown Connection Route 2 shuttle bus to M and 33rd
or 34th streets, walk up the hill 1 block on 33rd or 34th, then walk left on Prospect, and
then turn right on 36th. Or take a taxi. Main courses: $9–$15. Sandwiches: $7–$13.
AE, DC, DISC, MC, V. Hours: Mon–Thurs 11:30 a.m.–11 p.m., Fri 11:30 a.m.–midnight,
Sat 11 a.m.–midnight, Sun 9:30 a.m.–11 p.m.*

Tony Cheng's
$$ Chinatown   CHINESE/SEAFOOD

Tony Cheng couldn't decide between fish and meat, so he put Tony
Cheng's Seafood Restaurant on the second floor of this Chinatown building and Tony Cheng's Mongolian Restaurant on the first. The Seafood
Restaurant is a bit of a misnomer, because you can order poultry, beef,
pork, and vegetarian dishes there as well. But the seafood is the specialty,
and it always pays to check what's fresh, including what's swimming in the
tank. Downstairs, you pick your own ingredients for two different meth-
ods of cooking. Choose meats and vegetables for the chefs to sear quickly
on the grill. Or pick vegetables, meats, and seafood that you cook yourself
in a pot of boiling stock at your table. You finish the meal by eating the flavorful stock.

See map p. 126. 619 H St. NW (between 6th and 7th streets). ☎ *202-371-8669.
Reservations accepted. Metro: Gallery Place-Chinatown. Take the 7th and H streets
exit. Walk a half block east on H. Main courses: $11–$20. AE, MC, V. Open: Sun–Thurs
11 a.m.–11 p.m., Fri–Sat 11 a.m.–midnight.*

2 Amys
$$ **Upper Northwest** **PIZZA**

This is real Neapolitan pizza, particularly the "pizze d.o.c." offerings, which follow the recipes of the Italian government's *"denominazione di origine controllata"* regulations. The pizzas here have thin, chewy crusts. I like the d.o.c. Margherita, named after Italy's first queen and topped with tomato sauce, cheese, and basil. A Margherita "extra" enhances the flavor with whole, sweet, fresh cherry tomatoes. The d.o.c. versions are meatless, with fewer toppings than many Americans like. You can design your own pie from a list of two dozen toppings if you prefer. Be sure to sample the side dishes, such as the *polpettini al forno* (meatballs), *suppli a telefono* (breaded rice balls stuffed with cheese and fried), and deviled eggs with pesto sauce. The pizzas aren't big enough to make a shared meal, the way you're used to doing in a typical American pizzeria. But two can share a pizza when you add a couple of the sides or a salad. The restaurant is cheery, with shiny black-and-white tile and sunny paint on the walls. The décor makes for noise, which is one reason it's kid-friendly. Other reasons include the food, the highchairs, and the cheerful staff. For big folk, there's a wine bar in one corner.

See map p. 126. 3715 Macomb St. NW (just west of Wisconsin Avenue near Washington National Cathedral). ☎ *202-885-5700.* www.marketing-specialists.com/ 2Amysindex.htm. *Reservations not accepted. Metro: Tenleytown. Then take a 30-series Metrobus south on Wisconsin. Or take a 30-series bus from anywhere on its route. Or catch a cab. Pizzas: $8–$13, more if you add lots of ingredients. Sides and salads: $4–$6.75. MC, V. Open: Mon 5–10 p.m., Tues–Wed 11 a.m.–10 p.m., Thurs–Sat 11 a.m.–11 p.m., Sun noon–10 p.m.*

Vidalia
$$$$ **Downtown** **AMERICAN/SOUTHERN**

Maybe it's because I like jazz clubs, but it's never bothered me that Vidalia is located below street level. Others, however, seem to hesitate at the top of the stairs. So let me reassure you that at the bottom you find a cheerful restaurant with good food. Vidalia brought modern Southern cooking to Washington as Arkansan Bill Clinton was moving into the White House in the early 1990s. Proprietor/chef Jeffrey Buben calls Vidalia's cooking "American cuisine with a subtle southern influence." That means five-onion soup for an appetizer, shrimp and grits for the main course, and Georgia pecan pie with bourbon caramel sauce, vanilla bean ice cream, and a crisp praline chocolate cookie for dessert, for example. When Buben puts more emphasis on the modern, he comes up with dishes such as Tasmanian sea trout wrapped in phyllo with herb butter, crisp pork belly, honey cap mushrooms, beluga lentils, and pinot noir essence.

See map p. 126. 1990 M St. NW (between 19th and 20th streets). ☎ *202-659-1990.* www.vidaliadc.com. *Reservations recommended. Metro: Dupont Circle. From the Dupont Circle exit, walk 2 blocks south on 19th and then turn right on M. Main courses: $26–$33. AE, DC, DISC, MC, V. Open: Mon–Thurs 11:30 a.m.–2:30 p.m. and 5:30–10 p.m., Fri 11:30 a.m.–2:30 p.m. and 5:30–10:30 p.m., Sat 5:30 p.m.–10:30 p.m., Sun 5:30–10 p.m.*

Zaytinya
$$ Penn Quarter   MEDITERRANEAN

The worst thing about Zaytinya is that you can make reservations only for lunch and from 5:30 to 6:30 p.m. when patrons can be assured of a table before they head off to a nearby theater. This popular spot fills up rapidly after that. So the best solution may be to arrive here around 6:30 and then linger over several rounds of Mediterranean *mezes* (small plates) while enjoying the view of the bustling street scene outside the floor-to-ceiling windows. This strategy is especially good in spring or autumn, when you can watch night fall outside and the dining room become warmed by soft lighting inside. This stunningly attractive, modern restaurant is two stories high in the main dining room, with dark wood tables and chairs, white walls, and tiers of candles that cast soft light from the wall opposite the windows. Entrees are on the menu, but you should pass on them and let your waiter help you select *mezes* to share. If you're a vegetarian, you'll be pleased to note that 70 percent of these dishes were made for you. The *kolokithokeftedes* (zucchini-cheese patties) are light and tasty, fried crisp on the outside but creamy within. A nice alternative to the cooked *mezes* comes from one of the two salads that are based on tomatoes, cucumbers, red onions, and green peppers. Chef José Andrés is especially proud of the *manty nejla,* little pastas stuffed with beef in a yogurt sauce. The preparation is so labor-intensive that it can't turn a profit, he said, but it belongs on the menu as a statement of the restaurant's intentions.

See map p. 126. 701 9th St. NW (north of G Street). ☎ *202-638-0800.* www. zaytinya.com. *Reservations accepted only for lunch and 5:30–6:30 p.m. Metro: Gallery Place/Chinatown. From the 9th and G streets exit, look for the building with two stories of floor-to-ceiling windows and the big sign over the door that says "Zaytinya." Mezes: $4.50–$12. AE, DC, DISC, MC, V. Open: Sun–Mon 11:30 a.m.–10 p.m., Tues–Thurs 11:30 a.m.–11:30 p.m., Fri–Sat 11:30 a.m.–midnight.*

Dining and Snacking on the Go

Washington is full of workaholics who eat at their desks and tourists who eat on the run, so the city is full of places where you can grab snacks and light meals. Because Washington has so many parks — from huge expanses like the National Mall to small green areas suitable for alfresco dining scattered all around town — getting picnic food to go is a great idea.

Quick and cheap

Because of office workers downtown, you'll find an inexpensive lunch spot on nearly ever corner and at many points mid-block. Elsewhere, they're not as common. But you'll be hard-pressed to find a neighborhood that doesn't have a few modest eateries that are quick and cheap.

One of my favorites goes by the nonsense name **Booeymonger** (3265 Prospect St. NW at Potomac Street in Georgetown, ☎ **202-333-4810;** and 5252 Wisconsin Ave. NW at Jenifer Street near the D.C.-Maryland border in Upper Northwest, ☎ **202-686-5805**). The Wisconsin Avenue deli is a Price family hangout, because it's just a few blocks from home, the eat-in and takeout service is fast, and the food is good. (We've got Booeymonger frequent-eater cards!) My wife has a thing for the Manhattan — roast beef, spinach, bacon, cheddar cheese, and dressing on a baguette — and the carrot cake. In delis, I tend to go for hot pastrami on rye with mustard. When in a healthy mood, however, I order Booey's Pita Pan, a veggie and cheese sandwich. The menu has lots of sandwiches, salads, and sides to choose from (some with silly names), and you can get a full breakfast in the morning. The Georgetown Booey is open from 8 a.m. to midnight daily, the Wisconsin Booey is open from 7:30 a.m. to 1 a.m.

Another place I like a lot is **Chipotle** (1837 M St. NW, ☎ **202-466-4104**; 3255 M St. NW, ☎ **202-333-8377**; 1629 Connecticut Ave. NW, ☎ **202-387-8261**; 2600 Connecticut Ave. NW, ☎ **202-299-9111**; 4301 Wisconsin Ave. NW, ☎ **202-237-0602**; 601 F St. NW, ☎ **202-347-4701**; and 4771 Willard Ave., in the Friendship Heights shopping district, ☎ **301-654-6661**). I know it's a chain, but it's much more attractive — and the food is much better — than the typical fast-food joint. Burritos and tacos are made fresh as you order them in the cafeteria line and instruct the cooks on which ingredients you want. And you can grab a beer or margarita to quench your thirst.

Coffee shops

Besides a zillion branches of a certain Seattle coffee empire, Washingtonians have many sources for their caffeine fixes.

One of the most interesting is **Kramerbooks & Afterwords Cafe** (1517 Connecticut Ave. NW, just above Dupont Circle; ☎ **202-387-1400**). Bookish coffee spillers have been gathering at the cafe inside this bookstore since long before the national chains discovered how to sell food and drink with reading materials. You can get a caffeine or lit fix here just about any time you need one, because this place is open Monday through Thursday from 7:30 a.m. to 1 a.m., and 'round the clock from 7:30 a.m. Friday to 1 a.m. Monday.

The local chain of **Firehook Bakery & Coffeehouse** (1909 Q St. NW at Connecticut Ave., ☎ **202-588-9296**; 912 17th St. NW between I and K streets, ☎ **202-429-2253**; 441 4th St. NW between D and E streets, ☎ **202-347-1760**; 3411 Connecticut Ave. NW between Newark and Ordway streets, ☎ **202-362-2253**; 215 Pennsylvania Ave. SE between 2nd and 3rd streets, ☎ **202-544-7003**; 555 13th St. NW between E and F streets, ☎ **202-393-0952**; in the National Building Museum, 401 F St. NW at 4th Street; and in the Phillips collection, 1600 21st St. NW at Q Street) provides a great fix of fresh-made pastries and locally roasted coffee. Firehook makes the pastries and sells Quartermaine coffee, which is roasted nearby in suburban Maryland. Except for the museum locations, which operate according to the museums' schedules, the shops open at

Dining and Snacking on the Go

Atrium Café **30**
Ben & Jerry's **29, 37, 41**
Booeymonger **1, 7**
Bread & Chocolate **3, 14, 40**
Cafe Berlin **38**
Cascade Cafe **33**
Cheesecake Factory **1**
Ching Ching Cha **10**
Chipotle **1, 3, 8, 16, 21, 35**
Cold Stone Creamery **3**
Dean & Deluca **9**
Dolcezza Argentine Gelato Cafe **5**
Firehook Bakery **3, 15, 17, 22, 27, 34, 36, 39**
Fossil Cafe **30**
Garden Cafe **33**
Garden Terrace Lounge **12**
Gifford's **1, 28**
Häagen Dazs **37**
Kramerbooks & Afterwords **19**
Kron Chocolatier **1**
Lafayette Room **23**
Luna Grill and Diner **20**
Mezza Café **31**
Mitsitam Café **32**
Old Ebbitt Grill **24**
Park Hyatt Washington **13**
Pavilion Cafe **33**
Sky Terrace **25**
Smithsonian Jazz Café **30**
Sweet Licks **18**
Terrace Café **33**
Thomas Sweet **6**
Washington Harbour **11**
Washington National Cathedral **2**
Willard Room **26**
Wright Place **31**

6:30 a.m. weekdays. Some close on weekends. Call the location you're interested in for specifics.

Breakfast spots

To check out the power breakfast scene, head for a hotel dining room near the White House or Capitol. The **Lafayette Room** at the Hay-Adams (1 Lafayette Sq. at 16th and H streets NW; ☎ **202-638-6600**) and the **Willard Room** at the Willard InterContinental (1401 Pennsylvania Ave. NW between 14th and 15th streets; ☎ **202-628-9100**) are good places to start. So is the **Old Ebbitt Grill** (675 15th St. NW between F and G streets; ☎ **202-347-4800**).

At **Kramerbooks & Afterwords Cafe** (1517 Connecticut Ave. NW, just north of Dupont Circle; ☎ **202-387-1400**), you can crack a book with your soft-boiled egg.

If you want to jump-start *your* engine, not the economy's, try the **Luna Grill and Diner** (1301 Connecticut Ave. NW at N Street; ☎ **202-835-2280**). Another place for a fast, cheap — and good — breakfast is at **Booeymonger** (3265 Prospect St. NW at Potomac Street in Georgetown, ☎ **202-333-4810;** and 5252 Wisconsin Ave. NW at Jenifer Street in Upper Northwest, ☎ **202-686-5805**).

Tea for two (or one)

The United States has come a long way since the Boston Tea Party. Instead of throwing it into the harbor, Americans now drink it in great quantities. In Washington, several hotels are doing their part to perpetuate the upper-crust British tradition of high tea. In this context, *high tea* is a light meal with small, trimmed sandwiches (no crusts!), little cakes, and — of course — pots of fresh-brewed tea.

If you take high tea, you can pass on a big meal at dinnertime and opt for a snack later in the evening.

Get fancy and refined at the Four Seasons Hotel (2800 Pennsylvania Ave. NW at 28th Street; ☎ **202-342-0444**). Soak up the view of Rock Creek Park from the **Garden Terrace Lounge** and nibble on finger sandwiches, breads, tartlets, scones with Devonshire cream, fresh-brewed tea, and a nip of sherry (for medicinal purposes only). Teatime is 2 to 5 p.m. daily. Wednesday through Sunday, a pianist performs.

You can learn Chinese tea ritual at **Ching Ching Cha** (1063 Wisconsin Ave. NW near the C&O Canal in Georgetown; ☎ **202-333-8288**). The setting is serene and enhanced by classical Chinese music. The parlor lists more than two dozen teas from China and Taiwan, plus meals, snacks, and desserts. You also can purchase loose tea to take home. The restaurant is open Tuesday through Saturday from 11:30 a.m. to 9 p.m. and Sunday from 11:30 a.m. to 7 p.m.

Treating fine tea like fine wine, the **Park Hyatt Washington** (24th and M streets NW; ☎ 202 419 6755) has opened a "tea cellar" and offers rare teas that can sell for several hundred dollars a pot. (Others go for considerably less). Teas are available all day, tea with pastries daily 2:30 to 4:30 p.m.

You can tour and take tea at the **Washington National Cathedral** (Massachusetts and Wisconsin avenues NW; ☎ 202-537-8993) on Tuesdays and Wednesdays, except for some holidays. The tour starts at 1:30 p.m. inside the West Entrance on Wisconsin and finishes high up in the Pilgrim Observation Gallery, where you can gaze through arched windows at the city and beyond. Cost is $22 per person. Reservations are required — often far in advance — and are accepted up to six months ahead of time.

Where to find picnic supplies

Visitors intent on cramming in a lot of sights often prefer quick bites to spending an hour or two in a restaurant. Most delis and coffee shops — as well as many full-service restaurants — gladly pack your order to go.

Don't think of this to-go service as just fast food, however. Think of it as a picnic. You can find park benches all over the place, as well as many small park areas. I particularly like Lafayette Square, across Pennsylvania Avenue from the White House, and you can find lots of room on the Mall and around the Tidal Basin. (I'll pray for the pigeons and squirrels to leave you alone. You can do your part by not feeding them.)

Dean & Deluca's Georgetown shop (3276 M St. NW, east of 33rd Street; ☎ 202-342-2500) is a great place to put together a picnic. It offers a wide selection of sandwiches, salads, and desserts, as well as gourmet groceries. It's open daily from 10 a.m. to 8 p.m. You can picnic in Dean & Deluca's outdoor cafe, take your food south of M to the C&O Canal National Park, or go further south to the Georgetown waterfront.

Another option is to get food to go at the **Smithsonian museums,** then take it outside to eat on the Mall.

 You can find good, basic sandwich shops throughout the city — several per block in many places. Among those that I can vouch for, should you pass them in your wanderings, are **Au Bon Pain, Booeymonger, Bread & Chocolate, Chipotle, Corner Bakery, Firehook Bakery, La Madeleine, Vie de France,** and the **Wall Street Deli** — all with multiple locations.

Chocolates and sweets

Does your sweet tooth need a fix? Head for **Bread & Chocolate** (666 Pennsylvania Ave. SE, between 6th and 7th streets, on Capitol Hill, ☎ 202-547-2875; 2301 M St. NW, in the West End, ☎ 202-833-8360; or 5542 Connecticut Ave. NW, at Morrison Street, in Upper Northwest, ☎ 202-966-7413). This bakery/restaurant makes marvelous pastries.

Sample the strudels, tortes, and pies at **Cafe Berlin** (322 Massachusetts Ave. NE, east of 3rd Street; ☎ 202-543-7656), also located on the Hill.

Back in Upper Northwest, buy a cheesecake at the **Cheesecake Factory** (5345 Wisconsin Ave. NW, between Jenifer Street and Western Avenue; ☎ 202-364-0500). Choose among 35 varieties of calorie-laden, artery-clogging cheesecakes — or a bunch of other sweets. (You may find a slice too rich to consume in one sitting and want to share with your companions. I can't imagine why.) **Kron Chocolatier** (5300 Wisconsin Ave. NW; ☎ 202-966-4946) is across the street in the Mazza Gallerie. This shop sells all manner of world-class chocolate. Try the chocolate-dipped strawberries.

We all scream for ice cream

Washington's gone kind of ice-cream crazy, with lots of shops, many of them local, some of them unusual.

At the **Cold Stone Creamery** (3508 Connecticut Ave. NW, north of Ordway Street in Upper Northwest; ☎ 202-237-2605), you pick your ice cream flavor and goodies to mix into it — candy bar chunks, for example, or hot fudge sauce. The clerk scoops the ice cream onto a cold stone (natch) and then mashes your additives into it.

For another unique treat, check out **Dolcezza Argentine Gelato Cafe** (1560 Wisconsin Ave. NW, at Q Street in Georgetown; ☎ 202-333-4646). Here you get Argentinean ice cream, which is extra creamy and rich. For traditional U.S. ice cream in Georgetown, head for **Thomas Sweet** (3214 P St. NW, east of Wisconsin Avenue; ☎ 202-337-0616).

If the ice cream craving strikes you at Dupont Circle, walk on up to **Sweet Licks** (1704 R St. NW, west of 17th Street; ☎ 202-797-2736).

Gifford's, a locally made ice cream presence in the D.C. area since 1938, has shops in Penn Quarter (E and 10th streets NW; (☎ 202-347-7755) and Friendship Heights (21 Wisconsin Circle, just north of the intersection of Wisconsin and Western avenues NW; ☎ 301-652-8965).

On Capitol Hill, **Ben & Jerry's** (☎ 202-842-2887) and **Häagen-Dazs** (☎ 202-789-0953) both dish up their rich and creative flavors in Union Station. You'll also run into **Ben & Jerry's** at the Hill's Eastern Market (327 7th St. SE, between Pennsylvania Avenue and C Street; ☎ 202-546-2253) and Downtown in the Old Post Office Pavilion (1100 Pennsylvania Ave. NW, at 11th Street; ☎ 202-842-5882). Ben, Jerry, Häagen, and Dazs pop up in several other spots around town, as well.

Food court extraordinaire

The lower level of **Union Station** houses the largest and most diverse **food court** I've ever seen. Sure, you can buy hamburgers and pizzas, and if that's what the kids desire, that's fine. Those with more cosmopolitan tastes will want to take a stroll around the entire court before making their selections.

You can find the usual national chains, but also branches of local restaurants and a wide range of cuisines — Indian, Greek, Chinese, Cajun, Italian, barbecue, pizza, salads, pasta, sushi, deli items, baked goods, and gourmet coffee among the vast selection of edibles. If that doesn't satisfy you, you can take the escalator up to the next level, where other food establishments — from fast-food stands to full-serve restaurants — are scattered among the train gates and boutiques.

Meals on the Mall

You'll be spending lots of time in the museums along the National Mall — and trudging from one to the other. You can ease your hunger and quench your thirst in many of them. Some three million people eat in the Smithsonian Institution's cafeterias and restaurants each year. The food spots tend to be open when the museums are. All are happy to add to your American Express, Discover, MasterCard, or Visa bills.

The best place to eat on the Mall is the **Mitsitam Café** in the **National Museum of the American Indian.** I'm not talking relative to the mediocre offerings at most of the museums; I'm talking really good, Native American–inspired food, including sandwiches, entrees, soups, and desserts.

In addition to one of the world's great collections of fine art, the **National Gallery of Art** offers the next-best dining options on the Mall — the **Cascade Cafe** in the concourse between the East and West buildings, and the **Pavilion Cafe,** in the Sculpture Garden.

The Cascade Cafe with a view of a waterfall, is a large cafeteria with a wide choice of food. The dining area is bright and airy, the walls hung with prints from the gallery's collection. For $7.15, you can get one of the best dining deals in Washington — soup and half a big sandwich. I recommend the wild mushroom soup, which is spicy and rich. When I'm at the nearby D.C. courts building on jury duty — which, in Washington, comes every two years like clockwork — I often wander down here during lunch break.

The Pavilion Cafe is a glass-enclosed shelter in the Sculpture Garden. We stopped in one noon after a 7-inch snowfall, warmed ourselves with chili and tomato-herb bread, and gazed at the serene winter view outside. They hand out enormous salads here, and sandwiches so stuffed that a dining companion complained of the tuna salad sandwich: "There's too much tuna." In winter, you can sit inside and watch the ice skaters outside. In warm weather, you can eat at outdoor tables. Friday evenings from late May to mid-September, jazz groups perform here from 5 to 8:30 p.m.

Elsewhere in the gallery, you'll find an **espresso bar** that also serves *gelato, panini,* and sweets; the **Terrace Café,** overlooking the atrium, which offers salads, sandwiches, and desserts; and the **Garden Cafe,** which serves full meals à la carte or from a buffet. Susan likes the Garden Cafe for the setting, but I find the selection too small and the prices too large.

Here are your other options:

- **National Air and Space Museum:** The **Mezza Café** offers sandwiches, soups, and salads. The **Wright Place Food Court** is franchise village, with McDonald's, Donato's Pizza, and Boston Market. In nice weather, an outdoor kiosk sells snacks.

- **National Museum of Natural History:** At the **Fossil Cafe,** you can eat sandwiches, salads, and desserts at tables that are natural history exhibits themselves. The self-service **Atrium Café** offers fast foods. From 6 to 10 p.m. Fridays, you can eat, drink, and listen to live music at the **Smithsonian Jazz Café** for a $10 cover charge (kids 12 and younger free).

- **The Castle:** This cafe serves coffee, sandwiches, desserts, and snacks.

- **Hirshhorn Museum:** There's an outdoor cafe here from late spring through summer.

Drinks, with a view

Enjoy a cocktail while drinking in a primo view at the **Sky Terrace** of the Hotel Washington (515 15th St. NW, at Pennsylvania Avenue; ☎ 202-638-5900). Between May and October, this spot is a favorite for catching a sundowner. Keep it simple and stick to a cheese platter or a sandwich if you eat here. While you ogle the landscape, see how many buildings you can identify. You can almost peer into the East Wing of the White House.

For a view of the Potomac River — and of younger Washingtonians hustling for companionship of the opposite sex — mosey on down to Georgetown's **Washington Harbour** complex (3000 K Street, at Thomas Jefferson Street) on a warm evening. Grab a table at one of the outdoor watering holes, sip a drink, nibble on some appetizers, and watch the people strolling along the riverwalk, the boats sailing on the river, and the planes flying into and out of National Airport.

Index of Restaurants by Neighborhood

Union Station Food Court (Various Cuisines, $)

Chinatown
Eat First (Chinese, $$)
Tony Cheng's (Chinese, $$)

Downtown
Ben & Jerry's (Ice Cream)
Chipotle (Mexican, $)
Firehook Bakery (American, $)
Galileo (Italian, $$$$$)
Georgia Brown's (Southern, $$$$)
Lafayette Room (American, $$$$$)
Marrakesh (Moroccan, $$)
Nooshi (Asian, $)
The Occidental (American, $$$$$)
The Oceanaire Seafood Room (Seafood, $$$$)
Old Ebbitt Grill (American, $$$)
The Prime Rib (Steakhouse, $$$$$)
Sky Terrace (American, $$$)
Vidalia (American/Southern, $$$$$)
Willard Room (Modern American, $$$$$)

Dupont Circle
Bistrot Du Coin (French, $$$)
The Brickskeller (American, $$)
Chipotle (Mexican, $)
City Lights of China (Chinese, $$)
Firehook Bakery (American, $)
Hank's Oyster Bar (Seafood, $$$)
Kramerbooks & Afterwords (American, $$$)
Luna Grill & Diner (American, $$)
Malaysia Kopitiam (Malaysian, $$)
The Melting Pot (Fondue, $$$$)
Mimi's American Bistro (American, $$$)
Obelisk (Italian, $$$$$)
The Palm (Steakhouse, $$$$)
Pizzeria Paradiso (Pizza, $$)
Restaurant Nora (American/Organic, $$$$$)
Sette Osteria (Pizza/Italian, $$$)
Sweet Licks (Ice Cream)
Tabard Inn (Modern American, $$$)

Foggy Bottom/West End
Bread and Chocolate (American, $$)
Circle Bistro (Modern American, $$$)
Kinkead's (Seafood, $$$$)
Marcel's (French/Belgian, $$$$$)

Georgetown
Amma Indian Vegetarian Kitchen (Indian/Vegetarian, $)
Bistrot Lepic & Wine Bar (French, $$$)
Booeymonger (American, $)
Café La Ruche (French, $)
Ching Ching Cha (Chinese, $$)
Chipotle (Mexican, $)
Clyde's (American, $$)
Dean & Deluca (American, $$)
Dolcezza Argentine Gelato Cafe (Ice Cream)
Garden Terrace Lounge (American, $$$)
Garrett's (American, $$)
Harmony Cafe (Asian, $)
Martin's Tavern (American, $$$)
Michel Richard Citronelle (French/California, $$$$$)
Pizzeria Paradiso (Pizza, $$)
Sea Catch (Seafood, $$$$)
1789 Restaurant (American, $$$$$)
Thomas Sweet (Ice Cream)
The Tombs (American, $$)

Penn Quarter
Austin Grill (Southwestern, $$)
Café Atlántico (Latin American, $$$$)
Capital Q (Barbecue, $)
Clyde's (American, $$)
Jaleo (Spanish, $$)
Le Paradou (French, $$$$$)
Matchbox (Pizza/American, $$$)
Poste (Modern American, $$$$)
Rasika (Modern Indian, $$$)
Zaytinya (Mediterranean, $$)

Tidal Basin
CityZen (Modern American, $$$$$)

Upper Northwest

Austin Grill (Southwestern, $$)
Booeymonger (American, $)
Bread & Chocolate (American, $$)
Cheesecake Factory (American, $$$)
Chipotle (Mexican, $)
Clyde's (American, $$)

Cold Stone Creamery (Ice Cream)
Firehook Bakery (American, $)
Kron Chocolatier (Candy)
2 Amys (Pizza, $$)

U Street Corridor

Busboys and Poets (American, $$)

Index of Restaurants by Cuisine

American

Booeymonger (Georgetown/Upper Northwest, $)
Bread and Chocolate (Capitol Hill, West End, and Upper Northwest, $$)
The Brickskeller (Dupont Circle, $$)
Bullfeathers (Capitol Hill, $$)
Busboys and Poets (U Street Corridor, $$)
Cheesecake Factory (Upper Northwest, $$$)
Circle Bistro (Foggy Bottom/West End, $$$)
CityZen (Tidal Basin, $$$$$)
Clyde's (Georgetown, Penn Quarter, and Upper Northwest, $$)
Dean & Deluca (Georgetown, $$)
Firehook Bakery (Capitol Hill, Downtown, Dupont Circle, and Upper Northwest, $)
Garden Terrace Lounge (Georgetown, $$$)
Garrett's (Georgetown, $$)
Kramerbooks & Afterwords (Dupont Circle, $$$)
Lafayette Room (Downtown, $$$$$)
Luna Grill & Diner (Dupont Circle, $$)
Martin's Tavern (Georgetown, $$$)
Matchbox (Penn Quarter, $$$)
Mimi's American Bistro (Dupont Circle, $$$)
The Monocle (Capitol Hill, $$$$)
The Occidental (Downtown, $$$$$)
Old Ebbitt Grill (Downtown, $$$)
Poste (Penn Quarter, $$$$)
Restaurant Nora (Dupont Circle, $$$$$)
1789 Restaurant (Georgetown, $$$$$)

Sky Terrace (Downtown, $$$)
Tabard Inn (Dupont Circle, $$$)
The Tombs (Georgetown, $$)
Vidalia (Downtown, $$$$$)
Willard Room (Downtown, $$$$$)

Asian

Harmony Cafe (Georgetown, $)
Nooshi (Downtown, $)

Barbecue

Capital Q (Penn Quarter, $)

Brazilian

The Grill From Ipanema (Adams-Morgan, $$$)

Candy

Kron Chocolatier (Upper Northwest)

Chinese

Ching Ching Cha (Georgetown, $$)
City Lights of China (Dupont Circle, $$)
Eat First (Chinatown, $$)
Tony Cheng's (Chinatown, $$)

Fondue

The Melting Pot (Dupont Circle, $$$$)

French

Bistro Bis (Capitol Hill, $$$$)
Bistrot Du Coin (Dupont Circle, $$$)
Bistrot Lepic & Wine Bar (Georgetown, $$$)

Café La Ruche (Georgetown, $)
Le Paradou (Penn Quarter, $$$$$)
Marcel's (Foggy Bottom/West End,
$$$$$)
Michel Richard Citronelle
(Georgetown, $$$$$)
Montmartre (Capitol Hill, $$$)

German
Cafe Berlin (Capitol Hill, $$$)

Hamburgers
The Brickskeller (Dupont Circle, $$)
Bullfeathers (Capitol Hill, $$)
Clyde's (Georgetown, Penn Quarter,
and Upper Northwest, $$)
Old Ebbitt Grill (Downtown, $$$)

Ice Cream
Ben & Jerry's (Capitol Hill and
Downtown)
Cold Stone Creamery (Upper
Northwest)
Dolcezza Argentine Gelato Cafe
(Georgetown)
Häagen-Dazs (Capitol Hill)
Sweet Licks (Dupont Circle)
Thomas Sweet (Georgetown)

Indian
Amma Indian Vegetarian Kitchen
(Georgetown, $)
Rasika (Penn Quarter, $$$)

Italian
Galileo (Downtown, $$$$$)
Obelisk (Dupont Circle, $$$$$)
Sette Osteria (Dupont Circle, $$$)

Latin American
Café Atlántico (Penn Quarter, $$$$)

Malaysian
Malaysia Kopitiam (Dupont Circle, $$)

Mediterranean
Zaytinya (Penn Quarter, $$)

Mexican
Chipotle (Downtown, Dupont Circle,
Georgetown, Penn Quarter, and Upper
Northwest, $)

Moroccan
Marrakesh (Downtown, $$)

Organic
Restaurant Nora (Dupont Circle,
$$$$$)

Pizza
Matchbox (Penn Quarter, $$$)
Pizzeria Paradiso (Dupont
Circle/Georgetown, $$)
Sette Osteria (Dupont Circle, $$$)
2 Amys (Upper Northwest, $$)

Seafood
Hank's Oyster Bar (Dupont Circle,
$$$)
Kinkead's (Foggy Bottom/West End,
$$$$)
The Oceanaire Seafood Room
(Downtown, $$$$)
Sea Catch (Georgetown, $$$$)
Tony Cheng's (Chinatown, $$)

Southern
B. Smith's (Capitol Hill, $$$$)
Georgia Brown's (Downtown, $$$$)
Vidalia (Downtown, $$$$$)

Southwestern
Austin Grill (Penn Quarter and Upper
Northwest, $$)

Spanish
Jaleo (Penn Quarter, $$)

Steakhouse

The Palm (Dupont Circle, $$$$)
The Prime Rib (Downtown, $$$$$)

Vegetarian

Amma Indian Vegetarian Kitchen
(Georgetown, $)

Index of Restaurants by Price

$

Amma Indian Vegetarian Kitchen
(Georgetown, Indian/Vegetarian)
Booeymonger (Georgetown/Upper
Northwest, American)
Café La Ruche (Georgetown, French)
Capital Q (Penn Quarter, Barbecue)
Chipotle (Downtown, Dupont Circle,
Georgetown, Penn Quarter, and Upper
Northwest, Mexican)
Firehook Bakery (Capitol Hill,
Downtown, Dupont Circle, and Upper
Northwest, American)
Galileo Osteria (Downtown, Italian)
Harmony Cafe (Georgetown, Asian)
Nooshi (Downtown, Asian)
Union Station Food Court (Capitol Hill,
various cuisines)

$$

Austin Grill (Penn Quarter and Upper
Northwest, Southwestern)
Bread & Chocolate (Capitol Hill, West
End, and Upper Northwest, American)
The Brickskeller (Dupont Circle,
American)
Bullfeathers (Capitol Hill, American)
Busboys and Poets (U Street Corridor,
American)
Ching Ching Cha (Georgetown,
Chinese)
City Lights of China (Dupont Circle,
Chinese)
Clyde's (Georgetown, Penn Quarter,
and Upper Northwest, American)
Dean & Deluca (Georgetown,
American)
Eat First (Chinatown, Chinese)
Garrett's (Georgetown, American)
Jaleo (Penn Quarter, Spanish)

Luna Grill & Diner (Dupont Circle,
American)
Malaysia Kopitiam (Dupont Circle,
Malaysian)
Marrakesh (Downtown, Moroccan)
Pizzeria Paradiso (Dupont Circle and
Georgetown, Pizza)
The Tombs (Georgetown, American)
Tony Cheng's (Chinatown, Chinese)
2 Amys (Upper Northwest,
Italian/Pizza)
Zaytinya (Penn Quarter,
Mediterranean)

$$$

Bistrot Du Coin (Dupont Circle,
French)
Bistrot Lepic & Wine Bar
(Georgetown, French)
Cafe Berlin (Capitol Hill, German)
Cheesecake Factory (Upper
Northwest, American)
Circle Bistro (Foggy Bottom/West End,
Modern American)
Garden Terrace Lounge (Georgetown,
American)
The Grill From Ipanema (Adams-
Morgan, Brazilian)
Hank's Oyster Bar (Dupont Circle,
Seafood)
Kramerbooks & Afterwords (Dupont
Circle, American)
Martin's Tavern (Georgetown,
American)
Matchbox (Penn Quarter,
Pizza/American)
Mimi's American Bistro (Dupont
Circle, American)
Montmartre (Capitol Hill, French)
Old Ebbitt Grill (Downtown,
American)

Rasika (Penn Quarter, Modern Indian)
Sette Osteria (Dupont Circle, Pizza/Italian)
Sky Terrace (Downtown, American)
Tabard Inn (Dupont Circle, Modern American)

$$$$

Bistro Bis (Capitol Hill, French)
B. Smith's (Capitol Hill, Southern)
Café Atlántico (Penn Quarter, Latin American)
Georgia Brown's (Downtown, Southern)
Kinkead's (Foggy Bottom/West End, Seafood)
The Melting Pot (Dupont Circle, Fondue)
The Monocle (Capitol Hill, American)
The Oceanaire Seafood Room (Downtown, Seafood)
The Palm (Dupont Circle, Steakhouse)
Poste (Penn Quarter, Modern American)
Sea Catch (Georgetown, Seafood)

$$$$$

CityZen (Tidal Basin, Modern American)
Galileo (Downtown, Italian)
Lafayette Room (Downtown, American)
Le Paradou (Penn Quarter, French)
Marcel's (Foggy Bottom/West End, French/Belgian)
Michel Richard Citronelle (Georgetown, French/California)
Obelisk (Dupont Circle, Italian)
The Occidental (Downtown, American)
The Prime Rib (Downtown, Steakhouse)
Restaurant Nora (Dupont Circle, American/Organic)
1789 Restaurant (Georgetown, American)
Vidalia (Downtown, American/Southern)
Willard Room (Downtown, Modern American)

Part IV
Exploring
Washington, D.C.

The 5th Wave   By Rich Tennant

"I want a lens that's heavy enough
to counterbalance the weight on
my back."

In this part . . .

You're here to see the sights, and this part points you to the best. I start with the biggies — the Capitol, the Washington Monument, and the like. I also cover places that might be less familiar to you, such as the Phillips Collection and the Textile Museum. In case you're interested in buying as well as looking, I introduce you to the best of Washington's shopping scene. I also give tips on things to do outside of Washington, including some suggested itineraries — for the government groupie, for example, or the family with kids. If you don't want to take responsibility for your entire D.C. visit, I point you to some guided tours.

Chapter 11

Discovering Washington, D.C.'s, Best Attractions

*Y*ou came to Washington to see the sights, and this chapter gives you the scoop on Washington's premier attractions (memorials, galleries, topless bars — just wanted to see if you were paying attention — and so on).

The following reviews give you the lowdown on what you find at each place, as well as the specifics on hours, admission fees (if any), and any helpful tips for visiting an attraction.

One of the most pleasant things I reveal is that, in the capital of the land of the free, most of the attractions are free.

The Top Attractions from A to Z

For more information on the architecture and historical background of some of D.C.'s attractions, see Chapter 2.

American Art Museum
Penn Quarter

The most impressive art on display here may be the building itself, which was erected between 1836 and 1867 and which the American Art Museum now shares with the National Portrait Gallery. Walt Whitman described it as "the noblest of Washington buildings." Constructed to house the U.S. Patent Office, it's also been called a "temple to the industrial arts," one of the finest Greek Revival structures in the country, and simply "The Old Patent Office

The Top Attractions in Washington, D.C.

Kenyon St.
Irving St.
Columbia Rd.
Harvard St.
Girard St.
Fairmont St.
Euclid St.

Trinity College

McMillan Reservoir

Howard University

Bryant St.
Adams St.

Barry Pl.
13th St.

M **Rhode Island Ave.**
Red Line

U Street-Cardozo
Green Line

U STREET CORRIDOR

French St.

Shaw-Howard Univ.
Green Line

Florida Ave.

Rhode Island Ave.

BRENTWOOD PARK

New York Ave.
Red Line

DOWNTOWN

N St.
M St.

Mt. Vernon Sq./
Convention Ctr.
Green &
Yellow Lines

K St.
I St.
H St.
G St.

Mt. Vernon
Square

New York Ave.

Massachusetts Ave.

CHINATOWN

Union
Station

Union Station
Red Line

Metro Center
Red, Blue &
Orange Lines

Gallery Pl.-
Chinatown
Rd, Yellow
& Green Lines

PENN
QUARTER

Pennsylvania Ave.

Judiciary
Square
Red Line

F St.
E St.

Stanton
Square

Federal
Triangle
Blue &
Orange Lines

Archives-
Navy Mem'l
Green &
Yellow Lines

C St.

Constitution Ave.

NATIONAL MALL

Madison Dr.

NW
U.S. Capitol

NE

A St.
East Capit
A St.

Smithsonian
Blue &
Orange Lines

Jefferson Dr.
Independence Ave.

SW

CAPITOL
HILL

SE

Seward
Square

L'Enfant Plaza
Yellow, Green,
Blue &
Orange Lines

Federal Center SW
Blue &
Orange Lines

Capitol South
Blue &
Orange Lines

American Art Museum **17**
Arlington National Cemetery **2**
Bureau of Engraving
   and Printing **8**
Capitol **21**
Holocaust Memorial Museum **9**
Jefferson Memorial **7**
Korean War Memorial **5**
Library of Congress **23**
Lincoln Memorial **3**
National Air and Space
   Museum **19**
National Archives **16**
National Gallery of Art **18**
National Museum of
   American History **14**
National Museum of the
   American Indian **20**
National Museum of
   Natural History **15**
National Portrait Gallery **17**
National Zoo **1**
Franklin Delano Roosevelt
   Memorial **6**
Supreme Court **22**
Vietnam Veterans Memorial **4**
Washington Monument **10**
White House **12**
White House Visitors
   Center **13**
World War II Memorial **11**

Building." The Smithsonian Institution, which runs both museums, shut the place down in 2000 for what turned into a six-year renovation that cost several hundred million dollars. The result is stunning — both in the restoration of the marvelous structure and the creation of superb viewing space for the objects on display. The project restored marble floors, exposed hidden skylights, added 30,000 square feet of gallery space, and made it easier for visitors to move about the building. The galleries are extremely well-lighted, so it's easier to appreciate the art than it is in many other museums. A new glass-walled conservation center allows visitors to watch conservators at work. The museum owns 41,000 pieces of American art, beginning in the 17th century. The collection covers the gamut of what American artists have produced, including works by such notables as Charles Willson Peale, Gilbert Stuart, James McNeill Whistler, Robert Rauschenberg, Peter Paul Rubens, and Grandma Moses — along with folk art from many of America's ethnic groups. One of the most eye-popping pieces is a gigantic folk-art installation, covered with aluminum foil, titled *Throne of the Third Heaven of the Nations' Millennium General Assembly.* Don't miss it.

You can eat in the museum, but you shouldn't. The surrounding neighborhood is full of great places to eat, from cheap to very, very expensive. Check out the Penn Quarter index in Chapter 10.

See map p. 178. 8th St. NW (between F and G streets). ☎ *202-275-1500.* www.americanart.si.edu. *Metro: Gallery Place–Chinatown. The 9th and G streets exit is beside the museum, the 7th and F streets exit across the street. Admission: Free. Open: Daily 11:30 a.m.–7 p.m. Closed Dec 25.*

Arlington National Cemetery
Virginia

There's something overwhelming about the tens of thousands of simple grave markers that march in perfect formation across Arlington's hills and valleys. In their presence, it's impossible not to be moved by the enormity of the sacrifice of the military men and women who fought to preserve America's freedom and to enforce its sometimes-controversial foreign policies. More than 260,000 war dead and veterans (and their dependents) are buried here.

Stop first at the **visitor center,** look around, pick up a map, and then take the short walk to the memorial to the nearly two million women who have served in the military since the American Revolution. Return to the visitor center and buy a ticket for the **Tourmobile.** The sprawling cemetery is hilly. Unless you're in great shape and have lots of time, I don't advise covering it entirely on foot. The Tourmobile stops at the major sights. You can get off, explore the cemetery as long as you like, and then re-board to continue your tour. Before boarding for the first time, use the visitor center's restrooms — you won't find more until you get to **Arlington House,** where Robert E. Lee once lived with his wife, Mary Custis Lee, Martha Washington's great-granddaughter.

The first Tourmobile stop is at the grave of President John F. Kennedy, where his widow, Jacqueline Kennedy Onassis, also is buried, along with

The Mall

their two infants who died before the president. The president's brother, Robert F. Kennedy, who was assassinated during his own presidential campaign in 1968, is buried nearby. These gravesites have commanding views of the capital city.

The next Tourmobile stop is at the Tomb of the Unknowns, where the guard is changed every hour on the hour from October to March and every half-hour April to September. It's a somber ceremony.

When you get to Arlington House, also known as the Custis-Lee Mansion, you can take a free self-guided tour between 9:30 a.m. and 4:30 p.m., except December 25 and January 1. The Robert E. Lee Museum at the house opens at 8:30 a.m. The grave of Pierre L'Enfant, who drew up the plans for the capital at George Washington's request, is nearby. He was moved here from a pauper's grave and now enjoys a breathtaking panorama of his masterwork.

After you return to the visitor center, you can take a ten-minute walk to the Marine Corps Memorial, yet another moving scene that portrays the immortal photograph of Marines raising the U.S. flag on Iwo Jima during World War II.

Expect to spend two to three hours at these sights.

Remember that Arlington is a cemetery, so please conduct yourself — and be sure that your children conduct themselves — accordingly. Burials most likely will take place while you visit — two dozen occur many days.

See map p. 178. In Arlington, Virginia, across the Arlington Memorial Bridge from the Lincoln Memorial. ☎ *703-607-8052.* www.arlingtoncemetery.org. *Metro: Arlington National Cemetery. Tourmobile stops here. Admission: Free. Tourmobile tour: Adults $6, adults 65 and older $5, children 3–11 $3, younger free. Open: Daily Apr–Sept 8 a.m.–7 p.m., Oct–Mar 8 a.m.–5 p.m. Tourmobile leaves visitor center Apr–Sept 8:30 a.m.–6:30 p.m., Oct–Mar 8:30 a.m.–4:30 p.m.*

Bureau of Engraving and Printing
Tidal Basin

The buck may stop in the White House, but it starts here, where printers and engravers make money, postage stamps, Treasury bonds, and White House invitations. No free samples! However, you can purchase a souvenir (such as uncut or shredded currency) in the visitor center, and play with interactive displays.

March through August, you must get free, timed tickets on the day you tour, and people line up early. One person can get up to four tickets. The ticket kiosk is on Raoul Wallenberg Place on the 15th Street side of the building. The kiosk opens at 8 a.m. Monday through Friday, except Federal holidays, and tickets usually are gone by 9 a.m. Evening tours are offered May through August. Without tickets, you can skip the tour and enter the visitor center through the tour entrance on the 14th Street side. Tickets aren't required for tours September through February. Figure on spending an hour here (not including the wait to get in).

Monuments and Memorials

10th St.

11th St.

12th St.

13th St.

E St.

Pennsylvania Ave.

FBI Building

Federal Triangle
Blue & Orange
Lines

M

National Museum
of Natural History

Smithsonian
Blue & Orange Lines

M

12th St.

13th St.

Jefferson Dr.

Agriculture
Department

C St.

New York Ave.

G St.

F St.

14th St.

Constitution Ave.

Madison Dr.

National Museum
of American History

14th St

Bureau of
Engraving
and Printing

D St.

9

15th St.

Raoul Wallenberg Pl.

LAFAYETTE
PARK

Pennsylvania Ave. S.

The
White House

The Ellipse

50

10

Washington
Monument

Tidal Basin

Cherry Trees

8

17th St.

6

D St.

18th St.

Constitution Ave.

Reflecting Pool

WEST POTOMAC
PARK

Kutz Bridge

H St.

G St.

F St.

E St.

19th St.

Virginia Ave.

20th St.

20th St.

CONSTITUTION
GARDENS

4

21st St.

C St.

Independence Ave.

22nd St.

22nd St.

5

7

23rd St.

3

24th St.

25th St.

Potomac River

1/2 mi

0.5 km

0

0

Watergate

1

66

2

Arlington
Memorial Bridge

To Arlington
National Cemetery

FDR Memorial **7**

Holocaust Memorial
Museum **9**

Jefferson Memorial **8**

Kennedy Center
for the Performing
Arts **1**

Korean War Veterans
Memorial **5**

Lincoln Memorial **3**

Theodore Roosevelt
Island **2**

Vietnam Veterans
Memorial **4**

Washington
Monument **10**

World War II
Memorial **6**

Security has been tightened substantially at government facilities since the terrorist attacks of September 11, 2001. The Bureau of Engraving and Printing closes to the public when the Homeland Security Department raises the terrorist threat level to code orange.

Your U.S. representative and senators can help you with tickets to government buildings, such as the Bureau of Engraving and Printing. Phone them way ahead of time, tell them what you want to do, and ask what they can do for you.

See map p. 178. 14th and C streets SW. ☎ *866-874-2330 or 202-874-2330.* www.money factory.gov. *Metro: Smithsonian. From the Independence Avenue exit, walk west on Independence 1 long block and then left on 14th (to the tour entrance) or 2 blocks and then left on Raoul Wallenberg Place (for the ticket kiosk). Admission: Free. Tours: May–Aug Mon–Fri 9–10:45 a.m., 12:30–2 p.m., and 5–7 p.m.; Sept–Apr Mon–Fri 9–10:45 a.m. and 12:30–2 p.m.; visitor center Sept–Apr 8:30 a.m.–3 p.m., May–Aug until 7:30 p.m. Closed Federal holidays and Dec 25–Jan 1.*

Capitol
Capitol Hill

As the home to Congress and the most common symbol of American democracy, the Capitol belongs on every visitor's must-see list. The familiar architecture, the historic art inside, and the ornate decoration are other aspects that make the Capitol an interesting stop. Unfortunately, construction of a visitor center under the Capitol's East Lawn — along with various makeshift, post-9/11 security barriers — has turned much of the area around the Capitol into an eyesore and obstacle course. But take heart; the architect of the Capitol said he "expected" the center to be completed and opened by the time of your visit. (On the other hand, it was supposed to be done during 2005!)

The Capitol dominates the Washington landscape. The 180-foot-high dome is topped by a statue titled *Freedom.* Inside, the Rotunda serves as the heart of the Capitol. Above the Rotunda, in the canopy of the dome, you see Constantino Brumidi's fresco, *The Apotheosis of Washington,* which portrays the first president as a godlike character flanked by such allegorical figures as Liberty, War, Victory, and Fame. Statues of prominent Americans — and some not so prominent — fill Statuary Hall and stand throughout the building. Most importantly, of course, the building contains the House and Senate chambers, and the offices of top congressional leaders and some of the most powerful committees.

You can obtain free tickets for guided tours from a member of Congress or first-come, first-served at the Capitol Guide Service Kiosk along the curving sidewalk near First Street SW and Independence Avenue beginning at 9 a.m. Monday through Saturday. Lines can get quite long in spring and summer — and tickets can run out — which is why contacting your representative or senators ahead of time is a good idea. Expect to spend one to two hours here, not counting the time you wait to get in.

Your U.S. representative and senators can arrange for you to join a special Capitol Guide Service tour that's conducted before the public tours. Some

National Zoological Park

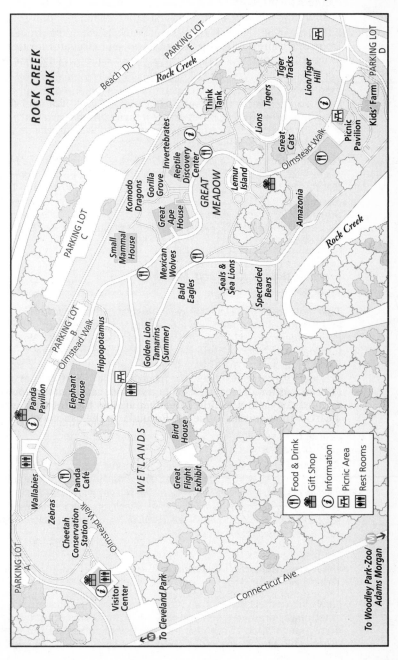

members of Congress — and their aides — are happy to lead constituents on tours themselves. Call your state's representative or senators far ahead of your visit and ask what they might do for you.

If the House or Senate is in session, you can watch the proceedings from a visitor's gallery. Call your representative or a senator for tickets.

If you do take a seat in a visitors gallery, don't be surprised if nothing exciting is going on. While the chambers fill for roll-call votes and during extremely important debates, usually only a handful of members is on the floor. You can witness the surreal scene of a grandiloquent senator propounding profoundly on the greatest issues of the day, with only one or two other members, one or two reporters, a few congressional staffers — and C-SPAN cameras — looking on.

See map p. 178. Capitol Guide Service Kiosk, near 1st Street SW and Independence Avenue. ☎ *202-225-6827. (Call senators at* ☎ *202-224-3121, representatives at* ☎ *202-225-3121.)* www.aoc.gov. *Metro: Capitol South. Walk north 1 block on 1st Street SE, turn left on Independence Avenue for 3 blocks, and then go right on 1st Street SW for 1 block. Admission: Free. Tours: 9 a.m.–4:30 p.m. Mon–Sat except Thanksgiving and Dec 25. First-come, first-served tour tickets distributed at kiosk beginning at 9 a.m.*

Franklin Delano Roosevelt Memorial
Tidal Basin

This monument to a U.S. president illustrates the latest trend in monument architecture. It is, shall I say, monumental in size — telling the 32nd president's biography as well as honoring him on a 7½-acre site. Walking through four open-air "rooms," one for each of Roosevelt's terms, you revisit the Great Depression, World War II, and other notable aspects of his 12-year presidency, the longest ever. The memorial features statues of his first lady, Eleanor, an important public figure in her own right, and Roosevelt's beloved dog Fala. Note how Fala's statue shines where visitors pet it.

You can see FDR's wheelchair and other memorabilia in the information center. Restrooms are located at each end of the memorial. Allow 30 minutes to an hour to visit.

See map p. 178. West Basin Drive SW at Ohio Drive. ☎ *202-426-6841.* www.nps.gov/fdrm. *Metro: Smithsonian. From the Independence Avenue exit, walk west on Independence until you're sure that you've gone too far and then turn left on West Basin Drive; total walking time about 30 minutes. The Tourmobile stops here, or you can take a taxi. Admission: Free. Open: Outdoor memorial always open; staffed daily 8 a.m.–midnight except Dec 25.*

Holocaust Memorial Museum
Tidal Basin

I have yet to meet a soul unmoved by a visit to this museum. Prepare to be emotionally drained when you leave. The museum recommends that children younger than 11 not visit the permanent collection, but they can view other exhibits. Prepare older children for what they'll see and hear.

The White House Area

The museum remembers the six million Jews who were murdered and the millions of others who were murdered or oppressed during the Holocaust. Multimedia exhibitions document this obscene chapter of history. Upon entering, each visitor picks up an identity card of a Holocaust victim, which personalizes the museum experience.

The self-guided tour begins with the rise of Nazism. Then, the Nazis' "Final Solution" is depicted. Aboard a freight car that was used to transport Jews to Treblinka, visitors listen to recordings of survivors. Another section is dedicated to the liberation of the concentration camps and to the non-Jews who, at great risk, hid Jews.

Time-specific tickets are required to view the permanent exhibits, which occupy the bulk of most visitors' time at the museum. They're available free beginning at 10 a.m. by the museum's 14th Street entrance for same-day visits, but usually are depleted quickly. One person can pick up ten passes. People often line up early. You can get tickets ahead of time for $1.75 from Tickets.com (☎ 800-400-9373; www.tickets.com).

Other exhibits don't require tickets. Among them is "Daniel's Story," which is appropriate for families even with young children. The museum recommends that parents also take children younger than 11 to the orientation film, the Wexner Learning Center, the Children's Tile Wall, and the Hall of Remembrance.

Most people spend two to three hours in the museum; many visitors spend a lot more time.

See map p. 183. 100 Raoul Wallenberg Place SW (south of Independence Avenue). ☎ 202-488-0400. www.ushmm.org. Metro: Smithsonian. From the Independence Avenue exit, walk west on Independence 2 blocks and then go left on Raoul Wallenberg Place. Admission: Free. Advance tickets: $1.75. Open: Daily 10 a.m.–5:30 p.m., extended hours until 7:50 p.m. Tues and Thurs from early April to mid-June. Closed Yom Kippur and Christmas.

Jefferson Memorial
Tidal Basin

This memorial is my favorite, partly because Thomas Jefferson is my favorite founding father and partly because the setting is marvelous. A 19-foot statue of Jefferson stands atop a six-foot pedestal inside the memorial's columned rotunda, which is akin to Jefferson's designs for his Monticello home and the University of Virginia. Jefferson quotations are carved into the memorial's interior.

The memorial, located on the southeast bank of the Tidal Basin, commands a spectacular view of the Washington Monument and the White House to the north. The scene is gorgeous in the spring when the cherry blossoms bloom, and awe-inspiring after dark with Jefferson's statue standing behind you and Washington's other illuminated landmarks glowing in the distance. A bookstore and restrooms are in the basement. Park rangers deliver talks upon request. Count on spending 15 to 45 minutes here depending on whether you listen to a ranger's talk — more if you get mesmerized by the view.

See map p. 183. East Basin Drive SW on southeast side of Tidal Basin. ☎ *202-426-6841.* www.nps.gov/thje. *Metro: Smithsonian. From the Independence Avenue exit, walk 2 blocks west on Independence and then left on Raoul Wallenberg Place to the Tidal Basin path. It's a 15- to 25-minute walk. A Tourmobile stop is at the memorial, or you can take a taxi. Admission: Free. Open: Always; staffed daily 9:30 a.m.–11:30 p.m.*

Korean War Veterans Memorial
National Mall

Before Vietnam, another undeclared war helped to drive a once-popular president (Truman) from office, cost more than 50,000 American lives, and left the nation in a mood more inclined to forget a conflict than to memorialize it. Finally, on the 42nd anniversary of the armistice that ended the fighting — but which has not yet officially sealed the peace — the Korean War Veterans Memorial was dedicated on July 27, 1995, by the presidents of the United States and South Korea, Bill Clinton and Kim Young Sam. Statues depicting an infantry unit on patrol are the focal point of the memorial. Park rangers give talks upon request. A bookstore, restrooms, and concessions are at the site. Allocate at least 15 minutes for touring.

See map p. 183. French Drive SW and Independence Avenue, southeast of the Lincoln Memorial. ☎ *202-426-6841.* www.nps.gov/kowa. *Metro: Foggy Bottom–George Washington University. Walk south 8 blocks on 23rd Street to the Lincoln Memorial and then left on French Drive. Or walk from the Tourmobile's Lincoln Memorial stop. Or take a taxi. Admission: Free. Open: Always; staffed daily 9:30 a.m.–11:30 p.m.*

Library of Congress
Capitol Hill

The general public can't borrow books at this library, the world's largest, but you can do research here (and I have). The collection — 130 million items on 530 miles of bookshelves — is built upon Thomas Jefferson's personal library of 6,487 volumes.

The main building, named for Jefferson, is an ornate Italian Renaissance structure that you can tour. If you saw the movie *All the President's Men,* you'll remember a mind-boggling overhead shot of Woodward and Bernstein doing research in the Main Reading Room, which you can view. Another highlight, the Great Hall, soars 75 feet from marble floor to stained glass ceiling. The *Gutenberg Bible* and the *Giant Bible of Mainz* are among artifacts on permanent display. The building also houses changing exhibits, as well as film showings and concerts.

Stop first at the Jefferson Building's visitor center, inside the ground level 1st Street SE entrance. Get tour tickets and ask what's going on, not only in the Jefferson Building, but in the library's nearby Madison and Adams buildings as well. Figure on spending one to two hours here if you take the tour. Naturally, at Congress's library, a representative or senator can get you into a special tour.

See map p. 183. 1st Street SE (between East Capital Street and Independence Avenue).
☎ *202-707-8000.* www.loc.gov. *Metro: Capitol South. Walk north on 1st Street 1½ blocks to Jefferson Building. Admission: Free. Open: Jefferson Mon–Sat 10 a.m.–5:30 p.m. Tours: Mon–Fri 10:30 and 11:30 a.m., 1:30, 2:30, and 3:30 p.m.; Sat 10:30 and 11:30 a.m., 1:30 and 2:30 p.m. Closed Federal holidays.*

Lincoln Memorial
National Mall

Okay, I confess: The Lincoln Memorial is up there with the Jefferson. If you were forced to pick the greatest president, Lincoln would be in the final four. And, like Jefferson's, Lincoln's memorial is an awe-inspiring place. Once again, you have an oversized sculpture of the president inside a structure that, in this case, has become as familiar as the Capitol and the White House. (It's on the back of the penny!) The Gettysburg Address and Lincoln's second inaugural address are inscribed on the walls. And the vista is spectacular, looking the length of the Mall, past the World War II Memorial and the Washington Monument to the Capitol.

The Lincoln Memorial has been the sight of some of America's most important political demonstrations, from Marian Anderson singing here in 1939, to Martin Luther King's "I Have a Dream" speech in 1963, to the Vietnam War protests. The Memorial has a visitor center and restrooms, and rangers give talks on request. You can spend 15 to 45 minutes — or more — here, depending on your interest, and it's awe-inspiring at night. From the back, you look into Arlington National Cemetery and see the perpetual flame on Kennedy's grave.

See map p. 183. West end of the Mall at 23rd Street between Constitution and Independence avenues. ☎ *202-426-6841.* www.nps.gov/linc. *Metro: Foggy Bottom. Walk south 8 blocks on 23rd Street. Tourmobile stops here, or you can take a taxi. Admission: Free. Open: Always; staffed daily 9:30 a.m.–11:30 p.m.*

National Air and Space Museum
National Mall

This museum is crammed with significant artifacts of flight and exhibits that teach the history and science of flight. You can stand beside John Glenn's *Friendship 7* capsule, in which he became the first American to orbit Earth, while gazing upon Neil Armstrong's *Columbia* command module, which first carried men to the moon. You can see Charles Lindbergh's ocean-crossing *Spirit of St. Louis,* Chuck *(The Right Stuff)* Yeager's sound-barrier-breaking *X-1,* a space station, a space rock . . . I have no room to do the collection justice.

Orville and Wilbur Wright's *Flyer* used to hang from the ceiling in the **Milestones of Flight Gallery,** near Glenn's and Armstrong's capsules. There, in a few feet of museum space, the 20th century progressed from "man cannot fly" to "man can walk on the moon" — in just 65 years by four guys who lived within 160 miles of each other in Ohio! Having covered Glenn the senator — and worked for newspapers in the Wright brothers' Dayton that circulated up to Armstrong's Wapakoneta — I always found that spot particularly meaningful. To mark the centennial of the Wrights' first flight — December 17, 1903 — the museum moved the *Flyer* to a special exhibit about "The Wright Brothers & the Invention of the Aerial Age." It's been extended for an indefinite run.

Because the Air and Space Museum is on every visitor's agenda, arriving when the doors open or late in the day is wise. Get a map at the information desk and decide whether you want to take a free guided tour, rent an audio tape tour, or fend for yourself. Next, purchase tickets for one of the movies on the multistory IMAX screen and consider buying tickets for the Albert Einstein Planetarium's tour of the universe.

An hour can slip by in what seems like seconds in this enormous, exhibit-packed place. Kids love it here. Allow *at least* two to three hours. If you're with me or my nephew Jason the pilot, you'll be here all day!

See map p. 178. Between Independence Avenue SW, Jefferson Drive, and 4th and 7th streets. ☎ *202-633-1000; tours and reservations 202-633-2563; IMAX Theatre and planetarium 877-932-4629 (202-633-4629); lectures and programs 202-633-2398.* www.nasm.si.edu. *Metro: L'Enfant Plaza. From the Smithsonian Museums exit, walk north 1 block on 7th Street SW, across Independence, then turn right. Admission: Free. Fees for IMAX Theatre, Einstein Planetarium. Open: Daily 10 a.m.–5:30 p.m. Closed Dec 25.*

National Archives
Downtown

The Declaration of Independence, the Constitution of the United States, the Bill of Rights, a 1297 version of the Magna Carta, and numerous other historical documents reside in the Archives, which has become much more visitor friendly because of a spectacular renovation. Those familiar with the old Archives, where you squinted to glimpse documentary treasures behind thick glass, will be especially pleased with the new Archives, where history is explained with multimedia presentations, interactive exhibits, and other state-of-the-art technologies. In the Charters of Freedom hall, for instance, visitors for the first time can see all four pages of the Constitution. The displayed documents have been made more easily seen by children and people in wheelchairs. Multimedia exhibits display documents and make their historical importance easier to understand. "Documents" today include photographs, films, and television recordings. Watch Harry Truman deliver the first televised presidential address — about a 1947 international food crisis. At the Archives gift shop, you can buy copies of documents as well as books, CDs, and games based on the institution's collections. Beyond being a tourist attraction, the Archives is the nation's record-keeper (official name: National Archives and Records Administration). Anyone can conduct research within the *billions* of documents the Archives preserves.

Figure on spending at least a half hour viewing the main exhibits. Be warned: If history interests you, this place could capture your attention for hours or days.

If you can plan six weeks in advance, the Archives recommends that you make a reservation by sending an e-mail to visitorservices@nara.gov. Waits of an hour or more may be encountered during March, April, May, Thanksgiving weekend, and the week between Christmas and New Year's. To join a guided tour, you must reserve by phoning ☎ 202-357-5450.

See map p. 178. 700 Pennsylvania Ave. NW (between 9th and 7th streets). ☎ 202-357-5000. www.archives.gov. *Metro: Archives-Navy Memorial. Walk across Pennsylvania Avenue. Admission: Free. Exhibitions daily 10 a.m.–9 p.m. Memorial Day weekend through Labor Day; to 5:30 p.m. daily after Labor Day through Mar; to 7 p.m. Apr through Memorial Day weekend. Closed Dec 25.*

National Gallery of Art
National Mall

The National Gallery is two buildings — East and West — connected by an underground walkway. The Gallery owns more than 100,000 works from the Middle Ages to the present. Important works are on exhibit throughout both buildings, and the gallery always is mounting special exhibitions, some of international importance.

The West Building is a treasure chest of European art from the 13th into the early 20th centuries and American art from the 18th to the early 20th. It includes the only painting by Leonardo da Vinci in the Western Hemisphere.

I.M. Pei designed the starkly modern East Building, which, appropriately, houses the gallery's 20th-century and contemporary art. An immense Calder mobile dominates the soaring central court. You also see works by Henri Matisse, Joan Miró, Pablo Picasso, and Jackson Pollock here.

In the Micro Gallery, near the Mall entrance to the West Building, you can use a computer terminal to identify the works you want to see and then print a map that shows you where they're located. In addition to the exhibits, the Gallery presents daily tours of the collection, a concert series, lectures, and films. The shops sell some of Washington's best souvenirs — reproductions of the gallery's masterworks in many forms. The Gallery even has a children's shop. You need at least two hours for a cursory taste of the National Gallery's treasures.

Families take note: Kids — as well as adults — enjoy the outdoor Sculpture Garden, across 7th Street from the West Building. It even has an ice-skating rink in the winter.

In addition to housing sculpture, the garden hosts live jazz performances 5 to 8:30 p.m. on Fridays from late May to mid-September.

See map p. 178. Constitution Avenue NW between 3rd and 7th streets. ☎ 202-737-4215. www.nga.gov. *Metro: Archives-Navy Memorial. Walk 1½ blocks east on Pennsylvania Avenue and then right on 6th Street. Admission: Free. Open: Mon–Sat 10 a.m.–5 p.m., Sun 11 a.m.–6 p.m. Closed Dec 25, Jan 1.*

National Museum of American History
National Mall

If the Smithsonian is the nation's attic — as it's often called — then this museum is the corner where the heirlooms are kept: three million pieces of vintage Americana.

A highlight here always has been the original Star-Spangled Banner, the giant flag that inspired the national anthem during the battle for Fort McHenry in Baltimore in 1814. You also can take a look at first ladies' gowns, a Samuel Morse telegraph, an Alexander Graham Bell telephone, George Washington's military uniform, Abraham Lincoln's top hat, Muhammad Ali's boxing gloves, Duke Ellington's sheet music, Julia Child's kitchen . . . even Howdy Doody. And that's not even scratching the surface.

Exhibition halls let you concentrate on things (agriculture equipment, power machinery, musical instruments), while others explore social phenomena (First Ladies' roles in politics, Americans at war, sports in American life).

The hands-on history and science rooms are designed for youngsters (or oldsters) five and older. Kids conduct experiments in the science room. In the history room, they can climb on a high-wheel bicycle or transmit a telegram. When the rooms are busy, you're given timed tickets that let you in later in the day.

You need at least two hours here, and this museum is another one in which you could spend an entire day and then come back for more.

The National Museum of American History closed for renovations in 2006 and was scheduled to re-open in summer 2008. In the interim, some of the museum's holdings were to be displayed in other Smithsonian facilities.

See map p. 178. Between Constitution Avenue NW, Madison Drive, and 12th and 14th streets. ☎ *202-633-1000.* http://americanhistory.si.edu. *Metro: Smithsonian. From the Mall exit, walk north across the Mall to the museum on your left. Admission: Free. Closed until summer 2008. Likely hours when reopened: Daily 10 a.m.–5:30 p.m. Closed Dec 25.*

National Museum of the American Indian
National Mall

The Smithsonian's newest museum has caused quite a stir. Not only has it proved to be enormously popular, it's also been quite controversial. Leaders of Indian organizations were intimately involved in the planning of the museum (including choosing the name), and critics complain that it's too heavy on Native American myths and too light on hard science.

You can decide for yourself by perusing the contents of the 250,000-square-foot facility which opened in fall 2004. The museum has acquired 10,000 years worth of artifacts from all the Americas — far more than can be displayed at one time. You also can shop at two museum stores and eat in the Mitsitam Café. ("Mitsitam" means "let's eat!" in the Delaware and Piscataway Indian language.) The cafe — the best place to eat on the Mall — serves Native foods from throughout the Western Hemisphere.

The museum's exterior architecture is designed to evoke a stone mass carved over time by wind and water.

See map p. 178. Independence Avenue SW at 4th Street. ☎ **202-633-1000.** www. nmai.si.edu. *Metro: L'Enfant Plaza. From the 7th Street/Maryland Avenue/ Smithsonian Museums exit, walk 2 blocks northeast on Maryland, then right on Independence and left on 4th. Admission: Free. Open: Daily 10 a.m.–5:30 p.m. Closed Dec 25.*

National Museum of Natural History
National Mall

Kids dig dinosaurs, right? And bugs. And giant 3D movies. So they gotta love this place! From the moment you walk in and encounter the huge African elephant in the Rotunda, your children will be squealing with delight. And the museum has plenty to interest the bigger folks, too. While the National Gallery may boast that it has artworks stretching back 800 years, artifacts at the Natural History Museum measure their years in *billions*.

When you're done ogling the elephant, pick up a museum map at the nearby information desk. Then consider buying tickets for the 90-foot-high IMAX Theatre. If you'd like to join a tour, they leave from the elephant exhibit in the Rotunda Tuesday through Friday at 10:30 a.m. and 1:30 p.m.

Children go gaga at the insect zoo, where they can touch creepy crawly critters and slither through a model of a termite mound, and they love to explore Dinosaur Hall. Other highlights, for visitors of all ages, include the Hall of Geology, Gems, and Minerals — where you find a moon rock, the 45.5 carat Hope Diamond, and many other baubles — and the exhibit on Ice Age mammals, which includes a giant ground sloth, a saber-toothed cat, and an American mastodon.

Humans are part of natural history, too, so the museum contains exhibits about evolution and various human cultures. One may argue that a high mark in human evolution was the development of jazz, and every Friday from 6 to 10 p.m. the museum presents live music with food, drinks, and IMAX films for a $10 cover (children 12 and younger free).

Plan on spending two to four hours here (not counting jazz night).

See map p. 178. Between Constitution Avenue NW, Madison Drive, and 9th and 12th streets. ☎ **202-633-1000.** www.mnh.si.edu. *Metro: Smithsonian. From the Mall exit, walk north across the Mall to the museum on your right. Admission: Free. Jazz night: $10 cover, children 12 and younger free. IMAX Theatre: $8.50 adult, $7.50 adults 60 and older, $7 children 2–12, younger free; some feature films $10. Open: Daily 10 a.m.–5:30 p.m., until 7:30 p.m. Memorial Day weekend through Labor Day weekend. Closed Dec 25.*

National Portrait Gallery
Penn Quarter

This gallery really is more about history than about art. Congress established it to collect portraits of folks who have made "significant contributions to the history, development, and culture of the people of the United

States." Because of the renovated facility (see American Art Museum review for details), the well-informed displays, and the eclectic nature of the collection, it's fun to learn history through portraits. All the presidents are here, of course, and many other powerful political leaders. But there also are significant contributors from other aspects of American life — Calvin Klein, for example, and Mia Hamm, Toni Morrison, Pocahontas, Frederick Douglass, Chief Joseph, Lucille Ball, Janis Joplin, Miles Davis, Jackie Robinson, Roberto Clemente, Susan B. Anthony, Cesar Chavez, Rosa Parks . . . and Shari Lewis with Lamb Chop. The portraits come in many media, not just oil on canvas. My favorite is a sculpture by cartoonist Pat Oliphant of President George H.W. Bush, appearing possibly naked, leaning forward to pitch a horseshoe. Think the Russian Portrait Gallery could portray Vladimir Putin that way? Is this a great country, or what?

See map p. 178. 8th Street NW, between F and G streets. ☎ *202-633-1000.* www. npg.si.edu. *Metro: Gallery Place–Chinatown. The 9th and G streets exit is beside the museum, the 7th and F streets exit across the street. Open: Daily 11:30 a.m.– 7 p.m. Closed Dec 25.*

National Zoo
Upper Northwest

Hands-down *the* most kid-friendly place in town, the National Zoological Park (that's "zoo" to you) shows off 2,000 critters big and small around 163 acres of hills and valleys, with most of the animals in compounds designed to resemble their natural habitat. Be sure to wear your walking shoes and comfortable clothing, 'cause you'll be doing lots of hiking here. The best time to see animal activity is early morning or around dusk; midday, many animals are napping and/or hiding away from zoo-goers.

Grab a map and schedule of events at the Education Building near the Connecticut Avenue entrance. Zookeepers conduct demonstrations and give talks throughout the park. It's always fun to be around at feeding time and when the elephants and seals put on performances.

Giant pandas have been the top attraction here since Richard Nixon was president and China sent a pair to mark the improvement in the two nations' relationship. It wasn't until mid 2005, however, that the current adult pandas — Mei Xiang and Tian Tian — finally produced an offspring who survived. Little Tai Shan immediately became the zoo's First Animal, and he has been a cutie to watch. Unfortunately, China gets to claim him sometime during 2007, so consider yourself truly fortunate if you get here in time to check him out. Otherwise, wish for his parents to get lucky again and provide us with another kid to observe.

The giant pandas' habitat is part of the zoo's newest improvement, the Asia Trail. Walk it and check out the new digs for sloth bears, red pandas, small-clawed otters, fishing cats, clouded leopards, and Japanese giant salamanders. Next planned for the trail: a better crib for the elephants, who currently share their 1930s-era Elephant House with a giraffe, three hippos, and two capybaras, which are gigantic rodents.

Hungry for other zoo highlights?

Remember that bar scene from Star Wars? Step into the other-worldly **Invertebrates House,** and you'll imagine that's where you've landed. Occupants range from octopuses and lobsters to cockroaches and ants. The spiny lobster especially looks like he could be running that bar, or ordering up some ethereal drink there.

At the **Think Tank,** you can look in as scientists study animal thinking, including inquiring into orangutans' language. Researchers test apes' ability to use and understand word symbols. Outdoors and 50 feet overhead, the apes use the **Orangutan Transportation System** to commute between the Think Tank and the Great Apes House. I've never seen them swinging there, but Julie's caught them perched on the towers the line is connected to as it runs above zoo walkways. Zoo officials assure that the apes are too good at swinging to fall and too smart to jump all that way to the ground. They may relieve themselves while up there, however, so don't stand beneath one.

The Amazon River Basin's tropical habitat is re-created in **Amazonia** to accommodate macaws, sloths, monkeys, avocadoes, cocoa trees, piranhas, poison frogs, and others. It's a great place to warm up in the winter. There are lizards and turtles and snakes, oh my, at the **Reptile Discovery Center.** Yucky for grownups, groovy for kids. More serene is the **Pollinarium,** where hummingbirds and butterflies flit about, pollinating plants.

Take your children to the **Kids Farm,** and they can pet or groom cattle, donkeys, and goats, check out chickens and ducks, and play with interactive educational displays. At the Pizza Garden, they can play on an oversized pie while learning about pizza ingredients, where they come from, and how they're grown. Tomatoes, basil, peppers, wheat, and other ingredients are grown here. For the parents, there are benches. Kids three to eight can crawl through **Prairie Playland** — which mimics the nearby prairie dog village — popping their heads up through openings and looking around just like the prairie dogs do.

The zoo is a large park with many walking paths and grassy areas where you can sit and picnic. Locals run and hike through here. D.C. organizations hold group picnics here. One zoo neighbor was such an avid zoo walker that his funeral was held here.

It's easy to spend the entire day here, and then want to come back for more. Take it easy. Flop for a while under a tree. Bring some food or grab lunch or a snack at one of the — let's call them "adequate" — refreshment stands.

If you eat at the Maine Cafe, go all the way to the back of the dining room and you'll find tables at windows that overlook nearby zoo facilities.

Despite its name, Woodley Park-Zoo is not the best Metrorail station to use on the way to the zoo. Here's what the locals do: On the way *to* the zoo, use the Cleveland Park station and then walk south on Connecticut Avenue from the East Side exit. When *leaving* the zoo, walk south on Connecticut to the Woodley Park-Zoo station. You walk a tad further, but more downhill and less uphill. The **L1, L2,** and **L4 Metrobuses** run from Dupont Circle all the way up Connecticut Avenue to Maryland, stopping at the zoo. The zoo provides parking, but charges $4 for the first hour, $12 for up to three hours, and $16 for more than three hours.

See map p. 178. 3001 Connecticut Ave. NW (north of Cathedral Avenue). ☎ *202-673-4821.* www.natzoo.si.edu. *Metro: Cleveland Park and Woodley Park-Zoo. Going to Zoo, walk down Connecticut from Cleveland Park. Leaving, walk down Connecticut to Woodley Park-Zoo. Admission: Free. Grounds open: Daily 6 a.m.– 8 p.m. Apr–Oct, until 6 p.m. Nov–Mar. Buildings open: Daily 10 a.m.–6 p.m. Apr–Oct, until 4:30 p.m. Nov–Mar. Closed Dec 25.*

Supreme Court
Capitol Hill

The majestic Supreme Court building looks as if it has been standing since the birth of the republic — the Roman Republic. In fact, the court was the last of the three government branches to get its own digs. The nine justices didn't move into this classic temple until 1935. Previously, they occupied a nook in the Capitol. This place is another one where a member of Congress — with lots of notice — can get you into a guided tour. Otherwise, you can wander around yourself, check out the exhibits on the ground floor, and attend a lecture in the courtroom.

By far, the best thing to do here is attend a one-hour argument. The topic can be front-page news around the world — defining freedom of speech, setting limits on the death penalty — or it can pick at arcane details of a commercial contract. No matter, it can be grand entertainment — with justices interrupting the lawyers, casting wry asides, or causing the courtroom to convulse in laughter with an on-the-money wisecrack. The court's right wing is most notable in the comment department. Antonin Scalia is the most humorous — or scathing, depending on the moment — justice. Clarence Thomas almost never opens his mouth.

The court hears arguments between 10 a.m. and 3 p.m. (sometimes only in the morning) on many Mondays, Tuesdays, and Wednesdays from October into late spring, usually two weeks on and two weeks off. Lines form on the plaza when arguments are being heard — one for listening to an entire argument, the other for taking a three-minute peek. Come early if the argument is big news. You can spend an hour here, more if you attend an argument or take a tour.

See map p. 178. 1 1st St. NE (at Maryland Avenue). ☎ *202-479-3211.* www.supreme courtus.gov. *Metro: Capitol South. Walk north 2½ blocks on 1st Street. Admission: Free. Open: Mon–Fri 9 a.m.–4:30 p.m. Lectures, when courtroom not in use, every hour on the half-hour 9:30 a.m.–3:30 p.m. Closed Federal holidays.*

Vietnam Veterans Memorial
National Mall

Depending on your age and your circumstances, this memorial can be the most emotional spot in Washington. The war divided the country, and the surviving soldiers came home feeling unappreciated. The private Vietnam Veterans Memorial Fund lobbied for a memorial on the Mall and raised money to build it. The organizers wanted to honor the soldiers and steer clear of the war's politics. Maya Lin — a Chinese-American Yale University student who grew up in Ohio — created the winning design.

Like the war, the simple memorial — a black granite V carved into the ground — was controversial. To appease those who wanted a more traditional patriotic monument, a flagpole and a statue of three soldiers was placed near the wall. Later a statue of three female military nurses, tending to a wounded soldier, was added.

Nevertheless, it's the Wall — with its 58,250 names of the dead and missing — that commands the attention of visitors and eloquently commemorates the soldiers' sacrifice. Park rangers are available to discuss the memorial and help if you're looking for individual names. So, usually, are Vietnam-era vets. You can find a bookstore, restrooms, and concessions in the area. You can spend as little as 15 minutes here, more as you're moved.

See map p. 183. Bacon Drive at Constitution Avenue NW, just northeast of the Lincoln Memorial. ☎ *202-426-6841.* www.nps.gov/vive. *Metro: Foggy Bottom. Walk south 7 blocks on 23rd Street, then left 1½ blocks on Constitution, and then right on Bacon. The Tourmobile stops at the nearby Lincoln Memorial, or you can take a taxi. Admission: Free. Open: Always; staffed daily 9:30 a.m.–11:30 p.m.*

Washington Monument
National Mall

This towering marble obelisk is one of the most recognizable sights in America. The view from the top is the most spectacular in Washington. You can get free time-specific tickets for riding the elevator to the top on the day of your visit at the monument's ticket kiosk near 15th Street and Madison Drive beginning at 8 a.m. One person may get up to six tickets. Tickets disappear quickly in spring and summer, and the line sometimes starts forming by 7:30 a.m., so arrive early. You can buy tickets in advance by calling ☎ 800-967-2283 or on the Internet at http://reservations.nps.gov. The charge is $1.50 per ticket, plus 50¢ per order.

The ride to the top takes just 70 seconds. You can stare out the windows as long as you like. You descend at a slower speed so that you can view the monument's interior. The grounds contain exhibits, a bookstore, restrooms, and concessions. On summer evenings, military bands perform here, and the monument provides a gleaming exclamation point for the Fourth of July fireworks.

You pass through security screening to enter the monument. Food, drinks, and large bags are prohibited. If you wear a pacemaker or other medical device that a magnetometer may affect, tell a ranger so that you can go through alternative screening. Figure on a 30-minute visit, not counting time in line.

See map p. 183. Between Constitution Avenue NW, Independence Avenue SW, and 15th and 17th streets. ☎ *202-426-6841; advance tickets 800-967-2283.* www.nps.gov/ wamo; *advance tickets* http://reservations.nps.gov. *Metro: Smithsonian. From the Mall exit, walk west on Jefferson Drive 2 long blocks. Admission: Free. Fee for* *advance tickets: $1.50 per ticket. Open: Daily 9 a.m.–4:45 p.m.; ticket kiosk 8 a.m.–4:30 p.m. or when tickets run out. Closed Dec 25.*

White House
Downtown

Is it just me, or does everybody wonder why, if security can screen passengers to get on airplanes, they can't screen visitors for White House tours? As I write this book, things are looser than during the first couple years after 9/11. But you still can't just walk up to the White House gate and get into a tour line. You must form a group of at least ten people and make a reservation — up to six months ahead — through a senator or representative. Check by Internet or phone to see whether things improve for your visit.

If you do get in, you'll see just a fraction of the president's mansion, which is not only the president's home and office but also work space for the highest ranking presidential aides and (usually) the White House press corps. (The press room is being remodeled as I write, and the press has been chased across the street to temporary digs.) The best time to visit is when the place is decorated wonderfully for Christmas.

If you can't get in, you'll have to content yourself with strolling the perimeter of the grounds, gazing through the fence, and marveling at the bizarre architecture of the Old Executive Office Building next door. You also can visit the **White House Visitor Center,** which, strangely enough, is located in the Great Hall of the Commerce Department building, on Pennsylvania Avenue between 14th and 15th streets. There, you find ranger talks, exhibits, a gift shop, and restrooms.

See map p. 178. 1600 Pennsylvania Ave. NW (between 15th and 17th streets). ☎ *202-456-7041.* www.whitehouse.gov/history/tours. *Metro: McPherson Square. From the Vermont Avenue–White House exit, walk 1 block south on Vermont and then across Lafayette Square. It's that big white house in front of you. Admission: Free for groups of at least ten who obtain tickets from a member of Congress. Tours: Tues–Sat 7:30 a.m.–12:30 p.m. Closed Federal holidays.*

See map p. 178. Visitor Center: 1450 Pennsylvania Ave. NW (between 14th and 15th streets). ☎ *202-208-1631.* www.nps.gov/whho. *Metro: Federal Triangle. Walk half block north on 12th Street and then go left on Pennsylvania 2½ blocks. Keep the parks on your right, and the visitor center will show up on your left. Admission: Free. Open: Daily 7:30 a.m.–4 p.m. Closed Thanksgiving, Dec 25, Jan 1.*

World War II Memorial
National Mall

Like the Mall's newest museum (the National Museum of the American Indian), the newest memorial arrived awash in controversy. First was the controversy over why it took so long to erect this memorial to the troops who fought America's biggest war — even after memorials to the later Korean and Vietnam conflicts were dedicated. It was opened finally on April 29, 2004, and was dedicated on May 29, two days before Memorial

Day. Second was the controversy over the location, smack dab in the middle of the Mall between the long-standing **Lincoln Memorial** and **Washington Monument.** Critics objected that it would disrupt the hallowed view from Lincoln's seat to the **Capitol** dome, which had been interrupted only by Washington's thin obelisk. Finally was the controversy over the design. After Maya Lin's spare plan for the **Vietnam Veterans Memorial** had been emulated in later memorials all around the country, the World War II Memorial came in big and bulky and ornate.

It's my personal judgment that the memorial does not damage the view. You can see it from Lincoln's steps, but you've always been able to see Washington's obelisk, too. I do agree with the critics that the memorial is way overdone. The giant plaza bakes in the summer (come in spring or fall). The memorial is too big, with too many elements — pillars, wreaths, arches, fountains, pools, stars, eagles, quotations, bas reliefs. The most telling critique I've heard focuses on symbolism, which is what memorials are about: There's a tall pillar with a wreath for each state and territory that fought in the war, which emphasizes separatism when in fact the country was never more unified.

The beauty of America, of course, is that each visitor can decide for himself. You can check Lincoln's view. You can study the new memorial up close. As with the Vietnam Memorial, the time you choose to spend here depends to a great extent on your personal relationship with this war. Plan on at least 15 to 30 minutes.

There are restrooms, water fountains, and an information kiosk near the memorial.

See map p. 183. 17th Street NW, between Constitution and Independence avenues. ☎ *202-619-7222.* www.nps.gov/nwwm. *Metro: Smithsonian. From the Independence Avenue exit, walk west to 17th, then turn right. Admission: Free. Open: Always; staffed daily 9:30 a.m.–11:30 p.m.*

Finding More Cool Things to See and Do

As a world capital — arguably *the world's capital* — Washington really does have something to interest everyone, or at least *nearly* everyone. In this section, I identify places of particular appeal to kids, historians, art aficionados, gardeners, and architecture buffs.

Especially for kids

If you have children with you, you should make a point to check out the following sights, perfectly suited for young visitors. Washington is both a fun and important destination for the younger members of the family, with most of the national monuments and museums having a child-focused aspect. Children love several of Washington's top sights. In the preceding section, be sure to check out the **Bureau of Engraving and Printing,** the **National Air and Space Museum,** the **National Museum of American History,** the **National Museum of Natural History,** and, of course, the **National Zoo.** Here are some more spots that are particularly attractive to kids — and, luckily, to their parents as well.

National Aquarium
Downtown

Kids can find relief from the heavy-duty sightseeing by ducking into this little hideaway in the Commerce Department building. Youngsters can watch sharks and other water creatures get along swimmingly. (It's lucky for the rest of the fish that a separate tank holds the piranhas.) Although this aquarium doesn't boast the latest in technological advances, it displays some 1,000 specimens of marine life (including alligators) in 80 exhibits. Kids can dip their hands into the touch tank and pet a horseshoe crab. Feeding time is 2 p.m. daily, different carnivores on different days. A visit here sets you back 45 minutes or more.

See map p. 202. 14th Street NW between Constitution and Pennsylvania avenues, in the Commerce Department building. ☎ *202-482-2825.* www.nationalaquarium.com. *Metro: Federal Triangle. Walk half block north on 12th Street, left on Pennsylvania 2 blocks, and then left on 14th. Admission: $5, seniors and military personnel $4, children two–ten $2, younger than two free. Open: Daily 9 a.m.–5 p.m.; last admission 4:30 p.m. Closed Thanksgiving, Dec 25.*

National Geographic Society's Explorers Hall
Downtown

The National Geographic Society explores the universe, so you can encounter exhibits on just about anything in Explorers Hall. Kids can be enthralled by some of the changing topics. As I'm writing this book, for example, featured exhibits include "Bizarre beasts: past and present" and photos by the 2006 wildlife photographer of the year. Call or check the Web site to find out what's going on before you decide to attend. While you're here, you also can check out the National Geographic Store's stock of nature books, photography, globes, maps, and back issues of the magazine. Plan on spending at least an hour.

See map p. 202. 17th and M streets NW. ☎ *202-857-7588.* www.nationalgeographic.com/explorer. *Metro: Farragut North. From the L Street exit, walk east on L 1 block and then go left at 17th. Admission: Free. Open: Mon–Sat 9 a.m.–5 p.m., Sun 10 a.m.–5 p.m. Closed Dec 25.*

National Postal Museum
Capitol Hill

This museum, dedicated to the history of stamps and the postal service, delivers, by extension, a large slice of American history. Interactive exhibits make it a hit with children. Tour a Southern Railway mail car, look up at mail planes, and discover the real story of the Pony Express. The museum is located in the old City Post Office Building, which operated from 1914 through 1986. There's a museum store and a functioning post office on site. Upstairs, part of the old post office has been transformed

More Cool Things to See and Do

Chesapeake and Ohio Canal Boat Rides **7**

Corcoran Gallery **12**

Frederick Douglass Historic Site **21**

Dumbarton Oaks **5**

Ford's Theatre **15**

Freer & Sackler Galleries **25**

Enid A. Haupt Garden **26**

Hirshhorn Museum and Sculpture Garden **27**

International Spy Museum **16**

Lafayette Square **9**

Mount Vernon **28**

National Airport **29**

National Aquarium **13**

National Building Museum **18**

National Geographic Explorers Hall **8**

National Museum of African Art **24**

National Museum of Women in the Arts **14**

National Postal Museum **19**

Newseum **23**

Octagon Museum **11**

Old Stone House **6**

Phillips Collection **4**

Renwick Gallery **10**

Textile Museum **3**

Union Station **20**

U.S. Botanic Garden **22**

Verizon Center **17**

Washington National Cathedral **1**

Woodrow Wilson House **2**

into a Capitol City Brewing Company pub, one of those places that caters to adults but is friendly to kids, with finger foods, burgers, and a children's menu. Plan on spending an hour or more in the museum.

See map p. 202. 2 Massachusetts Ave. NE (west of Union Station). ☎ 202-633-5555. www.postalmuseum.si.edu. *Metro: Union Station. From the Union Station Shops/Massachusetts Avenue exit, walk across 1st Street NE. Admission: Free. Open: Daily 10 a.m.–5:30 p.m. Closed Dec 25.*

Especially for teens

I have it on good authority, from teenagers who wish to remain anonymous, that the zoo is a cool place for teens to hang out. So is the Air and Space Museum (see "The Top Attractions from A to Z," at the beginning of this chapter, for both listings). Here are some other places where local teenagers like to go, and that visiting teens likely would enjoy as well.

International Spy Museum
Downtown

The interactive exhibits and gee-whiz spyware and spy lore grab young folks' attention and that of many older visitors as well. This museum has been very popular, so you're advised to purchase your time-specific tickets in advance. That's right, I said "purchase." This spot is a privately operated enterprise and one of the few museums in town where you have to pay to enter. That drops it way down the priority list when you're deciding how to spend your time in Washington. The crowds also can make it difficult to get to some of the interactive exhibits.

Because of the subject matter here — violence, deception, terrorism — the museum recommends that visitors be at least 12 years old, even though discounted tickets are available for children ages 3 to 11.

Once inside, you encounter the latest in interactive museum technology, along with old and new spy tools. You can see a Revolutionary War letter written by George Washington to authorize establishment of a spy network in New York in 1777. You can enter a mockup of an intelligence agency's 21st-century operations center, which displays information about the latest developments in espionage. Among the 68,000-square-foot museum's many artifacts are an Enigma cipher machine from World War II Germany, a U.S. Army M-209 cipher machine from the same era, a Soviet overcoat with a buttonhole camera, a CIA disguise kit, and (shades of Maxwell Smart!) a shoe with microphone and radio transmitter concealed in the heel.

Instruments of violence, as well as of intelligence-gathering, are on display. A U.S.-made bomb was disguised as a lump of coal to be planted in enemy coal bins during World War II; it exploded when shoveled into a locomotive's engine, a ship's boiler, or a factory's furnace. A double-barreled poison-gas gun enabled KGB agents to kill silently with a spray of cyanide. Another KGB weapon — a single-shot pistol — was disguised as a lipstick tube. On a lighter note, some exhibits explore the public's fascination with espionage — from Junior G-Man toys in the 1930s to James Bond and Austin Powers movies today.

The museum tells the story of spying from Biblical times to the present, with a heavy emphasis on the Cold War. Visitors are invited to adopt a secret identity and to try to maintain it under interrogation, to break codes, to identify disguised spies, to eavesdrop, and to be the target of eavesdroppers. There's a museum store, of course, and two eateries — **Spy City Cafe,** for quick meals, and **Zola,** a full-scale Modern American restaurant.

Peter Earnest (what a great name for a spy!), the museum's executive director, spent 36 years with the CIA. His advisory board includes former CIA and KGB officers. The museum is located in five restored buildings, one of which once housed a Communist Party district headquarters. It's within easy eavesdropping distance of the FBI across the intersection. The average visitor spends two hours with the permanent exhibits, an hour and a quarter in the special exhibits.

See map p. 202. 800 F Street NW (between 8th and 9th streets). ☎ *866-779-6873 or 202-393-7798.* www.spymuseum.org. *Metro: Gallery Place-Chinatown. From the 9th and G streets exit, walk 1 block south on 9th, cross F, and then turn left on F. Admission: Adults $16, children 5–11 $13, younger children free, seniors 65 and older and military and intelligence personnel $15. Hours vary, usually opening no later than 10 a.m., closing no earlier than 6 p.m. Last admission two hours before closing. Call or check Web site for specifics. Closed Thanksgiving, Dec 25, Jan 1.*

Georgetown

Teens have been making Georgetown their own since the days of pegged pants and poodle skirts. Shops, restaurants, and the overall scene entertain teenagers in this historic neighborhood, which is centered on the intersection of Wisconsin Avenue and M Street NW. The variety of people makes it perfect for people-watching. And — teens can be cruel — some youngsters get great joy from observing the frustration of drivers inching along in Georgetown's always-gummed-up traffic.

Commander Salamander (1420 Wisconsin Ave.), **Urban Outfitters** (3111 M St.), and **Up Against the Wall** (3219 M St.) are among the shops that cater to younger shoppers. The Commander ("Nobody calls it the Commander!" my teenager daughter admonishes me) offers punk-style clothing, colored wigs, and off-the-wall gifts — think "devil ducks," red rubber duckies with devil's horns. The Outfitters stock slightly offbeat clothing and accoutrements in a wide price range — fuzzy lamps (why not?) for decorating a teen's bedroom and lots of CD accessories. The Wall folks may be distinguished primarily by what's free — lots of loud music. Check out **Beyond Comics** (1419 Wisconsin Ave.) for comic books and related toys, dolls, T-shirts, and other such stuff. If your kids are suffering shopping-mall withdrawal, they can find scores of chain stores in **Georgetown Park** (3222 M St.); one of the best for young adults is **H&M,** which sells inexpensive but trendy clothing. I won't tell your teens about **Jinx Proof Tattoos and Piercing Parlor** (3289 M St.) or **Mrs. Natalie** the palm reader (1500 Wisconsin Ave.).

A kajillion restaurants are in Georgetown, give or take a few bazillion, many of them inexpensive and many ideal for carryout food. Before they actually entered college, Julie and her chums liked to sample college life by getting sandwiches at **Wisemiller's Grocery & Deli** (1236½ 36th St.), near the Georgetown University campus, then finding a seat on a convenient wall or set of steps, or heading to the little park south of M near 34th. **Dean & Deluca** (3276 M St.) is a great place for gourmet carryout, and it has outdoor tables.

Georgetown is especially well-stocked with ice cream parlors. **Dolcezza Argentine Gelato Cafe** (1560 Wisconsin Ave. at Q Street) scoops Argentinean ice cream. **Thomas Sweet** (3214 P St. east of Wisconsin) is locally grown. If your kids are into national brands, Georgetown entices them with **Ben & Jerry's** (3135 M St.) or **Häagen-Dazs** (3120 M St.).

The 30-series **Metrobuses** run along Pennsylvania Avenue, M Street, and Wisconsin Avenue. **Georgetown Connection** shuttle buses connect with the Dupont Circle, Foggy Bottom–George Washington University, and Rosslyn Metrorail stations. Another bus, the DC Circulator, runs from Union Station, through downtown, to Wisconsin Avenue and M.

Energetic teens have no trouble walking from the Foggy Bottom station, north on 23rd Street to Washington Circle, left around the circle to Pennsylvania Avenue, and then left on Pennsylvania to M.

Dupont Circle

Like Georgetown, Dupont Circle has all the necessities for people-watching, eating, and shopping. The park in the circle is a haven for chess players, recuperating bicycle messengers, and assorted other characters.

Beadazzled (1507 Connecticut Ave.) sells beads (you couldn't guess?) from $1 to $100 a piece, plus already-made jewelry and crafts. **Kramerbooks & Afterwords** (1517 Connecticut Ave.) is a bookstore where you can eat, drink, listen to music, and . . . well . . . browse for books. **Pizzeria Paradiso** (2029 P St.) is one of the two best pizza parlors in the city and also makes sandwiches to go. Look at any three doorways in the Dupont Circle area, and one probably leads into a place to eat. Dupont Circle has its own Metrorail Station, so it's really easy to get to.

Union Station

Young people are drawn to Union Station like iron filings to a magnet. Come here any afternoon or weekend if you don't believe me. Who'd have thought that a train station would morph into an upscale mall and entertainment center? Union Station has all the right stuff that young people crave: a nine-screen movie theater complex, more than 50 retailers, and a lower-level food court with dozens of vendors. You can eat in a restaurant or in the brightly decorated food court. Or you can carry your food outside to the fountain. A Metro stop is right in the basement.

Sports

If your teens are sports buffs, they'll find Washington to be one of the best professional sports towns in the country. We've got the NFL **Redskins,** the NBA **Wizards,** the NHL **Capitals,** the WNBA **Mystics,** the Major League Soccer **D.C. United** — and now, after three decades when the national pastime abandoned the nation's capital, the Major League Baseball **Nationals. Georgetown University** plays big-time college basketball. **The University of Maryland,** in suburban College Park, has been fielding nationally ranked basketball and football teams recently.

Verizon Center (601 F St. NW) is a superb arena and home to the Wizards, Mystics, Capitals, and some Georgetown games. **RFK Stadium** (2400 East Capitol St.) has gray hair and lacks the modern amenities of skyboxes for the rich, but it's still a beautiful setting for soccer and baseball. The cheap seats in the upper deck behind home plate are really pretty good. (Bring binoculars.) A Metrorail station is practically in Verizon Center's basement, and RFK has a station, too. The Redskins' **FedEx Field** (1600 FedEx Way, Landover, MD) is not easily accessible, but 'Skins tickets are nearly impossible to get anyway.

Music

Verizon Center and RFK Stadium also are venues for big-time pop-music concerts, as are other stages around town. To keep up with who's performing, check the ads and listings in the *Washington Post* — particularly the Friday "Weekend" section — as well as the *Post's* online entertainment guide (http://eg.washingtonpost.com).

Especially for history buffs

Deciding which attractions fall into this category is a tough call, because history infuses everything here. When you're done with the monuments, memorials, and federal buildings I cite earlier in this chapter, take a look at these attractions:

Ford's Theatre & Peterson House
Downtown

Closed for more than a century after President Lincoln was assassinated here on April 14, 1865, Ford's Theatre became a showcase for plays and concerts again in 1968. You can attend a performance here. And you can tour the scene, viewing the presidential box as it looked the night John Wilkes Booth shot the president during a performance of *Our American Cousin.*

In the basement, the **Lincoln Museum** displays the clothing Lincoln was wearing that night, the .44 caliber Derringer that Booth used, and other memorabilia associated with Lincoln and the assassination. Across the street, you can visit the place where Lincoln died, the Petersen House, 516 10th St. NW. You can spend about an hour touring the two locations.

See map p. 202. 511 10th St. NW (between E and F streets). ☎ *202-426-6924.* www.nps.gov/foth. *Performance information: 202-347-4833;* www.fords theatre.org. *Metro: Metro Center. From the 11th Street exit, walk 1 block south on 11th, go left on F, and then right on 10th. Admission: Free. Fee for performances. Open: Daily 9 a.m.–5 p.m. Closed Dec 25. Theater closed to tourists during perform- ances, rehearsals, and work on set.*

Frederick Douglass National Historic Site
Anacostia

This 21-room house was home to Frederick Douglass, the 19th-century abolitionist and civil rights leader, who was born a slave and eventually served as a District of Columbia Council member, D.C.'s U.S. marshal, and U.S. minister to Haiti. The home and visitor center feature original fur- nishings and tell the story of Douglass's remarkable life. Be sure to see the short film for an overview of his life. A bookstore and restrooms are on- site. Space is limited, so call ahead to find the best time to visit and to make a reservation. Plan to spend an hour here.

See map p. 202. 1411 W St. SE (at 14th Street). ☎ *800-967-2283 or 202-426-5961.* www.nps.gov/frdo. *Take a taxi. Admission: $2. Open: Mid-Apr to mid-Oct 9 a.m.– 5 p.m., mid-Oct to mid-Apr 9 a.m.–4 p.m. Closed Jan 1, Thanksgiving, Dec 25.*

Newseum
Downtown

Journalism has been called the "first rough draft of history," which is why I'm putting this institution in this section of this book. The Newseum hasn't reopened as I write this, so I have to rely on what the Newseum folks have announced rather than my own eyes. But, if it's anything like its prede- cessor — and it should be better! — everyone, including kids, will find a visit enjoyable and educational. People involved in the news business will love checking this place out. Everyone who is affected by news — and that's everyone — should come to get a better understanding of how and why the news is reported as it is. The earlier Newseum, across the Potomac River in Rosslyn, made the story of journalism come to life with state-of-the-art technology. This new Newseum, scheduled to open in fall 2007, will be state-of-the-artier. The institution will explore five centuries of news history and offer behind-the-scenes looks at how news is gathered and published in print and electronic media. Visitors will be able to watch television news feeds from around the world, see displays of 80 newspaper front pages each day, and have electronic access to more than 500. Freedom is the Newseum's key theme, and it will display key documents in freedom's evolution, including rare editions of the Magna Carta, the Federalist Papers, and the first pamphlet printing of the U.S. Constitution. Documenting another key moment in the march of freedom, the Newseum will display fragments of the Berlin Wall. Other features: an exhibit on revered radio and television newsman Edward R. Murrow, a documentary about the "Golden Age" of television news from 1954 to 1969, a gallery of Pulitzer Prize–winning photojournalism, a gallery devoted to news coverage of the 9/11 attacks, and a memorial to more than 1,600 journalists killed while reporting the news. The building also will house a food court and a Wolfgang Puck restaurant.

See map p. 202. 555 Pennsylvania Ave. NW (at 6th Street). ☎ *888-639-7386 or 703-284-3544.* www.newseum.org. *Metro: Archives/Navy Memorial. From the Metro exit, walk toward the Capitol on Pennsylvania Avenue 1 block. Opening in Fall 2007. Admission: Not determined. Open: Hours not determined.*

Old Stone House
Georgetown

In the heart of Georgetown — and easy to pass given its diminutive size — is one of Washington's oldest buildings. Built in 1765, it predates the United States and the District of Columbia. It's furnished as it was when Georgetown was a thriving tobacco port. Ask the ranger to tell you about the place. Most visitors are struck by the interior space, or lack thereof. Be sure to look out back at the lovely garden, abloom from April to November. You can also bring lunch and join picnickers who brown-bag it on the lawn. Plan to spend 15 minutes here, more if you do lunch.

See map p. 202. 3051 M St. NW (between 30th and 31st streets). ☎ *202-426-6851.* www.nps.gov/olst. *Take Georgetown Connection shuttle bus from Dupont Circle or Rosslyn Metrorail station to M and 30th or Thomas Jefferson Street or ride 30-series Metrobus or the Circulator. Admission: Free. House open: Daily noon–5 p.m. Garden open: Daily during daylight hours. Closed Dec 25.*

Woodrow Wilson House
North of Dupont Circle

After his term ended in 1921, Woodrow Wilson, America's 28th president, lived the last three years of his life in this Georgian Revival home, which was built in 1915. Depending on how you view Bill Clinton's current residency status, Wilson was the only president to live in Washington after his term expired. (Bill and Hillary bought a D.C. house after she was elected U.S. senator from New York, but their official residence is in the state she represents.) Many of the gifts Wilson received from world leaders — as well as his inaugural Bible, specs, and a shell casing from World War I — are among the artifacts displayed in the house. According to the docents, the residence/museum looks very much as it did when Wilson lived in it. Touring the place properly takes about an hour.

See map p. 202. 2340 S St. NW (between 23rd and 24th streets). ☎ *202-387-4062.* www.woodrowwilsonhouse.org. *Metro: Dupont Circle. From the Q Street exit, walk 2 blocks west on Q, right on Massachusetts Avenue 4 blocks, right on 24th Street 1 block, and then right on S. (Note: It's uphill.) Or take an N-series Metrobus up Massachusetts. Or take a taxi. Admission: $7.50, seniors $6.50, students $3, children younger than seven free. Open: Tues–Sun 10 a.m.–4 p.m. Closed major holidays.*

Especially for art lovers

Art galleries paint many D.C. neighborhoods, but the biggest concentration is in **Georgetown,** around 7th Street NW in the **Penn Quarter** neighborhood, and on the **National Mall.** For the Georgetown galleries, take the Metro to Foggy Bottom, walk north to Pennsylvania Avenue, then walk to where Pennsylvania ends at M Street. You also can take the Georgetown Connection shuttle bus from the Foggy Bottom, Dupont Circle, or Rosslyn Metrorail station, or ride the Circulator. Many galleries are on M and along Wisconsin Avenue between M and R streets. To reach the 7th Street galleries, between D and G streets, take the Metro to the Archives-Navy Memorial station and walk north on 7th.

The top gallery in town, of course, is the National Gallery, which I tell you about in the first section of this chapter. Also see the first section for the American Art Museum and the National Portrait Gallery. I can't tell you about all the other galleries around Georgetown, Penn Quarter, and the Mall, but these are some of the best:

Corcoran Gallery
Downtown

You can find Washington's first art museum — and D.C.'s largest private art museum — just a block from the White House. The Corcoran was founded in 1869 "for the purpose of encouraging the American genius." Its collection traces America's artistic development from colonial times to the present. It also contains a significant number of European works. Julie likes to come here to see the works of students in the Corcoran College of Art and Design. The Corcoran has a cafe, a noteworthy museum shop, and an auditorium which hosts concerts, films, and other activities. Tours of the collection leave from the information desk at noon Wednesday through Saturday, plus 7:30 p.m. Thursday, and 2:30 p.m. Saturday and Sunday. Figure on spending about an hour here.

See map p. 202. 500 17th St. NW (between New York Avenue and E Street).
☎ *202-639-1700.* www.corcoran.org. *Metro: Farragut West. From the 17th Street exit, walk 5 blocks south on 17th. Admission: $8, seniors and military personnel $6, students with ID $4, younger than 12 free, pay what you wish Thurs after 5 p.m. Open: Wed–Sun 10 a.m.–5 p.m., Thurs until 9 p.m. Open some Mon holidays. Closed Thanksgiving, Dec 25, and Jan 1.*

Freer and Sackler Galleries of Art
National Mall

Although these neighboring galleries store and display their collections in separate buildings, they're connected by underground exhibition space and together comprise the Smithsonian's Museum of Asian Art. The Freer also contains the world's finest collection of Whistlers (James McNeill Whistler, that is), and of some other American artists from the late 19th and early 20th centuries. If you've never seen the Peacock Room, that alone is reason to visit the Freer. Take the guided tour (from the information desk daily at

12:15 p.m. except Wed and Federal holidays) to discover the fascinating history behind Whistler's stunning dining room, created for a London town house and moved to the Mall after the owner's death. Sackler tours leave its info desk at the same time.

The Freer houses a world-renowned collection of art from Asia and the Near East. Highlights include Chinese paintings, Japanese folding screens, Korean ceramics, Buddhist sculpture, and Indian and Persian manuscripts. The Sackler's highlights include early Chinese bronzes and jades, Chinese paintings and lacquerware, ancient Near Eastern ceramics and metalware, South and Southeast Asian sculpture, and Islamic arts. Budget at least a half-hour for each museum.

See map p. 202. Between the Smithsonian Castle, Independence Avenue, and 12th Street. ☎ 202-633-4880. www.asia.si.edu. Metro: Smithsonian. From the Mall exit, walk southeast across Jefferson Drive. Admission: Free. Open: Daily 10 a.m.–5:30 p.m. Closed Dec 25.

Hirshhorn Museum and Sculpture Garden
National Mall

I get a charge out of standing directly beneath Kenneth Snelson's 60-foot-high "Needle Tower," just outside the Hirshhorn, and looking straight up. I must admit that much abstract and contemporary art is not to my taste. But some of it turns me on, and this aluminum-and-steel, TV-tower-like structure is one example.

If modern and contemporary art is *your* thing, then the Hirshhorn is your museum. All the top guns are here: Benton, Christo, Close, Gorky, Miró, O'Keeffe, Warhol, Bacon, de Kooning, Matisse . . . you get the — uh — picture. And, of course, the museum has many special exhibits. Across Jefferson Drive is the sunken Sculpture Garden, with more than 60 works by Rodin, Moore, Calder, and others (a particularly neat place in winter when the statues are draped in snow).

You can catch a museum tour at 10:30 a.m. and noon weekdays, noon and 2 p.m. weekends. Sculpture Garden tours are offered (weather permitting) Monday through Saturday at 10:30 a.m. June through September. Inquire at the information desk about tours of special exhibitions. No tours are given on holidays.

See map p. 202. Independence Avenue at 7th Street SW. ☎ 202-633-1000. www.hirshhorn.si.edu. Metro: L'Enfant Plaza. From the Smithsonian Museums exit, walk north 1 block on 7th and cross Independence. Admission: Free. Open: Daily 10 a.m.–5:30 p.m. Plaza: 7:30 a.m.–5:30 p.m. Sculpture Garden: 7:30 a.m.–dusk. Closed Dec 25.

National Museum of African Art
National Mall

Art from throughout Africa — traditional and contemporary — is the focus of this Smithsonian museum. In addition to mounting exhibits, the museum serves as a research and reference facility, with photo archives and a library. Its permanent exhibits include "The Art of the Personal Object," which explores the artistic content of everyday things, and "Ceramics," which shows traditional and modern works.

See map p. 202. 950 Independence Ave. SW (midway between 7th and 12th streets). ☎ *202-633-4600.* www.nmafa.si.edu. *Metro: Smithsonian. From the Independence Avenue exit, cross Independence and walk to the right. Admission: Free. Open: Daily 10 a.m.–5:30 p.m. Closed Dec 25.*

National Museum of Women in the Arts
Downtown

Housed in a landmark Downtown building that once served as a Masonic Temple, the privately managed National Museum of Women in the Arts has compiled a collection of 2,700 works by more than 800 artists since Wilhelmina Cole Holladay and Wallace F. Holladay began compiling their personal collection in the 1960s. That collection comprised the core of the museum when it was incorporated in 1981 and moved into its current quarters in 1987. The museum seeks to acquire the works of women artists of all periods and all nationalities.

See map p. 202. 1250 New York Ave. NW (at 13th Street). ☎ *800-222-7270* or *202-783-5000.* www.nmwa.org. *Metro: Metro Center. From the 13th Street exit, walk 2 blocks north on 13th. Admission: $8, seniors 60 and older and students $6, children 18 and younger free. Free for everyone first Sun of every month. Open: Mon–Sat 10 a.m.–5 p.m., Sun noon–5 p.m. Closed Thanksgiving, Dec 25, Jan 1.*

Phillips Collection
Dupont Circle

In the former home of collector and benefactor Duncan Phillips, you find the works of modern artists and of the earlier artists who influenced them. The Phillips bills itself as America's first museum of modern art, but it also believes in showing "the continuum of art and artists influencing their successors through the centuries." Duncan Phillips collected El Greco, for example, because he was the "first impassioned expressionist." The Phillips is noted for Impressionist and post-Impressionist paintings. You find Renoir's *Luncheon of the Boating Party* here, as well as works by such other notable artists as van Gogh, Monet, Degas, Gauguin, Cézanne, Rothko, Matisse, de Kooning, Hopper, and O'Keeffe.

When you tour the original galleries of the Phillips, you really do feel as if you're exploring a private collection in an elegant private home. An expansion completed in 2006 gives the Phillips modern exhibition space as well. In addition to increasing display space, that project added a 180-seat auditorium, a hands-on activity room, a courtyard, a new cafe, and a new shop, among other facilities. You can join an introductory tour of the collection on Saturday and of any special exhibition on Friday, both at 11 a.m. Classical music concerts are presented here at 4 p.m. Sundays October through May, lectures and other programs on Thursday evenings.

See map p. 202. 1600 21st St. NW (at Q Street). ☎ *202-387-2151.* www.phillips collection.org. *Metro: Dupont Circle. From the Q Street exit, walk 1 block west* on Q. Admission to the permanent collection is free weekdays. Admission varies Thurs evening, weekends, and to special exhibitions. Open: Tues–Sat 10 a.m.–5 p.m. (until 8:30 p.m. Thurs); Sun June–Sept noon–5 p.m., Oct–May until 7 p.m. Closed Federal holidays.

Renwick Gallery
Downtown

Across from the White House, this striking Second Empire building shows off American crafts from the 19th century to the present. Rotating exhibits from the gallery's permanent collection are displayed in the second floor galleries.

Among the more notable are Larry Fuente's *Game Fish,* with its glittering scales of game pieces, buttons, and beads, and Albert Paley's *Portal Gates,* made from forged steel, brass, copper, and bronze. Temporary exhibits of American crafts and decorative arts are shown on the first floor. Wood turning, leaded glasswork, and quilts are just a few of the crafts to be featured.

See map p. 202. 1661 Pennsylvania Ave. NW (east of 17th Street). ☎ *202-633-2850.* http://americanart.si.edu/renwick. *Metro: Farragut West. From the 17th Street exit, walk 2 blocks south on 17th and then left on Pennsylvania. Admission: Free. Open: Daily 10 a.m.–5:30 p.m. Closed Dec 25.*

Textile Museum
North of Dupont Circle

More than 17,000 objects, dating from 3,000 B.C. to the present, are held in the Textile Museum's collection. It all started with George Hewitt Myers's Chinese silks, tapestries, and hand-woven Oriental rugs. The gift shop is noteworthy, too, featuring silk scarves and ties, Tibetan rug squares, and other interesting items. Susan bought an Oriental rug mouse pad here.

See map p. 202. 2320 S St. NW (between 23rd and 24th streets). ☎ *202-667-0441.* www.textilemuseum.org. *Metro: Dupont Circle. From the Q Street exit, walk 2 blocks west on Q, right on Massachusetts Avenue 4 blocks, right on 24th Street 1 block, and then right on S. (**Note:** It's uphill.) Or take an N-series Metrobus up Massachusetts. Or take a taxi. Admission: Suggested donation $5. Open: Mon–Sat 10 a.m.–5 p.m., Sun 1–5 p.m. Closed Federal holidays, Dec 24.*

Stopping to smell the roses: Gardens and peaceful spots

You can find a lot of green spaces in and around Washington, many dating back to the founding of the city, and some even before that time. The temperate climate (well, in the spring and fall, anyway) means that the gardens are blooming pretty much throughout the year.

Dumbarton Oaks
Georgetown

If you're looking for a place to entertain both kids and grandparents, the Dumbarton Oaks gardens fit the bill. In fact, the first time Susan and I checked out this place, it was with my parents and our then-little daughter in tow. The big folks loved exploring the plantings. Julie loved running around and letting off steam.

Robert and Mildred Bliss — wealthy collectors of Byzantine and pre-Columbian art and of books on gardens — purchased this 19th-century mansion in 1920, then restored and expanded it over the years. In 1940, they donated the building, some of the grounds, their collections, and an endowment to Harvard University, which uses the property as a study center and museum.

The mansion hosted the Dumbarton Oaks Conversations — international discussions that laid the foundations for the United Nations — in 1944. The art from the Byzantine Empire is considered by many the most important Byzantine collection in America. Mildred Bliss employed noted landscape gardener Beatrix Farrand to design the gardens, which were envisioned as a unique American incorporation of elements from traditional French, English, and Italian gardens. They're in bloom from early spring through fall. Blooming starts in mid-March and April with cherry trees, forsythia, wisteria, azaleas, dogwood, lilacs, and magnolias and ends in October with chrysanthemums.

The mansion, with its art displays, has been closed during a lengthy renovation. It was scheduled to reopen during 2007.

See map p. 202. 1703 32nd St. NW (between R and S streets). Garden entrance at R and 32nd. ☎ *202-339-6401.* www.doaks.org. *Take Georgetown Connection Route 1 shuttle bus from Foggy Bottom–George Washington University Metrorail station to Wisconsin and R streets and then walk 1 block east on R. Or take a 30-series Metrobus to Wisconsin and R. Admission to gardens: $7, children and seniors $5, Nov to mid-Mar free. Open: Daily mid-March to Oct 2–6 p.m., Nov to mid-Mar 2–5 p.m. Closed inclement weather, Federal holidays, Dec 24.*

Enid A. Haupt Garden
The Mall

This 4.2-acre park, located between the Smithsonian Castle and Independence Avenue, is a pleasant place to rest when you're touring the National Mall. It's named for the woman who endowed it, an heir to the Annenburg publishing fortune and a one-time editor and publisher of *Seventeen* magazine who loved gardens and could afford to finance them.

The Haupt Garden actually is a collection of gardens that grow above the underground sections of the Arthur M. Sackler Gallery of Asian Art, the National Museum of African Art, and the S. Dillon Ripley Center's International Gallery. The Parterre is a large flower bed, lined with benches, in which designs are formed with the dirt, grass, shrubs, and flowers. The Moongate Garden was inspired by the Temple of Heaven in Beijing; it features a circular granite "island" and granite walkways that bridge the water. Catch your breath, rest your feet, and reflect before moving on to the next museum.

See map p. 202. Independence Avenue SW at 10th Street. ☎ *202-663-1000.* www.gardens.si.edu/horticulture/gardens/Haupt/hpt_home.htm. *Metro: Smithsonian. From the Independence Avenue exit, cross Independence and walk to the right. Admission: Free. Open: Daily dawn–dusk. Tours: May–fall Wed 1 p.m. from the south patio of the Castle.*

Lafayette Square
Downtown

Once part of the White House North Lawn and now separated from the lawn by Pennsylvania Avenue and the White House fence, Lafayette Square is a marvelous place for sitting, snacking, or even stretching out on the grass. Gazing to the south, you see the White House with the Washington Monument peeking over the roof in the near distance. To the west are historic houses that lead you to feel you're visiting a 19th-century town square. You can check out an ethnically diverse collection of statues — Marquis de Lafayette, for whom the square is named, the Comte Jean de Rochambeau, Thaddeus Kosciusko, Baron Frederick von Steuben, and Andrew Jackson on horseback.

The park attracts lunching workers from nearby office buildings, resting tourists, and a diverse collection of demonstrators who like to display their signs at the president's door. Over the centuries, the land has accommodated a farmhouse, an apple orchard, a cemetery, and a racetrack. According to the National Park Service, it's also home to "the highest density of squirrels per square acre ever recorded." Try to ignore the post-9/11 security barriers.

See map p. 202. Bordered by Pennsylvania Avenue NW and 15th, 17th, and H streets. Metro: McPherson Square. From the Vermont Avenue–White House exit, walk south 1 block on Vermont Avenue, cross H Street, and enter the park. Admission: Free. Open: 24 hours.

United States Botanic Garden
Capitol Hill

The nation's greenhouse sits in a sort of no-man's land just west of Capitol Hill, but not really on the National Mall. Because it's run by Congress, I call it a Capitol Hill attraction. And attractive it is, having just been through a major-major-major renovation.

About 4,000 plants are on display inside the Conservatory. More are in the gardens just outside the Conservatory and across Independence Avenue in Bartholdi Park. The park also contains the Bartholdi Fountain, created for the 1876 International Centennial Exhibition in Philadelphia by Frederic Auguste Bartholdi, the French designer of the Statue of Liberty.

Ask at the information desk about free 45-minute tours of the Conservatory that are conducted from time to time. Or you can just wander about on your own. The conservatory is particularly appealing in winter, when it serves as a tropical respite from the cold. It's a great place to visit in the Christmas season, when poinsettias brighten holiday spirits.

See map p. 202. 100 Maryland Ave. SW (at 1st Street). ☎ *202-225-8333.* www.usbg. gov. *Metro: Federal Center Southwest. Walk 3 blocks north on 3rd Street and then turn right on Maryland. Admission: Free. Open: Daily 10 a.m.–5 p.m.*

Especially for architecture buffs

Just about every building on the D.C. tourist itinerary has something to offer architecture enthusiasts. You can spend hours — days — studying the details of the great government buildings, such as the Capitol, the White House, the Supreme Court, and the Library of Congress. Many of the monuments are architectural triumphs, such as the Jefferson Memorial, the Lincoln Memorial, the Vietnam Veterans Memorial, and the Washington Monument, to name a few. If you take the train to Beaux Arts Union Station or fly into National Airport, you're instantly exposed to the fascinating architecture of these transportation hubs.

Mount Vernon
Virginia

One reason George Washington placed the capital where he did is its proximity to Mount Vernon, the Founding Father's plantation. This estate across the Potomac River is about 15 miles and more than 200 years away from modern-day D.C. A stop at the riverside mansion, meticulously restored down to the original paint colors on the walls, is the perfect complement to a visit in the federal district bearing George's name. The land was granted to Washington's great-grandfather in 1674. G.W. lived here most of his life, with time out for being a soldier and a president. He died and was buried here in 1799. What a setting! He certainly had an eye for prime real estate.

Mount Vernon is a typical 18th-century aristocratic estate. Learn about George and his times in the new orientation and education centers. Explore the house and grounds on your own. Guides are stationed throughout the mansion to answer your questions. Take a minute, especially with youngsters, to inspect the family kitchen and outbuildings where baking, weaving, and washing took place. George and other family members are interred in a tomb a short walk from the mansion.

Mount Vernon commemorates the **Presidents' Day** holiday, the third Monday in February, by admitting visitors for free and hosting a wreath-laying at Washington's tomb, with music and military exercises by the U.S. Army Old Guard Fife and Drum Corps. On February 22, Washington's actual birthday, anyone who is named George or was born on that date gets free admission.

From late November to early December, candlelight tours of the mansion are conducted from 5 to 8 p.m. Friday through Sunday. Costumed characters, including Martha Washington, speak with the tourists. Tickets go on sale November 1 and do sell out.

Mount Vernon hosts special events throughout the year, including hands-on activities for children. Call to find out what's going on during your visit. The grounds are a great place for little kids to explore — and run off energy — while their parents take turns touring the house.

Mount Vernon has a food court and a full-service restaurant, the **Mount Vernon Inn** (☎ **703-780-0011;** www.mountvernon.org/visit/dining).

If you have a car with you, this is one place to drive. Just go south on the George Washington Parkway until it ends at George Washington's home. You also can take Metrorail and bus. You can cruise to Mount Vernon on a Washington Sprit boat (☎ 202-554-8000; www.cruisetomountvernon. com). Or you can take a Gray Line bus tour that also stops in Alexandria (☎ 800-862-1400; www.grayline.com).

See map p. 202. At the southern end of the George Washington Parkway in Virginia. ☎ 703-780-2000. www.mountvernon.org. Metro: Huntington. From the Huntington Avenue exit, take Fairfax Connector bus to Mount Vernon. Admission: $13, seniors 62 and older $12, children 6–11 accompanied by an adult $6, younger free. Candlelight tours: $15, children younger than 11 $8. Open: Daily Apr–Aug 8 a.m.–5 p.m.; Mar and Sept–Oct 9 a.m.–5 p.m.; Nov–Feb 9 a.m.–4 p.m.

National Airport
Virginia

Because travelers often heed advice to get to the airport early, they find themselves with lots of time on their hands. If you have extra time, you may want to tour National Airport on your way out of town. Here's how much of an attraction this place is: Just before the new terminal opened in 1997, thousands of Washingtonians showed up for an open house.

What you find here is the historically interesting old Terminal A and the modern new terminal. Because of heightened security, only ticketed passengers are allowed access to the gate concourses. But you can see much of the interesting stuff from outside those security checkpoints.

State-of-the-art when it opened in 1941, Terminal A was designed to be both "modern" and reflective of the area's Colonial and Neoclassical architecture. It was built on a curve and features a multilevel waiting room with picture windows that look over the runways to the Washington skyline across the Potomac River. It will be restored to its 1941 condition and continues to house gates, ticket counters, and concessions.

The new terminal also offers picture-window views of Washington landmarks. The first things you notice, of course, are the glass and metal in the walls, ceilings, and roof, with 54 domes designed to suggest Thomas Jefferson's contributions to architecture. Works by 30 artists are incorporated into the floors, walls, windows, and other elements of the terminal in various materials, including stained glass, marble, terrazzo, cast bronze, hammered aluminum and copper, painted steel, porcelain, enamel, paint on board, and paint on canvas. As a practical, functioning airport, it's easy to navigate and has an unusually good collection of eating and shopping spots.

See map p. 202. Off George Washington Memorial Parkway in Arlington, Virginia. ☎ 703-417-8000. www.metwashairports.com/national. Metro: National Airport. Admission: Free. Open: 24 hours.

National Building Museum
Downtown

The best place to begin an architecture tour of Washington is the National Building Museum, dedicated to architecture, design, engineering, construction, and urban planning. The museum itself occupies a fascinating building. Designed in 1881 and opened in 1887, it was constructed to house the Pension Bureau, a predecessor of today's Department of Veterans Affairs.

Among the building's most striking features is a 3-foot-high terra-cotta frieze that wraps for 1,200 feet around the entire exterior. Designed by Caspar Buberl, the frieze depicts a parade of Civil War soldiers. Working before the advent of modern air-conditioning and efficient electric lighting, architect Montgomery C. Meigs employed a system of windows, vents, and open archways to bathe the Great Hall in light and air. The Great Hall has a central fountain and eight 75-foot-tall Corinthian columns that are among the tallest interior columns in the world. Its monumental dimensions and spectacular appearance make the Great Hall a popular site for major events, including presidential inaugural balls. (If you'd like to host a party here, rental fees start at $11,000.)

The focus of the museum is on the building process, architectural styles, and construction techniques. The collection contains 40,000 photographs, 68,000 prints and drawings, 100 linear feet of documents, and 2,100 objects such as construction materials and architectural fragments. Planned special exhibits include "Reinventing the Globe: A Shakespearean Theater for the 21st Century," in which five architects and set designers create hypothetical Shakespearean theaters for this century (through Aug 27, 2007), "House and Home: 400 Years of Domestic Architecture" (opening spring 2008), and "Designing the World of Tomorrow: America's World's Fairs of the 1930s" (opening late 2008 or early 2009). A long-term exhibit is "Washington: Symbol and City," which tells the story of how the nation's capital grew to its current form.

Family-oriented programs are scheduled throughout the year; call or check the museum's Web site for details. Exhibits sometimes contain interactive elements aimed at youngsters. In the Building Zone, kids ages three to six can erect their own structure.

See map p. 202. 401 F St. NW (between 4th and 5th streets). ☎ **202-272-2448.** *www.nbm.org. Metro: Judiciary Square. From the F Street exit escalator, look in front of your nose. Admission: Free, but a $5 donation is requested. Open: Mon–Sat 10 a.m.–5 p.m. and Sun 11 a.m.–5 p.m. Guided tours Mon–Wed 12:30 p.m., Thurs–Sun 11:30 a.m., 12:30 and 1:30 p.m. Tours of exhibitions Fri–Sun 2:30 p.m. Call or check Web site for tours of current exhibitions. Closed Jan 1, Thanksgiving, Dec 25, and during special events.*

The Octagon Museum
Foggy Bottom

The Octagon is a museum of architecture and an architecturally interesting building. It's also a place where international history was made.

President and Mrs. Madison fled to this mansion after the British set fire to the White House during the War of 1812. It was here that Madison received and signed the Treaty of Ghent, which ended that war. The OSS, predecessor to the CIA, set up shop in the Octagon during World War II, and the National Trust for Historic Preservation was headquartered here immediately afterward.

Built between 1799 and 1801, the Octagon is one of the oldest structures in the Capital and one of the best examples of Federal architecture in the country. The Octagon was designed by William Thornton, the first architect of the U.S. Capitol. Strangely, it doesn't have eight sides. While it's not known how the Octagon acquired its name, it may have come from the round entrance hall. According to the American Architectural Foundation, round rooms in the 18th century often were formed from eight angled walls that were plastered smooth into a circle and were referred to as "octagon salons." The house was built for John and Ann Ogle Tayloe, who raised 15 children in the Octagon and continued to live here until their deaths — John's in 1828, Ann's in 1855.

Visitors can tour the house and explore exhibits. If you tour the building, you see the Octagon as it looked during the last 11 years of John Tayloe's life. The museum collection includes more than 100,000 architectural drawings, 30,000 historic photographs, 760 pieces of decorative arts, and nearly 14,000 archeological artifacts and architectural fragments from the building and its grounds, as well as scrapbooks, sketchbooks, manuscripts, and models.

The Octagon was closed to the general public for a long-term improvement project which began in 2006. During that project, pre-arranged tours were available only to groups of at least ten. Call to find out if that's changed at the time of your visit.

See map p. 202. 1799 New York Ave. NW (at 18th Street). ☎ *202-638-3221.* www.archfoundation.org/octagon. *Metro: Farragut West. From the 18th Street exit, walk 5 blocks south on 18th. Admission, when open, was: $5, children and seniors $3. When open, hours were: Tues–Sun from 10 a.m.–4 p.m. Closed Thanksgiving, Dec 25, and Jan 1.*

Union Station
Capitol Hill

This is Washington's back-to-the-future headquarters. After years of blight, Union Station has become the most bustling hub in town. The train is the very best way to travel in the Washington–New York corridor today. Hordes of subway travelers use the Metrorail station here daily. Maryland and Virginia commuter trains converge here. Cabs line up for business. Tour buses come and go. And — as I detail in Chapter 12 and elsewhere in the book — Union Station is a great place for shopping, eating, movie-going, and teens hanging out. More than 25 million people pass through this place every year.

The building is, indeed, a railroad palace. It was designed in grand Beaux Arts style by Daniel Burnham, who gathered inspiration from the Diocletian Baths and the Arch of Constantine in Rome. When construction was completed in 1908, Union Station occupied more land area than any other U.S. building and there was no bigger train station in the world. Presidents really used the President's Room (now home to B. Smith's Restaurant), and kings, queens, and other world leaders passed through with regularity.

Airplanes and interstate highways drove the station into a long decline. But a monumental renovation campaign led to a spectacular reopening in 1988, and now you can gaze upon the grandeur that welcomed travelers nearly a century ago — with a lot of new amenities.

A fountain and statue of Columbus stand outside the building, along with a replica of the Liberty Bell. The facade is festooned with eagles. Inside, sculptures of Roman soldiers by Augustus Sant-Gaudens stand guard over the Main Hall, which features a 96-foot high barrel-vaulted ceiling. The East Hall boasts stenciled skylights. At the east end of the East Hall, be sure to peek into B. Smith's to see the soaring ceilings and ornate architecture of the President's Room.

See map p. 202. 50 Massachusetts Ave. NE (at 1st Street). ☎ *202-289-1908.* www.unionstationdc.com. *Metro: Union Station. Admission: Free. Station open 24 hours. Most shops and food court spots open 10 a.m.–9 p.m. Mon–Sat and noon–6 p.m. Sun. Some restaurants close later.*

Washington National Cathedral
Upper Northwest

The cathedral, founded to serve all faiths (though it's affiliated with the Episcopal denomination), raises its towers higher than anything else in Washington and can be seen throughout D.C. and into the Virginia suburbs. President Theodore Roosevelt and the bishop of London participated in the laying of the foundation stone, which came from a field near Bethlehem, in 1907. Like its European predecessors, this cathedral — officially named the Cathedral Church of Saint Peter and Saint Paul — wasn't built in a day. Constructed in the traditional "stone-on-stone" method (no structural steel), the building was completed in 1990.

You can find much to see and do here, outside as well as inside. Guided tours of the cathedral leave from the west entrance off Wisconsin Avenue daily. Check this Web site (www.cathedral.org/cathedral/visit/tour.shtml) for details of this and other tours. You can rent an audio tour or wander about on your own. Whatever you do, be sure to check out the gardens as well as the interior.

The real business of the church — weddings, funerals, worship services, and the like — supersedes touring. Some programs are offered on irregular schedules, so calling before you visit is wise. Kids 6 to 12 enjoy the Gargoyle's Den, held in the crypt classroom Saturday from 10 a.m. to 2 p.m. They can try stone carving, make a gargoyle, work with stained glass and mosaics, and learn about cathedral construction. After the workshop, children can join a supervised scavenger hunt around the cathedral. Children should have adult companions. Fee varies from $1 to $5. Youngsters 10 and older enjoy the gargoyle tour, 2 p.m. on the fourth Sunday of each month from April through October, also 6:30 p.m. on the fourth Thursday May through July, $5. Bring binoculars, and look for Darth Vader.

The cathedral is a bit off the standard tourist path, but you can grab a good lunch or dinner at several neighborhood restaurants:

- ✔ **2 Amys** (see review in Chapter 10). This place serves the best pizza in town — real Neapolitan pizza, with thin, chewy crust. It's a great spot for kids.

- ✔ **Cactus Cantina** (3300 Wisconsin Ave. NW, north of Macomb Street; ☎ 202-686-7222), a large, boisterous Tex-Mex spot with an outdoor dining area, where my daughter once encountered President Bush II and his entourage.

- ✔ **Cafe Deluxe** (3228 Wisconsin Ave., south of Macomb; ☎ 202-686-2233), a bistro with indoor and outdoor tables and an eclectic menu of New American and traditional comfort foods with a twist: burgers, chicken pot pie, grilled meatloaf with Creole sauce, pan roasted halibut with corn and asparagus sauté, and penne pasta with chicken and asparagus.

You can take tea after a tour of the Cathedral itself on Tuesdays and Wednesdays, except for some holidays. Tour begins at 1:30 p.m. inside the west entrance off Wisconsin Avenue. Tea is served at tour's end in the Pilgrim Observation Gallery, where you can gaze through arched windows at the city and beyond. It costs $22 per person, and you need to make reservations as early as six months ahead of time by calling ☎ **202-537-8993.**

See map p. 202. Massachusetts and Wisconsin avenues NW. (You can't miss it!) General info ☎ 202-537-6200; recorded info 202-364-6616. www.cathedral.org/cathedral. *Take an N-series Metrobus up Massachusetts Avenue from Dupont Circle. Or catch a 30-series bus, which runs along Pennsylvania Avenue, M Street, and Wisconsin Avenue. Or take a taxi. Admission: Free, offerings accepted. Fees vary for tours, programs. Open: Mon–Fri 10 a.m.–5:30 p.m., June–Labor Day until 7:45 p.m.; Sat 10 a.m.–4:30 p.m.; Sun 8 a.m.–6:30 p.m. Cathedral tours Mon–Sat 10–11:30 a.m. and 12:45–3:15 p.m.; Sun 12:45–2:30 p.m. Other tours (gardens, gargoyles, and so on) at various times. Services Sun 8, 9, 10, 11 a.m., 4 and 6:30 p.m.; Mon–Sat 7:30 a.m., noon, and 2:30 and 5:30 p.m.*

Seeing Washington by Guided Tour

Travelers with limited time and/or limited mobility can benefit from taking a general orientation tour. So can visitors who like to check out the forest before inspecting the trees. Guided tours also make sense for those with kids in tow, seniors, and travelers with special interests. In Washington, you can tour historic, cultural, and even scandal-ridden sites. And you can do it by bus, bike, boat, motorized scooter, and foot — for an hour or for a day or more.

General orientation tours

Tourmobile (☎ 202-554-5100; www.tourmobile.com) takes the prize as the best general tour operator in the city. The area's largest sightseeing organization is licensed by the National Park Service and operates its trams year-round.

The company's **American Heritage Tour** makes about two dozen tram stops on or near the Mall and Pennsylvania Avenue, then heads off to Arlington Cemetery for another four stops. You can get off and on the trams as often as you like during the day. Some visitors remain on board for an entire loop, listening as the Tourmobile guide points out places of interest and discusses their history, then take a second go-round, getting off at spots that interest them.

Using Tourmobile is an excellent way to familiarize yourself with the major tourist areas. One-day tickets cost $20 for adults, $10 for kids 3 to 11, and free for younger tots. You can purchase tickets from the driver or at ticket booths at select boarding points along the tram route. Tourmobile runs from 9:30 a.m. to 4:30 p.m. daily except December 25 and January 1. Final reboarding is 3:30 p.m.

If you find the prospect of tackling both D.C. and Arlington in one day too taxing, Tourmobile offers a separate Arlington Cemetery Tour. The cost is $6 for adults, $5 for seniors 65 and older, $5 for children 3 to 11, and free for those younger. You can purchase tickets at the Arlington Cemetery Visitors Center. This tour departs the visitor center daily except December 25 from 8:30 a.m. to 6:30 p.m. from April through September and 9:30 a.m. to 4:30 p.m. the rest of the year.

Old Town Trolley (☎ 202-832-9800; www.historictours.com/washington) operates much like Tourmobile, except you ride in a bus outfitted to look like an old-time trolley car. You can get on and off the trolley whenever the spirit moves you. It takes about two and a quarter hours for a trolley to complete one loop. First departure from Union Station is at 9 a.m. Trolleys stop running at 5:30 p.m., 4:30 p.m. in winter. (Inquire about the final departure from the last stop you plan to use.) Trolleys don't run July 4, December 25, Thanksgiving, the Sunday of Memorial Day weekend, and during the Marine Corps Marathon. Prices are $32 for adults, $16 children ages 4 to 12, younger kids are free.

For the same prices, the Trolley will take you on a two-and-a-half-hour **Monuments by Moonlight** tour that lets you see D.C.'s memorials and monuments illuminated in all their nighttime glory — at least during part of the tour. The guides let you in on such secrets as which president's ghost haunts Congress. (Which ones don't?) The tour departs nightly from Union Station at 6:30 p.m. during fall and winter and 7:30 p.m. in spring and summer. It doesn't run January 1, July 4, Thanksgiving, December 25, or December 31. Reservations are required. The best time to take this tour is late fall and winter, when the entire Moonlight Tour actually takes place after dark.

Tourmobile Route

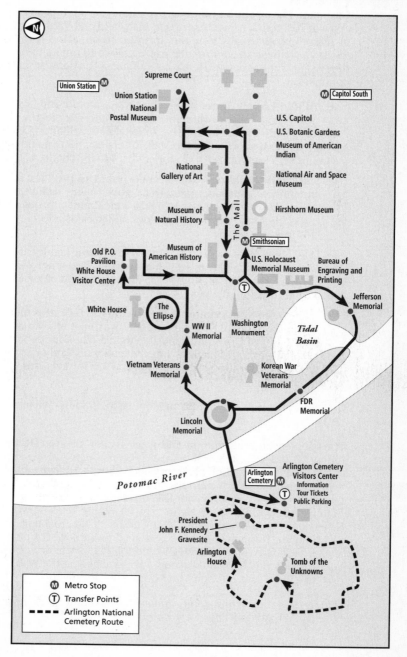

You can buy discounted tickets at the Old Town Trolley Web site.

Gray Line (☎ 800-862-1400; www.grayline.com) offers an extensive array of D.C. tours, as well as trips to Maryland and Virginia attractions by motor coach, usually from the Gray Line terminal in Union Station. Always call ahead to confirm departure times and points because they're subject to change. Here's a sampling of the company's touring options.

- ✔ **L'il Red Trolley Tours** are similar to Tourmobile and Old Town Trolley and make a continuous loop around Washington. Some stops include the Capitol, the National Zoo, Arlington Cemetery, and several spots along the Mall. Riders can hop on and off as they choose. The tour costs $25 for adults, $10 for children.

- ✔ The **Public Buildings Tour** is a nine-hour trek past and through monuments, museums, memorials, government buildings, and historical sites. The tour starts at 8:30 a.m. Monday through Saturday and costs $45 for ages 12 and older, $22 for kids 3 to 11, younger kids free.

- ✔ Gray Line starts its three-hour **after-dark tour** nightly at 7:45 p.m. except on January 1, July 4, Thanksgiving, December 24, December 25, and December 31. Cost is $35 for ages 12 and older, $17 for ages 3 to 11, free for younger.

- ✔ A nine-hour **Combination Tour** takes in top D.C. sites plus visits to Arlington National Cemetery, George Washington's Mount Vernon home, and Old Town Alexandria, Virginia. The tour departs at 8:30 a.m. daily except Thanksgiving, December 25, January 1, and July 4. It costs $57 for those 12 and older, and $28 for kids 3 to 11, younger free.

Gray Line also runs excursions to Monticello, Colonial Williamsburg, and Gettysburg.

The people who bring you the Old Town Trolley also run **DC Ducks** tours (☎ 202-832-9800; www.historictours.com/washington), an entertaining combination of history and silliness. Utilizing amphibious vehicles that transported troops and supplies during World War II, they take visitors past several major D.C. attractions before plunging into the Potomac to float past more sights. The 90-minute keels-on-wheels tours depart daily on the hour from Union Station 10 a.m. to 4 p.m. in spring and summer. Tours may be cancelled in bad weather, so it pays to phone ahead. Tickets cost $28 for ages 13 and up, $14 for children 4 to 12. Younger kids ride free and discounts are available at the Web site. The drivers will be wise-quacking, and eventually so will you.

DC Ducks seating is first-come, first-seated, so show up early or you may have to wait another hour for your ride.

River tours

Hit the deck and see the capital city's pretty face from the Potomac — on a real boat, not a duck. For a 45-minute narrated float, take one of the Capitol River Cruises' boats from Georgetown's Washington Harbour dock (bottom of 31st Street). The cruise runs hourly noon to 8 p.m. every day April through October, and until 9 p.m. Memorial Day through Labor Day. The cost is $12 for adults and $6 for kids 3 to 12. Call ☎ 800-405-5511 or 301-460-7447 or visit its Web site at www.capitolriver cruises.com.

Canal rides

Board a mule-drawn canal boat for a trip along the historic C&O Canal. *The Georgetown* is berthed in (where else?) Georgetown, near the Chesapeake and Ohio Canal National Historical Park visitor center (1057 Thomas Jefferson St. NW, just south of M Street). From early April through October, the boat plies the canal for delightful one-hour rides, manned (and womaned) by volunteers in period clothing, while National Park Service rangers narrate. Schedules vary, so call ☎ 202-653-5190 or check the Web at www.nps.gov/choh for details. Tickets are $8, seniors $6, kids $5.

Bike tours

Several guided bicycle tours are available through **Bike the Sites** (☎ 202-842-2453; www.bikethesites.com). The Capital Sites Tour covers everything between the Lincoln Memorial and the Supreme Court. The journey lasts three hours and covers 7 to 8 miles of easy pedaling, nearly all on flat land. Other tours of between two and three and a half hours focus on landmarks at night, monuments, sculptures, and D.C.-based movies. There also are special tours for families with kids. The guide stops frequently so bikers can consume some history and humor with their granola bars. Most tours cost $40, $30 for kids 12 and younger, and include bike, helmet, water, and snack. Tours leave from a purple and yellow kiosk on 12th Street NW between Pennsylvania and Constitution avenues, across 12th from the Federal Triangle Metrorail Station. Call for times and to make reservations.

If you want a bike to explore Washington on your own, Bike the Sites will be happy to rent one to you.

Chapter 12

Shopping the Local Stores

. . . .

In This Chapter

▶ Visiting the big brands and unique local shops
▶ Exploring great shopping neighborhoods
▶ Hitting the outdoor markets
▶ Shopping for specific needs

. . . .

I know that shopping isn't your top reason for coming to Washington. And I know that, to the extent you'd like to taste some of the shopping Washington has to offer, you don't want to visit the same national chains you can find back home. So, as I consider the shopping that you may want — or need — to do here, I'll clue you in to the local shops, as well as the familiar names.

Surveying the Shopping Scene

You won't find much clothing, furniture, or fashion made in D.C. Washington focuses more on making laws, rules, regulations, and headlines. But the Washington area does have artists and craftspeople whose work is displayed in D.C. galleries. And certain shops seek out interesting products that aren't found in run-of-the-mill retail establishments.

You'll find the best buys to be had are at the **museum and gallery shops,** because they make an effort to sell things related to their collections — things you can't locate in your average suburban shopping mall.

It's impossible to talk about the best times to find sales or general shopping hours anymore. Shoppers demand sales, so the typical retailer puts on some kind of sale most of the time. Retailers also set their shopping hours according to their perceptions of their customers' work schedules and shopping habits, and as part of special promotions.

 Call ahead if you want to know a certain store's hours. Otherwise, you can be fairly confident that most D.C. stores will be open at least from late morning to early evening. You're more likely to find late-night shops in late-night entertainment areas.

Don't forget to factor in your contribution to the local government's coffers when you consider the price of an item. The sales tax is 5.75 percent in Washington, 5 percent in Maryland, and 4.5 percent in Virginia. Thank you for your support!

Checking Out the Big Names

Washington lost its last local department store name — Hecht's — when Federated Department Stores decided to tag everything **Macy's** or Bloomingdale's. Hecht's old flagship store Downtown, at the Metro Center Metrorail Station, is now a Macy's (1201 G St. NW; ☎ 202-628-6661). Hecht's old Friendship Heights store — which previously had been Woodward & Lothrop, another deceased local business — was torn down, and a new Bloomingdale's is being built on the site.

Neiman Marcus (☎ 202-966-9700; www.neimanmarcus.com) — the Texas-based emporium that sells six-figure Christmas gifts and is picketed regularly by antifur activists — anchors one side of **Mazza Gallerie**, an urban shopping mall at 5300 Wisconsin Ave. It's right at the Friendship Heights Metrorail Station.

Lord & Taylor, best known for women's clothing, is at 5255 Western Ave. NW, also near the Friendship Heights Metrorail Station (☎ 202-362-9600; www.lordandtaylor.com).

Saks Fifth Avenue's Maryland store is a rather regal structure that stands oddly alone in the midst of its own large parking lot at 5555 Wisconsin Ave. (☎ 301-657-9000; www.saksfifthavenue.com). The **Saks Fifth Avenue Men's Store** sits across Mazza Gallerie's main lobby from Neiman Marcus, at 5300 Wisconsin Ave. NW (☎ 202-363-2059).

Taking It to the Street

Old-fashioned markets of various kinds are still alive and kicking in Washington. The early dog gets the flea — or something like that — when shoppers battle for bargains at flea markets. Don't be afraid to bargain for your bargain. A lot of folks think that's the main reason to frequent flea markets. The best one in Washington is Capitol Hill's **Eastern Market** (7th Street SE, between C Street and North Carolina Avenue; ☎ 202-544-0083; www.easternmarket.net; Metro: Eastern Market). It's a riot of activity on weekends. Scores upon scores of farmers, grocers, artists, craftsmen, and vendors peddle their wares inside the historic market building and in the open spaces and storefronts that surround it. Chefs join the locals and party-givers who shop here on Saturday, when the produce and flowers are especially plentiful. Activity occurs all week long inside the Victorian-era building, where various butchers, bakers, fishmongers, and grocers have their permanent stands in the South Hall. The North Hall has been turned into an arts-and-crafts center, open

Shopping in Washington, D.C.

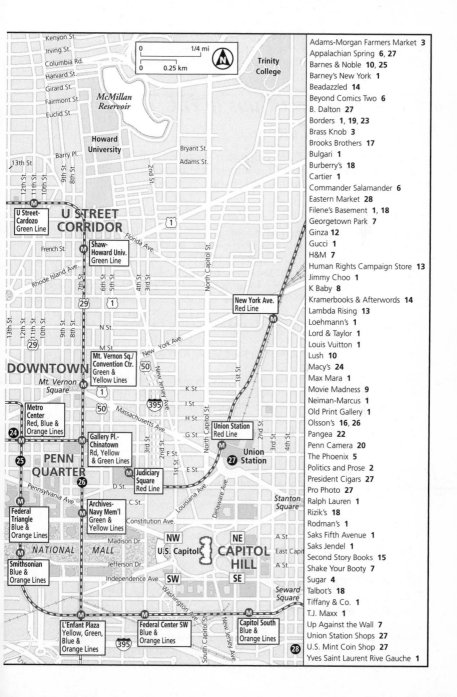

Adams-Morgan Farmers Market **3**
Appalachian Spring **6, 27**
Barnes & Noble **10, 25**
Barney's New York **1**
Beadazzled **14**
Beyond Comics Two **6**
B. Dalton **27**
Borders **1, 19, 23**
Brass Knob **3**
Brooks Brothers **17**
Bulgari **1**
Burberry's **18**
Cartier **1**
Commander Salamander **6**
Eastern Market **28**
Filene's Basement **1, 18**
Georgetown Park **7**
Ginza **12**
Gucci **1**
H&M **7**
Human Rights Campaign Store **13**
Jimmy Choo **1**
K Baby **8**
Kramerbooks & Afterwords **14**
Lambda Rising **13**
Loehmann's **1**
Lord & Taylor **1**
Louis Vuitton **1**
Lush **10**
Macy's **24**
Max Mara **1**
Movie Madness **9**
Neiman-Marcus **1**
Old Print Gallery **1**
Olsson's **16, 26**
Pangea **22**
Penn Camera **20**
The Phoenix **5**
Politics and Prose **2**
President Cigars **27**
Pro Photo **27**
Ralph Lauren **1**
Rizik's **18**
Rodman's **1**
Saks Fifth Avenue **1**
Saks Jendel **1**
Second Story Books **15**
Shake Your Booty **7**
Sugar **4**
Talbot's **18**
Tiffany & Co. **1**
T.J. Maxx **1**
Up Against the Wall **7**
Union Station Shops **27**
U.S. Mint Coin Shop **27**
Yves Saint Laurent Rive Gauche **1**

Tuesday through Friday 11 a.m. to 5 p.m., Saturday and Sunday from 8 a.m. The indoor market is open Tuesday through Saturday from 7 a.m. to 6 p.m., Sunday 9 a.m. to 4 p.m. The outdoor farmers' market is open 8 a.m. to 6 p.m. Saturday and Sunday. There's an arts-and-crafts fair from 10 a.m. to 5 p.m. Saturday, a flea market those same hours on Sunday.

Hunting Down Best Buys in D.C.'s Prime Shopping Zones

During your time in D.C., perhaps as a break from all that sightseeing, you may want to check out the following shopping areas. Each neighborhood has its own unique characteristics.

Adams-Morgan

Adams-Morgan is jammed with restaurants, clubs, and interesting shops — and with people trying to get into them. The heart of this ethnically diverse neighborhood beats at 18th Street NW and Columbia Road. Take Metrorail to the Woodley Park-Zoo-Adams-Morgan Station, walk south 1 long block on Connecticut Avenue, left 5 long blocks on Calvert Street, and then bear right a half block to 18th and Columbia. In evenings and on weekends, you can take the no. 98 Metrobus from the station to Calvert and Columbia. It runs from 5:59 p.m. to 3:15 a.m. weeknights, from 9:50 a.m. to 3:15 a.m. Saturdays, and from 6:05 p.m. to 12:15 a.m. Sundays. After dark, it's best to take the bus or a taxi.

You can enjoy a number of secondhand and one-of-a-kind stores here selling clothing, antiques, foodstuffs, and other items. On Saturday, you can find a **farmers' market** at 18th Street and Columbia. Check out a haunt of decorators and do-it-yourselfers at **The Brass Knob** (2311 18th St. NW; ☎ 202-332-3370), for architectural acquisitions recovered from demolished houses and office buildings.

When you enter a Metrorail station to begin your trip, get a transfer ticket from the machine on the mezzanine level. Hand the bus driver the transfer and 35¢.

Carry exact fare; the drivers don't make change. You don't get a discount when you transfer from bus to train. Transfers between buses are free within a two-hour period.

Connecticut Avenue/Dupont Circle

The shopping on Connecticut Avenue changes flavor as you walk north from the Farragut North Metrorail Station at K Street to the Dupont Circle Metrorail Station and beyond. Between K and M streets, where many lawyers and lobbyists ply their not-unrelated trades, you can browse such traditional clothiers as **Brooks Brothers** (1201 Connecticut Ave.; ☎ 202-659-4650); **Talbot's** (1122 Connecticut Ave.; ☎ 202-887-6973);

and **Burberry's** (1155 Connecticut Ave.; ☎ **202-463-3000**). Clothing bargain hunters will like **Filene's Basement** (1133 Connecticut Ave.; ☎ **202-872-8430**). Women who need a little something to wear to a black-tie affair at the White House shop at **Rizik's** (1100 Connecticut Ave.; ☎ **202-223-4050**), which has been offering designer garments and excellent service since 1908.

As you get closer to Dupont Circle, shoppers and shopkeepers are less likely to be wearing suits and carrying briefcases and more likely to be outfitted in jeans and unnatural hair colors. Check out the galleries, booksellers, secondhand stores, and specialty boutiques in this lively neighborhood, which is one of Washington's major entertainment centers, home to many nonprofit organizations, and the heart of D.C.'s gay community. Try **Kramerbooks & Afterwords** for books, food, and drink into the wee hours (1517 Connecticut Ave.; ☎ **202-387-1400**). The staff at **Beadazzled** (1507 Connecticut Ave.; ☎ **202-265-2323**) can help you make a necklace from a large selection of beads. In search of a kimono and fan? Look no further than **Ginza** (1721 Connecticut Ave.; ☎ **202-331-7991**). **Lambda Rising** (1625 Connecticut Ave.; 202-462-6969) is D.C.'s leading gay/lesbian-oriented bookstore. The **Human Rights Campaign,** America's largest gay rights political action organization, runs a store at 1629 Connecticut Ave. (☎ **202-232-8621**).

Georgetown

Many art galleries, antiques stores, and specialty shops help make Georgetown one of Washington's liveliest neighborhoods from morning until after midnight. This community is truly diverse, sporting some of the city's most expensive residences, Georgetown University, and its student rooming houses. Folks from all walks of life stroll the commercial blocks defined by M Street NW, Wisconsin Avenue, and nearby side streets. You see old women with blue hair and young women with blue hair — just different tints. Walk from the Foggy Bottom–George Washington University Metrorail Station, or take a 30-series Metrobus, Circulator bus, or Georgetown Connection shuttle. You'll recognize the major national chain stores when you walk past them, so let me concentrate on some others — local, or at least unusual.

- ✔ **Movie Madness** (1083 Thomas Jefferson St.; ☎ **202-337-7064**) sells movie posters.

- ✔ **Commander Salamander** (1420 Wisconsin Ave.; ☎ **202-337-2265**) sells punkish clothing, colored wigs, and off-the-wall gifts. This store is popular with teens.

- ✔ **The Phoenix** (1514 Wisconsin Ave.; ☎ **202-338-4404**) has been selling Mexican folk art and bric-a-bracs, handcrafted silver jewelry, and those peasant blouses once favored by Joan Baez since 1955.

- ✔ For some comic relief — and more — check out **Beyond Comics** (1419 Wisconsin Ave.; ☎ **202-333-8650**) for comic books and the toys, dolls, T-shirts, and other paraphernalia that the comic characters spawn.

✔ **Up Against the Wall** (3219 M St.; ☎ 202-337-9316) sells trendy clothes for teens and young adults.

✔ **Shake Your Booty** (3225 M St.; ☎ 202-333-6524) supplies boots — and shoes — to folks inclined to shake their thing.

✔ **Lush** (3066 M St. NW; ☎ 202-333-6950), popular in Great Britain, opened one of its first U.S. stores here to sell fresh-made bath bombs, soaps, and other natural beauty products.

✔ **H&M** (3222 M St. NW; ☎ 202-298-6792), from Sweden, a hip international chain store, offers trendy, inexpensive clothing for the whole family.

✔ **Old Print Gallery** (1220 31st St. NW; ☎ 202-965-1818) offers the area's largest selection of antique prints and maps.

✔ **K Baby** (3112 M St. NW; ☎ 202-333-3939) targets babies — and their mommies who crave high-end clothing and nursery accessories.

✔ **Sugar** (1633 Wisconsin Ave. NW; ☎ 202-333-5331) boutique attracts celebrities in search of hot designers' clothes plus jewelry made by local designers.

✔ **Appalachian Spring** (1415 Wisconsin Ave. NW; **202-337-5780**) carries a wide selection of American crafts made of wood, glass, and fiber.

✔ If you suffer mall withdrawal, you can find a slew of upscale national chains at **Georgetown Park** (3222 M St.; ☎ 202-342-2688).

Union Station

A magnificent railway terminal, **Union Station** (50 Massachusetts Ave. NE; ☎ 202-289-1908; www.unionstationdc.com; Metro: Union Station) serves Washington in multiple ways — train station, Metrorail station, intercity bus depot, tour bus departure point, taxi stand, fast-food court, full-service restaurant station, and super shopping destination. National chains are well represented here. But you also encounter some unique shops as well.

The most interesting spot here is the **East Hall Gallery.** The gallery's central open area contains small stands that sell a variety of jewelry, arts, and crafts. Encircling the open area are stores, one of which, **Appalachian Spring** (☎ 202-682-0505), is a favorite of my family. My daughter acquired a wonderful monkey puppet (whom she named "Fred") here when she was young. Each time we return, we check to assure ourselves that Fred's younger relatives do, indeed, still hang out here. The quilt on Susan's and my bed comes from the Appalachian Spring Georgetown store, the first, which opened in 1964. Originally, Appalachian Spring dealt exclusively in arts and crafts from the

Appalachian Mountains. Now it carries original works from throughout the United States.

Right outside the East Hall is a **coin shop** operated by the **U.S. Mint** (☎ 202-289-0609). Elsewhere in the station are a cigar shop that goes by the moniker **President Cigars** (☎ 202-289-2559) and a **Discovery Channel Store** (☎ 202-842-3700), run by the TV/Internet empire that's headquartered in Washington's Maryland suburbs.

If you get hungry here, you'll have no trouble finding something to eat. Several full-service **restaurants** are scattered around the station. (See Chapter 10 for **B. Smith's.**) The lower-level **food court** is enormous and offers a wide variety of cuisines.

Upper Wisconsin Avenue

Just outside the Friendship Heights Metrorail Station is what I call **Washington's Rodeo Drive.** A few blocks of Wisconsin Avenue, on both sides of the Washington-Maryland border, provide retail space for some of the best-known names in up-up-up-scale shopping. (I happen to live near here, so I'll tell you about the downscale stores — where I shop — as well.)

If Tiffany and friends appeal to you, gather up your titanium credit cards and follow me. I've already mentioned **Saks Fifth Avenue, Saks's men's store, Neiman Marcus,** and **Lord & Taylor.** Also ready to sell you expensive goods in this neighborhood are **Saks Jandel** (5510 Wisconsin Ave.; ☎ 301-652-2250); **Tiffany & Co.** (5481 Wisconsin Ave.; ☎ 301-657-8777); **Yves Saint Laurent Rive Gauche** (5510 Wisconsin Ave.; ☎ 301-656-8868); **Ralph Lauren** (5471 Wisconsin Ave.; ☎ 301-718-4223); **Barney's New York** (5471 Wisconsin Ave.; ☎ 301-634-4061); **Max Mara** (5471 Wisconsin Ave.; ☎ 301-656-0581); **Louis Vuitton** (5555 Wisconsin Ave.; ☎ 301-656-2191); **Cartier** (5471 Wisconsin Ave.; ☎ 301-654-5858); **Jimmy Choo** (5481 Wisconsin Ave.; ☎ 240-223-1102); **Gucci** (5481 Wisconsin Ave.; ☎ 301-986-8902); and **Bulgari** (5481 Wisconsin Ave.; ☎ 301-966-8610).

Now, just so you don't get the wrong idea about my neighborhood, let me tell you that you can have an eclectic shopping experience here if you want it. Neiman's and Saks's men's stores are major anchors of the **Mazza Gallerie** (5300 Wisconsin Ave.) shopping mall. So is discounter **Filene's Basement** (☎ 202-966-0208). Across Jenifer Street from Mazza and across 44th Street from Lord & Taylor sits another discounter, **T.J. Maxx** (☎ 202-237-7616). Across Wisconsin from Mazza is another indoor mall, **Chevy Chase Pavilion.** Next door is **Loehmann's** (5333 Wisconsin Ave. NW; ☎ 202-362-4733), an off-price mecca since the first store opened in Brooklyn in 1921. New merchandise, including a small amount for men, appears regularly, and women flock to the famous Back Room for their favorite designers' clothes at 30 percent to 65 percent off regular retail.

The easiest way to get to the area is to take Metrorail to the Friendship Heights Station and follow the signs to the Western Avenue exits. After you go through the Metro gate and up the escalator, you find yourself in a sort of rotunda, with four exits to choose from. The hard left takes you to the Western Avenue and 44th Street exit and Mazza Gallerie. The soft left takes you to the Wisconsin and Western avenues exit, from where you can walk up Wisconsin toward the upscale stores in Maryland. Straight ahead is the Western Avenue and Military Road exit, which takes you toward Clyde's restaurant and the new Collection of Chevy Chase shopping area where some of the upscale stores are located. The doors to your right take you right into Chevy Chase Pavilion.

This neighborhood presents you with numerous dining options. See reviews of **Clyde's, Booeymonger,** and **Chipotle** in Chapter 10. You can get good, *huge* meals at the **Cheesecake Factory** (5335 Wisconsin Ave.; ☎ 202-364-0500) in the Pavilion, but you may have to wait at meal times because they don't take reservations. At **Maggiano's Little Italy** (5333 Wisconsin Ave.; ☎ 202-966-5500), they take reservations but don't seem to know what they're for; you can make a reservation, show up on time, and still have to wait. What really irks me, in addition to that, is that while they think nothing of keeping you waiting, they won't seat you until your entire party has arrived, even if you're only one short. Another Italian option is **Lia's** (4445 Willard Ave., just west of Wisconsin, 1 block north of Western; ☎ 240-223-5427). Yet another is **Famoso** (5471 Wisconsin Ave.; ☎ 301-986-8785), in the Collection of Chevy Chase shopping area.

In the front end of Maggiano's, the **Corner Bakery** (☎ 202-237-2200) serves sandwiches, salads, and pastas. **Chadwick's** (5247 Wisconsin; ☎ 202-362-8040) is a neighborhood hangout; I find the burgers, salads, and crab cakes to be best. **Bambule** (5225 Wisconsin Ave.; ☎ 202-966-0300) serves tapas and has comfortable lounge seating and outdoor dining in good weather. **Cosi** (5252 Wisconsin Ave.; ☎ 202-537-9000) sells soups, salads, and sandwiches, as does **Panera** (4459 Willard Ave.; ☎ 301-951-5858) near Lia's. Fancier and more expensive is the French/Mediterranean restaurant **Matisse** (4934 Wisconsin Ave.; ☎ 202-244-5222). The best way to enjoy the wonderful Indian food at **Indique Heights** (2 Wisconsin Circle, above the bus terminal at the Western-Wisconsin intersection; ☎ 301-656-4822) is to order from the small-plates menu. Also on the circle are **Potomac Pizza** (19 Wisconsin Circle; ☎ 301-951-1127) and **Gifford's Ice Cream** (21 Wisconsin Circle; ☎ 301-652-8965).

For a look at a real Friendship Heights neighborhood institution, walk south on Wisconsin Avenue to Garrison Street and check out **Rodman's** (5100 Wisconsin Ave.; ☎ 202-363-3466). It's sort of a 21st-century general store. Someone from our house comes here nearly every day — to buy milk or bread or wine or toothpaste or bath beads or toilet paper or a kitchen gadget or a birthday card or to get a watch repaired or to pick up a prescription. This place is, after all, a pharmacy . . . and an international food emporium and an electronics shop. Okay, you get the picture.

(And you can get film and developing services, including digital prints.) If you need something that fits on a shelf, you just may find it here. If you're here at the right time, you may catch Roy Rodman roaming the aisles, negotiating a deal with a wholesaler on his portable phone. I was here once, after a blizzard, when grocers around town were running out of basics, and I noticed with surprise that Rodman's had lots of milk. I commented on this irony to a clerk, who told me that a milk truck had broken down in front of the store the day before, and Mr. Rodman had negotiated to buy the whole load.

Shopping for Specialties in D.C.

Are you looking to buy a specific product rather than to browse a shopping area? Check this section to find what you're looking for.

Bookstores

Washington is a literary town, so you can buy books in lots of places. Here's a sampling:

- ✔ It's off the beaten tourist path, but **Politics and Prose** (5015 Connecticut Ave. NW; ☎ **202-364-1919**) is a wonderful bookstore. It's a neighborhood institution in a neighborhood that happens to have lots of writers. So, beyond the books for sale, something is always going on here. C-SPAN is taping a writer who's reading from or talking about his book. An author is signing books or celebrating a new publication. (The coming-out party for the first book Susan and I wrote was here.) You may bump into George Will or Tim Russert while browsing in the current affairs section. A funky coffee house is in the lower level. Take an L-series Metrobus from Dupont Circle or catch a cab.

- ✔ Before it became a universal requirement that bookstores house cafes, **Kramerbooks & Afterwords** (1517 Connecticut Ave. NW; ☎ **202-387-1400**) was serving up food, drink, and live music with its printed products. I'm talking full bar, breakfast, lunch, dinner, and late supper. This place is open from 7:30 a.m. to 1 a.m. daily, and around the clock from Friday morning until 1 a.m. Monday. Brunch is served Saturday and Sunday, including all night. Did I mention that they sell books?

- ✔ **Olsson's Books & Records** is Washington's local bookstore chain, with two shops in the city and others in the suburbs, including one at Reagan National Airport (☎ **703-417-1087**). The stores survive in an era dominated by national chains by focusing on their communities. Each store's manager stocks reading matter and music that he knows his clientele is most interested in. You'll find more theater, film, and music at the location that's next door to the Shakespeare Theater in the Penn Quarter arts and entertainment district (418 7th St. NW; ☎ **202-638-7610** for books, 202-638-7613 for music), and more ecology and politics for the activists who work around Dupont Circle at that branch (1307 19th St. NW; ☎ 202-785-1133 for books, 202-785-2662 for music).

✔ Bargain hunters and collectors browse the shelves of **Second Story Books** by Dupont Circle (2000 P St. NW; ☎ 202-659-8884). It's Washington's premier used and rare books store and also has two locations in the suburbs. Proprietor Allan Stypeck is a host of "The Book Guys" nationally syndicated radio show. Together, the three stores have more than a million books, manuscripts, maps, prints, paintings, and vintage posters.

✔ You can get your **Borders Books & Music** fix downtown at 600 14th St. NW (☎ 202-737-1385) and 1801 L St. NW (☎ 202-466-4999), in Upper Northwest's Friendship Heights shopping area (5333 Wisconsin Ave. NW; ☎ 202-686-8270), and at National Airport (☎ 703-416-1590).

✔ **Barnes & Noble** stores are downtown (555 12th St. NW; ☎ 202-347-0176) and in Georgetown (3040 M St. NW; ☎ 202-965-9880).

✔ There's a **B. Dalton** in Union Station (☎ 202-289-1724).

Cameras

If you need to get a camera repaired, want to buy some photographic equipment, or need expert advice on the best film for what you plan to shoot (if you're among the dwindling crowd that still uses film), here are two reputable companies that buy, sell, and repair equipment and sell and process film.

✔ **Penn Camera** is at 1015 18th St. NW (☎ 202-785-7366).

✔ I've bought a camera, other equipment, and film — and sought advice — from **Pro Photo** (1902 I St. NW; ☎ 202-223-1292). I was referred there in the first place by a professional photographer.

Music and Gifts

So what you really want is music for your ears? **Olsson's, Borders,** and **Barnes & Noble** sell music as well as books. See the previous section for details.

A really unusual and interesting spot to look for unique gifts is **Pangea Artisan Market and Cafe** (2121 Pennsylvania Ave. NW; ☎ 202-872-6432). It's run by the World Bank to support artisans in developing countries. You'll find high-quality handbags, jewelry, table settings, and other crafts. You also can learn about the people who make them. And, yes, you can eat at the cafe.

Bibliophiles, music lovers, and collectors shouldn't overlook the museum and gallery stores.

Index of Stores by Merchandise

Antiques
The Brass Knob (Adams-Morgan)

Books
Barnes & Noble (Upper Northwest, Downtown)
B. Dalton (Union Station)
Borders Books (Upper Northwest, Downtown)
Kramerbooks & Afterwords (Dupont Circle)
Lambda Rising (Dupont Circle)
Olsson's (Dupont Circle, Downtown, Reagan National Airport)
Politics and Prose (Upper Northwest)
Second Story Books (Dupont Circle)

Cameras and Film
Penn Camera (Downtown)
Pro Photo (Downtown)

Clothing and Shoes
Barney's New York (Upper Northwest/Maryland)
Brooks Brothers (Downtown)
Burberry's (Downtown)
Commander Salamander (Georgetown)
Gucci (Upper Northwest/Maryland)
H&M (Georgetown)
Jimmy Choo (Upper Northwest/Maryland)
K Baby (Georgetown)
Max Mara (Upper Northwest/Maryland)
Ralph Lauren (Upper Northwest/Maryland)
Rizik's (Downtown)
Saks Fifth Avenue Men's Store (Upper Northwest)
Saks Jandel (Upper Northwest/Maryland)
Shake Your Booty (Georgetown)
Sugar (Georgetown)
Talbot's (Downtown)
Up Against the Wall (Georgetown)
Yves Saint Laurent Rive Gauche (Upper Northwest/Maryland)

Crafts
Beadazzled (Dupont Circle)

Department Stores
Lord & Taylor (Upper Northwest)
Macy's (Downtown)
Neiman Marcus (Upper Northwest)
Saks Fifth Avenue (Upper Northwest/Maryland)

Discount Shopping
Filene's Basement (Downtown, Upper Northwest)
Loehmann's (Upper Northwest)
T.J. Maxx (Upper Northwest)

Gifts and Souvenirs
Appalachian Spring (Georgetown, Union Station)
Ginza (Dupont Circle)
Pangea (West End)
The Phoenix (Georgetown)
U.S. Mint Coin Shop (Union Station)

Jewelry
Cartier (Upper Northwest/Maryland)
Tiffany & Company (Upper Northwest/Maryland)

Malls
Chevy Chase Pavilion
Georgetown Park
Mazza Gallerie
Union Station

Markets
Eastern Market (Capital Hill)
Farmers Market (Adams-Morgan)

Miscellaneous

Beyond Comics 2 (Georgetown)
Discovery Channel Store (Union Station)
Human Rights Campaign Action Center and Store (Dupont Circle)
Louis Vuitton (Upper Northwest/Maryland)
Lush (Georgetown)
Movie Madness (Georgetown)
Old Print Gallery (Georgetown)
President Cigars (Union Station)
Rodman's (Upper Northwest)

Chapter 13

Following an Itinerary: Three Great Options

So many sights, so little time! Is that your problem? Allow me to help with some suggested itineraries for seeing the top Washington sights in just three days, for seeing government in action, and for exploring D.C. with kids.

Refer to Chapter 10 for restaurant reviews and Chapter 11 for details about the top sites.

Exploring Washington in Three Days

Direct from the Rectangular Office (sorry, mine's not oval), here is a three-day agenda for visiting the cream of Washington's top sights and getting a taste of the city.

As of this writing, the **White House** is not open for tours by the general public. If it does reopen — or if you're in a group that qualifies for a tour — you'll want to put it on your itinerary, too. Call ☎ **202-456-7041** or check www.whitehouse.gov/history/tours for information and updates.

Save your Washington time for touring — not for standing in line — by buying advance tickets to the **Washington Monument** and the **Holocaust Museum.**

Day one

Start your Washington touring by getting an overview on the **Tourmobile.** Get on board at the stop closest to your hotel (drivers sell tickets) or at **Union Station.** Ride the whole route, taking in the sights from the comfort of your seat. Then continue on the Tourmobile to the **Smithsonian Institution** museum on the **National Mall** that interests you most. (Depending on where you first boarded the Tourmobile, you may save time by getting off across the Mall from your museum destination rather than riding all the way to the museum's door.) Spend some time at that museum and have lunch there or at a nearby museum on the Mall.

In the afternoon, take the Tourmobile to **Arlington National Cemetery** and transfer to Tourmobile's Arlington tour. Get off at each of the stops to visit the **Kennedy gravesites,** witness the changing of the guard at the **Tomb of the Unknowns,** and explore **Arlington House.**

Have dinner in **Georgetown.** After dinner, stroll M Street and Wisconsin Avenue to absorb the Georgetown nightlife. Treat yourself to an ice cream cone at **Dolcezza Argentine Gelato Cafe** or **Thomas Sweet.**

Day two

If the **Supreme Court** is hearing arguments today, get in line on the court plaza before 10 a.m. and take a look. One line lets you take a quick peek; the other enables you to see the entire hour-long performance. Whether or not you take in an argument, plan on touring the Court, the **Capitol,** and the **Library of Congress.**

Before you leave home, contact your representative or a senator for tickets to the special congressional tours conducted in each of these buildings.

Act like an insider and grab lunch in a **congressional cafeteria.** Enter any House or Senate office building and ask a guard for directions.

When you're done on Capitol Hill, if you have time, visit another **museum on the Mall** or the **American Art Museum and National Portrait Gallery** in the Old Patent Office Building. Then return to the Hill for a quick, inexpensive dinner in **Union Station's spacious lower-level food court** or at one of the informal restaurants that are scattered around the building. Afterward, take Gray Line's three-hour **Washington After Dark Tour,** which leaves from the bus line's terminal in the station.

Day three

Use your advance tickets for a morning visit to the **Holocaust Museum** and a late afternoon ride to the top of the **Washington Monument.** In between, try to squeeze in some time at the **National Gallery of Art,** where the **Cascade Cafe** inside or the **Pavilion Cafe** in the **Sculpture Garden** are good places for lunch. After you leave the Washington Monument, stroll down the Mall to take in the **memorials** to those who fought in **World War II, Vietnam,** and **Korea,** as well as the **Lincoln Memorial.**

If fine dining interests you and you don't mind paying for it, eat at **Kinkead's,** one of Washington's very best restaurants and one of my favorites. Otherwise, check out the reviews for the $ and $$ restaurants in Chapter 10. In warm weather, cap off your D.C. visit by having a drink with a view on the **Sky Terrace** at the top of the Hotel Washington.

Washington for Government Groupies

Many put their faith in oysters and chocolate, but Henry Kissinger declared that — based on personal experience — power is the greatest aphrodisiac. Should you agree with Henry — the former secretary of state, national security adviser, and all-around powerful person — join the government groupie patrol at the following sights. (Even if you're not a government groupie or a political junkie, you may want to tag along just to see where all those tax dollars of yours go.)

Contact your U.S. representative or one of your senators far in advance of your visit to Washington. Ask him or her for **VIP touring tickets** and for a pass to the visitors galleries in the **House and/or Senate chambers.** Also ask about stopping by to see the office — or all three of them — while you're in town.

Government Groupie Morning is much like Day Two of the three-day tour. If the **Supreme Court** is hearing arguments today, get in line on the court plaza before 10 a.m. As a government groupie, you'll want to witness the entire hour-long event. When you're not in the courtroom, tour the Court, the **Capitol,** and the **Library of Congress.** If they're in session, stop by the chambers to watch Congress at work.

You'll definitely want to have **lunch in a government cafeteria.** Ask a guard in any House or Senate office building for directions. If you feel more judicial than legislative, eat in the Supreme Court cafeteria.

Post-9/11 security has wreaked havoc on Government Groupie Day by severely restricting tours of the **White House** and the **Pentagon.** To get into the White House as I write this book, you have to be in a group of at least ten people and make reservations through a member of Congress. The Pentagon also is restricted to certain groups. Check the White House status at ☎ **202-456-7041** or www.whitehouse.gov/history/tours or the Pentagon at ☎ **703-697-1776** or pentagon.afis.osd.mil. If you can't get into the president's mansion, you can stop by the **White House Visitor Center** — which is at 1450 Pennsylvania Ave. NW — and then take a stroll over to 1600 Pennsylvania and gaze longingly through the fence.

Now, head back to the Hill and grab a drink at **Bullfeathers** (410 1st St. SE at D Street), a popular hangout for House staffers, or the **Dubliner** (520 North Capitol St. NW at F Street), which draws folks from the Senate side. For dinner, drop some bucks at one of these government groupie gathering places:

> ✔ **The Monocle,** a dining spot for senators, Senate staffers, the occasional Supreme Court justice, and others who have business on the Senate side of Capitol Hill.

> ✔ **The Palm,** where you may run into Larry King or James Carville or at least see their caricatures on the wall.

Touring Washington Family Style

Don't despair if the grandparents change their minds about staying with the children so that you can enjoy a nice, relaxing adult vacation. Bring the younger generation along! Washington is a very kid-friendly place. Just take lots of breaks and carry snacks.

With kids younger than eight . . .

Go directly to the **National Zoo.** Do not pass go. Do not collect $200. Go to the zoo. Pick up a map and schedule of events at the Education Building near the Connecticut Avenue entrance when you arrive. Children particularly enjoy watching the **animals being fed** and the **training sessions.** The more active the animals, the more enthralled the kids will be. That makes the **seals** and the **monkeys** good bets. Check out the **Orangutan Transportation System,** to see whether any apes are using their high-strung cable to swing from building to building right over your head. Small kids sometimes find it easier to identify with the small animals in the **Small Mammal House.** Children also seem to have a strange fascination with the lizards and snakes at the **Reptile Discovery Center.** Exclusively for kids are the **Kids Farm,** where they can groom animals and engage in other hands-on activities, and the **Prairie Playland,** which kids three to eight can crawl through. Everyone, of course, loves the **pandas.**

If you don't spend the entire day at the zoo (It can happen!), head for the **National Mall** and the old-fashioned **carousel** in front of the Smithsonian's **Arts and Industries Building.** Other kid-friendly happenings on the Mall include:

> ✔ The **Insect Zoo** and **Dinosaur Hall** in the **Museum of Natural History**

> ✔ Just about any of the airplanes and space vehicles in the **Air and Space Museum**

> ✔ The **sculpture gardens** outside the **National Gallery** and the **Hirshhorn Museum**

In addition, not far from the Mall is the **National Aquarium,** where children can pet a horseshoe crab in the touch tank.

With kids eight and older . . .

The **National Zoo** and the **Air and Space Museum** work for kids of all ages (including me!). So do the **IMAX Theatre** presentations in Air and Space and the **Natural History** museums. Buy a **kite** in Air and Space and fly it on the Mall — a long-standing tradition. These older kids also like the **Bureau of Engraving and Printing** tour.

The beauty of Washington for families is that it's hard to have an interest that isn't represented in the city somewhere. Ask your youngsters what they're interested in, and you should be able to find a museum — or at least a museum section — that's dedicated to the subject. Washington also has **sports, music, movies,** and **pizza.**

With teens . . .

Touring Washington with teens is easy (knock on wood). At the very least, they'll be interested in the places they've read about in their history classes.

To be a bit more specific: The gadgets and pop culture references at the **International Spy Museum** are especially attractive to teens. Lots of teens enjoy people-watching, and the sidewalks of **Georgetown** teem with watchable people. Lots of Georgetown shops cater to the teen and young-adult crowd as well. Let them explore the enormous variety of eatables at the **Union Station food court.**

To avoid feeling like you're dragging your teens around the city, ask them to thumb through this book, especially Chapter 11, and let them take the lead in planning some of your family's activities. See Chapter 11 for specific ideas.

Chapter 14

Going Beyond Washington: Three Great Day Trips

*P*oliticians work their butts off to get elected so they can come to Washington. Then they spend as little time here as possible — heading back home for as many Fridays through Mondays as they can, so they can maximize their time with their constituents and be reelected to come back. You can play that game, too, getting out of Washington for a day — even overnight — to check out some nearby attractions. This chapter describes three destinations within an hour or less of the White House (in case that's where you stay).

Day Trip #1: Discovering Old Town in Alexandria, Virginia

Like Georgetown, Alexandria was a bustling river port before anyone had even dreamed of a District of Columbia — or of a United States for D.C. to be the capital of. When the time came to plan for revolution, George Washington and other Founding Fathers did some important planning in what is now called Alexandria's **Old Town,** which is where you'll want to spend your time. The river and 18th-century buildings are still here to put you in touch with Alexandria's history. There are both inexpensive and fine-dining restaurants, along with countless shops selling a wide variety of goods. The waterfront is still active, though primarily with pleasure craft. The local economy now bustles with overflow from the capital city up the river, tourism, and a rather large artists' colony operating in an old military weapons plant. In February, locals and visitors unpack their powdered wigs for the giant Washington's Birthday Parade.

Old Town Alexandria

Potomac River

WASHINGTON, D.C.

VIRGINIA

Old Town Alexandria

0   1/8 mi

0   125 meters

FOUNDERS PARK

WATERFRONT PARK

Quay St.

Union St.

Lee St.

Prince St.

Duke St.

Wolfe St.

Fairfax St.

Royal St.

Franklin St.

Wythe St.

Pendleton St.

Oronoco St.

Princess St.

Queen St.

Market Square

King St.

Pitt St.

St. Asaph St.

Gibbon St.

To Mount Vernon, Woodlawn, and Gunston Hall

↑ To Reagan National Airport and Washington, D.C.

Alexandria Black History Resource Center

Washington St.

Columbus St.

Alfred St.

Patrick St. (Rte. 1 North)

← To I-95 and U.S. 1

← From I-95 and U.S. 1

Cameron St.

Henry St. (Rte. 1 South)

Lafayette St.

Payne St.

West St.

King St.

Duke St.

Roundhouse St.

Wilkes St.

Gibbon St.

Franklin St.

Hamilton Ln.

Hooff's Run

Cameron St.

Peyton St.

AFRICAN AMERICAN HERITAGE PARK

Jamieson Ave.

Ballenger Ave.

King Street Blue Line Yellow Line

Daingerfield Rd.

Diagonal Rd.

Alexandria Archaeology Museum **25**
Alexandria Farmer's Market **15**
A Likely Story **2**
Arts Afire **5**
Barkley Square **23**
Carlyle House **18**
Christmas Attic **22**
Elder Crafters **12**
Gadsby's Tavern **13**
Gossypia **16**
Hard Times Cafe **3**
House in the Country **19**
King Street Metrorail Station **1**

Lee-Fendall House **11**
La Cuisine **17**
Majestic Cafe **8**
Misha's Coffee **9**
My Place in Tuscany **4**
Old Town Hotel **14**
Pauline Books and Media **7**
Potomac Riverboat Company **24**
Ramsay House **20**
Ten Thousand Villages **10**
Torpedo Factory **25**
Union Street Public House **21**
Vermilion **6**

Getting to Old Town

If you drive to Old Town, go west on Independence Avenue. As you approach the Lincoln Memorial, watch closely for signs to Arlington Memorial Bridge. After you cross the bridge, turn right out of the traffic circle and then exit left, following the signs to National Airport. After you pass the airport, the parkway becomes Washington Street in Alexandria. The heart of Old Town is along **King Street,** both left and right of Washington Street.

Thumbs down on driving here in rush hour, when the 8 miles from D.C. may feel more like 80. And be warned that traffic almost always creeps on Old Town's narrow streets, and finding parking is a hassle, especially on weekends.

Out-of-town visitors can get **free 24-hour parking** permits at the **Ramsay House Visitors Center** (221 King St., east of Fairfax Street; ☎ 800-388-9119 or 703-838-5005; www.funside.com). Park your car at a two-hour meter and put in some change. At the visitor center, give your license plate number and show identification that proves you're from out of the area. Then put the pass in your car. You can renew it once. Old Town has about 20 **parking lots and garages.**

If you're coming for the day and don't have luggage in tow, **Metrorail** is a better transportation bet. Take the Yellow Line train toward Huntington or a Blue Line toward Franconia-Springfield. Get off at the **King Street Station.** You're now at the western edge of Old Town. You can start strolling east on King to explore everything Old Town has to offer. (The first couple blocks don't look like much, but you'll soon start using words like quaint and charming to describe what you're seeing.) Or you can catch a **DASH bus** (☎ 703-370-3274; www.dashbus.com) at the Metrorail Station. The 2, 5, and 7 buses travel from the station to near the eastern end of King Street. Fare's a buck — or 35¢ with a Metrorail transfer; up to two kids age four and younger ride free with an adult. The Dash About shuttle takes passengers for free between the Metro station and the visitors center Friday 7 p.m. to midnight, Saturday 10 a.m. to midnight, and Sunday 11 a.m. to 10 p.m.

Taking a tour

Alexandria offers so many tours they bump into each other as they move around town. The **Ghost and Graveyard Tour** seems to be the most popular, but I like the **Horse-Drawn Carriage Ride** better.

A guide wearing 18th-century clothes and carrying a lantern leads Alexandria Colonial Tours' **Ghost and Graveyard Tour** (☎ 703-519-1749; www.alexcolonialtours.com), which, of course, takes place at night. A guide leads the group through Old Town's old streets, with patter that's a mixture of real cultural history and old-time stories. The stories describe Alexandria residents who supposedly died in some unfortunate way that caused them to return to haunt the living. The group is "abandoned" in a graveyard, but it's not too hard to find your way out. The one-hour tour starts from the Ramsay House Visitors Center, 221 King St. (east of Fairfax Street), at 7:30 and 9 p.m. Friday and Saturday, and 7:30 p.m. Sunday from mid-March to mid-November, weather permitting. During June to November, tours also are scheduled on Wednesday and Thursday at 7:30 p.m. Tickets are $8 for tourists 13 and older, $6 for military personnel, $5 for children ages 7 to 12, and free for those younger than 7.

Another fun way to see Old Town is in a horse-drawn carriage. **Olde Towne Horse and Carriage** (☎ **703-765-8976**) offers rides Wednesday through Sunday except when it's raining, snowing, above 90 degrees or below 40. You'll clip-clop slowly through Old Town's quieter back streets. It's a quiet, relaxing excursion. You have to call ahead for reservations. Tickets cost $10 per person for a 15- to 20-minute ride. For $75, you can rent the whole carriage to take up to six people on a one-hour ride.

As a river city, Alexandria also offers a number of **boat tours** from the marina at Cameron and Union streets.

With the **Potomac Riverboat Company** (☎ **877-511-2628,** 703-548-9000; www.potomacriverboatco.com), you can cruise to, tour, and return from George Washington's Mount Vernon home; see Washington's monuments from the water; or take a water taxi trip between Alexandria and 31st Street NW in Georgetown. Prices range from $11 to $32, $11 to $30 for seniors 60 and older, and $7 to $19 for children. Boats run on varied schedules from April through October.

Seeing the sights

Write, call, or stop at the **Ramsay House Visitors Center** (221 King St., east of Fairfax Street; ☎ **800-388-9199** or 703-838-5005; www.funside. com), a replica of the early-18th-century house built by William Ramsay, a Scottish merchant and a founder of Alexandria. The center provides brochures, maps, and a special events calendar. Pick up the free **Official Visitors Guide,** which contains, among other things, directions for an **Old Town walking tour.** You also can purchase admission tickets for many historic homes and sights. Ramsay House is open daily from 9 a.m. to 5 p.m., except Thanksgiving, December 25, and January 1.

If you plan to visit historic Gadsby's Tavern, Carlyle House, and Lee-Fendall House, you can save a bit by buying the Tricorn Ticket, which gets you into all three places for $9 for adults and $5 for children 11 to 17.

The two buildings that comprise **Gadsby's Tavern** (134 N. Royal St., south of Cameron Street; ☎ **703-838-4242;** www.gadsbystavern.org) were constructed in 1785 and 1792 and were operated by John Gadsby from 1796 to 1808. Many Revolutionary leaders slept, ate, met, and were entertained here — including George and Martha Washington, John Adams, Thomas Jefferson, James Monroe, and the Marquis de Lafayette. The buildings and furnishings have been restored to their 18th-century appearance. Guided tours are conducted a quarter before and past each hour: April through October Tuesday through Saturday from 10 a.m. to 5 p.m., Sunday and Monday from 1 to 5 p.m.; November through March Wednesday through Saturday from 11 a.m. to 4 p.m. and Sunday 1 to 4 p.m.; closed Thanksgiving, December 25, and January 1. Tours cost $4 for adults, $2 for children 11 to 17, free for younger children who are with a paying adult. The tavern is still functioning, so you can eat here daily from 11:30 a.m. to 3 p.m. and 5:30 to 10 p.m., or take Sunday Brunch from 11 a.m. to 3 p.m. Come for the atmosphere rather than expecting gourmet cooking. The ham and crab in puff pastry is pretty good.

We heard a fascinating and thorough recounting of the history and architecture of the **Carlyle House** (121 N. Fairfax St., south of Cameron Street; ☎ 703-549-2997; www.carlylehouse.org) during a 45-minute tour of this impressive 18th-century mansion. It was built of stone in 1752 by John Carlyle, a Scottish merchant and another founder of the city. It is said that the home's Colonial Georgian architecture is patterned on a Scottish country house. British Gen. Edward Braddock set up headquarters here for a while during the French and Indian War, and five colonial governors met here to plan the campaign against the French and Indians along the Ohio River. You can take a break from touring by relaxing in the gardens out back. Tours are conducted on the hour and half hour Tuesday through Saturday from 10 a.m. to 4 p.m. and Sunday noon to 4 p.m. Tickets cost $4 for adults, $2 for children ages 11 to 17, and free for younger kids.

Historical figures from the 18th to the 20th centuries owned the property on which the **Lee-Fendall House** (614 Oronoco St., east of N. Washington Street; ☎ 703-548-1789; www.leefendallhouse.org) stands. Gen. "Light Horse Harry" Lee — a Revolutionary War leader and the father of Confederate Gen. Robert E. Lee — sold the lot for the house to his cousin Philip Richard Fendall in 1784. The last of the Lee family moved out in 1903. In 1937, the house became the property of United Mine Workers President John L. Lewis, one of the most important labor leaders in U.S. history. Lewis lived here until his death in 1969. The house is restored to its Victorian appearance when Lee family members lived here during the 1850 to 1870 period. The house is open Tuesday through Saturday from 10 a.m. to 4 p.m. and Sunday from 1 to 4 p.m. Admission is $4 for adults, $2 for students ages 11 to 17, and free for younger children. Phone ahead if you plan a weekend visit because the house sometimes closes for private functions.

Shopping in Old Town

Right after World War I and again during World War II, the **Torpedo Factory** (105 N. Union St., at Cameron Street; ☎ 703-838-4565; www.torpedofactory.org) did manufacture torpedoes. Now, it's an arts center, with 82 working studios, six galleries, and more than 165 painters, sculptors, weavers, and other artists who work in full view of the public. Visitors are invited inside the artists' studios to observe and make purchases. While you're here, take a look at the unearthed artifacts on

display in the **Alexandria Archaeology Museum** (☎ 703-838-4399; oha.
ci.alexandria.va.us/archaeology), which occupies space in the
factory. The factory is open daily from 10 a.m. to 5 p.m. Admission is
free. It's also free to visit the museum, which is open Tuesday through
Friday from 10 a.m. to 3 p.m., Saturday from 10 a.m. to 5 p.m., and
Sunday from 1 to 5 p.m. Both facilities are closed Easter, Thanksgiving,
July 4, December 25, and January 1.

Farmers have been displaying their produce in Alexandria's Market
Square since the city was born. Today, the **Farmers' Market** (301 King
St., between Royal and Fairfax streets) occupies the square in front of
City Hall from 5:30 to 10:30 a.m. every Saturday year-round. As befitting
a market in a 21st-century tourist area, the market offers arts and crafts,
as well as fruits, vegetables, and baked goods. It's a great place to nibble
your breakfast while strolling around and looking at what's for sale. Get
some coffee, some fresh-squeezed orange juice, and a couple of pastries.
You can find a place to sit on a wall or some steps if you have trouble
chewing and walking — and juggling several cups and bags — at the
same time.

I can't begin to do justice to the multitude of shops that stretch from the
river to the King Street Metrorail Station. So I'll just highlight a few of the
most interesting ones.

Ten Thousand Villages (915 King St.; ☎ 703-684-1435; www.tenthousand
villages.com) is a unique shop that sells fair-trade crafts from around
the world — mostly from poorer countries or neighborhoods. The shop
is part of a global organization that pays the craftsmen or farmers
(coffee is sold here) a fair wage for their work, which is more than they
usually earn. But the prices remain attractive. Also importing folk arts
and crafts — most from Latin America — is **Gossypia** (325 Cameron St.;
☎ 703-836-6969; www.gossypia.com). Here you encounter decorative
items, rugs, pillows — and bridal dresses. **Elder Crafters** (405 Cameron
St.; ☎ 703-683-4338) offers works by crafters older then 55. Some of you
might think that's a bit early to be called "elder," but AARP is out recruiting 50-year-olds now, so there you go. You can find a wide range of products here, from the kind of simple crafts you run into at a church bazaar
to gorgeous quilts with price tags that flirt with $1,000. Much of the stuff
here is kid-oriented — clothes, toys, and the like. **Arts Afire** (1117 King
St.; ☎ 703-838-9785; www.artsafire.com) sells primarily — but not
exclusively — American-made arts and crafts. It probably won't surprise
you to learn that **My Place in Tuscany** (1127 King St.; **703-683-8882;**
www.myplaceintuscany.com) sells brightly colored handmade ceramics from Italy.

For real decadence, leap over to **Barkley Square Gourmet Dog Bakery
& Boutique** (1 Wales Alley; ☎ 703-519-7565), which proffers exactly
what its name implies. Get your dog some gourmet biscuits, or some
fancy toys, or some exclusive clothing.

If cooking's your thing, drop in on **La Cuisine** (323 Cameron St.; **703-836-4435**). The foodies there sell cooking utensils, cookbooks, spices, oils, and chef's clothing. **Misha's Coffeehouse and Coffee Roaster** (102 South Patrick St.; **703-548-4089**) roasts coffee (surprise!) on the premises and sells brewed coffee for consumption inside or on a bench on the sidewalk.

A Likely Story (1555 King St.; ☎ **703-836-2498**; www.alikelystory books.com) is a children's bookstore, as well as a place to buy toys, games, puzzles, stuffed animals, and other kid stuff. A really big religious bookstore, **Pauline Books and Media** (☎ **703-549-3806**), sits at 1025 King St.

The Christmas Attic (125 S. Union St.; ☎ **703-548-2829**; www.christmas attic.com) is an enormous Christmas store, open year-round, that became so big and successful it opened a second shop (107 N. Fairfax St.; ☎ **703-548-4267**). The second shop is called **House in the Country,** but you can find some pretty uncountrified things here. "Christmas" is defined broadly enough there to encompass other holidays, evidenced by their stock of scary Halloween accoutrements, among others.

Where to dine in Alexandria

One of the best places to dine in Alexandria is **Vermilion** (1120 King St., west of Henry Street; ☎ **703-684-9669**; www.vermilionrestaurant.com), a warm and comfortable Modern American spot. Try to get a table by a second floor window, where you can look down at the activity along King Street while savoring the quiet, soft atmosphere inside. In keeping with the name, most of the interior is done in shades of red — a red brick wall, red fabric draped from the ceiling and along another wall. The floor is a warm wood. Gas lights glow along the brick wall, and candles burn on the tables. Start your meal by chewing on some of the superb French bread while enjoying a generous serving of steamed mussels in a rich, salty, buttery sauce. The baby spinach salad's also good. For a main course, opt for the tender, tasty pork chop if it's on the changing menu. Lots of revelers crowd into the downstairs bar, which has its own menu, but it's a bit too smoky for my nostrils. Main courses run from $17 to $30. Vermilion is open daily from 11:30 a.m. to 3 p.m. Dinner is 5:30 to 10 p.m. Sunday through Thursday and until 11 p.m. Friday and Saturday. Reservations are recommended.

For a break from Alexandria's 18th- and 19th-century history, sample a bite of 20th-century history at the **Majestic Cafe** (911 King St, between Patrick and Alfred streets; ☎ **703-837-9117**; www.majesticcafe.com). As you approach the Majestic, the Art Deco facade and the movie-theater-like neon sign proclaim its movie-theater-like name. An earlier Majestic Cafe fed Alexandrians a couple blocks away in the 1930s and 1940s, and at this site from 1949 to 1978. In 2001, the Majestic reopened as a Modern American restaurant with strong Southern influences. It quickly became one of Alexandria's best dining sites. Just as this edition of *Washington, D.C. For Dummies* was heading for the printer, the Majestic's management changed hands. But it should retain its high quality because it's going to be run by the folks who operate another one of Alexandria's top spots, Restaurant Eve. The menu was slated to include traditional American dishes and home-style deserts. Main courses at dinner are expected to cost between $15 and $22. Approximate operating hours are to be 11:30 a.m. to 2:30 p.m. daily for lunch, 5:30 to 10 p.m. Sunday through Thursday for dinner, and until 11 p.m. Friday and Saturday. Reservations are recommended.

The **Hard Times Cafe** (1404 King St., at West Street; ☎ **703-837-0050;** www.hardtimes.com) earns a spot in my family's heart because of the bizarre focus of its menu — Texas and Cincinnati chili. When Susan and I lived in Dayton, Cincinnati chili parlors were all around, and I developed a fondness for the spicy stuff. For the uninitiated, Texas chili is made with coarse-ground or chunked beef. Cincinnati chili, originally concocted by Greek immigrants, uses fine-ground beef in a tomato sauce with sweeter spices, including cinnamon. Adding to Cincinnati chili's uniqueness is the tradition of serving it with spaghetti, beans, onions, and cheese (a "five-way") — or any combination thereof. Keeping up with the new times, the Hard Times folks now offer vegetarian chili. Hard Times opens at 11 a.m. daily and closes at 11 p.m. Sunday through Thursday and midnight Friday and Saturday. A bowl of chili costs $7, more when you add those optional ingredients. Chili dogs cost $6.79. Reservations are not accepted.

The **Union Street Public House** (121 S. Union St., between King and Prince streets; ☎ **703-548-1785;** www.usphalexandria.com) has long been a favorite for its casual, neighborhood saloon ambience, bar food, and local beer. Old brickwork, gas lamps, and polished wood enhance the pubby-clubby atmosphere. Dinner entrees — crab cakes, fish and chips, lobster, ribs, and pasta — range from $10 to $25, with sandwiches from $8 to $15. A kids' menu is available. The restaurant is open Monday through Thursday from 11:30 a.m. to 10:30 p.m.; Friday and Saturday from 11:30 a.m. to 11:30 p.m.; and Sunday from 11 a.m. to 10:30 p.m., with Sunday brunch from 11 a.m. to 3 p.m. The bar stays open till 1:40 a.m., and serves a light menu until midnight Sunday through Thursday and 1 a.m. Friday and Saturday. Reservations accepted for parties of eight or more, except Friday and Saturday evenings.

Spending the night in Alexandria

The best-located hotel in Alexandria is the **Old Town Hotel** (480 King St., east of Pitt Street; ☎ **800-368-5047** or 703-549-6080). This six-story, red brick hotel stands a block from Market Square in the heart of Old Town. The décor — from the lobby to the rooms — is replica colonial. Rooms tend to be large. Some have balconies overlooking a courtyard. The hotel offers a pool, exercise equipment, and the usual in-room amenities. On-site parking costs $10 a night. There's free shuttle service to National Airport and the King Street Metrorail Station. Rack rates start at $249 for a double. But deep discounts are available during off-peak times.

Day Trip #2: Visiting Annapolis, Maryland

One more historic and lower key alternative to Washington is Annapolis, another port since the 18th century. Annapolis remains a hub for maritime businesses, pleasure boaters, and the U.S. Navy. This is the home of the **U.S. Naval Academy,** as well as of St. John's College, which is noted for its unique Great-Books-based curriculum and its consistent victories over the midshipmen in an annual croquet tournament. Annapolis also serves as Maryland's capital, so it's not exactly a sleepy town. But stroll among the historic buildings and sit for a while by the water, and you'll feel some serenity that's harder to find in the big city.

A vocal and active preservation group oversees the historic district, some think with an iron fist. But the efforts have paid off handsomely: No high-rises, billboards, fast-food restaurants, or out-of-place modern buildings interfere with the architectural integrity of downtown.

Getting there

Traveling to Annapolis is a rare time during your Washington visit when a car comes in handy. The drive from downtown D.C. takes about an hour. Leave Washington to the east via New York Avenue, which is U.S. 50, and follow 50 all the way. As you approach Annapolis, take Exit 24, Rowe (rhymes with cow) Boulevard. From there, you can follow signs to the visitor center, which is near two parking garages in the Historic District.

Tune your radio to **1620 AM** as you approach the city for warnings about **parking** during special events.

On-street parking is a buck an hour from 10 a.m. to 7:30 p.m. daily. After two hours, you must move the car. You'll find it a lot easier to park in a garage or at the Navy-Marine Corps Stadium, which is off Rowe at Taylor Avenue.

Stadium parking is $5 all day. A free shuttle to the visitor center, Historic District, and City Dock leaves the stadium on the hour and half hour from 6:30 a.m. to 8 p.m. weekdays and 10 a.m. to 6 p.m. weekends. Another shuttle runs more frequently to the visitor center and government buildings. Shuttles don't run on some holidays. Call ☎ **410-263-7964** for information.

The **Gotts Court Garage,** off Calvert or Northwest street by the visitor center, is $1.25 to a maximum $10 on weekdays and $4 on weekends. Off Main Street closer to the City Dock, the **Hillman Garage** charges $10 maximum every day and tends to fill earlier.

The local traffic agents are as vigilant as vultures awaiting fresh road kill. You really don't want to park in an illegal spot.

Annapolis

A. L. Goodies General Store **15**
Annapolis Marriott Waterfront **20**
Annapolis Pottery **9**
Aurora Gallery **7**
Avoca Handweavers **14**
Banneker–Douglass Museum **3**
Café Normandie **11**
Chick and Ruth's Delly **12**
City Dock **22**
Dawson Gallery **6**
Gibson's Lodgings **25**
Gotts Court Garage **1**
Government House **4**
Griffin's **17**
Hillman Garage **13**
Historic Annapolis Foundation **19**
Kunta Kinte Memorial **24**
Maryland Federation of Art
    Gallery **10**
Maryland Inn **8**
Paca House **16**
Riordan's **18**
State House **5**
Storm Brothers Ice Cream
    Factory **23**
U.S. Naval Academy **26**
Visitors Bureau **2**
Visitor Information Booth **21**

Dillon's Bus Service (☎ **800-827-3490** or 410-647-2321; www.dillonbus. com) operates limited service between D.C. and Annapolis for $4.25 one way. **Greyhound's** (☎ **800-229-9424;** greyhound.com) limited service is $16 one way, $31 round-trip.

Seeing the sights

Annapolis is a working state capital whose history stretches back more than 300 years. More than 1,500 historic buildings are scattered among the narrow brick streets and alleys. The city is almost always crowded with people working, playing, sailing, eating, and studying.

To work out how you want to spend your time in Annapolis, write or call the **Annapolis and Anne Arundel County Conference and Visitors Bureau,** 26 West St., Annapolis, MD 21401 (☎ **888-302-2852,** 410-280-0445), open 9 a.m. to 5 p.m. daily except Thanksgiving, December 25, and January 1, or surf over to www.visit-annapolis.org. Once you arrive in town, you can get information from the bureau's visitor center, which is just off Church Circle. You also can pick up maps and literature and ask questions at the visitor information booth next to the public restrooms at the City Dock. It's open the same hours from April to early October, then limited hours on weekends through November.

Three Centuries Tours (☎ **410-268-7600**) leads several different walking itineraries of the Historic District, the Capitol, and the Naval Academy.

Discover Annapolis Tours (☎ **410-626-6000;** www.discoverannapolis. com) shuttles visitors through 350 years of history and architecture aboard minibuses with big windows. The hour-long tour leaves from the Visitor Center at 26 West St., the 40-minute tour from History Quest at 99 Main St. Call or check the Web site for departure times, which vary according to the season. The hour-long tour costs $15 for adults, $7 for ages 11 to 15, $3 for younger kids. The shorter tour costs $13, $6, and $3. This tour is good for persons with disabilities, those who can't walk long distances, and the terminally lazy. All others should get out there and walk!

The **Historic Annapolis Foundation** (☎ **800-603-4020** or 410-297-6656; www.annapolis.org) rents four different **digital audio tours** at 99 Main St. The tours cover Annapolis highlights, Annapolis during the Revolution, Annapolis in the Civil War, and African-American Annapolis. You'll spend one to three hours on a tour. Call to find out when the recordings are available.

Watermark Cruises (☎ **410-268-7600;** www.watermarkcruises.com) sails from the City Dock to view Annapolis Harbor, as well as the U.S. Naval Academy and the banks of the Severn River. Go with the flow. The 40-minute narrated tour leaves every hour on the hour from noon to 3 p.m. weekdays and 11 a.m. to 6 p.m. weekends late March to mid-May; from 11 a.m. to 4 p.m. weekdays and 11 a.m. to 7 p.m. weekends mid-May to early September; and from noon to 4 p.m. weekdays and 11 a.m.

to 6 p.m. weekends from early September to early October. Tours are offered on an irregular basis afterwards. Cost is $10 for adults and $4 for ages 3 to 11, free for younger kids. Cruises lasting 90 minutes are offered at 12:30, 2:30, and 4:30 p.m. daily mid-May to early September, weekends mid-April to mid-May and early September to early October. Call about other offerings, such as an all-day cruise on the Chesapeake Bay.

You don't need a guide to walk the length of City Dock to the water and enjoy the panorama from **Susan Campbell Memorial Park.** Get a double-scooper from **Storm Brothers Ice Cream Factory** (130 Dock St.; ☎ 410-263-3376) and drip across the street to the sea wall along **Ego Alley,** appropriately named for the informal parade of boats and flesh that takes place on summer weekends. Where Ego Alley dead-ends, across from **Market House,** is a life-size bronze of *Roots* author **Alex Haley** reading to several children. The sculpture commemorates the landing of Haley's ancestor, Kunta Kinte, aboard the slave ship *Lord Ligonier* in 1767.

Check out the architecture as you ascend **Main Street** from City Dock to **Church Circle** and the harbor view from the **Maryland Inn** (58 State Circle; ☎ 410-263-2641). Independently owned businesses are **A.L. Goodies General Store** (112 Main St.; ☎ 410-269-0071) for souvenirs, T-shirts, and fudge; **Avoca Handweavers** (141 Main St.; ☎ 410-263-1485) for woolens and household accessories from the British Isles; and **Chick and Ruth's Delly** (165 Main; ☎ 410-269-6737), an Annapolis institution since the 1960s. (See the next section, "Where to dine," for more information.)

History buffs may want to detour to the **Banneker-Douglass Museum** (84 Franklin St.; ☎ 410-514-7618; www.bdmuseum.com), dedicated to preserving Maryland's African-American heritage; it's named for Benjamin Banneker, who helped survey and lay out the District of Columbia, and Frederick Douglass, who escaped slavery to become a leader of the abolition movement. From the top of Main Street, go left at Church Circle and then left at Franklin. The museum is housed in the old **Mount Moriah A.M.E. Church.** The museum's exhibits change periodically. Call ahead to find out about current shows. It's open Tuesday through Friday from 10 a.m. to 3 p.m. and Saturday from noon to 4 p.m. Admission is free.

If you go right onto Church Circle from Main Street and right again at School Street to State Circle, you discover Annapolis as state capital. The **State House** (☎ 410-974-3400), the oldest state capitol building in continuous use, still watches over the town below. Construction began in 1772, and the original section was completed in 1779. It served as the U.S. Capitol from November 1783 to August 1784 when the Continental Congress met in the Old Senate Chamber. View the grounds and public areas on your own or take the free tour, daily at 11 a.m. and 3 p.m. When you exit the rear of the building, cross **Lawyers Mall,** with its statue of **Thurgood Marshall,** to **Government House,** the official residence of Maryland's governor. Because the governor lives here, you can't just walk in to tour.

On State Circle are some of the town's premier shops and galleries. **Annapolis Pottery** (no. 40; ☎ 410-268-6153; www.annapolispottery. com) is a workshop/gallery with a wide selection of attractive and functional pieces. The **Maryland Federation of Art Gallery** (no. 18; ☎ 410-268-4566; www.mdfedart.org), in a restored 1840 building with exposed brick and modern lighting, mounts solo and small group exhibits of multimedia works and three national shows per year.

From State Circle, turn down Maryland Avenue, with its many home design and antiques shops, boutiques, and galleries. Reminiscent of a gentler era and a lot less touristy than Main Street, Maryland Avenue merits exploration. Shops line the cobblestone street from State Circle to Prince George Street. Stop in the **Aurora Gallery** (no. 67; ☎ 410-263-9150) a few doors from the State House, with its American-made crafts, pottery, jewelry, paintings, and sculpture (some created by the artist-owners). The **Dawson Gallery** (no. 44; ☎ 410-269-1299) sells 18th-, 19th-, and early-20th-century American and European paintings. Among the gallery's better-known customers is Harrison Ford, who purchased paintings here while filming *Patriot Games* in Annapolis.

Anyone who's been in Annapolis five minutes knows it's a sailing mecca. Many people come here from all over the country to learn to sail. If you're one of them, try the **Annapolis Sailing School** (601 6th St.; ☎ 800-638-9192, 410-267-7205; www.annapolissailing.com), where I'm told you can learn the basics in a weekend.

If you're not going to take the helm yourself, feel the wind on your face aboard the 74-foot schooner *Woodwind* (☎ 410-263-7837; www. schoonerwoodwind.com), which sails from 80 Compromise St. Several cruises run at varying times daily mid-April through October. Call or check the Web site for details. The two-hour cruise costs $31 to $34, $29 to $32 for seniors 60 and older, and $20 for kids younger than 12.

Annapolis lays claim to numerous fine examples of 18th- and 19th-century architecture. As you tour, notice the colored plaques on many buildings designating their historic status and the period in which they were built. (An explanation is provided in the *Annapolis Visitors Guide,* available at the visitor center.) Check out the **William Paca House and Garden** (186 Prince George St.; ☎ 410-267-7619; www.annapolis.org/ paca-house.html). Paca (pronounced *Pay*-ca) was a wealthy planter who signed the Declaration of Independence. The Georgian mansion, built between 1763 and 1765, nearly succumbed to the wrecker's ball in 1965. The Historic Annapolis Foundation stepped in, restoring the house and gardens to their former grandeur. Tours are offered once an hour on the half hour Monday through Saturday from 10 a.m. to 5 p.m. and Sunday from noon to 5 p.m. from late March through December, and Friday through Sunday noon to 5 p.m. from late January to late March. It's closed Thanksgiving Day and December 25. Call or check the Web site for details. Admission to the garden is $5. Garden plus house tour is $8, seniors $7, children 6 to 17 $5, younger kids free.

Many people use the words "Annapolis" and **"U.S. Naval Academy"** interchangeably. Whatever you call it, the academy is a must-see. If you park downtown, it's a five-minute walk from City Dock via Randall Street to King George Street and Gate 1, the visitors' entrance. Since September 11, 2001, tourists aren't permitted to drive onto the academy grounds (or "onboard," as the sailors say). The exception is a vehicle with a handicapped license plate or permit, which is allowed on campus through Gate 1 after an inspection. To get information before you arrive, call ☎ **410-263-6933** or visit the academy's Web site for tourists at www. navyonline.com.

At the **Armel-Leftwich Visitor Center,** just inside Gate 1, you can watch the short film *To Lead and to Serve,* check out the interactive exhibits, peruse the gift shop, and join a guided tour of the academy. The center displays a sample midshipman's room; *Freedom 7,* the space capsule in which Navy Commander Alan Shepard became the first American to take a suborbital flight into space; a howitzer gun; the original wooden figurehead of the USS *Delaware,* and an exhibit on the life and times of John Paul Jones, the Revolutionary War commander.

The center is open daily from 9 a.m. to 5 p.m. March through December and 9 a.m. to 4 p.m. January and February. It's closed Thanksgiving, December 25, and January 1. Tours cost $8, seniors 62 and older $7, elementary and secondary school students $6, preschoolers free. July through August, the tours run from 9:30 a.m. to 3 p.m. Monday through Saturday, and 12:30 to 3 p.m. Sunday. From December through March, they run Monday through Saturday from 10 a.m. to 2:30 p.m. and Sunday from 12:30 to 2:30 p.m. April through June and September through November, the tours run Monday through Friday from 10 a.m. to 3 p.m., Saturday from 9:30 a.m. to 3 p.m., and Sunday from 12:30 to 3 p.m. During the academic year (Sept–May), try to hook up with a morning tour that allows you to see noon meal formation in front of Bancroft Hall.

For information and tickets to athletic events, call the Naval Academy Athletic Association (☎ **800-874-6289;** www.navysports.cstv.com).

Where to dine

Café Normandie (185 Main St.; ☎ **410-263-3382**) is a cozy, plant-filled French bistro. Come for a hearty breakfast on weekends (eggs, omelets, and French toast). All week, it's is a good place for lunch (tomato-crab or onion soup, grilled chicken, or crepes), or dinner (shrimp, beef many ways, seafood-filled crepes). The best desserts are ice-cream or fruit-filled crepes. The restaurant is open Monday through Friday from 11 a.m. to 10:30 p.m., Saturday from 8 a.m. to 11 p.m., and Sunday from 8 a.m. to 10 p.m. Dinner main courses run from $13 to $28. Reservations are recommended.

From May to October, visit **Cantler's Riverside Inn** on Mill Creek (458 Forest Beach Rd.; ☎ **410-757-1311;** http://cantlers.com) and dig into a pile of steamed fresh Maryland blue crabs. This place is packed in summer, especially on weekends. The best strategy is to arrive at off times. Have an early or late lunch or a *very* early dinner. Otherwise, you may find the crabs AWOL. When the crabs are out of season, try the steamed shrimp, and fried or broiled fish. The inn is about a 15-minute ride from City Dock. Cantler's opens daily at 11 a.m. and closes at midnight Friday and Saturday and 11 p.m. the rest of the week. Reservations accepted only for parties of ten or more Monday through Thursday.

With its long wooden bar, chatty bartender, high-decibel noise level, and garage-sale accessories, **Riordan's** (26 Market Space; ☎ 410-263-5449; www.riordans.com) is a quintessential neighborhood saloon. The servers are pleasant and efficient, the food is consistent and reasonably priced, and the beer is cold. Start with cheddar-bacon potato skins or a seafood appetizer and then move on to a burger or roast beef sandwich. The soups are, um, super, especially the New England clam chowder and crab vegetable. The à la carte Sunday brunch (mimosa or glass of champagne included) is an Annapolis tradition — and a bargain, with entrees all less than $10. At lunch and dinner, a kids' menu lists burgers, chicken tenders, and pasta. Hours are Monday through Saturday from 11 a.m. to 1:30 a.m. and Sunday 10 to 1:30 a.m. Sandwiches and entrees run $8 to $15.

Chick and Ruth's Delly (165 Main St.; ☎ 410-269-6737; www.chickand ruths.com) has anchored the corner of Main and Conduit streets since the 1960s, before Annapolis became a yuppie outpost. Come for the breakfast platters (served all day), the tasty sandwiches (named for Maryland politicians and local characters), milkshakes, malts, or banana splits. Try the *delly fries* (home fries with plenty of pepper and onions). The kitschy décor — orange Formica countertops and bagel light-pulls are décor? — is pure 1950s. So are the cheeky waitresses and the prices. Except for the crabs, almost everything's under $10. The Delly is open Sunday through Thursday 6:30 a.m. to 11:30 p.m., Friday and Saturday till 12:30 a.m.

Griffin's (22–24 Market Space; ☎ 410-268-2576; www.griffins-city dock.com) feels like a pub, stocks a dozen or more draft beers, and dishes out enormous portions. It serves up creative cooking, as well. On a recent visit, Susan, Julie, and I agreed that the portobello mushroom sandwich was very good. The greens in a very good — and very interesting — salad were topped with coconut-breaded shrimp, almonds, and dried cranberries. The fries came as they're supposed to — crunchy on the outside, warm and soft in the middle. Sandwiches range from $7.50 (burger) to $15 (crab cakes), and main courses are $12 (ribs) to $27 (steak). Griffin's is open 11 a.m. to 2 a.m. Monday through Saturday, 10 a.m. to 2 a.m. Sunday.

Spending the night in Annapolis

The Annapolis Marriott Waterfront (80 Compromise St.; ☎ 888-773-0786 or 410-268-7555; www.annapolismarriott.com) stands just where its name proclaims. Most of the rooms have water views, and some have waterfront balconies. If you bring a boat, you can tie it up at the Marriott's dock. This comes at a price. Rack rates start at $319 double.

For rooms around $200 or less, try Gibson's Lodgings (110 Prince George St.; ☎ **877-330-0057** or 410-268-5555; www.gibsonslodgings.com) — two historic town houses and a late-20th-century addition. These facilities also are conveniently located a block from the city dock.

Day Trip #3: Taking a Trip to Baltimore

Washington and Baltimore have long shared their residents. Some D.C. workers live in Baltimore and commute because the cost of living is lower. Between the time the Baltimore Colts snuck away to Indianapolis and the Cleveland Browns deserted Cleveland to become the Baltimore Ravens, Baltimore football fans had to content themselves with following the Washington Redskins. For more than three decades, D.C. baseball fans made the trek up to watch the Baltimore Orioles, because the nation's pastime deserted the nation's capital until the Montreal Expos moved to Washington in 2005 to become the Nationals. The Washington Wizards NBA team used to be the Baltimore Bullets. And, to the extent Baltimore has hockey fans, they have to go to D.C. to watch the NHL Capitals.

There are more reasons for a Washington visitor to travel up to Baltimore for a day or two — starting with the food, the harbor, the history, the art, and fun for kids.

Getting there

Baltimore's an easy jaunt from D.C. by any mode of transportation. To **drive** from downtown Washington, take New York Avenue (U.S. 50) east. Shortly after you leave the city, go north on the Baltimore-Washington Parkway (Maryland 295), which will take you right into downtown Baltimore. After you pass the Ravens' and Orioles' stadiums, turn right on West Pratt Street to get to the **Inner Harbor.** Several **parking** garages stand near the Inner Harbor. The closest has entrances on Calvert and South streets, to the left off Pratt as you pass the Inner Harbor while following the directions above. The downtown-to-downtown drive shouldn't take more than an hour, depending on both cities' traffic conditions, of course.

Maryland Rail Commuter (☎ 800-325-7245; www.mtamaryland.com) runs MARC trains between Baltimore's Penn Station and D.C.'s Union Station for $7 one way on weekdays. **Amtrak** (☎ 800-872-7245; www.amtrak.com) runs trains every day for as low as $14 one way. **Greyhound** (☎ 800-231-2222; www.greyhound.com) also charges about $14 for the bus ride. The trip takes about an hour on MARC trains, 30 to 40 minutes on Amtrak, 55 to 95 minutes by bus.

Seeing the sights at Inner Harbor

There's lots to do within a very compact area at the **Inner Harbor**. First, you can check in at the **Baltimore Visitor Center** (401 Light St.; ☎ 877-225-8466) for info on the best things to see in the city. If you need it, the folks here also can help you book a hotel room, make restaurant reservations, and buy tickets to attractions and events.

Harborplace (along Pratt and Light streets at the Inner Harbor; ☎ 410-332-0060; www.harborplace.com), built right along the water, is a large, modern shopping-eating-drinking complex. You'll find more than 100 **shops, restaurants,** and fast-food spots here — most of them national chains. This is not where to go for Baltimore's best cooking. But it's fun to grab a seat and a **drink** on one of the balconies that overlook the water. Musicians often perform along the Inner Harbor's walkways — I caught a very good doo-wop group one evening.

Your children will find lots to do in this area. Luckily, you'll find that accompanying them is pretty interesting, too.

Baltimore's **National Aquarium** (501 E. Pratt Street; ☎ 410-576-3800; www.aqua.org) puts Washington's little basement fish tank to shame. The aquarium's 115,000 square feet of floor space hold tanks with more than a million gallons of water. More than 14,000 creatures call this place home — not just fish, but frogs, crocodiles, and other water-loving animals as well. The big hit with kids is the dolphin show. In addition to entertaining you, the trainers explain how they get these water-dwelling mammals to do their tricks.

This kids are going to want to sit in the front row and squeal with delight when the soaring dolphins splash them. You, on the other hand, will want to be sure to sit in the splash-free zone.

Tickets are $22, seniors 60 and older $21, children 3 to 11 $13, younger kids free. Add in the dolphin show, and the prices jump to $25, $24, and $14. Friday after 5 p.m. you can get in for $8. The aquarium is open January, February, November, and December Saturday through Thursday 10 a.m. to 5 p.m., Friday till 8 p.m. Though closing hours are the same March through June and September through October, opening hours are at 9 a.m. July to late August the aquarium is open daily 9 a.m. to 8 p.m. Closing time during the last week or so of August is 6 p.m. Saturday through Thursday. Closed Thanksgiving, December 25.

Another kid-magnet stands at the other end of Harborplace — the **Maryland Science Center** (601 Light St.; information line ☎ 410-685-5225, live operator 410-685-2370; www.mdsci.org). This place is jam-packed with interactive exhibits that parents like to play with almost as much as the kids. (Did I say "almost"?)

The center is run by the Maryland Academy of Sciences, which has been promoting science since 1797. The academy aims to teach while

Baltimore

Admiral Fell Inn 14
American Visionary
    Arts Museum 2
Another Period
    in Time 17
Baltimore Museum
    of Art 7
Bonaparte Breads 15
Broadway Market 16
Charleston 11
Corduroy Button 13
Dudley & Max 12
Fort McHenry 1
Gertrude's 7

Hyatt Regency
    Baltimore 5
InterContinental Harbor
    Court 4
La Tavola 10
Maryland Science
    Center 3
National Aquarium 9
Obrycki's 18
Port Discovery 8
Rocky Run Tap & Grill 7
Silk Road 15
Ten Thousand Villages 12
Walters Art Museum 6

entertaining, so a lot of painless education occurs here. The dinosaur exhibit, for example, addresses evolution and climate change. The largest skeleton on display — 45 feet long, 15 feet tall — goes by the marvelous name "giganotosaurus." Interactive activities include a paleontological dig. Another exhibit — called TerraLink — is full of high-tech, hands-on activities that show how the Earth's environment, water, and land interact. You see how volcanoes erupt, how wind shapes sand dunes, and how tornadoes and hurricanes go about their destructive work. Other exhibits deal with the human body, medicine, magnetism, light, sound, and the Chesapeake Bay's ecosystem. There's a planetarium and an IMAX theater. The Kids Room was specifically designed for children younger than eight. Memorial Day through Labor Day, the center is open daily 10 a.m. to 5 p.m. The rest of the year, it's open Tuesday through Friday 10 a.m. to 5 p.m., Saturday 10 a.m. to 6 p.m., and Sunday 11 a.m. to 5 p.m. Closed December 25. Tickets cost $15, seniors 60 and older $14, children 3 to 12 $10. Additional charges for planetarium, films, and special exhibitions.

Not far from the aquarium and the science center is yet a third place for children, **Port Discovery** (35 Market Place; ☎ **410-727-3042;** www.port discovery.com). It's a marvelous three-story play land for kids ages two to ten.

The first thing you see when you walk in the door is a mini soccer pitch. There's a gigantic climbing area with giant slides and a zip line. Kids can build things with giant (I keep using that word!) tinker toys. There also are interactive educational exhibits and arts-and-crafts programs.

Port Discover is open October through May Tuesday through Friday 9:30 a.m. to 4:30 p.m., Saturday 10 a.m. to 5 p.m., Sunday noon to 5 p.m.; Memorial Day through Labor Day Monday through Saturday 10 a.m. to 5 p.m., Sunday noon to 5 p.m., Fridays early July through late August till 8 p.m.; after Labor Day through September Friday 9:30 a.m. to 4:30 p.m., Saturday 10 a.m. to 5 p.m., Sunday noon to 5 p.m. Closed Thanksgiving and December 25. Tickets cost $11, children younger than two are free.

Taking in Baltimore's art scene

Baltimore boasts a rich cultural heritage. Here are three of the best places to check out the city's art.

Consider the three buildings themselves to be part of the art at the **Walters Art Museum** (600 N. Charles St.; ☎ **410-547-9000;** www.the walters.org). The newest addition, opened in 1974 and renovated in 2001, presents a starkly modern face, with a four-story glass entryway, glass atrium, and hanging staircase. Henry Walters's original gallery, built between 1904 and 1909, was modeled on Italian Renaissance and baroque palaces. The sculpture court features a marble floor, columns, and a two-story skylight. Touring the third building, which was constructed between 1848 and 1850, is like perusing a private art collection in a mansion. Don't fail to climb the spiral staircase which leads to a stained glass dome.

The collection of more than 28,000 objects stretches from ancient Egypt to late-19th-century Europe. Works also come from Greece, Rome, the Islamic world, Asia, and America. In addition to paintings and sculptures, the Walters shows off rare books, mummy masks, medieval armor, and Art Deco jewelry. You'll find works by Monet, Manet, Delacroix, Raphael, El Greco, and other masters.

The Walters puts on many children's programs. Call ahead to see what might be on tap during your visit.

The Walters is open Wednesday through Sunday 11 a.m. to 5 p.m., and till 8 p.m. Friday. Closed most federal holidays and December 24. Admission is free.

All three of these museums have in-house eating facilities. At the Baltimore Museum of Art, **Gertrude's** (☎ **410-889-3399;** www.john shields.com/restaurant/rest/gertrudes.html) is a popular destination in its own right for crab cakes and Sunday brunch. The museum also can give you a map that shows other restaurants in the area. A lot of them are moderately priced to attract Johns Hopkins University students. There's good crab soup and interesting fry-bread sandwiches at **Rocky Run Tap & Grill** (3105 St. Paul St.; ☎ **410-235-2501;** www.rocky run.com), a typical college pub.

Maryland's largest art museum, the **Baltimore Museum of Art** (10 Art Museum Dr.; ☎ **443-573-1700;** www.artbma.org) houses a distinguished and eclectic collection. The Cone Collection was assembled by two Baltimore sisters — Claribel and Etta Cone — who bought works by Matisse and Picasso from the artists at their studios, and also acquired paintings by Cézanne, Gauguin, van Gogh, and Renoir.

Among the vast array of other items you won't have time to see in one visit are painting and sculpture from around the world and throughout history, decorative arts, furniture, silver, textiles, and folk art. Period rooms from six Maryland houses have been reassembled here, and there is a gallery of miniature rooms with furnishings. Among the artists represented: Manet, van Dyck, Rembrandt, Rodin, Botticelli, Warhol, Johns, Rauschenberg, Lichtenstein, Calder, as well as photographers Man Ray, Alfred Stieglitz, and Edward Weston.

If you've got kids in tow, check at the information desk for children's activities.

The museum is open Wednesday through Friday 11 a.m. to 5 p.m., Saturday and Sunday 11 a.m. to 6 p.m., and till 9 p.m. on the first Thursday of each month. Closed January 1, July 4, Thanksgiving, and December 25. Admission is free. There's a fee for some special exhibitions.

Baltimore's most unusual arts spot is the **American Visionary Arts Museum** (800 Key Hwy.; ☎ 410-244-1900; www.avam.org). It is essentially a showcase for art by amateurs — or, as the museum itself puts it, "art produced by self-taught individuals, usually without formal training, whose works arise from an innate personal vision that revels foremost in the creative act itself." It's not folk art, the museum says, because it's not tied to any long-lived cultural tradition. So, what kind of art do you encounter here? Well, before you enter the building you'll have a hard time missing the 55-foot-tall, multicolored, wind-powered "Giant Whirligig." Most of the inside space is devoted to changing exhibitions. Examples of what you might find: sculptures made of toothpicks or bottle caps, decorated funeral urns, or installations covered with aluminum foil. At first glance, this all seems quite whimsical and silly. But the museum is dead serious about the motivations and messages of these untaught artists. Exhibition themes can be heavy — even disturbing. Because much of what's here is obviously attractive to children, the museum warns you when material is inappropriate for young eyes.

The museum is open Tuesday through Sunday 10 a.m. to 6 p.m. Closed Thanksgiving and December 25. Admission is $12; seniors 55 and older, children 7 and older, and students $8; younger than 6 are free.

Touching through Baltimore's history

The Star Spangled Banner still waves — or at least a replica does — at **Fort McHenry** (2400 E. Fort Ave.; ☎ 410-962-4290; www.nps.gov/fomc), 3 miles southeast of the Inner Harbor and across the Patapsco River from Fells Point, which we will visit next. It was from here that U.S. troops prevented British warships from approaching Baltimore during the War of 1812. The battle occurred near the end of the war, in September 1814, and was observed by Francis Scott Key, a prisoner on a British ship. Key penned the poem that later was set to music and became the U.S. national anthem.

The fort stayed in service until the 1920s, when it became a national park, later redesignated as a national monument and historic shrine. It looks pretty much as it did when Key watched the battle and wondered if the flag still flew. You can wander through all the buildings in the fort, walk around the perimeter and down to the riverside, and check out the exhibits in the visitor center. The fort is open early June through early September daily 8 a.m. to 7:45 p.m., till 4:45 p.m. the rest of the year. Admission to the fort is $7, children 15 and younger free. No charge to enter the visitor center and grounds around the fort.

While the Inner Harbor development is new, glittery, and synthetic, **Fells Point** (☎ 410-675-6750; www.fellspoint.us) remembers the city's gritty origins and growth as an important maritime center. Today, more than 30 million tons of cargo pass through Baltimore's port every year. Back in 1726, William Fell founded a shipbuilding company in Baltimore's oldest neighborhood which later took his name. Cobblestone streets are still lined with 18th and 19th century houses here today. Streets carry old English names, such as Shakespeare, Fleet, and Thames.

If you were a fan of the old television show *Homicide: Life on the Street,* you'll recognize the beat-up entrance to the police station on Thames Street that served as that show's precinct headquarters. The **Broadway Market,** on Broadway between Lancaster and Fleet streets, is a collection of shops, delis, restaurants, and greasy spoons that serve up flowers, fruit, deli meats, baked goods, candy, coffee, pizza, sandwiches, fried chicken, and other simple food. The best thing to do in this neighborhood is to wander among the **antique shops, clothing boutiques, restaurants,** and **bars,** primarily along Broadway and Thames, south of Fleet. **Corduroy Button** (1628 Thames St.; ☎ 410-276-5437) sells children's clothing. **Dudley & Max** (1625 Thames St.; ☎ 410-522-7735) sells clothing and other things for pets. **Another Period in Time** (1708 Fleet St.; ☎ 410-675-4776) is an antique shop. **Silk Road** (905 S. Ann St.; ☎ 410-675-1705) sells Oriental rugs, textiles, and home furnishings. There's a **Ten Thousand Villages** at 1621 Thames St. (☎ 410-342-5568). (See the Alexandria shopping section for more details about this chain of fair-trade stores.)

You might do a double-take when a horse-drawn cart full of produce goes clip-clopping by. These streets sport a broad range of eating establishments of various ethnic extractions, and I saw no evidence of a fast-food chain. See the next section for a review of **Bonaparte's** charming French cafe, and "Spending the Night in Baltimore" for a review of the **Admiral Fell Inn.**

Where to dine

I think it's in the Constitution that if you go to Baltimore you must eat crab. One of the classic places to do so is **Obrycki's** (1727 E. Pratt St.; ☎ 410-732-6399; www.obryckis.com),which has specialized in Maryland blue crab since the 1940s. Everything here is about the food. You eat at a plain table with paper napkins and paper placemats. The cavernous dining room, broken up by red brick archways, is filled with happy customers. If you close your eyes, you might think you're on a construction site. But it's just the sound of determined diners hammering away at their hard-shell crabs to get at the delectable meat inside. There are easier ways to eat crab here, and I confess to taking those routes. The cream of crab soup is excellent, the bowl brimming with crab meat. The lump crab meat sautéed in butter is rich and delicious. The baked potato is cooked to perfection. The bread pudding makes an excellent dessert. Obrycki's bakes its own version of Key lime pie, which is more tart than most. Main courses cost from $15 (for grilled chicken breast, but who would want that here?) to $30 (for a seafood combination). Obrycki's opens daily at 11:30 a.m. In spring and fall it closes Monday through Friday at 10 p.m., Saturday at 11 p.m., and Sunday at 9:30 p.m. In summer it stays open till 11 p.m. Monday through Saturday. The restaurant closes from mid-November to mid-March.

Baltimore, which has a Little Italy, may be as well known for Italian cooking as for crab. To sample the Italian, try **La Tavola** (248 Albemarle St.; ☎ 410-685-1859; www.la-tavola.com), which serves excellent food at reasonable prices. Start with the *antipasto Italiano,* a generous selection of Italian meats and cheeses over a bed of arugula. An excellent pasta course is perfectly-al-dente rigatoni, with sautéed eggplant and mozzarella in a flavorful tomato sauce. *Mafalde alla Fiorentina* is a hearty dish of wide pasta served with spinach, raisins, pine nuts, and ricotta cheese, seasoned with nutmeg and cinnamon. Service here is both warm and professional, the atmosphere in the dining room serene. Main courses cost from $12 (pasta with tomato sauce) to $22 (for a couple of seafood dishes). La Tavola opens at 11:30 a.m. Tuesday through Sunday, closes at 10:30 p.m. Friday and Saturday, 10 p.m. Sunday and Tuesday through Thursday.

Bright and cheerful **Bonaparte Breads** (903 S. Ann St.; ☎ 410-342-4000) is a pleasant place to grab lunch or take a snack break while you're tooling around Fells Point. Order a sandwich at the counter and grab a leather upholstered chair by the floor-to-ceiling windows that look toward boats tied up at the dock across the narrow street. In nice weather, you may see pleasure boaters conducting their version of a tailgate party — sharing food and drinks with friends beside their boats. You'll be tempted to stay here a long time. The chairs are comfy, and the room is attractive. An ornate clock — the kind you used to see all the time outside banks — is suspended from one of the yellow walls. The floor is tile, the ceiling wood. I was disappointed in the tomato quiche. But the tuna salad, on an excellent baguette, was quite good — and big enough for two to share. Fruit tarts, like those served here, are one of my major weaknesses. Most of the soups, sandwiches, and quiches are $7 to $8. Bonaparte is open daily 8 a.m. to 6 p.m., but only breads and pastries are available after 3 p.m.

As I write this, the hottest restaurant in town is **Charleston** (1000 Lancaster St.; ☎ 410-332-7373; www.charlestonrestaurant.com). It's expensive, excellent, and unusual. Charleston's name explains its roots, as a Modern American restaurant with Southern influences. Some of that stays on the menu today — gulf shrimp with andouille sausage and grits, for instance. But owners Cindy Wolf and Tony Foreman shut the place down for a bit in 2005 to refurbish both the dining room and the menu. Now Chef Wolf offers diners a large number of choices of small plates with which to build their own meals — three to six courses for $67 to $102, with dessert thrown in for free. Wolf also offers a chef's menu, and looking at a recent one is probably the best way to get an idea of what this restaurant is all about: bisque of lobster, crab, and shrimp; scrambled eggs with white truffle; salmon tartare with cucumber and sesame seeds; grilled lamb tenderloin with basmati rice, lentils, and cucumber yogurt; morbier cheese; and a crème brûlée trio of vanilla bean, roasted chestnut, and cinnamon caramel flavors. Charleston is open Monday through Saturday from 5:30 to 10 p.m.

Spending the night in Baltimore

You can't beat the location of the **Hyatt Regency Baltimore** (300 Light St.; ☎ **888-591-1234** or 410-528-1234; www.hyatt.com). It's just across the street from Harborplace — and it's got its own bridge to get there. We had a spectacular view of the Inner Harbor from the glass-enclosed elevator that lifted us to our room, and from the room itself. The just-renovated rooms are large, and the beds extremely comfortable. The rooms have all the expected amenities. The hotel has several restaurants, including the top-floor Pisces with a more-than-spectacular view. You can order room service from 6 a.m. till midnight, swim in the outdoor pool in the summer, work out in the gym, jog on the track, play on the tennis courts, or soak in the hot tub. Rack rates start at $399, but I've found deals as low as $149 off peak. Self-parking is $27, valet $36.

Just down the street from the Hyatt is the even more luxurious **Inter-Continental Harbor Court** (550 Light St.; ☎ **800-824-0076** or 410-234-0550; www.harborcourt.com). Independently owned and operated since it opened in 1986, the Harbor Court joined the InterContinental chain in 2006. The sitting room of the entrance lobby is called the Library, and its walls are lined with old books. Pull a few off the shelves, and you may be surprised to find that many are in foreign languages. Standard rooms come with bay window, easy chair, table, and desk. One-bedroom suites have a living-dining area, two bay windows, and an enormous bath. For $3,500 you can bed down in the Presidential Suite, containing such accoutrements as a grand piano, wet bar, full kitchen, sitting and dining areas, and one or two bedrooms. I always wonder what kind of people shell out $3,000 or more for a hotel room. In this case, the most recent occupant was Bruce Willis, in town to film another *Die Hard* movie (no. 412, I think). The Harbor Court has a large indoor pool, spa, fitness center, outdoor tennis court, racquetball court, two restaurants, and a lounge. Double rooms start at $359. Discounts to below $200 are sometimes available.

You say you've fallen in love with Fells Point and don't want to leave? Well, get yourself a room at the **Admiral Fell Inn** (888 S. Broadway; ☎ **410-522-7377**; www.admiralfell.com), cobbled together from eight adjoining buildings, some dating to the 18th century. Because the Admiral's rooms are in different buildings — from different centuries — they differ in design and furnishing. There's a partial canopy bed here, four-poster with lace canopy there, two rooms sharing a balcony over there. One bi-level suite has a downstairs living room with a working fireplace, an upstairs bedroom, a microwave, a fridge, and a Jacuzzi. Each room is named for a Maryland historical figure, and a plaque outside the door displays a brief biography. All rooms have television, air-conditioning, and a private bathroom. Photos of Baltimore, most for sale, decorate the inn's walls. There's a nautical-themed bar, a basement restaurant with exposed stone walls, and a library with wood-burning fireplace.

Rates run from $199 for a standard room to $500 for a suite. The inn tacks on an additional $10-a-day "destination fee" that covers unlimited local and domestic long distance phone calls, high-speed Internet access, access to a hotel computer and printer, newspaper, and a shuttle to various parts of town. Valet parking costs $25. Ask about packages.

Part V
Living It Up After Dark: D.C. Nightlife

The 5th Wave   By Rich Tennant

"Yes, we are going to hear Pachelbel's Canon next, but maybe I should explain..."

In this part . . .

When it comes to nightlife, D.C. ain't New York. For many Washingtonians, this is first, foremost, and almost always a place to work. Period. But that doesn't mean you can't enjoy D.C. after dark. This part gives you the low-down on where to find the best shows, concerts, neighbor-hood watering holes, and music/dance clubs — plus I'll tell you about D.C.'s high culture (symphony, opera, and dance), which is top-notch and constantly getting better. Washington is the land of freebies, even when it comes to music and thea-ter, so you can scratch your cultural itch without opening your wallet.

Chapter 15

Applauding the Cultural Scene

- -

In This Chapter

▶ Getting information and tickets
▶ Dining before the curtain goes up
▶ Knowing what's hot on the cultural scene
▶ Taking in a play, concert, or dance performance

- -

*U*nlike the famous cherry trees, Washington's cultural scene knows no particular season and blooms year-round. Over the years, a dazzling array of theatrical venues has sprouted for residents and visitors alike.

Getting the Inside Scoop on the D.C. Arts Scene

 You could spend your entire Washington visit in the **John F. Kennedy Center for the Performing Arts** (2700 F St. NW, between New Hampshire Avenue and Rock Creek Parkway; concerts ☎ **800-444-1324** or 202-467-4600, tours 202-416-8340; www.kennedy-center.org) and partake of just about every type of performance you enjoy.

The center, a living memorial to the martyred president, is both a performance venue and a tourist attraction in its own right. It also was a long time a-coming.

President Eisenhower signed legislation creating a "national cultural center" in 1958. Kennedy himself was an ardent fundraiser for the project. After Kennedy's assassination, Congress designated the center as his memorial. President Johnson broke ground in 1965. The center finally opened in 1971, during the Nixon presidency, with a performance of Leonard Bernstein's "Requiem" for Kennedy.

The Performing Arts Scene in Washington, D.C.

Arena Stage **11**
Carter Barron Ampitheatre **1**
Discovery Theater **10**
Folger Shakespeare Library **12**
Ford's Theatre **7**
Kennedy Center **4**
National Theatre **5**
Shakespeare Theatre **8**
Source Theatre **2**
Ticket Place **9**
Warner Theatre **6**
Wolf Trap **3**
Woolly Mammoth Theatre **9**

Fabulous freebies

The best news for those traveling on a tight budget is that **free performances** are as much a part of Washington as spin doctors and negative campaign advertising.

The **Kennedy Center** offers free shows on the Millennium Stage in the Grand Foyer daily at 6 p.m. Audiences enjoy midsummer nights' freebies when the **Shakespeare Theatre** plays outdoors in Rock Creek Park's Carter Barron Amphitheatre, off 16th Street and Colorado Avenue NW. The **National Symphony** and **military bands** present free outdoor concerts at several sites from Memorial Day through Labor Day. The National Mall has become an outdoor theater for screening **classic movies** in the summer. The **Washington National Opera** occasionally projects a live performance onto a screen on the Mall. Horrendous weather unfortunately discouraged all but a few true buffs from taking in *Madame Butterfly* in November 2006.

Today, the center is a world-class cultural venue, with **concert hall, opera house, movie theater,** and other facilities. It's home to the **National Symphony** and the **Washington National Opera.** It also hosts numerous local and traveling troupes in all the performing arts.

The halls outside the performance venues are truly grand. More than 40 nations donated building materials and works of art. Great views are to be had from the top-floor restaurants and promenade. You can attend performances here, including daily free performances on the **Millennium Stage.** And you can take a tour.

The center is open daily from 10 a.m. until 30 minutes after last performance. Tours are conducted Monday through Friday from 10 a.m. to 5 p.m. and Saturday and Sunday from 10 a.m. to 1 p.m. Admission is free to the building. You pay, of course, for tickets to most performances.

The **box office,** in the Kennedy Center Hall of States, is open Monday through Saturday 10 a.m. to 9 p.m., and Sundays and holidays from noon to 9 p.m. For a 10-percent surcharge, you can place a phone order from 10 a.m. until 9 p.m. daily by calling ☎ **800-444-1324** or 202-467-4600. Tickets can be purchased online, again with a 10-percent surcharge, at www.kennedy-center.org/tickets. You can get further ticket information from 10 a.m. to 9 p.m. daily by calling ☎ **202-467-4600.**

Free shuttle service is available from the Foggy Bottom–George Washington University Metrorail Station every 15 minutes from 9:45 a.m. until midnight Monday through Friday, 10 a.m. until midnight Saturdays, noon until midnight Sundays, and 4 p.m. until midnight on federal holidays. Look for signs to the left as you get off the station escalator.

 You can obtain tickets for "VIP" tours of the center from members of Congress.

Half-price tickets for some Kennedy Center performances are available in limited numbers to full-time students through graduate school, seniors 65 and older, enlisted military personnel in grades E-1 to E-4, and people on fixed incomes below $5,000 a year or with permanent disabilities. If you have a disability, you can order tickets by phone. Others must get them at the box office. Tickets are available in advance for opening nights and some other performances. The rest are sold on performance day, beginning at noon for matinees and 6 p.m. for evening shows. Except for elementary and secondary school students, you must produce proof of eligibility — student or military ID card, Medicare card, driver's license, or other government document indicating age or income. Those with disabilities can show an ID card obtained from Kennedy Center.

All these events occur at just one venue. Year-round, on any given day, you can count on finding performing artists on many stages in Washington.

The play's the thing

In a city that generates more than its share of political theater, dramatic and musical theater also thrives.

Broadway-bound shows and resurrected classics account for much theatrical activity at the **Kennedy Center** (See contact information above.) **Arena Stage** (1101 6th St. SW, at Maine Ave; ☎ 202-488-3300; www.arena stage.org), on the other hand, presents new works, reinterprets older works, and offers a diverse mix of shows. Now more than 50 years old, Arena can brag about a distinguished life so far: It was the first not-for-profit theater in the United States, the first regional theater to transfer a production to Broadway, the first regional theater invited by the U.S. State Department to tour behind the Iron Curtain, and the first regional to win a Tony.

D.C.'s diminutive Theater District — I don't think I'll compare it to Broadway — spans a portion of Downtown and Penn Quarter, east of the White House. The most active stages are:

- ✔ **National Theatre** (1321 Pennsylvania Ave. NW, between 13th and 14th streets; ☎ 800-447-7400 or 202-628-6161, children's programs 202-783-3372; www.nationaltheatre.org).

- ✔ **Warner Theatre** (513 13th Street NW, between E and F streets; ☎ 202-783-4000; www.warnertheatre.com).

- ✔ **Ford's Theatre** (511 10th St. NW, between E and F streets; ☎ 202-347-4833; www.fordstheatre.org).

- ✔ **Studio Theatre** (1501 14th St. NW, at P Street; ☎ 202-332-3300; www.studiotheatre.org), which focuses on contemporary works by young artists, but is not limited to that. The 2004 season included *Tommy,* The Who's rock opera, for instance.

✔ **Woolly Mammoth Theatre Company** (641 D St. NW, between 6th and 7th streets; ☎ 202-393-3939; www.woollymammoth.net), which moved into new quarters in Penn Quarter in mid-2005. Woolly presents plays that "explore the edges of theatrical style and human experience."

✔ **Shakespeare Theatre** (450 7th St. NW, between D and E streets; ☎ 202-547-1122; www.shakespearetheatre.org). These thespians perform the bard and other playwrights at their marvelous theater complex in Penn Quarter. Catch them for free in the summer at Carter Baron Amphitheater (16th Street and Colorado Avenue NW; ☎ 202-426-0486; www.nps.gov/rocr/cbarron).

✔ The **Folger Shakespeare Library** (201 E. Capitol St. SE, at 2nd Street; ☎ 202-544-7077; www.folger.edu/whatson.cfm) provides D.C.'s most interesting setting for theater-going. It's a replica of an Elizabethan theater. While Shakespeare's plays obviously provide the core of the Folger's offerings, works by other playwrights are performed as well, and the theater presents poetry readings and concerts of early European music.

Hearing the sounds of music

The **National Symphony Orchestra,** one of the world's best, plays in the Kennedy Center Concert Hall (2700 F St. NW, between New Hampshire Avenue and Rock Creek Parkway; ☎ **800-444-1324,** 202-467-4600; www.kennedy-center.org/nso). In summer, these musicians take some of their concerts outdoors. Leonard Slatkin is the musical director, with other world-renowned conductors and musicians making guest appearances. The symphony's performances frequently sell out, so make your reservations early.

Hot time: Summer in the city

If you visit Washington in summer and enjoy classical music, check out the **National Symphony's free concerts** on the **West Lawn of the Capitol,** on the Sunday of the Memorial Day and Labor Day weekends, and on July 4. You also can catch a free concert by the **NSO** several times in summer at the **Carter Barron Amphitheatre** in Rock Creek Park (16th Street and Colorado Avenue NW; ☎ **202-426-0486;** www.nps.gov/rocr/cbarron). These events are some of the top perks of summer in this city. The Capitol Lawn concerts are enormously popular, so you need to arrive early and be prepared to go through security screening. The symphony also performs outdoors in summer at **Wolf Trap Farm Park for the Performing Arts** (1551 Trap Rd., Vienna, Virginia, off the Wolf Trap exit from the Dulles Toll Road; ☎ **703-255-1800;** www.nps.gov/wotr; more details in Chapter 18).

The rousing **Fourth of July concert** on the **West Lawn of the Capitol** features the **National Symphony,** guest artists, celebrity hosts, and an enthusiastic audience. The evening ends with a bang when the 1812 Overture accompanies the **fireworks** display on the Mall (or vice versa, depending on your viewpoint). Arrive early, be braced for crowds, and bring something to sit on. You also can catch a live broadcast of the concert on public television.

Beat some of the crowds at all these concerts by showing up the night before for the dress rehearsal.

A night at the opera

Washington's opera aficionados are thrilled that superstar tenor Placido Domingo is general director of the **Washington National Opera** (2700 F St. NW, between New Hampshire Avenue and Rock Creek Parkway, in Kennedy Center; ☎ **800-876-7372,** 202-295-2400; www.dc-opera.org). Under Domingo's leadership, the troupe mounts classic shows and pushes the envelope with modern material. The 2006–07 season, for instance, included such standards as Puccini's *Madame Butterfly* and Wagner's *The Valkyrie* — as well as the North American première of *Sophie's Choice,* Nicholas Maw's adaptation of the William Styron novel that was made into a hit movie starring Meryl Streep. When performances sell out, the opera sells standing room tickets at the box office and by phone (☎ **800-444-1324** or 202-467-4600) for $25.

Enjoying an evening of dance

The best in the dance world grace Washington's stages. Such world-class troupes as the Kirov, the Royal, the Joffrey, the Bolshoi, and the American Ballet Theatre came here for the 2006–07 season alone. The city also is quite proud of its own **Washington Ballet** (☎ **202-362-3606;** www.washingtonballet.org), which performs in several venues, including Kennedy Center. Every Christmas season, the ballet performs the *Nutcracker* at the Warner Theater.

Finding Out What's Playing and Getting Tickets

If you want to take in a play, concert, or dance performance during your D.C. visit, it pays to do a little homework before you arrive. Surf to the *Washington Post* Web site (www.washingtonpost.com) and click on "City Guide" near the top of the home page. You also can peruse the *Post's* daily Style section, Sunday Arts section, and Friday *Weekend* magazine.

Tickets, please!

Competition for tickets to a popular performance can be keen. To get the best seats (or any seats!) for a hit show, you need to buy tickets as far in advance as possible.

If you order tickets over the phone, ask about the seat location; at the box office, ask to see a diagram of the theater.

The best pre-theater dining

If you're catching a theater performance, be seated for dinner no later than 6 p.m., as most curtains go up at 7:30 or 8 p.m. Choose someplace near the theater, in case the service is slow. (Wouldn't you rather sprint a couple of blocks than hail a cab and maybe miss Act I?) When you arrive at the restaurant, tell the host or waiter (or both) that you're going to an event and need to be out by a certain time. Order soon after you're seated and save the soufflé and other dishes requiring lots of preparation for a non-theater evening.

Many restaurants offer pre-theater, fixed-price menus. This dinner usually includes an appetizer or salad, entree, and dessert. Pre-theater specials usually are available from 4:30 or 5 p.m. to 6 or 6:30 p.m. You can spend considerably less than you would if you ordered à la carte.

If you have tickets for a show, consider the following pre-theater deals:

- ✔ **Marcel's** (2401 Pennsylvania Ave. NW, at 24th Street; ☎ 202-296-1166) has the coolest pre- (and post-) theater deal. This highly acclaimed restaurant serves you dinner between 5:30 and 7 p.m., sends you by limo to the Kennedy Center for your show, and then brings you back to the restaurant for dessert after the show, all for $48.

- ✔ The pre-theater dinner at **Circle Bistro** (1 Washington Circle NW, at 23rd Street and New Hampshire Avenue; ☎ 202-293-5390) is served from 5 to 7 p.m. and costs $35.

- ✔ Near the Shakespeare and Ford's theaters, **Café Atlántico** (405 8th St. NW, between D and E streets; ☎ 202-393-0812; www.cafeatlantico.com), serves its pre-theater meal for $28 from 5 to 6:30 p.m.

- ✔ The restaurants in the **Kennedy Center** don't offer pre-theater specials, but they certainly are handy places to eat before a show. Reservations are recommended at the full-service **Roof Terrace Restaurant** (2700 F St. NW; ☎ 202-416-8555; www.kennedy-center.org/visitor/restaurants.html). They're not accepted at the **KC Cafe**, which also is located on the roof terrace level.

See Chapter 10 for reviews of other restaurants. Ask restaurants near your theater whether they offer a pre-theater special.

To order tickets to most events, call **Ticketmaster** (☎ 800-551-7328 or 202-397-7328) or visit Ticketmaster's Web site www.ticketmaster.com. Expect to pay an outlandish surcharge. **Tickets.com** (☎ 800-400-9373; www.tickets.com) pretty much covers what Ticketmaster doesn't. Like Ticketmaster, expect to pay a high surcharge. If your hotel has a concierge, he or she should be able to get tickets to many events. You may have to pay a surcharge, and you should tip the concierge for the service.

For cut-rate tickets to same-day performances, go to **Ticket Place,** which moved in 2004 to a new location at 407 7th St. NW between D and E streets, near the Gallery Place/Chinatown and Archives/Navy Memorial Metrorail stations. Ticket Place sells same-day (and some advance-sale) tickets for 62 percent of face value. The ticket booth is open Tuesday to Friday between 11 a.m. and 6 p.m. or Saturday between 10 a.m. and 5 p.m. Some tickets are sold on the Internet (www.ticketplace.org) for 67 percent of face value Tuesday to Friday noon to 4 p.m. Ticket Place doesn't sell tickets by phone but does provide recorded information at ☎ **202-842-5387.** Because Ticket Place is closed Sunday and Monday, tickets for those days sometimes can be purchased on Saturday. If you can't find a bargain here, you can pay big-time for Ticketmaster service at the same location.

 Some theaters set aside tickets for seniors and full-time students and sell them the day of the performance. If you don't ask, you don't get! Gamblers are advised to arrive at the box office a half-hour before curtain time; sometimes unclaimed reserved tickets are available. If you're determined to attend a performance that's sold out, ask about SRO (standing room only) tickets. If someone leaves at intermission, you may get lucky and snag a seat.

Curtain calls

Some people blame it on the preponderance of military officers and bureaucrats in D.C. For whatever reason, Washingtonians are a punctual lot, so you usually can count on the curtain rising on time. A good general rule is to arrive at least 15 minutes early so that you can visit the restroom and buy your overpriced snack. (I've seen the line to the ladies room snake all the way to Kentucky five minutes before a performance. Seldom, it seems, does that happen to us men.) Many venues will not seat latecomers until a break in the program occurs — which may mean intermission.

Dressing the part

A night at the theater no longer demands a suit and tie or dress and high heels. Most Washington theatergoers are a shade or two less formal and flamboyant. Knock yourself out and preen your feathers if that's your style, but the usher will show you to your seat no matter what your attire — well, within reason. When in doubt, follow your mother's advice and "wash behind your ears, comb your hair, and look presentable." Try slacks or a skirt, a shirt or blouse, a jacket or sweater, a tie if you want. Now, go make your entrance.

Finding Things for the Kids

 Washington offers wonderful cultural opportunities for families, especially during the school year. Look to the following for entertaining productions that are geared to youngsters.

- ✔ The **Discovery Theater** (in the Ripley Center, just west of the Smithsonian Castle, 1100 Jefferson Dr. SW; ☎ 202-357-1500; www. discoverytheater.si.edu) presents live performances for children of all ages.

- ✔ The **Kennedy Center** (2700 F St. NW, between New Hampshire Avenue and Rock Creek Parkway; ☎ 800-444-1324 or 202-467-4600; www.kennedy-center.org/programs/family) presents many youth and family programs. These include plays and musicals for children and special concerts.

- ✔ Tickets are free for the children's program "Saturday Morning at the **National Theatre**" (1321 Pennsylvania Ave. NW, between 13th and 14th streets; ☎ 202-628-6161; www.nationaltheatre.org/ saturday/saturday.htm). Get them — first-come, first-served — a half hour before each of the 9:30 and 11 a.m. programs. Recent programs included *Mother Goose and her Fabulous Puppet Friends,* *Red Riding Hood,* and *Romeo and Juliet* adapted for kids.

- ✔ The **Washington Ballet**'s *Nutcracker,* performed during the Christmas season at the Warner Theatre (513 13th St. NW, between E and F streets; ☎ 202-783-4000; www.warnertheatre.com), is a treat for everyone in the family. Tickets are sold through Ticketmaster (☎ 800-551-7328 or 202-397-7328; www.ticketmaster.com).

- ✔ The "petting zoo" before the **National Symphony Orchestra's Family Concerts** (2700 F St. NW, between New Hampshire Avenue and Rock Creek Parkway; ☎ 800-444-1324 or 202-467-4600; www. kennedy-center.org/nso/programs/family) is a treat for budding young musicians and even those who don't know they're budding yet. The concerts are designed to appeal to anyone seven or older. During the "zoo," one hour before each concert, kids can go up to the stage and handle instruments. After 3 p.m. concerts, performers stay to answer children's questions and to tell stories about what it's like to be a musician.

Chapter 16

Bars, Stars, and Gee-tars: D.C. at Night

*F*eeling thirsty for a chilled cocktail and some hot jazz? Longing to find a pub that stores 1,000 beers in its fridge? Itching to rock the night away? Longing for laughs? Rest assured, after the lights go off in the White House, you can take the party elsewhere, such as Adams-Morgan, Georgetown, Dupont Circle, or the ever-more-booming Penn Quarter. It's true that a segment of Washingtonians think a hit night is popcorn and C-SPAN reruns. But lots of young people and a large cosmopolitan population have spawned clubs, bars, and other nightspots that appeal to D.C.'s multicultural citizenry.

Before you head off to strut your stuff, keep in mind that Washington's subway system doesn't run around the clock. But Metrorail does run later — and earlier — than it used to. The system opens at 5 a.m. weekdays and 7 a.m. weekends. It closes at midnight Sunday through Thursday and 3 a.m. Friday and Saturday. Check when the last train leaves from the station you plan to use at the end of your night of revelry. Leave yourself plenty of time to get to the station, or you may find yourself having to hail a cab. Be aware: D.C. cabs, plentiful during business hours, make like Cinderella's coach at night.

For a comprehensive listing of the entertainment happenings, see the "Weekend" section of the Friday *Washington Post.* The free *City Paper* — available in bookstores, restaurants, bars, and cafes all around town — is another good source for information on what's going on.

Focusing on the Music: The Best Jazz Clubs

D.C.'s premier jazz club is **Blues Alley** (1073 Wisconsin Ave. NW, in the alley south of M Street; ☎ **202-337-4141;** www.bluesalley.com) in Georgetown. All the top touring artists come here. Dizzy Gillespie, Charlie Byrd, Stanley Turrentine, Ahmad Jamal, and Ramsey Lewis cut live albums at the club. As I write this, the club's menu of upcoming performers includes Larry Coryell, Oregon, Mose Allison, Bucky Pizzarelli, Stanley Clarke, and Arturo Sandoval. Blues Alley bills itself as a jazz supper club and serves Creole cuisine, steak, and seafood from 6 p.m. and lighter fare after 10 p.m. Reservations are recommended, and the best way to get good seats is to book an early dinner. This place isn't cheap. In addition to the ticket charge, which varies with the popularity of the musicians, there's a $2.50 cover and $10 minimum. The aforementioned Allison was fetching $24, Pizzarelli $35, and Clarke more than $50. If you opt for dinner, entrees run from $17 to $23. The club offers half-price admission to students and congressional staff with ID for some 10 p.m. shows Sunday through Thursday. Shows start at 8 and 10 p.m. most nights.

The **Bohemian Caverns** (2001 11th St. NW, at U Street; ☎ **202-299-0801;** www.bohemiancaverns.com) is a renovation and expansion of the Crystal Caverns, which showcased such jazz greats as Duke Ellington, Pearl Bailey, Miles Davis, John Coltrane, Ella Fitzgerald, and Billie Holiday from the '20s to the '60s. A full-service restaurant resides within this multistoried jazz club. Call ahead for information on performances, which aren't scheduled every night. The club has a business-casual dress code. Cover is usually $10 to $20.

Friday nights on Capitol Hill, upstairs at **Mr. Henry's** (601 Pennsylvania Ave. SE, at 6th Street; ☎ **202-546-8412**) is the place for jazz. This comfortable, popular restaurant is known as a gathering plays for gays and lesbians, but it attracts lots of straight men and women for the music, the food, and the laid-back atmosphere. You pay an $8 minimum to enter the room where the music plays from 8:30 p.m.

Some restaurants and cafes present live jazz along with their food and drink. Look them up in Chapter 10 for details. Traditional jazz groups play on Friday and Saturday nights at **B. Smith's,** in Union Station. **Georgia Brown's** serves a jazz brunch Downtown from 10 a.m. to 2:15 p.m. Sundays. **Kinkead's,** in Foggy Bottom/West End, offers live jazz from 6:30 to 10 p.m. Tuesday through Saturday. From late May to mid-September, jazz groups perform outdoors from 5 to 8:30 p.m. at the **Pavilion Cafe** in the **National Gallery of Art's Sculpture Garden.** From 6 to 10 p.m. Fridays, a portion of the **National Museum of Natural History** becomes the **Smithsonian Jazz Café,** with food, drink, and live music for a $10 cover (kids 12 and younger free).

Turning Up the Volume: Rock and Pop Venues

Many rockers believe the **9:30 Club**'s (815 V St. NW, at Vermont Avenue; ☎ 202-393-0930; www.930.com.) state-of-the-art sound system makes it the best place to hear pop music. It's sure not the seats — there are very few!

Pink, Cat Power, Sheryl Crow, Shawn Colvin, R.E.M., Red Hot Chili Peppers, Ice-T, Alanis Morissette — and Tony Bennett! — have played here. The cover charge depends on the act. Call or check the Web site to find out when performances are scheduled. The club's only open when someone's playing, and you're wise to get advance tickets for big-name acts. Tickets are available through the club's Web site and at the box office, which is open Monday through Friday from noon to 7 p.m., and during shows. When there's a show, doors open Sunday through Thursday at 7:30 p.m., Friday and Saturday at 9 p.m. The first act starts 45 to 75 minutes later. The 9:30 is in the U Street Corridor, an up-and-coming entertainment district. But the club's corner is still a pretty skuzzy looking place. Stick with the crowd on your way to and from the nearby Vermont Avenue exit of the U Street/Cardozo Metrorail Station. Don't go wandering down any dark side streets. If you drive, park in the garage across the street for $10. It's wise to make a parking reservation with the club, which runs the garage. Or, just take a cab.

The coolest felines purr at the **Black Cat** (1811 14th St. NW, between S and T streets; ☎ **202-667-7960**). You don't pay a cover charge in the Red Room bar, which has pool tables, pinball machines, a jukebox with an eclectic selection of music, and a laid-back atmosphere. The ground floor Backstage hosts poetry readings and films. The menu at the Food for Thought Cafe satisfies vegans, vegetarians, and carnivores alike. Things get hopping upstairs at Mainstage, the concert room which showcases underground/alternative performers and has a dance floor that holds 400. The Black Cat does not limit its musical tastes. Hip hop, techno, swing, and folk are all heard here. Performers have included Bright Eyes, the Roots, Cherry Poppin' Daddies, Foo Fighters, Korn, We Are Scientists, Yeah Yeah Yeahs, and — conceding nothing to nearby 9:30 — Pete Seeger. Cover charge in the concert room depends on the act. You can get tickets at Ticketmaster (☎ **800-551-7328**; www.ticketmaster.com), and at the box office (cash only). Backstage tickets are sold at the door only. Mainstage and Backstage open Sunday through Thursday at 8:30 p.m., Friday and Saturday at 9:30 p.m. Mainstage opening act starts 30 minutes later. Hours at the Red Room are Sunday through Thursday 8 p.m. to 2 a.m., Friday and Saturday 7 p.m. to 3 a.m. The cafe opens at the same times, and closes an hour earlier.

The big-big-big stars — the kind that can draw tens of thousands to a single concert — stop at the big-big-big venues. When Simon and Garfunkel brought their reunion tour to town in late 2003, for example, they set up shop at what is now called **Verizon Center** (601 F St. NW, at 6th Street; ☎ **202-661-5000**; www.verizoncenter.com). Verizon Center

Washington, D.C., Clubs and Bars

Black Cat **6**
Blue Bar **26**
Blues Alley **14**
Bohemian Caverns **27**
B. Smith's **31**
Capitol Steps **20**
Chi Cha Lounge **5**
Club Heaven & Hell **3**
Clyde's **13**
Dubliner **30**
Garrett's **11**
Georgia Brown **17**
Habana Village **2**
Halo **7**
Improv **16**
JR's Bar and Grill **8**
Kelly's Irish Times Pub **29**
Kinkead's **15**
Madam's Organ **1**
Mr. Henry's **33**
9:30 Club **28**
Old Ebbitt Grill **18**
Omega DC **10**
Pavilion Cafe **22**
Phase One **35**
Platinum **24**
Remington's **34**
RFK Stadium **32**
Russia House **4**
Sky Terrace **19**
Smithsonian Jazz Cafe **21**
Tabard Inn **9**
The Tombs **12**
Verizon Center **25**
Zanzibar **36**
Zola **23**

also is where Bruce Springsteen and his fellow political-activist performers finished their ill-fated "Vote for Change" tour on the eve of the 2004 election. More recently, Bob Seger, Justin Timberlake, the Who, and Christina Aguilera have been on the center's schedule. Most nights, this is where you find the Washington Wizards National Basketball Association team, the Washington Capitals National Hockey League team, the Washington Mystics Women's NBA entry, and some Georgetown University basketball games.

Odd fact: When this used to be called MCI Center, it picked up the nickname the "Phone Booth." When naming rights went to another telephone company, the official name changed but the nickname stuck.

When the Phone Booth's 20,000-plus concert seats aren't enough, superstars take their acts to **Robert F. Kennedy Memorial Stadium** (East Capitol Street at 22nd Street; ☎ 202-547-9077; www.dcsec.com), which can accommodate 55,000 or more. The Rolling Stones rocked RFK, as do some giant music festivals. As a sports stadium, RFK is home to the D.C. United Major League Soccer club and the Washington Nationals Major League Baseball team. A new baseball park was scheduled to open on South Capitol Street on Capitol Hill in 2008. A new soccer field also was being discussed, so some wonder what RFK's future will look like.

Another site for mammoth events is **FedEx Field** (I-495 Exit 16, Maryland; ☎ 301-276-6000; www.redskins.com/fedexfield), which seats more than 90,000 for Redskins games. It's in the middle of nowhere, a mile from the nearest Metrorail station, Morgan Boulevard.

Shaking Your Groove Thing: Dance Clubs

Do you wanna dance? If so, see the preceding section of this chapter for details about **Black Cat,** where rockers go to dance as well as listen to top-name performers. Then consider these other venues, where dancing's the thing.

As you may expect, **Club Heaven & Hell** (2327 18th St. NW, at Columbia Road; ☎ 202-667-4355) welcomes both angels and devils. Check your wings and pitchforks at this door in Adams-Morgan. Here, it's Heaven that sizzles. It's a loud dance hall on the upper level (of course) that features different styles of music on different nights, sometimes live, sometimes DJ-generated. On weekends, the pearly gates don't close until 3 a.m. (2 a.m. Sun–Thurs). Doors open at 7:30 p.m. Hell, downstairs, is a dark bar with jukebox and pool table.

Another Adams-Morgan nightspot, **Madam's Organ** (2461 18th St. NW, south of Columbia Road; ☎ 202-667-5370; www.madamsorgan.com) — the owner likes puns — was once named one of the 25 best bars in America by *Playboy* magazine. Madam's has a varied musical menu, with shows starting between 9 and 10 p.m. On Monday, it's funky jazz.

Wednesday it's bluegrass (with local TV news anchor Doug McKelway sometimes sitting in on banjo). On other nights, you might encounter blues, R&B, jazz, reggae, salsa, merengue, and/or a magician. You can eat sandwiches, snacks, and "soul food" here. Redheads get half price on Rolling Rock. The second floor bar is called "Big Daddy's Love Lounge & Pick-Up Joint." The place describes itself as a "blues bar and soul food restaurant where the beautiful people go to get ugly." If you want noise, body heat, and dancing, Madam's is the spot for you. Or you can go outside on the roof deck to cool off — or order something from the tiki bar! Madam's is open Sunday through Thursday from 5 p.m. to 2 a.m. and Friday and Saturday from 5 p.m. to 3 a.m. Cover usually is between $3 and $7.

Platinum (915 F St. NW, between 9th and 10th streets; ☎ **202-393-3555;** www.platinumclubdc.com) is an upscale club with three dance floors where the young and beautiful move to varied music. Check the Web site for what's playing when you want to go. Platinum has a VIP lounge that takes table reservations and expects you to spend a lot on liquid refreshments. It's open 10 p.m. to 3 a.m. Thursday through Saturday, and 9 p.m. to 2:30 a.m. on Sunday, usually with a $10 to $20 cover. Admission is free before 11 p.m. on Saturday and Sunday if you register first on the Web site.

If you'd like a view with your dancing, salsa on down to **Zanzibar** (700 Water St. SW, between 7th and 8th streets; ☎ **202-554-9100;** www. zanzibar-otw.com). Actually, you'd best take a cab. This large, popular dance club comes with picture windows that look out onto the boats tied up in the Washington Channel. You can cool down on outdoor decks during nice weather. Inside, year-round, the club sports multiple rooms, bars, and dance floors on several levels. A fair number of tables and comfortable seating are situated around the place. This club draws an international, integrated clientele — especially Latin Americans and those who like to dance to Latin music. Hours, special programs, and cover charges vary. Call or check the Web site for details.

Hanging Out: D.C.'s Best Bars

After a rough day of sightseeing, kicking back with your favorite aperitif can be therapeutic.

If you're looking for a romantic spot where you can share some quiet music with someone special, settle into the **Blue Bar** at the Henley Park Hotel (926 Massachusetts Ave. NW, west of 9th Street; ☎ **202-638-5200**) at the northwest edge of Penn Quarter. A pianist performs Thursday, Friday, and Saturday evenings. The bar is softly lighted and is comprised of a collection of cubicle-like spaces that enable you and your companion to feel a sense of privacy while you listen to the music. The bar has no cover charge. The bar opens at 11:30 a.m. daily and closes at midnight Sunday through Thursday and 1 a.m. Friday and Saturday. A light menu is available.

The well-worn comfort of the **Tabard Inn** (1739 N St. NW, between 17th and 18th streets; ☎ 202-833-2668; www.tabardinn.com/rest.htm) near Dupont Circle makes it a perfect spot for a drink all year. It's even better in the winter, when you can cozy up to the fireplace. Every Sunday, live jazz plays from 7:30 to 10:30 p.m. The **Old Ebbitt Grill** (675 15th St. NW, between F and G streets; ☎ 202-347-4800) has the feel of an old-fashioned men's club, and as the evening wears on, that feeling grows. This downtown tavern is big and has multiple bars, so you ought to be able to find a spot that satisfies you. You have lots of choices in the nibbles department as well. The lounge at **Zola** (800 F St. NW; ☎ 202-654-0999), with floor-to-ceiling windows looking at the street action in the Penn Quarter arts and entertainment district, is a highly popular spot for after-work unwinding. Zola prints an innovative cocktail and wine list. It closes at 10 p.m. Sunday and at midnight the rest of the week.

Enjoy a panoramic view of Washington with your cocktail at the **Sky Terrace** atop the Hotel Washington (515 15th St. NW, at Pennsylvania Avenue; ☎ 202-638-5900), just a block from the White House. From April through October, weather willing, this outdoor restaurant is a wonderful vantage point for watching the sun set over the city or the lights come on at D.C.'s landmarks. You can order a meal or just get a drink until 12:30 a.m. daily.

For a beer with some atmosphere, drop in at a longtime Georgetown hangout. **Clyde's** (3236 M St. NW, between Wisconsin Avenue and Potomac Street; ☎ 202-333-9180) has helped to define eating and drinking in Georgetown since 1963. A 1996 renovation replaced much of its old-time-tavern atmosphere with the appearance of your typical, late-20th-century, family-friendly theme bar (airplane models dangling from the ceiling in one room, for example). But it's still a comfortable spot for a beer and a burger — whether bar munchies or a full meal. Clyde's is open Monday through Thursday from 11:30 a.m. until midnight, Friday 11:30 a.m. to 1 a.m., Saturday 10 a.m. to 1 a.m., and Sunday 9 a.m. until midnight.

If you prefer that worn, college-bar mystique, stroll east on M Street for about 2 blocks to **Garrett's** (3003 M St. NW, at 30th Street; ☎ 202-333-1033; www.garrettsdc.com) where the street-level bar will remind you of some place where you drank and dug the jukebox in your past — except that this jukebox is linked to the Internet and has a near-limitless selection of songs. Listen, there's Bob Dylan spittin' out "Rainy Day Woman" like it's 1966. Upstairs you find two more bars, a golf game, and a nice little restaurant. It's open Monday through Thursday 11:30 a.m. to 1:30 a.m., Friday and Saturday noon to 2:30 a.m., Sunday noon to 1:30 a.m.

Georgetown's main college bar is **The Tombs** (1226 36th St. NW, at Prospect Street; ☎ 202-337-6668), which occupies the basement of a mid-19th-century house at the edge of the Georgetown University campus. Students, faculty, and other neighborhood residents frequent this comfortable, attractive pub, which once counted a young Bill

Clinton among its regulars. The food is unusually good for a college hangout because of its relationship with the excellent 1789 Restaurant upstairs. The Tombs is open Monday through Thursday from 11:30 a.m. to 1:15 a.m., Friday from 11:30 a.m. to 2:15 a.m., Saturday from 11 a.m. to 2:15 a.m., and Sunday from 9:30 a.m. to 1:15 a.m.

Going International: Latin, Irish, and Russian Hot Spots

Want to add a little international flavor to your Washington nightlife? If your tastes run to dancing and things Latin, you'll enjoy **Zanzibar,** described earlier in this chapter. If you're interested in Latin dancing lessons, check when they're being offered at **Habana Village** (1834 Columbia Rd. NW, between Biltmore Street and Belmont Road; ☎ 202-462-6310), an Adams-Morgan nightspot where salsa and merengue are big Wednesday and Thursday from 6:30 p.m. to 3 a.m., and Friday and Saturday till 2:30 a.m. The **Chi Cha Lounge** (1624 U St. NW, between 16th and 17th streets; ☎ 202-234-8400) entertains with Latin drinks, music, and tapas. Oh, and also water pipes — but for smoking tobacco only. Chi Cha has a $15 minimum and is open Sunday through Thursday from 5:30 p.m. to 1:30 a.m., and Friday and Saturday till 2:30 a.m.

The Irish have been influential in American politics for a long time, so it stands to reason that America's capital would have its share of Irish pubs. On Capitol Hill, side-by-side competition occurs between the **Dubliner** (4 F St. NW, at North Capitol Street; ☎ 202-737-3773; www. dublinerdc.com) and **Kelly's Irish Times Pub** (14 F St. NW, between North Capitol Street and New Jersey Avenue; ☎ 202-543-5433). Both spots parcel out Irish beer, Irish food, and live Irish music. Both offer sidewalk tables in nice weather. You find lots of Capitol Hill denizens here — congressional staffers, journalists, lobbyists, and the occasional legislator. The Times also attracts 20-somethings with a pop jukebox in the basement and is open Sunday through Thursday from 11 a.m. to 1:30 a.m. and Friday and Saturday until 2:30 a.m. Live music starts Friday and Saturday at 10 p.m. The Dubliner is open daily from 11 a.m. until the crowd thins out after midnight. Live music starts at 9 p.m. Monday through Saturday and 7 p.m. Sunday.

Pretend you're part of the post-Soviet oligarchy at **Russia House Restaurant and Lounge** (1800 Connecticut Ave. N.W., at S Street; ☎ 202-234-9433; www.russiahouselounge.com). This is truly a remarkable spot, spun out of an organization founded to promote U.S.-Russia business. The décor is elegant, designed to evoke the era of the czars. There are, of course, large selections of vodkas, Russian beers and caviars. You can order a full Russian meal in the restaurant.

Laughing the Night Away: Comedy Clubs

The best comedy in Washington is homegrown. **The Capitol Steps** (www.capsteps.com) did, in fact, blossom on the Capitol steps. Congressional staffers with talent saw the humor around them and turned it into an enduring musical act. (Motto: "We put the mock in democracy.") I'm talking about songs like "It's a Whole Newt World," "Send in the Clones," "Don't Cry for Me, Judge Scalia," "Enron-Ron-Ron," and "Papa's Got a Brand New Baghdad." Following defeat of the Senate Democratic leader in the 2004 election, the Steps penned "Hang Down Your Head, Tom Daschle." Following the Democratic resurgence in 2006, they came up with "Springtime for Liberals" (to the tune of "Springtime for Hitler" from *The Producers*) and "Everything's Run by Pelosi" ("Everything's Coming up Roses"). They've been doing this act since the early '80s ("The Wreck of the Walter Fritz Mondale," "Dutch, the Magic Reagan"). Now, they have a regular gig every Friday and Saturday at 7:30 p.m. in the amphitheater of (don't you love irony?) the Ronald Reagan Building, 1300 Pennsylvania Ave. NW, between 13th and 14th streets. You can purchase the $35 tickets from Ticketmaster (☎ **800-551-7328** or 202-397-7328; www.ticketmaster.com), at the Ticketmaster outlet at the D.C. Visitor Information Center in the Reagan Building or at the door after 6 p.m. on the night of the performance.

Headliners on the national comedy club circuit (and subheadliners, too, if the truth be known) perform at **The Improv** (1140 Connecticut Ave. NW, between L and M streets; ☎ **202-296-7008**; www.dcimprov.com). Ellen DeGeneres, Jerry Seinfeld, and Robin Williams have performed here. So have a whole bunch of people I've never heard of, supposedly with Comedy Central credentials. (Where does Tony Rock, Chris's younger brother, fit in?) Drinks and light meals are available. Show times are Tuesday through Thursday at 8:30 p.m., Friday and Saturday at 8 and 10:30 p.m., and Sunday at 8 p.m. The cover varies with the lineup, and there's also a two-item (food or drink) minimum. You can make reservations in person at the box office, by phone, or from the Web site. You must be age 18 to enter.

Painting the Town Rainbow: The Gay and Lesbian Scene

Gays' full participation in the Washington community is only half reflected in the city's nightlife. There is a large and varied collection of night spots for gay men, but just one dedicated to women — although many attract both sexes. As you might expect, Dupont Circle has the most gay-oriented night spots, but gay-focused clubs are scattered throughout the city. Some attract a substantial straight clientele as well.

Among the most popular is **JR's Bar and Grill** (1519 17th St. NW, between P and Q streets; ☎ **202-328-0090**; www.jrswdc.com). The bar draws upscale gay men and has a big-screen TV at the bar and pool tables on the balcony. JR's is open Sunday through Thursday from 4 p.m. to 2 a.m. and Friday and Saturday from 2 p.m. to 3 a.m.

Also attracting gay men in Dupont Circle is **Omega DC** (2122 P St. NW, between 21st Street and Twining Court, entrance off Twining Court; ☎ 202-223-4917), which scatters parties over two floors with several rooms. There's a piano bar, a cigar/martini bar, two more bars, a pool table, and a 60-inch video screen. Omega DC is open Sunday from 7 p.m. to 2 a.m., Monday through Thursday from 4 p.m. to 2 a.m., Friday from 4 p.m. to 3 a.m., and Saturday from 7 p.m. to 3 a.m.

Halo (1435 P St. NW, between 14th and 15th streets; ☎ 202-797-9730; www.halodc.com), about 4½ blocks from Dupont Circle, is one of D.C.'s newest and most popular night spots for gay men and women. Named Washington's best gay and lesbian bar by voters in the 2005 *Washington Post* online readers' poll — and best neighborhood bar, best place to meet men, and best happy hour by *The Washington Blade* in 2006 — Halo actually attracts neighborhood residents of all orientations. They come to this comfortable place to relax, talk, eat, and sip cocktails. Halo is open Monday through Thursday 5 p.m. to 2 a.m., Friday and Saturday 5 p.m. to 3 a.m., and Sunday 2 p.m. to 2 a.m.

Capitol Hill boasts **Remington's** (639 Pennsylvania Ave. SE, between 6th and 7th streets; ☎ 202-543-3113; www.remingtonswdc.com), a country-western bar that offers Western dance lessons and attracts mostly gay men. It's open Monday to Thursday from 4 p.m. to 2 a.m., Friday and Saturday from 4 p.m. to 3 a.m., and Sunday from 5 p.m. to 2 a.m.

Mr. Henry's (601 Pennsylvania Ave. SE, at 6th Street; ☎ 202-546-8412) lures a mixed gay/straight clientele for meals and for jazz Friday nights on the second floor. This Capitol Hill institution is open Monday through Saturday 11:15 a.m. until midnight and Sunday 10 a.m. until midnight. There's an $8 minimum to hear jazz on the second floor from 8:30 p.m. Friday.

Capitol Hill also is home for Washington's oldest bar for lesbians, **Phase One** (525 8th St. SE, between F and G streets; ☎ 202-544-6831). Like Halo, this is a comfortable neighborhood bar. It's got a pool table and small dance floor and attracts gay women of all ages. It's open Thursday from 7 p.m. to 2 a.m., Friday and Saturday till 3 a.m. There's live music Thursday nights.

Noting the paucity of night spots specifically for lesbians, Bridget Hieronymus has created **A Different Kind of Ladies Night.** Actually, it's "nights." These essentially are happy hours for women that Hieronymus organizes frequently in various bars around town. She describes her goal as replicating a "hip, funky, martini-type bar where women could sit around and actually talk and mingle and have a drink." Venues agree to offer drink specials and charge no cover. To find the next gathering, check her Web site www.adifferentkindofladiesnight.com.

Part VI
The Part of Tens

The 5th Wave   By Rich Tennant

"That? That's schedule LVES-1. We've never had to use it. But, if anyone actually discovers how to grow money on trees, Uncle Sam's got a form to get his fair share of the leaves."

In this part . . .

A h, tradition. The Part of Tens is to *For Dummies* books what monument hopping is to Washington — essential. In this part, I list the top ten views in D.C. and the top ten reasons to (gulp) drive around the city.

Chapter 17

Top Ten D.C. Views

In This Chapter

▶ Discovering great places to see D.C. in all its splendor

▶ Looking from the monuments instead of at them

▶ Climbing to high spots that overlook the city

▶ Finding scenic spots for panorama photos

*T*he monuments, monumental buildings, memorials, parks, fountains, and flowers make Washington a stunning city to look at. If you flew down the Potomac River into National Airport, you've already seen the most impressive view. Here are ten others. Don't forget your camera.

Washington Monument

It's pretty widely agreed that the best view of Washington — that doesn't come from a flying machine — comes from the top of the **Washington Monument** (between Constitution Avenue NW, Independence Avenue SW, and 15th and 17th streets; ☎ 202-426-6841; www.nps.gov/wamo; advance tickets 800-967-2283 or http://reservations.nps.gov). You take the fast elevator to the top, wander from window to window to get a panoramic view, then ride down more slowly so you can take a gander at the monument's interior. The elevator runs daily 9 a.m. to 4:45 p.m. The monument's closed December 25. See the monument's listing in Chapter 11 for details on getting tickets.

Old Post Office Tower

Ride the elevator to the top of the **Old Post Office Tower** (Pennsylvania Avenue NW at 11th Street; ☎ 202-606-8694; www.nps.gov/opot). From the observation deck, 270 feet above the street, you can see a view of downtown and beyond. Many people think this view is second only to the vista from the Washington Monument (see preceding section).

While you're here, take a look at the interior workings of the tower clock and bells and visit the ninth-floor exhibit room. The tower is open Monday through Friday from 9 a.m. to 4:45 p.m., and weekends and holidays 10 a.m. to 5:45 p.m. From the first weekend in June through Labor

Top Washington, D.C., Views

Day, it stays open till 7:45 p.m. Monday through Friday. Because the observation deck is exposed to the elements, the tower may close in bad weather.

Arlington National Cemetery

When you ride the Tourmobile through **Arlington National Cemetery** (☎ 703-607-8052; www.arlingtoncemetery.org), be sure to get off at Arlington House and walk around. One of the best panoramas of Washington is viewed from the lawn here or from Pierre L'Enfant's grave below the house. (For details on riding the Tourmobile through Arlington, see Chapter 11.)

Washington National Cathedral

Washington's highest points above sea level are the towers of the Washington National Cathedral (Massachusetts and Wisconsin avenues NW; ☎ 202-537-6200; www.cathedral.org/cathedral), so the views from those spots are among the best in the city. Unfortunately, tourists can't go all the way to the top. But the view from the **Pilgrim Observation Gallery** is still pretty cool. One way to partake of that view is to have tea in the gallery. (See Chapter 10 for information on making reservations.) Or you can visit on your own from 10 a.m. to 5:30 p.m. Monday through Friday (till 7:45 p.m. June–Labor Day), 10 a.m. to 4:30 p.m. Saturday, and 8 a.m. to 6:30 p.m. Sunday. See the Cathedral's listing in Chapter 11 for details.

Lincoln Memorial

Take a break from reading the Gettysburg Address on the wall and gaze at the Reflecting Pool, the Mall, the World War II Memorial, the Washington Monument, and the Capitol from the steps of the **Lincoln Memorial** (23rd Street NW, between Constitution and Independence avenues, on the National Mall; ☎ 202-426-6841; www.nps.gov/linc). Then walk around to the back of Lincoln's place for a view across the Potomac River of Arlington National Cemetery and the eternal flame marking John F. Kennedy's grave. The Lincoln Memorial is always open, and the view is particularly impressive after dark. See Chapter 11 for more details.

Jefferson Memorial

One of the reasons the **Jefferson Memorial** (East Basin Drive SW, on southeast side of Tidal Basin; ☎ 202-426-6841; www.nps.gov/thje)

is my favorite is the marvelous view here in spring, when the cherry blossoms color the land around the Tidal Basin, and after dark year-round, when Washington's many alabaster buildings and monuments gleam in their floodlights. Especially prominent is the White House, where Jefferson once lived, and the monument to his fellow revolutionary and president, George Washington.

Roof Terrace of the Kennedy Center

You don't need orchestra seats to visit the **Kennedy Center** (2700 F St. NW, between New Hampshire Avenue and Rock Creek Parkway; ☎ 800-444-1324 or 202-467-4600; www.kennedy-center.org). In fact, one of the best shows in town plays night and day, and it's free. Although you may want to dine in the **Roof Terrace Restaurant** (reservations ☎ 202-416-8555) or the **KC Cafe** (no reservations), which also is located on the roof terrace level, you can feast on the view from the promenade *outside* the restaurants without spending a cent. Circle the promenade once for a 360-degree vista. The center is open daily from 10 a.m. until 30 minutes after the last performance. See Chapter 15 for more details.

Sky Terrace

Come to this open-air rooftop restaurant for the view, not the food. If you do eat at the **Sky Terrace** (in the Hotel Washington, 515 15th St. NW, at Pennsylvania Avenue; ☎ 202-638-5900), pick something simple, like a sandwich. Or just have a drink. You're here for the bird's-eye view of the White House at the next block and the rest of Washington further into the distance. Arrive by 5:30 p.m. if you want to beat out the locals and other tourists for a seat. The Sky Terrace is open daily 11:30 a.m. to 12:30 a.m. late April to mid-October.

Washington Harbour

Walk along the **riverfront promenade** at Washington Harbour, below K Street at Thomas Jefferson Street in Georgetown, and gaze across the Potomac toward Virginia. Dead ahead is Theodore Roosevelt Island. To the left, you can make out the Watergate and, beyond it, the Kennedy Center. To the right, Key Bridge connects Georgetown with Arlington, Virginia. If you're so moved, grab an outdoor seat at one of the harbor's restaurants and have a sip or a snack.

West Front of the Capitol

One of the many victims of increased D.C. security is the marvelous view from the steps and terrace on the West Front of the Capitol. It's one of the best places to watch the sun set over the Washington Monument, Lincoln Memorial, and Potomac River. Seeing Washington's marble landmarks bathed in golden light, with purple and pink streaking the sky over the Potomac, is an awesome sight. The view at others times of the day and after dark ain't too shabby either. Now you can catch a glimpse of that view when you take a Capitol tour. Or you can walk across the West Lawn to the base of the steps and check out a lower-level perspective. (See the Capitol's listing in Chapter 11 for touring information.)

Chapter 18

If You Must Drive: Ten D.C. Roadside Attractions

In This Chapter

▶ Finding the places worth the drive

▶ Discovering parks away from the Mall

▶ Sightseeing along the parkway

▶ Figuring out how to get there from here

I know: If you've read any other chapter in this book, you've seen my repeated warnings that you should not drive in Washington. This chapter, though, goes contrary to that advice because I'm actually giving you ten reasons *to* drive. I'll just call this chapter — as members of Congress do in the *Congressional Record* — a revision and extension of my remarks. If you happen to have a car, you can find some sights that are worth driving to. I'm not really advocating that you drive *in* central D.C. but encouraging you to use your car to reach sights and attractions that are mostly outside the District.

National Arboretum

The best time to visit the **National Arboretum** (3501 New York Ave. NE, east of Bladensberg Road; ☎ 202-245-2726; www.usna.usda.gov) is from late April into late May, when the azaleas are in full riot, and crabapples, dogwoods, peonies, roses, and irises also bloom. If you can't make it during that timeframe, though, don't worry: The National Arboretum always has something to see, such as magnolias in early spring and holly berries in winter. Some man-made items will grab your attention as well, such as 22 sandstone columns that were removed from the East Portico of the Capitol during a renovation and now stand like an ancient ruin in the arboretum.

This 446-acre site is a research and educational facility of the Agricultural Department's Research Service. Stop at the Administration Building to pick up a map and guide, and to find out what's blooming.

If the azaleas are in flower, you *have* to drive Azalea Road. You won't believe the cascade of colors! Pack a picnic.

From downtown D.C., go northeast on New York Avenue all the way to the arboretum's entrance (to the right). Watch carefully for the sign after you cross the big Bladensberg Road intersection. Returning to downtown is trickier because of traffic patterns. I suggest using the R Street exit from the arboretum, which is near the Administration Building. Turn left on Bladensburg and then right on Maryland Avenue, which carries you right to the Capitol. Watch out for the jog around Stanton Park Square at 6th and C streets. Arboretum grounds are open daily (except Dec 25) from 8 a.m. to 5 p.m. Admission is free.

Clara Barton National Historic Site

Hard as it is to believe, when **Clara Barton**'s last home (5801 Oxford Rd., Glen Echo, Maryland, southwest of Macarthur Boulevard; ☎ **301-320-1410**; www.nps.gov/clba) became part of the National Park Service in 1975, it was the first National Historic Site dedicated to the accomplishments of a woman. The founder of the American Red Cross lived here from February 28, 1897, until she died in her bedroom on April 12, 1912, at the age of 90. Until she resigned as Red Cross president in 1904, her residence was also the Red Cross headquarters and a warehouse for disaster supplies.

To reach the site, go west on M Street out of Georgetown, then turn left on Canal Road, which becomes Clara Barton Parkway. Then follow the signs to the Clara Barton National Historic Site. The interior of the house is shown by guided tour daily on the hour, with the first tour at 10 a.m. and the last tour at 4 p.m. (closed Thanksgiving, Dec 25, and Jan 1). Admission is free.

Because of traffic patterns, the easiest way to return to D.C. is to follow Macarthur Boulevard till it ends at Foxhall Road. Bear right on Foxhall, then turn left where Foxhall ends at Canal Road, and you'll be on your way into Georgetown.

 Don't leave Washington before 9:30 a.m. weekdays, when a portion of Canal Road is inbound only.

Glen Echo Park

 The National Park Service and a lot of volunteers have worked magic at **Glen Echo Park** (7300 Macarthur Blvd., Glen Echo, Maryland, at Oxford Road; ☎ **301-320-1400,** recorded information 301-634-2222; www.glenechopark.org and www.nps.gov/glec), which stands essentially next door to Clara Barton's house. Glen Echo is an abandoned amusement park that operated from about 1900 to 1968. I used to describe it as a

D.C. Roadside Attractions

Chesapeake and Ohio Canal National Historical Park **1**
Clara Barton National Historic Site **4**
Glen Echo Park **4**
Great Falls Park **2**
National Air & Space Museum Udvar-Hazy Center **3**
National Arboretum **6**
Theodore Roosevelt Island **5**
Wolf Trap **3**

very strange place. When I walked around here — especially in winter when it's deserted — I felt like an archaeologist exploring some reasonably well-preserved ruin: You see the remains of the swimming pool over here, the abandoned bumper car pavilion over there . . .

But the restoration is proving wondrous. The centerpiece is a marvelous working carousel — with 40 horses, 4 rabbits, 4 ostriches, 1 giraffe, 1 deer, 1 lion, 1 tiger, 2 circus chariots, more than 1,000 lights, and lots of mirrors. Equally impressive is the Art Deco Spanish Ballroom, a large dance hall filled with polished wood and looking as enticing as it must have when it opened in 1933 and Swing was becoming king. Trolley cars, like those that brought Washingtonians out to the amusement park, are on display.

Glen Echo once again rings with the laughter of children who come here for the many arts programs, puppet shows, and other performances — and, of course, the carousel. Adults of all ages participate in many arts programs as well, such as pottery classes. And the ballroom once again fills with music during dances and dance classes. Most dances are preceded by an instruction period for beginners. Call or explore the Web site for details on the many other activities.

The park grounds and parking lot are open daily 6 a.m. to 1 a.m., except Thanksgiving and December 25. The carousel operates May and June Wednesday and Thursday 10 a.m. to 2 p.m.; Saturday and Sunday noon to 6 p.m.; July and August Wednesday through Friday 10 a.m. to 2 p.m., Saturday and Sunday noon to 6 p.m.; September Saturday and Sunday noon to 6 p.m. Park admission is free. Carousel tickets are $1. There are fees for other activities. Bring a picnic.

To get to Glen Echo Park, follow the directions to Clara Barton's house. You can't miss it: It's the abandoned amusement park with the stone tower and trolley cars parked out front!

Chesapeake and Ohio Canal National Historical Park

The **C&O Canal National Historical Park** (11710 Macarthur Blvd., Potomac, Maryland, at the end of the road; ☎ **301-767-3714;** www.nps. gov/choh) actually stretches along the old canal from Georgetown to Cumberland, Maryland. In this chapter, I'm talking about the section of the park at the Great Falls of the Potomac River in Maryland. My family comes here regularly to picnic, stroll the boardwalk out to the falls, and hike along the canal and into the bordering hills. The setting is beautiful. You can brush up on your history at the visitor center in the old Great Falls Tavern, which served canal boat passengers. You can bring a picnic or buy simple foods at the park refreshment stand. From early April till the end of October, you can take an hour-long ride on a replica of a canal boat. July through August, the boat floats Wednesday through Friday at 11 a.m., 1:30 p.m., and 3 p.m.; Saturday and Sunday a 4:30 p.m. ride is added. April through June, and September and October, the trips start Wednesday through Friday at 11 a.m. and 3 p.m., Saturday and Sunday also at 1:30 p.m. Tickets cost $2.

To get to Great Falls, follow the directions to Clara Barton's house (see the section "Clara Barton National Historic Site," earlier in this chapter), but stay on the Clara Barton Parkway until it ends at Macarthur Boulevard. Follow Macarthur to the left until it ends in the park.

The park is open daily during daylight hours, and the visitor center operates daily from 9 a.m. to 4:45 p.m. Park and center close Thanksgiving, December 25, and January 1. Admission is $5 per vehicle for a three-day pass, $3 per individual who comes by bike or walking.

Great Falls Park

Directly across the Potomac River from the C&O Canal Park's Great Falls area is Virginia's **Great Falls Park** (9200 Old Dominion Dr., McLean, Virginia, at Georgetown Pike; ☎ **703-285-2965;** www.nps.gov/grfa). You see the same falls from the opposite side, can picnic and hike, and can check out some additional history at Virginia's park. A substantial visitor center offers history and nature exhibits. Before he presided over the successful launch of a new nation, George Washington presided over a failed attempt to build a canal on this side of the Potomac. Remnants are visible.

Go west on M Street out of Georgetown, left on Canal Road, left over Chain Bridge, right on Virginia Route 123 (Chain Bridge Road), and then right on Virginia Route 193 (Georgetown Pike). Turn right at Old Dominion Drive at the sign to the park.

The park is open daily from 7 a.m. until dark. The visitor center is open daily 10 a.m. to 4 p.m., and stays open somewhat later in spring and summer. Admission is $5 per vehicle for a three-day pass, $3 per individual who comes by bike, horseback, or walking. There are riding trails in the park, but it's BYOH (bring your own horse).

Wolf Trap

The name here says it all: **Wolf Trap Farm Park for the Performing Arts** (1551 Trap Rd., Vienna, Virginia, off the Wolf Trap exit from the Dulles Toll Road; ☎ **703-255-1800;** www.nps.gov/wotr). At the Filene Center — a roofed, open-air theater with outdoor lawn seating as well — big-name artists perform before audiences of up to 7,000 from May through September. The **Meadow Pavilion** and the **Theatre in the Woods** host workshops in theater and other arts and crafts. Performances are held throughout the year in the **Barns of Wolf Trap,** a 352-seat indoor theater built in two restored 18th-century barns.

The word eclectic was created to describe Wolf Trap's performance schedule: the National Symphony Orchestra, the Wolf Trap Opera, pop, rock, country, folk, Broadway musicals, operettas, and lots of stuff for kids and for aging boomers. It's becoming a summer tradition for my sister and her husband to come for a visit that includes a trip to Wolf Trap for some '50s/'60s/'70s group that's still keeping the candle burning — the Kingston Trio, the Doobie Brothers, the Beach Boys, or Brian Wilson on his "Smile" tour. Peter, Paul, and Mary have performed here several times. We used to take Julie here for kids festivals. Most recently, she thought it would be fun to come for the *Mikado*. (She was right!) Wolf Trap has a restaurant (reservations are strongly advised), refreshment stand, and lots of space for picnicking — and holding festivals — on the 117 acres of farm and forest land. You can bring your own food and drink, including alcoholic beverages, but you can't take them inside the roofed part of the theater. To find out which performances might appeal to you, phone ☎ 703-255-1868 or surf to www.wolf-trap.org.

Drive west on Constitution Avenue to westbound I-66. Watch for signs to Virginia Route 267 local exits (the Dulles Toll Road). After you're on 267, watch for signs to Wolf Trap. Admission to the park is free. Fees for performances vary.

Don't get on the toll-free Dulles Access Highway, which is restricted to airport traffic. There's no exit before the airport, and you can be fined if you're caught using the highway for anything other than airport business.

Theodore Roosevelt Island

This little island in the middle of the Potomac River is a memorial to the 26th president's history as an outdoorsman and advocate of conservation. **Theodore Roosevelt Island National Memorial** (George Washington Memorial Parkway; ☎ 703-289-2500; www.nps.gov/this) contains 91 acres of woods, 2.5 miles of trails, and a memorial plaza with an outsized statue of Roosevelt. It's a pleasant respite that's actually inside the city limits. It also helps to dramatically illustrate how the Republican Party has changed since it was led by this man, who arguably was our most environmentalist president. In 2005, the Republican chairman of the House Resources Committee proposed selling it to developers! He didn't succeed.

Drive west on Constitution Avenue and continue straight across the Theodore Roosevelt Memorial Bridge to the George Washington Memorial Parkway (northbound). The Roosevelt Island parking lot is to your right immediately after you enter the parkway. *Don't miss it!* The only entrance is from the northbound lanes. The park is open daily from dawn to dusk, and admission is free.

George Washington Memorial Parkway

You can explore numerous interesting places along the **George Washington Memorial Parkway** (☎ 703-289-2500; www.nps.gov/gwmp; e-mail: gwnp_superintendent@nps.gov; mailing address: George Washington Memorial Parkway Headquarters, Turkey Run Park, McLean, VA 22101), which runs along the south and west bank of the Potomac River from I-495 northwest of D.C. to Mount Vernon. Write, phone, or e-mail parkway headquarters before your visit to ask for a map/brochure to be mailed to you. Otherwise, look for it at National Park Service facilities along the parkway. You also can ask whether parkway brochures are available at other park service sites you visit in the Washington area.

Here are some spots worth a stop along the parkway:

- ✔ **Turkey Run:** Explore 700 acres of forest and hiking trails.

- ✔ **Dyke Marsh:** This 380 acres of tidal marsh, floodplain, and swamp forest comprises the largest remaining freshwater tidal wetlands in the Washington Metropolitan area and attracts bird-watchers.

- ✔ **Fort Hunt:** Batteries here guarded the river approach to Washington from 1898 to 1918.

- ✔ **Fort Marcy:** The earthwork remnant is just one example of the many forts that surrounded Washington during the Civil War.

- ✔ **Netherlands Carillon:** The 50-bell, 127-foot-tall carillon was given by the Dutch to express gratitude to the United States after World War II. The bells strike the hour daily from 10 a.m. to 6 p.m. Carillonneurs present concerts Saturdays and national holidays from 2 to 4 p.m. in May and September and 6 to 8 p.m. in June, July, and August. During concerts, visitors are welcome to go up in the tower to watch the carillonneur perform. Automated concerts occur daily at noon and 6 p.m. On May 5, Dutch Independence Day, you hear "The Netherlands' National Anthem." On July 4, by act of Congress, the largest bell tolls 13 times at 2 p.m. Patriotic songs are played at 9:04 a.m. September 2, the moment the Japanese armistice ended World War II. At 6 p.m. New Year's Eve, you can toast to "Auld Lang Syne." (A bit early, don't you think?)

- ✔ **Marine Corps Memorial:** This oversized sculpture of the famous World War II photograph, by Joe Rosenthal, shows Marines raising the U.S. flag during the battle for Iwo Jima.

- ✔ **Gravelly Point:** This is a popular spot for watching airplanes take off and land at National Airport. If you have a boat, put it in the Potomac here and view Washington's landmarks from the water.

The parkway also provides access to Arlington National Cemetery (see Chapter 11 for details), Mount Vernon (see Chapter 14), and Theodore Roosevelt Island (see earlier in this chapter). At Alexandria, the parkway runs through the city as Washington Street.

From D.C., drive west on Constitution Avenue and continue straight across the Theodore Roosevelt Memorial Bridge to the George Washington Memorial Parkway (northbound). Or drive west on Independence Avenue; as you pass the Lincoln Memorial, watch closely for signs to the Arlington Memorial Bridge. After you cross the bridge, turn right out of the traffic circle and then exit left to continue southbound or go straight to go northbound. The southbound route also is marked to National Airport.

Do not sightsee along the parkway during rush hour. This road is a major commuter artery on weekdays. Drive here on the weekend or from mid-morning until mid-afternoon during the week. Also note: Some spots are accessible only from the northbound or southbound lanes.

Rock Creek Park

This marvelous urban park (☎ 202-895-6070; www.nps.gov/rocr; mailing address: 3545 Williamsburg Lane NW, Washington, DC 20008) winds its way from the Potomac River near the Kennedy Center all the way up to D.C.'s most northern tip. Write or phone the park headquarters before your visit to request a map/brochure. In the park, you can find information desks and activities at the following locations:

- ✔ The **Nature Center** (5200 Glover Rd. NW, south of Military Road; www.nps.gov/rocr/planyourvisit/naturecenter.htm) is open Wednesday through Sunday from 9 a.m. to 5 p.m. and is closed Thanksgiving, December 25, January 1, and July 4. The Nature Center features exhibits on plants, animals, and habitats in the park. It's the starting point for guided and self-guided nature walks. The hands-on Discovery room appeals to youngsters, as does the **planetarium**'s kid-oriented shows on Wednesdays at 4 p.m. Other planetarium presentations occur Saturdays and Sundays at 1 and 4 p.m. Restrooms are available.

- ✔ **Peirce Barn** (Tilden Street at Beach Drive) is open weekends from noon to 4 p.m. Programs here tell about nearby Peirce Mill, an early-19th-century water-powered grist mill that is closed for repairs. Restrooms are available.

You can also ask for the Rock Creek Park brochure and map at other National Park Service sites in the Washington area.

The park offers a wide range of outdoor activities, such as hiking, horseback riding, bicycling, picnicking, golf, tennis, and boating. The Nature Center, Planetarium, and Peirce Barn conduct numerous programs for children. The 4,000-seat **Carter Barron Amphitheatre** (16th Street and Colorado Avenue NW; ☎ 202-426-0486; www.nps.gov/rocr/cbarron) hosts numerous outdoor performances, both paid and free, including free summer concerts by the National Symphony Orchestra and free plays by the Shakespeare Theatre.

Rock Creek Park Area

To enter the park from central D.C., drive northwest on Virginia Avenue to Rock Creek Parkway and turn right.

 Rock Creek Parkway and Beach Drive are major commuter routes during workday rush hours. South of Connecticut Avenue, the parkway is one-way south from 6:45 a.m. to 9:30 a.m. Monday through Friday and one-way north from 3:45 p.m. to 6:30 p.m. those days. On weekends and holidays, portions of Beach Drive are clogged with a different kind of traffic — bicyclists, in-line skaters, walkers, and runners. The drive is closed to motor vehicles from Broad Branch Road to Military Road, from Picnic Grove 10 to Wise Road, and from West Beach Drive to the D.C.-Maryland border from 7 a.m. to 7 p.m. on holidays and from 7 a.m. Saturday until 7 p.m. Sunday on weekends.

National Air and Space Museum Steven F. Udvar–Hazy Center

You can fit only so many flying machines into a building in the middle of Washington, so the Air and Space Museum decided to expand out into the countryside — in a corner of Washington Dulles International Airport, about 25 miles away, to be exact. The product of this expansion is the **Steven F. Udvar–Hazy Center** (14390 Air and Space Museum Parkway, Chantilly, Virginia, off Virginia Route 28, south of the airport's main entrance; ☎ 202-633-1000; www.nasm.si.edu/museum/udvarhazy), an enormous structure that opened in late 2003 and nearly quintupled the museum's display space.

There's now plenty of room for such large artifacts as the Enola Gay, the B-29 Superfortress that dropped the first atomic bomb; the Space Shuttle Enterprise, the first shuttle, which was used in tests; and the SR-71 Blackbird reconnaissance plane, the fastest and highest-flying jet aircraft ever built, with a top speed of more than 2,200 mph at altitudes exceeding 85,000 feet. About 270 aircraft and spacecraft now call Udvar-Hazy home, as do more than 1,500 smaller items. It also has an aircraft control tower, flight simulators, and a giant-screen IMAX Theatre. Knowledgeable docents enrich the visitor's experience by explaining displays and answering questions. You'll spend one to two hours here — more if you really study the exhibits.

Drive west on Constitution Avenue to westbound I-66. Watch for signs to Virginia Route 267 local exits (the Dulles Toll Road). Just before you get to the airport, take Exit 9A to Virginia Route 28, and then drive south 3½ miles to the Air and Space Museum Parkway. Follow signs to the museum. Admission is free, but you'll pay $12 for on-site parking. IMAX tickets cost $8.50 to $10. Phone ☎ 877-932-4629 for information about the films. The museum is open daily from 10 a.m. to 5:30 p.m., except December 25.

Appendix

Quick Concierge

- -

Fast Facts

AAA

The most centrally located AAA office is at 701 15th St. NW, between G and H streets (☎ 202-331-3000). For emergency road service, call ☎ 800-222-4357.

American Express

An American Express Travel Service office is located downtown at 1501 K St. NW at 15th Street (☎ 202-457-1300). Open Monday through Friday, 9 a.m. to 5:30 p.m.

Area Codes

If you're calling a D.C. number from outside D.C., dial **202**. If you're in D.C. and calling D.C., no area code is needed. Dial **703** for suburban Virginia. For most close-in Maryland suburbs, dial **301**. Annapolis and Baltimore are **410**, and some **443** area codes are showing up.

ATMs

It's hard to walk a block in D.C. without encountering an ATM. They're located in or near hotels, restaurants, attractions, and Metro stations. Most, if not all, bank branches have them, many located outside. For specific locations, call Cirrus (☎ 800-424-7787) or PLUS (☎ 800-843-7587), depending upon which network is listed on your ATM card, or consult www.visa.com or www.mastercard.com.

Baby Sitters

Many hotels will secure a bonded sitter for your brood. Ask the concierge or at the front desk. White House Nannies (☎ 301-652-8088 or 800-266-9024; www.whitehousenannies.com) sends sitters to hotels on short notice. Reserving ahead of time saves you money.

Business Hours

D.C. banks tend to be open from 9 a.m. to 5 p.m. Monday through Friday, with some opening on Saturday morning. It's really impossible to talk about typical hours for stores anymore. Most will open by 10 a.m. and not close before 5 p.m. Monday through Friday. Many are open into the evening and on Saturday, and some open Sunday afternoon. You'll tend to find more stores open at night in areas with substantial nightlife, such as Georgetown.

Camera Repair

If your shutter won't shut, head to Pro Photo, 1902 I St. NW (☎ 202-223-1292), or Penn Camera, 1015 18th St. NW (☎ 202-785-7366).

Congress

Call the Capitol switchboard to locate a senator (☎ 202-224-3121) or member of the House (☎ 202-225-3121).

Convention Center

The Washington Convention Center (☎ 800-368-9000 or 202-249-3000; www.dcconvention.com) occupies the area between N, K, 7th, and 9th streets NW.

Credit Cards

If your card is lost or stolen, call American Express (☎ 800-221-7282), MasterCard (☎ 800-307-7309), or Visa (☎ 800-847-2911). To obtain the phone number for other cards, call the toll-free information operator at ☎ 800-555-1212.

Dentists

In a dental emergency, call the District of Columbia Dental Society Referral Service at ☎ 202-547-7615.

Doctors

Ask your hotel's concierge or the front desk for the name of a physician who treats hotel guests. Or try the physicians referral services at George Washington University Hospital (☎ 888-449-3627), Washington Hospital Center (☎ 202-877-3627), or Georgetown University Hospital (☎ 202-342-2400).

Emergencies

For police, fire, and ambulance, call ☎ 911. The 24-hour poison control hotline is ☎ 202-222-1222. To contact the police when it's not an emergency, dial ☎ 311.

Hospitals

For life-threatening emergencies, call ☎ 911. For emergency-room treatment, contact one of the following hospitals: Children's National Medical Center (111 Michigan Ave. NW, at 1st Street, about 2½ miles due north of the Capitol; ☎ 202-884-5203); George Washington University Hospital (900 23rd St. NW, at I Street Downtown; ☎ 202-715-4911); Georgetown University Hospital (3800 Reservoir Rd. NW, at 38th Street in Georgetown; ☎ 202-444-2119); or Sibley Hospital (5255 Loughboro Rd. NW, between Macarthur Boulevard and Dalecarla Parkway in Upper Northwest; ☎ 202-537-4080). If you have a car, an emergency is not the time to drive in D.C. In life-threatening circumstances, call ☎ 911 for an ambulance. Otherwise, I suggest you take a taxi.

Hotlines

For help with a wide range of problems, call the Answers Please information and referral service (☎ 202-463-6211) or the D.C. Mental Health Department Access Help Line (☎ 888-793-4357). Other hotlines include the House of Ruth Domestic Violence Hotline (☎ 202-667-7001), the D.C. Rape Crisis Center (☎ 202-333-7273), and the Poison Control Center (☎ 800-222-1222).

Information

For tourist information, contact the D.C. Convention Visitor Information Center, 1300 Pennsylvania Ave. NW, Washington, DC 20004 (at 13th Street, in the Ronald Reagan Building and International Trade Center; ☎ 866-324-7386; www.dcvisit.com). For D.C. telephone directory information, dial ☎ 411; for telephone numbers outside the Washington area, dial the area code plus 555-1212. See the "Where to Get More Information" section later in this chapter.

Internet Access and Cybercafes

Check your e-mail at Kramerbooks & Afterwords Café (1517 Connecticut Ave. NW, just above Dupont Circle; ☎ 202-387-1400), or at any D.C. public library: Martin Luther King, Jr., Library (901 G St. NW, at 9th Street Downtown; ☎ 202-727-0321); West End Branch (1101 24th St. NW, at L Street; ☎ 202-724-8707); Georgetown Branch (3260 R St. NW, at Wisconsin Avenue; ☎ 202-282-0220); and Southeast Branch (403 7th St. SE, at D Street on Capitol Hill; ☎ 202-698-3377). Call for hours, which vary. Many Starbucks offer wireless Internet access. You can search for other Washington cybercafes at www.cybercaptive.com and www.cybercafe.com.

Liquor Laws

You must be 21 to drink alcohol in D.C. Restaurants and bars can serve alcohol Sunday through Thursday from 9 a.m. to 2 a.m. and Friday and Saturday from 9 a.m. to 3 a.m. Retail stores can sell beer, wine, and liquor from 9 a.m. to 10 p.m. Monday through Saturday. Beer and wine can be sold Sunday as well.

Maps

Free city maps are available at many hotels and tourist sites and at the Washington Visitor Information Center, on the ground floor of the Ronald Reagan International Trade Center Building, 1300 Pennsylvania Ave. NW, between 13th and 14th streets (☎ 866-324-7386; www.dcvisit.com).

Pharmacies

CVS pharmacies abound in Washington. It seems like you can find one on every corner. To locate the one nearest to you, call ☎ 888-607-4287 or click the Store Finder link at www.cvs.com. CVS 24-hour pharmacies are located at 2240 M St. NW, between 22nd and 23rd streets in West End (☎ 202-296-9876 pharmacy, 202-296-9877 main); 4555 Wisconsin Ave. NW, between Albemarle and Brandywine streets in Upper Northwest (☎ 202-537-1587); 6 Dupont Circle on the western side of the circle (☎ 202-785-1466). Rite Aid has a 24-hour pharmacy, at 1815 Connecticut Ave. NW, 2½ long blocks north of the Dupont Circle Metro's Q Street exit (☎ 202-332-1718; www.riteaid.com).

Police

In case of emergency, dial ☎ 911. To locate the nearest police station or for nonemergency business, call ☎ 311.

Post Office

For the nearest Post Office, ask at your hotel's front desk, click on "Locate a Post Office" at www.usps.com, or phone

☎ 800-275-8777. For ZIP Code information, call the same number or click "Find a ZIP Code" at the same Web site.

Radio Stations

Some of Washington's top AM radio stations are WMAL, 630, news/talk/entertainment; WAVA, 780, Christian/conservative talk; 820 WTOP, news/sports/traffic/weather; WTEM, 980, sports; WUST, 1120, ethnic/international; WWRC, 1260, liberal talk; WYCB, 1340, gospel; WOL, 1450, black talk; WTWP, 1500, *Washington Post* radio; WPGC, 1580, gospel. Among the top FM stations are WAMU, 88.5, NPR; WPFW, 89.3, Pacifica; WCSP, 90.1, C-SPAN; WETA, 90.9, NPR; WKYS, 93.9, hip-hop/R&B; WARW, 94.7, classic rock; WPGC-FM, 95.5, urban contemporary; WHUR, 96.3, adult urban contemporary and classic; WASH, 97.1, adult light rock; WMZQ, 98.7, country; WHFS, 99.1, Spanish adult contemporary; WBIG, 100.3, classic rock; WWDC, 101.1, rock/alternative rock; WMMJ, 102.3, urban adult contemporary; WTOP, 103.5, news/sports/traffic/weather; WGMS, 104, classical; WAVA, 105.1, Christian/conservative talk; WJZW, 105.9, smooth jazz/easy listening; WJFK, 106.7, talk; WTPW, 107.7, *Washington Post* radio.

Restrooms

One of the great things about being a tourist in Washington is that you're never far from clean, safe, and free restrooms — a particular benefit when you're traveling with young children. You can find them in all the government buildings, all the Smithsonian museums, the major monuments, and the larger food courts. One place you won't find them easily is inside the Metrorail system. In a truly extreme emergency, ask a Metrorail station attendant to let you use the station facility. Most stations have restrooms that are supposed to be available to the public on request, but Metrorail resists wide use.

Safety

Like any big city, Washington has street crime. Luckily for you, the areas most frequented by tourists are the safest. Post-9/11 concerns have heightened governments' attention to security, especially around government buildings, monuments, museums, Metrorail, and other places where large numbers of visitors are likely to gather. In Adams-Morgan, the U Street Corridor, and on Capitol Hill at night, stick to the well-lighted, highly populated, main commercial blocks. In fact, it's best to stay out of dark, deserted places all over town. The Mall used to feel safe round the clock, but a couple of well-publicized muggings after dark in 2006 challenged that complacency. If Metro's service has stopped for the night, and you still are out on the town, take a taxi. Know your destination before you get out of the cab. Hold your kids' hands on city streets and sidewalks, on all Metro escalators, and on Metro platforms. Lock your hotel room door, car doors, and trunk. Don't leave luggage or other items visible in your car when you park it. Lock valuables in a hotel safe deposit box (if not in your room, at the front desk). Keep a tight hold on your pocketbook and camera. Hold onto your purse in a restaurant. Carry your cash and credit cards in a front pocket or a concealed money pouch. Leave the family jewels at home; what you do bring, don't flash. Don't leave a purse or other bag unattended in public. Not only might you lose it to a purse snatcher, you might lose it to law enforcement officials who worry there might be a bomb inside.

Smoking

By law, Washington's restaurants and bars now are smoke-free, except for cigar and hookah bars and outdoor areas such as sidewalk cafes. The ban also covers offices and apartment building lobbies. The law allows you to smoke in your hotel room. Establishments, of course, are free to impose stricter limitations of their own, and smoke-free hotel rooms have become pretty ubiquitous.

Taxes

Sales tax on merchandise is 5.75 percent in D.C., 5 percent in Maryland, and 4.5 percent in Virginia. Restaurant taxes are 10 percent in D.C., 5 percent in Maryland, and 4.5 percent in Virginia. Hotel taxes are 14.5 percent in D.C., 5 percent (plus another 1-percent to 10-percent local tax) in Maryland, and about 10 percent in Virginia.

Taxis

D.C. taxis don't have meters. You're charged according to the zones you travel through — $6.50 within one zone, $8.80 for two, and so on. See Chapter 4 for a more detailed explanation of this complicated fare system. Washington cabs usually are easy to hail on the street. When I need to order a cab, I call **Diamond** (☎ 202-387-6200, 202-797-5916, 202-797-5915, or, for airport service, 202-387-2600).

Time Zone

Washington is in the Eastern time zone. For the correct time, dial ☎ 202-844-2525. For the official U.S. time, go to the National Institute of Standards and Technology's Internet clock at www.nist.time.gov.

Transit Info

For Metrorail (subway) and Metrobus information, call ☎ 202-637-7000 or visit the Metrorail Web site www.wmata.com.

Weather

For the D.C. weather conditions and forecast, call ☎ 202-936-1212, listen to WTOP 1500 am "on the 8s" (8 after the hour, 18 after, and so on), watch the Weather Channel, or surf over to www.weather.com.

Toll-Free Numbers and Web Sites

Airlines

Aeroflot
☎ 888-686-4949
www.aeroflot.com

Air Canada
☎ 888-247-2262
www.aircanada.com

Air France
☎ 800-321-4538
www.airfrance.com

Air Jamaica
☎ 800-523-5585
www.airjamaica.com

AirTran
☎ 800-247-8726
www.airtran.com

Alaska Airlines
☎ 800-252-7522
www.Alaskaair.com

American Airlines
☎ 800-433-7300
www.aa.com

ANA
☎ 800-235-9262
www.ana.co.jp/eng

ATA
☎ 800-435-9282
www.ata.com

Austrian Airlines
☎ 800-843-0002
www.aua.com

British Airways
☎ 800-247-9297
www.british-airways.com

Continental Airlines
☎ 800-523-3273
www.continental.com

Delta Air Lines
☎ 800-221-1212
www.delta.com

Ethiopian Airlines
☎ 800-445-2733
www.flyethiopian.com

Frontier Airlines
☎ 800-432-1359
www.frontierairlines.com

Icelandair
☎ 800-223-5500
www.icelandair.com

JetBlue
☎ 800-538-2583
www.jetblue.com

KLM (through Northwest)
☎ 800-225-2525
www.nwa.com

Korean Air
☎ 800-438-5000
www.koreanair.com

Lufthansa
☎ 800-645-3880
www.lufthansa.com

MAXjet
☎ 888-435-9629
www.maxjet.com

Mexicana
☎ 800-531-7921
www.mexicana.com

Midwest
☎ 800-452-2022
www.midwestairlines.com

North American
☎ 800-359-6222
www.northamericanair.com

Northwest Airlines
☎ 800-225-2525
www.nwa.com

Pan Am Clipper Connection
☎ 800-359-7262
www.flypanam.com

SAS
☎ 800-221-2350
www.scandinavian.net

Saudi Arabian Airlines
☎ 800-472-8342
www.saudiairlines.com

South African
☎ 800-722-9675
www.flysaa.com

Southwest Airlines
☎ 800-435-9792
www.southwest.com

Spirit
☎ 800-772-7117
www.spiritair.com

Sun Country
☎ 800-800-6557
www.suncountry.com

TACA
☎ 800-535-8780
www.grupotaca.com

Ted
☎ 800-225-5833
www.flyted.com

United Airlines
☎ 800-241-6522
www.ual.com

US Airways
☎ 800-428-4322
www.usairways.com

USA 3000
☎ 877-872-3000
www.usa3000.com

Virgin-Atlantic
☎ 800-862-8621
www.virgin-atlantic.com

Major hotel and motel chains

Best Western International
☎ 800-780-7234
www.bestwestern.com

Comfort Inns
☎ 877-424-6423
www.hotelchoice.com

Courtyard by Marriott
☎ 888-236-2427
www.courtyard.com

Days Inn
☎ 800-329-7466
www.daysinn.com

Doubletree Hotels
☎ 800-445-8667
www.doubletree.com

Econo Lodge
☎ 877-424-6423
www.hotelchoice.com

Fairfield Inn by Marriott
☎ 800-228-2800
www.fairfieldinn.com

Four Seasons Hotels and Resorts
☎ 800-819-5053
www.fourseasons.com

Hampton Inn
☎ 800-445-8667
www.hampton-inn.com

Hilton Hotels
☎ 800- 445-8667
www.hilton.com

Holiday Inn
☎ 888-465-4329
www.holiday-inn.com

Howard Johnson
☎ 800-446-4656
www.hojo.com

Hyatt Hotels and Resorts
☎ 888-591-1234
www.hyatt.com

InterContinental
☎ 888-424-6835
www.interconti.com

Marriott Hotels
☎ 800-236-2427
www.marriott.com

Motel 6
☎ 800-466-8356
www.motel6.com

Quality Inns and Resorts
☎ 877-424-6423
www.hotelchoice.com

Radisson Hotels International
☎ 888-201-1718
www.radisson.com

Ramada Inn
☎ 800-272-6232
www.ramada.com

Red Roof Inn
☎ 800-733-7663
www.redroof.com

Renaissance Hotels and Resorts
☎ 800-468-3571
www.renaissancehotels.com

Residence Inn by Marriott
☎ 800-331-3131
www.residenceinn.com

Ritz-Carlton
☎ 800-241-3333
www.ritzcarlton.com

Sheraton Hotels and Resorts
☎ 888-625-5144
www.sheraton.com

Super 8
☎ 800-800-8000
www.super8.com

Travelodge
☎ 800-578-7878
www.travelodge.com

Westin Hotels
☎ 800-937-8461
www.westin.com

Wyndham
☎ 877-999-3223
www.wyndham.com

Major car-rental agencies

Alamo
☎ 800-462-5266
www.goalamo.com

Avis
☎ 800-331-1212
www.avis.com

Budget
☎ 800-527-0700
www.budgetrentacar.com

Dollar
☎ 800-800-3665
www.dollarcar.com

Enterprise
☎ 800-261-7331
www.pickenterprise.com

Hertz
☎ 800-654-3131
www.hertz.com

National
☎ 800-227-7368
www.nationalcar.com

Thrifty
☎ 800-847-4389
www.thrifty.com

Where to Get More Information

If I haven't packed enough information into this book for you, you can consult the following resources for additional details.

Tourist information offices

✔ Call or write the **Washington, D.C., Visitor Information Center,** on the ground floor of the Ronald Reagan International Trade Center Building, 1300 Pennsylvania Ave. NW, at the Federal Triangle Metrorail Station (☎ 866-324-7386; www.dcvisit.com), and ask for a free copy of the *Washington, D.C., Visitors Guide,* which contains information about visitor services, hotels, restaurants, sights, transportation, and tours. The organization's Web site contains lots of info and updates you on events.

✔ For everything you want to know about the many Smithsonian Institution facilities, check out the **Smithsonian Information Center,** in the "Castle," 1000 Jefferson Dr. SW, on the National Mall, near the Smithsonian Metrorail Station (☎ 202-633-1000; TTY 202-357-1729; www.si.edu/visit/infocenter/start.htm; e-mail: info@si.edu). The center also has information about events elsewhere in the city.

Newspapers and magazines

✔ You can find the *Washington Post* online at www.washington post.com. The Web site provides up-to-the-minute news, weather, visitor information, restaurant reviews, and online discussions of various subjects. Near the top of the home page, click "City Guide" for voluminous information about attractions, lodging, and nightspots, as well as restaurant reviews.

✔ For another informed perspective on all those things visitors like to know about a city, visit the Web site of *Washingtonian,* D.C.'s leading local magazine (www.washingtonian.com). At the top of the home page you'll see links to information about restaurants, art, sports, and other topics that might interest you. Check out *Washingtonian*'s lists of D.C.'s 100 best restaurants, "cheap eats," and "dirt-cheap eats."

Other sources of information

✔ Go to the Web site www.nps.gov/parks.html to access information about **National Park Service** facilities. You can find detailed information about all National Park Service sites, as well as individual listings for sites in the Washington area by name (Washington Monument, for example). Or click on "Geographic Search" for a list of all facilities in the Washington area.

✔ If you're looking for information about **National and Dulles airports,** go to the Web site www.metwashairports.com. It contains everything you want to know about flight schedules, flight status, ground transportation, terminal maps, and airport facilities. **Baltimore/Washington International Airport**'s Web site is at www.bwiairport.com.

✔ At the **Washington Metropolitan Area Transit Authority** Web site (www.wmata.com), you can find timetables, maps, fare schedules, and more information useful to riders of Washington's **buses** and **subway.**

✔ I particularly like the online **map of the area around each Metrorail station** that you can find at www.stationmasters.com. Click on "go to the Metrorail system map," then click the station you're interested in.

Index

See separate Accommodations and Restaurant Indexes following this index.

General Index

• *A* •

• C •

downtown
accommodations in, 123
description of, 82–83
restaurants in, 128, 169
driving in Washington, D.C.
problems with, 33, 97
renting a car for, 64–66
roadside attractions, 301–310
driving to Alexandria, Virginia, 246
driving to Annapolis, Maryland, 252
driving to Baltimore, Maryland, 259
driving to Washington, D.C.,
50–52, 53, 78–79
"drops a bill", 19
drugstores
CVS pharmacy locations, 68, 313
in Rodman's, 234–235
Dudley & Max (Baltimore), 265
Dulles airport, 44–46, 76–77, 318–319
Dumbarton Oaks, 213–214
Dupont Circle
accommodations in, 123
attractions for teenagers in, 206
description of, 83
map of, 129
restaurants in, 128, 129, 169
shopping in, 230–231
Dyke Marsh, 307

• E •

East Hall Gallery, 232
Easter Egg Roll at White House, 27
Eastern Market, 38, 227
"economy-class syndrome", 69
Ego Alley (Annapolis), 255
"1812 Overture", U.S. Army Band
performance of, 29
Elder Crafters (Alexandria), 249
"eleventh commandment", 19
e-mail, 70–71
emergencies
lost or stolen wallet, 41–42
medical emergencies, 68
phone numbers for, 312
Engraving and Printing, Bureau of, 14

Enid A. Haupt Garden, 214–215
event calendar, 25–30, 276–277

• F •

families
accommodations for, 39, 55–56,
106–107
attractions for, 14, 55, 56–57, 200–207
baby sitters for, 311
itinerary for, 242–243
performing arts for, 56, 279–280
restaurants for, 12, 142, 152
trip planning for, 57
Farmers' Market (Alexandria), 249
"fat cat", 19
FedEx Field, 207, 286
Fells Point (Baltimore), 264–265
Festival of American Folklife,
Smithsonian, 28
Filene's Basement, 231, 233
finances. *See* money
Foggy Bottom
accommodations in, 123
description of, 83–84
restaurants in, 169
Folger Shakespeare Library, 276
food. *See* cuisine; restaurants
food courts, 166–167
Ford's Theatre & Peterson House,
207–208, 275
Fort Hunt, 307
Fort Marcy, 307
Fort McHenry (Baltimore), 264
Fourth of July Celebration, 28, 276–277
Franklin Delano Roosevelt
Memorial, 186
Frederick Douglass National Historic
Site, 208
Freedom statue, 184
Freer and Sackler Galleries of Art,
210–211
Friendship Heights, shopping in, 38
*Frommer's Washington, D.C. with
Kids* (Rubin), 56

• N •

• S •

• *Y* •

• *Z* •

Accommodations Index

Restaurant Index

BUSINESS, CAREERS & PERSONAL FINANCE

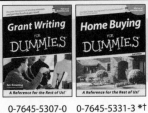

0-7645-5307-0   0-7645-5331-3 *†

Also available:
- Accounting For Dummies †
  0-7645-5314-3
- Business Plans Kit For Dummies †
  0-7645-5365-8
- Cover Letters For Dummies
  0-7645-5224-4
- Frugal Living For Dummies
  0-7645-5403-4
- Leadership For Dummies
  0-7645-5176-0
- Managing For Dummies
  0-7645-1771-6

- Marketing For Dummies
  0-7645-5600-2
- Personal Finance For Dummies *
  0-7645-2590-5
- Project Management
  For Dummies
  0-7645-5283-X
- Resumes For Dummies †
  0-7645-5471-9
- Selling For Dummies
  0-7645-5363-1
- Small Business Kit For Dummies *†
  0-7645-5093-4

HOME & BUSINESS COMPUTER BASICS

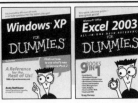

0-7645-4074-2   0-7645-3758-X

Also available:
- ACT! 6 For Dummies
  0-7645-2645-6
- iLife '04 All-in-One Desk Reference
  For Dummies
  0-7645-7347-0
- iPAQ For Dummies
  0-7645-6769-1
- Mac OS X Panther Timesaving
  Techniques For Dummies
  0-7645-5812-9
- Macs For Dummies
  0-7645-5656-8
- Microsoft Money 2004 For Dummies
  0-7645-4195-1

- Office 2003 All-in-One Desk
  Reference For Dummies
  0-7645-3883-7
- Outlook 2003 For Dummies
  0-7645-3759-8
- PCs For Dummies
  0-7645-4074-2
- TiVo For Dummies
  0-7645-6923-6
- Upgrading and Fixing PCs
  For Dummies
  0-7645-1665-5
- Windows XP Timesaving
  Techniques For Dummies
  0-7645-3748-2

FOOD, HOME, GARDEN, HOBBIES, MUSIC & PETS

0-7645-5295-3   0-7645-5232-5

Also available:
- Bass Guitar For Dummies
  0-7645-2487-9
- Diabetes Cookbook For Dummies
  0-7645-5230-9
- Gardening For Dummies *
  0-7645-5130-2
- Guitar For Dummies
  0-7645-5106-X
- Holiday Decorating For Dummies
  0-7645-2570-0
- Home Improvement All-in-One
  For Dummies
  0-7645-5680-0

- Knitting For Dummies
  0-7645-5395-X
- Piano For Dummies
  0-7645-5105-1
- Puppies For Dummies
  0-7645-5255-4
- Scrapbooking For Dummies
  0-7645-7208-3
- Senior Dogs For Dummies
  0-7645-5818-8
- Singing For Dummies
  0-7645-2475-5
- 30-Minute Meals For Dummies
  0-7645-2589-1

INTERNET & DIGITAL MEDIA

0-7645-1664-7   0-7645-6924-4

Also available:
- 2005 Online Shopping Directory
  For Dummies
  0-7645-7495-7
- CD & DVD Recording For Dummies
  0-7645-5956-7
- eBay For Dummies
  0-7645-5654-1
- Fighting Spam For Dummies
  0-7645-5965-6
- Genealogy Online For Dummies
  0-7645-5964-8
- Google For Dummies
  0-7645-4420-9

- Home Recording For Musicians
  For Dummies
  0-7645-1634-5
- The Internet For Dummies
  0-7645-4173-0
- iPod & iTunes For Dummies
  0-7645-7772-7
- Preventing Identity Theft
  For Dummies
  0-7645-7336-5
- Pro Tools All-in-One Desk
  Reference For Dummies
  0-7645-5714-9
- Roxio Easy Media Creator
  For Dummies
  0-7645-7131-1

* Separate Canadian edition also available
† Separate U.K. edition also available

Available wherever books are sold. For more information or to order direct: U.S. customers
visit www.dummies.com or call 1-877-762-2974.
U.K. customers visit www.wileyeurope.com or call 0800 243407. Canadian customers visit
www.wiley.ca or call 1-800-567-4797.

SPORTS, FITNESS, PARENTING, RELIGION & SPIRITUALITY

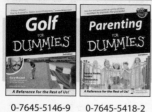

0-7645-5146-9   0-7645-5418-2

Also available:
- Adoption For Dummies
  0-7645-5488-3
- Basketball For Dummies
  0-7645-5248-1
- The Bible For Dummies
  0-7645-5296-1
- Buddhism For Dummies
  0-7645-5359-3
- Catholicism For Dummies
  0-7645-5391-7
- Hockey For Dummies
  0-7645-5228-7

- Judaism For Dummies
  0-7645-5299-6
- Martial Arts For Dummies
  0-7645-5358-5
- Pilates For Dummies
  0-7645-5397-6
- Religion For Dummies
  0-7645-5264-3
- Teaching Kids to Read
  For Dummies
  0-7645-4043-2
- Weight Training For Dummies
  0-7645-5168-X
- Yoga For Dummies
  0-7645-5117-5

TRAVEL

0-7645-5438-7   0-7645-5453-0

Also available:
- Alaska For Dummies
  0-7645-1761-9
- Arizona For Dummies
  0-7645-6938-4
- Cancún and the Yucatán
  For Dummies
  0-7645-2437-2
- Cruise Vacations For Dummies
  0-7645-6941-4
- Europe For Dummies
  0-7645-5456-5
- Ireland For Dummies
  0-7645-5455-7

- Las Vegas For Dummies
  0-7645-5448-4
- London For Dummies
  0-7645-4277-X
- New York City For Dummies
  0-7645-6945-7
- Paris For Dummies
  0-7645-5494-8
- RV Vacations For Dummies
  0-7645-5443-3
- Walt Disney World & Orlando
  For Dummies
  0-7645-6943-0

GRAPHICS, DESIGN & WEB DEVELOPMENT

0-7645-4345-8   0-7645-5589-8

Also available:
- Adobe Acrobat 6 PDF
  For Dummies
  0-7645-3760-1
- Building a Web Site For Dummies
  0-7645-7144-3
- Dreamweaver MX 2004
  For Dummies
  0-7645-4342-3
- FrontPage 2003 For Dummies
  0-7645-3882-9
- HTML 4 For Dummies
  0-7645-1995-6
- Illustrator CS For Dummies
  0-7645-4084-X

- Macromedia Flash MX 2004
  For Dummies
  0-7645-4358-X
- Photoshop 7 All-in-One Desk
  Reference For Dummies
  0-7645-1667-1
- Photoshop CS Timesaving
  Techniques For Dummies
  0-7645-6782-9
- PHP 5 For Dummies
  0-7645-4166-8
- PowerPoint 2003 For Dummies
  0-7645-3908-6
- QuarkXPress 6 For Dummies
  0-7645-2593-X

NETWORKING, SECURITY, PROGRAMMING & DATABASES

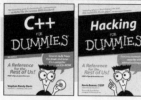

0-7645-6852-3   0-7645-5784-X

Also available:
- A+ Certification For Dummies
  0-7645-4187-0
- Access 2003 All-in-One Desk
  Reference For Dummies
  0-7645-3988-4
- Beginning Programming
  For Dummies
  0-7645-4997-9
- C For Dummies
  0-7645-7068-4
- Firewalls For Dummies
  0-7645-4048-3
- Home Networking For Dummies
  0-7645-42796

- Network Security For Dummies
  0-7645-1679-5
- Networking For Dummies
  0-7645-1677-9
- TCP/IP For Dummies
  0-7645-1760-0
- VBA For Dummies
  0-7645-3989-2
- Wireless All In-One Desk Reference
  For Dummies
  0-7645-7496-5
- Wireless Home Networking
  For Dummies
  0-7645-3910-8